Race and Classification

Race and Classification

The Case of Mexican America

Edited by Ilona Katzew and Susan Deans-Smith

with a Preface by William B. Taylor

Stanford University Press
Stanford, California

Stanford University Press
Stanford, California

Portions of "'Dishonor in the Hands of Indians, Spaniards, and Blacks': Painters and
the (Racial) Politics of Painting in Early Modern Mexico" were originally printed in
Mexican Soundings: Essays in Honor of David A. Brading, eds., Susan Deans-Smith and
Eric Van Young, Institute of the Study of the Americas © 2007, as "'This Noble and
Illustrious Art': Painters and the Politics of Guild Reform in Early Modern Mexico City"

An earlier version of "Moctezuma through the Centuries" was originally published
in *El imperio sublevado. Monarquía y naciones en España e Hispanoamérica,* eds., Víctor
Mínguez and Manuel Chust, Consejo Superior de Investigaciones Científicas © 2004,
as "Moctezuma a través de los siglos"

This book has been published with the assistance of the Program for Cultural
Cooperation between Spain's Ministry of Culture and United States Universities,
a University Co-Operative Society Subvention Grant awarded by the University
of Texas at Austin, and the Los Angeles County Museum of Art.

Library of Congress Cataloging-in-Publication Data

Race and classification : the case of Mexican America / edited by Ilona Katzew and Susan
Deans-Smith ; with a preface by William B. Taylor.
    p. cm.
  "This book originated with a conference organized by the Los Angeles County Museum
of Art in conjunction with the exhibition Inventing Race: Casta Painting and Eighteenth-
Century Mexico, on May 1, 2004"—Acknowl.
  Includes bibliographical references and index.
    ISBN 978-0-8047-6140-6 (cloth : alk. paper)—ISBN 978-0-8047-6141-3 (pbk. : alk. paper)
   1. Racism—Mexico—History—Congresses. 2. Racism—Southwestern States—History—
Congresses. 3. Ethnicity—Mexico—History—Congresses. 4. Ethnicity—Southwestern
States—History—Congresses. 5. Mexico—Race relations—Congresses. 6. Southwestern
States—Race relations—Congresses. 7. Race in art—Congresses. 8. Race in literature—
Congresses. I. Katzew, Ilona. II. Deans-Smith, Susan, 1953–

  F1392.A1R33 2009
  305.800972—dc22

               2008041876

Typeset by Thompson Type in 10/14 Minion Pro.

Cover: Adriana Katzew, *Mexican field worker standing/Campesino mexicano de pie,* from
the series *Y se repite,* 2008, digital photomontage

For Adriana uva-beenie-grape, with love
(Ilona Katzew)

For Jc'q, Doodle, Fee, Sidda, and Harold Stringfellow the Star
(Susan Deans-Smith)

Contents

Preface

THE *CASTA* PAINTINGS made in Mexico during the eighteenth century have fascinated scholars and a wider public in recent years. The dozens of sets of these paintings illustrate racial mixture in family settings, with parents and children combining Spanish, African, and Indian ancestry in a bewilderingly fractionalized calculus. This recent interest in the paintings has led to path-breaking cross-disciplinary scholarship that reveals much about what they are, where they are found, and who they were for. It also invites the question of why we are especially interested in them now. Neither the why of their making or of our interest in them has a simple answer.

The occasion for the symposium that led to this collection of informed and provocative essays was a major exhibition of *casta* paintings at the Los Angeles County Museum of Art in 2004, curated by Ilona Katzew. In the spirit of the "Inventing Race" theme and the California venue of the exhibition, participants across disciplines in the social sciences and humanities gathered to consider the enduring significance of race in Mexico, the United States, and a southwestern "Mexican America," with *casta* paintings serving as a touchstone. The essays share a basic approach and several themes. All view race as a social and political construction, with a history that valorizes whiteness; all recognize that racial classification is always about more than just race; and all contribute to historical thought about a "third space" straddling national boundaries that Ilona Katzew and Susan Deans-Smith highlight in their introduction.

Casta paintings amount to a pictorial artifact of Spain's and New Spain's entry into eighteenth-century notions of a more secular modernity. They were also a comforting elaboration on official racial policy for anxious, or perhaps oblivious, elite patrons. The paintings are mysterious objects, with surprises yet to be discovered, but certain features of them have become clear. As María Elena Martínez suggests, they express the shift from a conception of race and purity of blood attached to religious lineage (placing a premium on "old" Christian ancestry), to a more secular, biological conception. The paintings themselves are strikingly secular, without the traditional religious content and purpose of most colonial Mexican painting. Priests, churches, and devotional culture are almost entirely absent, while the classifying predilections of Enlightenment natural history and applied science are fully present.

The contrast between these paintings and familiar forms of racism in the United States, based on a sharp black and white divide that hardly acknowledges miscegenation, is striking. *Casta* paintings openly recognize racial mixing, describing colonial Mexican society in a way that reached beyond the two "republics" of Spaniards and Indians. They acknowledge that the legal fiction of three forever separate racial stocks did not hold true, and that there were many free people of color; but, with the possible exception of several early sets, especially Miguel Cabrera's stunning portraits of gorgeous people in all the hypothetical racial combinations, they are not a celebration of race mixture or harbingers of José Vasconcelos's grandiose vision of racial synthesis. This was no rainbow coalition of cultural diversity two centuries before Jesse Jackson. On the contrary, *casta* paintings put people in their racialized place, imposing order on unsanctioned mixing that had spilled far beyond legal limits. Like the early history of race in the United States, the *castas* validated white superiority in their own way. The mixing of races depicted in the paintings imagines a whitening process in which the Indian side of the family tree recedes, with descendants whitened, both racially and culturally. The paintings depict black and white mixture moving in the same, uplifting direction, but never quite getting there.

Casta paintings contain some other fictions and silences suited to the taste of their patrons, many of them peninsular Spaniards if the large number of late eighteenth-century sets sent to Spain is an indication. They are pleasing pictures, often in bright colors—attractive furnishings for an aristocrat's salon—not clinical studies or mug shots. The elites who commissioned and displayed the paintings are not portrayed in them except occasionally as types. In effect, they stand apart from this society of racial ambiguities as connoisseurs and classifiers. Also missing are the institutions of external discipline and enforcement—police, soldiers, jails, sweat shops, and chain gangs.

The paintings offer airbrushed images of healthy, clean, industrious people, dressed in their Sunday best, living (except for some of the darker *casta* unions across the white and black line) in harmony at home. There is little in these paintings to trouble the casual viewer; they were Hallmark cards of their day. For peninsular patrons returning to Spain, the paintings were souvenirs of exotic America. As one such patron of the genre, Archbishop Francisco Antonio Lorenzana, put it, "Two worlds has God placed in the hands of our Catholic monarch, and the New does not resemble the Old, not in its climate, its customs or its inhabitants . . . In the Old Spain only a single caste of people is recognized, in the New many and different." Some of the intermediate *casta* designations must have satisfied an imagined more than a functioning order. Did strangers pass on the street and say or think, "Aha, I see you are a *barsino*. You're 45/64 Indian, 11/64 African, and 8/64 Spaniard." Probably not.

This elaborate description of race in colonial Mexican society did not displace old racial dualities that were deeply embedded in law and everyday life. The fundamental racial distinction in Mexico remained Spaniard (white, European) and Indian (now more politely "indígena"), as it does today. In the early nineteenth century, Manuel Abad y Queipo—another peninsular prelate— noted the gradations of race that caught Lorenzana's eye, but he added that there were few such gradations in wealth. People were either rich or wretched, and the wretched were mainly the Indian majority. Anyone who has lived in central or southern Mexico will recognize the depth of prejudice against Indians and the ambivalence about Indian ancestry that can still peek through conventions of public life. Indian warriors and villagers in homespun may serve as emblems of the nation, but they can be a source of shame and object of prejudice there, too. A bitter argument erupted one day in 1964 in the stairwell of my Mexico City apartment building between the *portera* (concierge) of the building who lived in cramped quarters on the ground level and the inebriated male tenant of the maid's quarters on the roof. Both were middle-aged, dark complected, and living on modest means. The shouting and profanities between them went on for several minutes, culminating in what both parties regarded as the terminal insult, hurled at the *portera: india bestia,* beastial Indian. The man was dead to the *portera* from then on.

Paradoxically, *casta* paintings represent a growing elite consciousness of race in Spanish America during the eighteenth century when it would have been clear that social realities spilled beyond the boundaries of a simple, segregated racial structure of Spaniard, Indian, and black African. Elite racism in the late eighteenth century was marked also by royal decrees that forbade cross-racial marriages and made it more difficult for *castas* to be recognized as Spaniards. But Bourbon authorities elaborated on a *sistema de castas*—they did not invent it. As Ian Haney López notes in his essay, the marking of racial differences is about power and class more than about race. This verity is expressed in the *casta* paintings' placement of the uneducated and poor in the lower ranks of the racial hierarchy, and in the submerged duality of Spaniard and Indian. It is equally true of the history of race in Mexico and the United States during the nineteenth and twentieth centuries. Power dislikes irregularity and disorder, and the Spanish Bourbons exercised their power by classifying, making uniform laws and regulations, and seeking to reform America in the image of Spain.

As different as the Spanish Bourbons were from their Hapsburg predecessors, they expressed the preoccupations of power in similar views of race and social order. Seventeenth-century Hapsburg administrators were anxious about what one of them called the "mixto imperio," an evocatively ambivalent phrase. *Imperio* (empire) suggests authority, good order, and unity. "Mixto," or "jumbled," suggests disorder, irregularity, exceptions, and complications that undermine good order. Old categories of race were blurring in the seventeenth century, and the two "republics" of Spaniards and Indians could no longer contain most of colonial life. Descendants of Native Americans were not acting like the Indians Spanish authorities had in mind; they had become childish instead of childlike. Slave women dressed like Spanish aristocrats. Some Spanish women from respectable families dressed as men and became famous for unladylike acts of lethal violence. There were too many *forasteros*—people without a fixed place in society or a permanent residence in their place of birth. The vagrants and other misfits among them included thousands of poor Spaniards, *gente perdida* (godforsaken people). Hapsburg imperial authorities recognized that people of mixed racial ancestry were numerous, but chose not to define a place for them in law, and to rely on customary relationships worked out in local situations. Irregularities were contained, in part, by punishment or by folding people into the old categories. Exceptions were made to the rules of race—some individuals who would otherwise be classified as *mestizos, mulatos,* and *castizos* "passed" as Spaniards or Indians or appeared in legal records with several different racial designations.

"Baroque" was a cultural expression of these social and political irregularities and the growth of domestic economies and regional affiliations that distanced Spanish America from Spain in the seventeenth and eighteenth centuries. It was an art of faith with few rules and many exceptions, layered complexities, free-flowing ornamentation, dramatic gestures, fragments, and asymmetry that gained its coherence in the *conjunto*—everything together, seen whole, in which no space is untouched. It was not an orderly sum of its parts, and American churches, painting, and sculpture were not just like the European models that inspired them. Part of the appeal of *casta* paintings in our time of post-modern "neo-Baroque" awareness is that they seem to undermine the neat racial dichotomies of white and black, European and Indian in a Baroque spirit. Some scholars in the United States and Europe celebrate the hybridities, irregularities, and flamboyance of then and now; others lament the unfinished, chaotic, even pathological fragmentations as overripe imitation and oppressive decadence, the remains of a blasted landscape left behind by the failures of colonialism and modernity. When Latin America's own intellectuals reflect on *lo barroco,* they have had in mind much more than an art style. Fifty years ago José Lezama Lima, Alejo Carpentier, and Leopoldo Castedo celebrated the Baroque in Latin America as a creative spirit, a way of being in a volatile world of inequalities, mixture, clash, religious sentiment, and political retreat that became popular across the social spectrum, expressing local realities, ingenuity, and a measure of freedom, and lasting far beyond its time in Europe. *Lo barroco* may have flowered first in the seventeenth century, they observed, but its improvisations, elaborations, and small subversions have never gone away. There is a touch of irony, then, in embracing *casta* paintings now as another Baroque subversion, for they express, above all, Bourbon modernity's earnest wish to put things and people in order.

A Dialectics of Race in Our Time

Perceptions and practices have changed, but how race matters today in the American Southwest has a recent past as well as deeper genealogies. Two striking changes since the 1960s inform most of these essays and my perspective on the subject. A defining book for the first change—the Chicano awakening in the late 1960s and 1970s—is Carey McWilliams's *North from Mexico: The Spanish-Speaking People of the United States.* It is still an instructive book. Although *North from Mexico* attracted little attention when first published in 1948, its probing, long view of prejudice and racial violence in the region struck a chord in college classrooms when it was reissued in 1968. McWilliams offered a panorama of race relations that focused on Mexicans and the "Anglo"/"Hispano" divide, with a message that the Southwest had been Mexican long before it was American. And the book validated the thirst for volition and action among Mexican American youth. In his introduction to the 1968 edition, McWilliams wrote, "there has been a new burst of interest in Mexican-Americans, which, in large part, has come about as a result of activities and developments for which they themselves are responsible." Haney López's essay shares this vision: "the future of race in the United States depends on how Hispanics come to be seen and to see themselves, in racial terms." But, like an Old Testament prophet of doom, McWilliams shadowed his celebration of self-making with an apocalyptic conclusion: "The explosion at Alamogordo unlocked the latent richness of the mineral resources of the Southwest . . . Here, in the heart of the old Spanish borderlands, the oldest settled portion of the United States, a new world has been born and the isolation of the region has been forever destroyed. Like the peoples of the world, the peoples of the borderlands will either face the future 'one and together' or they are likely to find themselves sifting on the siftings in oblivion."

Cause for such a bleak and urgent vision is as obvious as ever sixty years later, especially in disaster-prone, effervescent California, but the essays in this collection describe a present and future of race that is not like McWilliams's. Instead of a line patrolled and circumvented, the U.S.-Mexican frontier dissolves into a vast, expanding territory of sustained interaction and mixing of people, with its own vertiginous multiplicity of combinations and layers of inequality, possibility, and prejudice, shaped partly by the ways race in Mexico has long resisted categorization and by the insistent claim in deed, if not always in words: "I am here. I exist. I am many things." In this Mexican America categories like Mexican, Indian, black, and white are confounded and reshaped. "Mexicans" in the United States proclaim themselves to be not just Mexicans (though they may learn of themselves as Mexicans in new ways by living in Mexican America), but *yucatecos, oaxaqueños, michoacanos, norteños, sureños, guatemaltecos, salvadoreños,* and *hondureños;* people from Papantla, Tlacolula, or a *ranchito* near Apatzingán; and Americans.

Two words, *pocho* and *nepantla,* are keys to the sense of a Mexican America place I find in these pages. *Pocho* has long been a derogatory term in Mexico for Mexicans who left for the United States and lost their native fluency in Spanish and things Mexican; "bastardized Mexicans," in Guillermo Gómez-Peña's pungent shorthand. "Pocho" appears in Gómez-Peña's reflections with a very different edge than it had in José Antonio Villarreal's *Pocho,* another required reading of the 1970s. Villarreal's coming of age novel first appeared in 1959 to a warm if limited response, but the 1970 edition became a best seller in the Southwest. The novel chronicles Richard Rubio's boyhood in Santa Clara,

California, during the 1930s and early 1940s, the son of a fearless, violent, and incorruptible Villista fighter in the Mexican Revolution who crossed the border and settled into an inconspicuous life of a fruit picker, small farmer, and family man. Born in the United States, Richard has his boyhood adventures in a multicultural neighborhood, but he is something of a sissy, given more to words and questions than to decisive action, and uneasy with the fractured multiplicity of his past and present. Like his father, Richard longs for Mexico, but for him it is "the faraway unknown" and "he knew that he could never be wholly Mexican." He declares "I'm an American," but is always marked off as a Mexican by strangers, and his father reminds him "do not ever forget that you are Mexican." He is saddened by the loss of Mexican traditions in his family and his own assimilation, but does little to change the situation. "He withdrew into his protective shell of cynicism." At the end of the novel we find Richard, finally, about to take action and enlist in the navy during World War II. But he is also on the threshold of a new homelessness ("he knew that for him there would never be coming back" to his neighborhood), still longing for a place. In the novel, "pocho" amounts to this longing for a lost place and cause for regret.

Students I knew at the University of Colorado in the early 1970s related strongly to Richard's predicament, the loss of traditions, and the prejudice Villarreal described, but they were impatient with Richard's dithering cynicism, existential loneliness, and lack of *indigenista* pride. Many of them acted to reclaim for themselves the Spanish language, traditional celebrations, foods, and Mexican history. Theirs was a quest for something lost. They delved into pre-Columbian lore, declared themselves Mexican in racial terms that embraced the Native American side of their heritage as a badge of honor, sought Aztlán (the legendary homeland of the Aztecs) in the American Southwest, invoked Vasconcelos's *raza cósmica,* Mexican *indigenismo,* and *mestizaje,* protested discrimination, attended Corky González's fishermen's dinners at the Crusade for Justice, and sometimes wore brown berets and thought of themselves as latter-day Joaquín Murrietas. Those were heady times, but the *mestizaje* model of racial mixture carried with it a certain static, dislocated outlook that had been expressed, among many other places, in Octavio Paz's *Labyrinth of Solitude:* Mexicans were torn between Spanish and Native American pasts, destined to replay without resolution the original sin of the Spanish Conquest, compounded by the treachery of La Malinche.

Villarreal leaves Richard in a virtual *nepantla*—a nowhere place, caught between home and away, between past and future, not much different from the situation described in Julio Cortázar's distressing story, "Axolotl" (1968), in which the Spanish Conquest severed time for Native Americans, leaving the survivors in a state of suspended animation, like a central Mexican *axolotl* (an amphibious creature) immobilized in a terrarium, unable to move, a captive with endless time to think and look out at limited surroundings. *Nepantla* on this side of the border in the 1980s stood especially for the double displacement and victimization of the Spanish Conquest in sixteenth-century Mexico and the fractured relocation in the United States exemplified by Villarreal's novel.

Old habits of thought and discrimination have not disappeared, but the landscape of race today and in these essays reflects a different California and various Southwests in which about a quarter of the population is foreign-born and many are first generation Americans. La Malinche is no longer the one-dimensional traitor of her people, whoever "her people" might be; all native peoples in Mexico are not Aztecs or victims; and Afro Mexicans are being recognized and speaking up. Tellingly, the word *nepantla* as the nowhere place does not appear in these pages, and *pocho* is reworked by "transdisciplinary" performance artist Gómez-Peña as a "term of empowerment" and fertile ambiguity in his turbocharged vision of an ever-changing "post Mexican" present and future. Proclaiming the death of the *mestizaje* model, Gómez-Peña revels in mixed, situational identities and multiple crises that spill across familiar racial categories in America. His kind of agency is not just confrontation and violation. "We can reinvent our identities [and] pick and choose from cultural selves," he declares. His Mexican America is the home of countless trespasses and many overlapping subcultures—holes in the fence, he calls them. At one moment he is an Indian chief in feather headdress and football shoulder pads, fingering the barrel of an AK-47 as if it were the neck of a guitar; at another he is a black-caped, mustachioed, macho cowboy with a bare midriff and a fan.

Even the U.S. census for 2000 acknowledged some of the mind-bending complexities of race in contemporary America. Noting that "the racial make-up of the country has changed since 1977" when racial categories for the census were last revised, the Census Bureau now allows respondents to identify themselves by more than one race (American Indian or Alaska Native; Asian; Black or African American; Native Hawaiian or Other Pacific Islander; White; and now a sixth category, "Some Other Race"). Two categories for ethnicity also were included, "Hispanic or Latino" and "Not Hispanic or Latino," with people who identify as Hispanics and Latinos invited to pick their race(s).

Compare this to the 1930 census which treated "Mexican" as a race, and the contemporary confusion is just about complete.

Expressions of dynamic confusion and diversity are almost as numerous now as the idea itself implies. Richard Rodríguez is no Gómez-Peña, but his message about race in America in *Brown: The Last Discovery of America* (2002) is similar in its subversion: "I write about race in America in hopes of undermining the notion of race in America. Brown bleeds through the straight line, unstaunchable—the line separating Black from white, for example. Brown confuses. Brown forms at the border of contradiction." And self-described "artistic and alternative historian" Enrique Chagoya's "Borderlandia" imagines Superman mixing it up with Aztec gods or kings. Current events and ancient history are simultaneous in his art rather than sequential and chronological. It is a world of interminglings where "all cultures meet and mix in the richest ways, creating the most fertile ground for the arts ever imagined," in a world of gut-wrenching inequities and improprieties, "perfectly capable of total destruction." Chagoya also "think[s] in terms of opposites to balance each other, a dialectical interaction . . . that hopefully could trigger some laughter." This complex, ever-changing vision is evident, too, in the remarkable painted walls of Los Angeles—"mural art capital of the world" and home to the exhibition of *casta* paintings that inspired this book—from the 1970s and early 1980s with the work of Judith Baca, Yreina Cervantes, Judithe Hernández, and Los Four, to David Botello, George Yepes, and the East Los Streetscapers, to the disparate themes and alternative histories of more recent mural paintings, almost always with Mexico, Central America, and five hundred years of contact and connection across cultures somehow in the picture. Intentionally or not, these walls talk back to *casta* paintings.

Dynamic confusion and racial classification are not a new counterpoint, but the unclassifiable diversity recognized by Gómez-Peña and Chagoya is not the seventeenth-century anxiety of the *mixto imperio* or the attempts by eighteenth-century elites to fix a social order that had escaped the bounds of a rudimentary racial classification. *Casta* paintings were a monologue; the Mexican America of these essays is a murmur of many voices. It affirms what *casta* paintings denied—that identity is a moving target. Whether many people find Chagoya's sought-after dialectical synthesis in this "third space" beyond imposition and substitution, "with a different logic of resistance and contamination," as Gómez-Peña puts it, remains to be seen. Most immigrant parents are too busy trying to make a living to have much time for cultural synthesis;

old racial simplicities have not disappeared; and apocalyptic observers of the California scene envision a bleak dystopia ahead. Perhaps this dynamic Mexican America will soon blur the old racial-national boundaries beyond recognition. It is certainly full of possibilities and surprises, perhaps of many heterotopias more than either a dystopia or utopia. In any case, the emerging "third space" of Mexican America is no longer confined to the Southwest and a few cities elsewhere—Chicago, Detroit, Washington, D.C., and New York. It is almost everywhere now, from Dubuque to Kennett Square, Charlottesville, Cozad, Wichita, and Walla Walla; and it is not only Mexican.

William B. Taylor
University of California, Berkeley

Acknowledgments

THIS BOOK ORIGINATED with a conference organized by the Los Angeles County Museum of Art in conjunction with the exhibition *Inventing Race: Casta Painting and Eighteenth-Century Mexico,* on May 1, 2004. The goal of the symposium was to place the creation of *casta* paintings in a historical context and discuss how issues of racial classification and racial "perceptions" continue to shape our lives. Although the exhibition focused exclusively on the colonial era, lessons were constantly being drawn with the present by the press and the public, particularly in a city such as Los Angeles. Like so many other places in the United States, Los Angeles is a city with one foot firmly anchored in the future, and the other in the past. In this megalopolis people from a multiplicity of backgrounds come together, and yet there is also a profound sense of dislocation. Issues of race and racial categorization are especially poignant in Los Angeles, a place where the histories of Mexico and the United States are deeply intertwined. The purpose of the conference, and now this volume, was to discuss some of these issues in contemporary times, and to assess how many of our concepts of place and selfhood are rooted in the Iberian past, if not before.

After many years of thinking about collaborating on a project given our shared interests in history and art history, we were finally able to join forces on editing this volume. For both of us this has been a highly collegial and rewarding experience—a bond of several years now. Together, we first wish to thank David Theo Goldberg, director of the University of California Humanities Research Institute, a noted expert on race, who co-organized the symposium with the Los Angeles County Museum of Art. He was supportive of the project since its inception and played a key role in its fruition. We are especially thankful to the various authors who participated in the conference and subsequently turned their contributions into publishable manuscripts. Bringing together their perspectives from across disciplines—art history, the history of science, social and cultural studies, legal studies, performance art, and so forth—has been most gratifying and enriching.

More than half of the contributions to the volume originated as papers at the conference (and as a performance by Guillermo Gómez-Peña). We are extremely grateful to Gómez-Peña, Ramón Gutiérrez, Ian Haney López, and María Elena Martínez, for preparing their papers and for their patience while we completed the task of editing the book. Jaime Cuadriello, Alexandra Minna Stern, Adriana Katzew, and Jennifer González (who interviewed Gómez-Peña and co-wrote with him the text in this volume), graciously joined the project midstream making the editorial process remarkably pleasant. William B. Taylor, a leading light in the field of Latin American history, who always teaches by example, kindly agreed to write the preface for the volume, and lucidly succeeded in putting the entire project—the book and the larger subject of classification—in perspective with his incisive and thoughtful commentaries. Many of the contributions, including our own, benefited from the generous and well articulated advice of the manuscript's outside readers, including Claudio Lomnitz and Stanford's anonymous reader. We also wish to thank Christopher Leland Winks for his assistance in translating Cuadriello's essay, and to Jennifer Boynton for her wonderful editorial skills. The Los Angeles County Museum of Art not only made it possible for many of the contributors to participate in the symposium in Los Angeles, but also generously provided funding that enabled us to obtain some of the illustrations that appear in the book. We also thank the University of Texas at Austin, and the Program for Cultural Cooperation Between Spain's Ministry of Culture and United States Universities for their generous subventions. We would be remiss if we did not also thank Sarah Crane Newman, Margaret Pinette, and the people at Thompson Type for their remarkable assistance in all phases of the editing and production process. Finally, our deepest appreciation goes to Norris Pope at Stanford University Press for encouraging us to complete the book and for seeing it through. Gracias.

Contributors

Jaime Cuadriello is Professor of Art History and Researcher at the Universidad Nacional Autónoma de México, Mexico City. He has curated a number of groundbreaking exhibitions on colonial Mexican art and is the author of several books and essays, including *Los pinceles de la historia. El origen del reino de la Nueva España, 1680–1750* (1999), *Zodíaco mariano: 250 años de la declaración pontificia de María de Guadalupe como patrona de México* (2004), and *Las glorias de Tlaxcala. La conciencia como imagen sublime* (2004), which was awarded first prize from the Association of Latin American Art.

Susan Deans-Smith is Associate Professor of History in the Department of History at the University of Texas at Austin. She is the author of *Bureaucrats, Planters and Workers: The Making of the Tobacco Monopoly in Bourbon Mexico* (1992), *Mexican Soundings. Essays in Honour of David A. Brading* (2007) co-edited with Eric Van Young, and numerous articles on the social and cultural history of colonial Mexico. Recent awards include a National Endowment for the Humanities faculty fellowship for her current research on artists, artisans, and the Royal Academy of San Carlos in colonial Mexico. She currently serves on the editorial board of the *Colonial Latin American Review*.

Guillermo Gómez-Peña is a performance artist/writer and the director of the artist collective La Pocha Nostra. He was born in Mexico City in 1955 and came to the United States in 1978. Since then he has been exploring cross-cultural issues with the use of performance, multilingual poetry, journalism, video, radio, and installation art. A MacArthur Fellow and American Book

Award winner, Gómez-Peña is a regular contributor to National Public Radio, a writer for newspapers and magazines in the United States, Mexico, and Europe and a contributing editor to *The Drama Review* (NYU-MIT). He is the author of several books, including most recently *Ethno-Techno: Writings on Performance, Activism and Pedagogy* (2005).

Jennifer González is Associate Professor in the History of Art and Visual Culture Department at the University of California, Santa Cruz. Her writings, including on race and digital culture, have appeared in *Frieze, Diacritics, Inscriptions, Art Journal, Bomb, The Cyborg Handbook,* and *Race in Cyberspace.* Recipient of the Joanne Cassullo Fellowship, she also teaches at the Whitney Museum Independent Study Program. Her book *Subject to Display: Reframing Race in Contemporary Installation Art* was awarded a publication grant from the Andrew Wyeth Foundation.

Ramón A. Gutiérrez is the Preston and Sterling Morton Distinguished Service Professor of History at the University of Chicago. He was the founding chair of the Ethnic Studies Department and the Center for the Study of Race and Ethnicity at the University of California, San Diego. He is the author of many publications, among them *Contested Eden: California Before the Gold Rush* (1998), *Mexican Home Altars* (1997), *When Jesus Came the Corn Mothers Went Away: Marriage, Sexuality and Power in New Mexico, 1500–1846* (1991), and is currently working on a synthetic history of the Chicano Movement.

Ian Haney López is Professor of Law at the University of California, Berkeley, where he teaches in the areas of race and constitutional law. Among his groundbreaking publications are *White by Law: The Legal Construction of Race* (1996) and *Racism on Trial: The Chicano Fight for Justice* (2003). His numerous articles have appeared, among other places, in the *Yale Law Journal,* the *California Law Review,* and the *Pennsylvania Law Review;* his work has also been featured in over two dozen anthologies and encyclopedias, and he has published opinion pieces in the *New York Times* and the *Los Angeles Times.* His current research examines the emergence and operation of a new racial paradigm of color-blind white dominance.

Adriana Katzew is Assistant Professor in the Art and Art History Department and Director of the Art Education Program at the University of Vermont, Burlington. Her research focuses on the intersection between Chicanas/os visual culture, education, and activism. She received her doctorate from Harvard University Graduate School of Education and her law degree from the University of Pennsylvania Law School. She is an artist working in photography and mixed media that explore issues of identity and memory, whose work on Mexican migrant workers was recently awarded a prize by *En Foco*.

Ilona Katzew is Curator of Latin American Art at the Los Angeles County Museum of Art, where she has organized several exhibitions, including *Inventing Race: Casta Painting and Eighteenth-Century Mexico*. Her books include *New World Orders: Casta Painting and Colonial Latin America* (1996), winner of the prestigious Henry Allen Moe Prize, New York Historical Society; *Casta Painting: Images of Race in Eighteenth-Century Mexico* (2004), which received a book award by the Association of Latin American Art; and *Una visión del México del Siglo de las Luces. La codificación de Joaquín Antonio de Basarás* (2006). Her upcoming exhibition *Contested Visions: The Image of the Indian in Colonial Mexico and Peru* was awarded a planning grant by the National Endowment for the Humanities.

María Elena Martínez is Associate Professor of Latin American History at the University of Southern California, Los Angeles, where she teaches courses on Latin American history, the Iberian Atlantic, early modern religion and race, and gender and sexuality in Spanish America, and is co-director of the Tepoztlán Institute for the Transnational History of the Americas, 2008–2009. She has written a number of seminal articles on the intersection of race, gender, and religion in colonial Latin America, including an award-winning study on the presence of Africans in New Spain for *William and Mary Quarterly*. She is the author of *Genealogical Fictions: "Limpieza de Sangre," Religion, and Gender in Colonial Mexico* (2008).

Alexandra Minna Stern is the Zina Pitcher Collegiate Professor in the History of Medicine, Associate Director of the Center for the History of Medicine, and Associate Professor of Obstetrics and Gynecology, History, and American Culture at the University of Michigan, Ann Arbor. She is the author of *Eugenic Nation: Faults and Frontiers of Better Breeding in Modern America* (2005), which won the 2006 Arthur Viseltear Prize for outstanding book in the history of public health from the American Public Health Association. She has received grants from the National Institutes of Health, the Centers for Disease Control and Prevention, and the National Endowment for the Humanities to support projects on the history of eugenics, genetics, and infectious diseases.

Race and Classification

Introduction:
The Alchemy of Race
in Mexican America

Susan Deans-Smith and Ilona Katzew

WRITING IN 1774 about the racially mixed population of colonial Mexico or "the kingdom of New Spain" as it was known, the Spanish merchant and antiquarian don Pedro Alonso O'Crouley (1740–1817) observed:

> [A] pure-bred Indian is as untainted in blood as a Spaniard, with whom there is no incompatibility as there is with the Negro; although their mixture continues, it is uncontaminated through all the degrees of descent and back to the original starting point . . . To those contaminated with the Negro strain we may give over-all, the name of *mulatos,* without specifying the degree or the distance direct or indirect from the Negro root or stock, since . . . be it the first union with an Indian or Spaniard or a mixture of these, that it always results in some kind of *mulato* mixture, which even the most effective chemistry cannot purify.[1]

Some 130 years later, Dr. Alfred P. Schultz, a proponent of Social Darwinism and its "scientific" arguments that emphasized the virtues of racial purity, described the negative consequences of racial mixing in his book *Race or Mongrel* (1908). In his chapter devoted to the "South American Mongrel," Schultz observed:

> As long as Gothic blood prevailed in Spain, Spain was great. After the Moorish wars were over, the Spaniards and the Portuguese fused with the Moors that remained. The Moors introduced Arabian and negro blood . . . These Iberian-Gothic-Arabian-negro mongrels colonized South America, Mexico, Central America, and the West Indies . . . Mexico is a country inhabited by whites,

Indians, and white-Indian mongrels . . . Of natives there are practically two classes in Mexico; those of Spanish origin . . . men of whom the white race has no reason to be proud; far superior, however, to the other four-fifths of the population . . . [who] are animals, and their only human qualities are their super-human mendacity and their ability to consume pulque.[2]

Shortly after the appearance of Schultz's volume, the Mexican writer, intellectual, and politician José Vasconcelos (1881–1959) published his popular if controversial essay *La raza cósmica* (*The Cosmic Race*) (1925).[3] Critical of Eurocentric racial theories that emphasized the degenerate and inferior characteristics of mixed races, Vasconcelos contended that:

No contemporary race can present itself alone as the finished model that all the others should imitate. The mestizo, the Indian, and even the Black are superior to the White in a countless number of properly spiritual capacities. Neither in antiquity, nor in the present, have we a race capable of forging civilization by itself. The most illustrious epochs of humanity have been precisely, those in which several different peoples have come into contact and mixed with each other.[4]

Combined, these three observers convey the central themes of this collection of essays: the naming, classification, and imaging—the making and marking—of race over almost five centuries within the geographical space of what the historian Américo Paredes (1915–1999) has termed "Greater Mexico."[5] The area of Greater Mexico or what we call Mexican America comprises what was originally the viceroyalty of New Spain (colonial Mexico), one of the kingdoms that made up Spain's composite monarchy and empire between 1521 and 1821, and its northern territories that eventually became the U.S. states of Arizona, California, New Mexico, and Texas after the Mexican-American War of 1846–1848. The loss of territory and redrawing of borders following the Mexican-American War may have created two contiguous nation-states—Mexico and the United States—but far from being simply separate bounded and bordered national binary spaces what also developed was a Greater Mexico, and what the historian David Gutiérrez has aptly defined as a "third space"—one that coexists with the nation-states of Mexico and the United States.[6] The concept of Greater Mexico captures the porosity of political borders and the enduring presence and influences of Mexico and Mexicans in the United States despite the loss of national territory. As Paredes observed: "Every Mexican knows that there are two Mexicos . . . One . . . is found within the boundaries of the Mexican republic. The second Mexico—the *México de Afuera* (Mexican abroad) as Mexicans call it—is composed of all the persons of Mexican origin in the United States."[7]

The idea for this volume stems from the symposium *Race and Classification: The Case of Mexican America,* held in conjunction with the exhibition *Inventing Race: Casta Painting and Eighteenth-Century Mexico* at the Los Angeles County Museum of Art in 2004.[8] The pictorial genre known as *casta* painting was invented in Mexico in the eighteenth century. The works depict the complex process of racial mixing among the three main groups that inhabited the colony: Amerindians, Spaniards, and Africans. (The small Asian population resident in colonial Mexico are conspicuously absent.) The paintings give visual form (albeit idealized) to the *sistema de castas* (caste system) of colonial Mexican society. The basic premise of the genre as conveyed through the inscriptions on the paintings is that the successive combination of Spaniards and Indians (Indians were considered pure in colonial legislation) would result in a vigorous race of unadulterated white Spaniards. The mixture of Spaniards or Indians with blacks, however, would only lead to racial degeneration and the impossibility of returning to a white racial pole (fig. I.1).[9] The works naturalize the hierarchical arrangement of society through the familial metaphor where different forms of subordination are clearly articulated—that of child to woman and woman to man, and of subaltern races to Spaniards. Many of the ideas regarding racial purity and racial degeneration that have characterized Greater Mexico are ciphered in this pictorial genre. The paintings were popular among Spanish colonial officials, the Catholic clergy, enlightened thinkers, and naturalists, and they continue to attract the attention of scholars of race. The purpose of the symposium, however, was not to focus on *casta* painting per se, but to think through and around the genre as a particular manifestation in the historical development of racial thinking and imaginings that have marked colonial and contemporary Mexican America.

To this end, the collection of essays offered here represent contributions from a range of disciplines, including social and cultural history, art history, legal studies, and performance art. This volume does not pretend to be comprehensive nor does it aim to advance revisionist interpretations about racial theory. Our intention is to provide fresh perspectives on the subject of race and racial classification as refracted through their particular development and manifestation in Greater Mexico, and to provide departure points for discussion and further inquiry. The essays range from the earliest decades of

Figure I.1. Luis de Mena, Casta Painting, eighteenth century, Oil on canvas, 120 × 104 cm. Museo de América, Madrid.

Spanish colonial rule of Mexico in the sixteenth century and the coming-into-being of a multiracial colonial population to the transnational condition of Latinos in the United States in the twentieth and twenty-first centuries. This broad chronological sweep encompasses the dissolution of the Spanish empire and the creation of new territorial borders and nation-states. The chronological and geographical frameworks allow readers to keep in focus the simultaneous influences and exchanges between imperial power and colony in the case of colonial Mexico, and between and across "borders"—national and international—in the case of contemporary Mexico and the United States, that contributed to the shaping of racial narratives and ideologies in the region.[10] Together the essays introduce students and specialists to the development of racial thinking in different historical periods and localities within Greater Mexico, and their shifts and continuities over time. The volume is divided into three broad sections that focus respectively on the development of racial categories and systems of classification in colonial Mexico, the development of racialized national rhetorics in the nineteenth century in Mexico and the United States, and finally the various ways in which racial identities in the United States are constructed and challenged.

The past decade has witnessed the rapid growth of progressively sophisticated historiographical and anthropological literatures on race and identity in general and on Mexico, the borderlands, and Latin America in particular. It would be neither possible nor desirable to summarize such a vast literature. There are, however, several important themes and revisionist arguments which emerge from the recent literature that we wish to emphasize and with which the contributors engage in varying ways. First, the literature has deepened and historicized the concept of "race" and "racism" through a more critical questioning of how racial differences are conceptualized and how their discourses are generated and perpetuated over the centuries even as the ideological bases of such differences may change. Particularly important here are recent discussions that challenge assertions that the concept of "race" did not exist prior to the eighteenth century, as well as those that posit a shift from cultural constructions of race to the dominance in the nineteenth and twentieth centuries of the biological discourses of "scientific racism."[11] As the historians Ania Loomba and Jonathan Burton have argued particularly for the early modern period: "early modern discourses clearly indicate that ideas about "culture" and "biology" do not occupy separate domains and that they develop in relation to one another. Thus, the bifurcation of "culture" and "nature" in many analyses of race needs to be questioned."[12] Second, scholars have increasingly recognized the malleability of racial hierarchies and their classificatory systems, as well as the fluidity of racial identities through reconstructions of how individuals' lives were and are shaped by such classifications (what Peter Wade describes as "the lived experience of mestizaje").[13] The making and marking of racial differences and identities results not simply from one variable—phenotype or skin color—but from constellations of variables such as honor, religion, gender, occupation, local networks, and social practices which combine to determine an individual's or group's position in society.[14] Third, scholars stress the importance of local and regional contexts when discussing the imperial/colonial and national/transnational circuits of knowledge to produce distinctive (sometimes contradictory) constructions of race and racial identities: that is, how subordinate populations have understood popular racial discourses and classifications and how their actions in turn can shape elite racial ideologies.[15] Scholars are also challenging how concepts such as racial mixing or *mestizaje,* racial democracy, and citizenship which employ a rhetoric of *inclusion,* in practice produce *exclusionary* mechanisms which mask racial inequalities, discrimination, and marginalization within multiracial societies.[16] Otherwise stated, the construction of policies, laws, and practices that eliminate race as a criterion and proclaim racial equality in official rhetoric does not mean that in practice racializing and racial thinking disappear. The implementation of cultural distinctions continues to erect boundaries and distinctions that perpetuate racial discrimination or "cultural racism."[17]

The essays in the volume forcefully demonstrate an enduring problem and paradox faced by states—past and present—and ruling elites that threads its way from the beginnings of Spanish colonialism in Mexico, into the formation of Mexican nationalism and the narrative of *mestizaje,* to the contested definition and expression of Mexican American identities within a multicultural United States in the twenty-first century: the tension "between notions of incorporation and differentiation that were weighted differently at different times."[18] In so doing, the essays foreground the tenacity of "race" and of racial thinking—how race continues to matter. As the historian Thomas C. Holt has noted: "[r]acism's powerful hold . . . appears to arise not from some parasitic attachment on the surface of an otherwise healthy body politic but from viral growths within the living whole. Race yet lives because it is part and parcel of the *means* of living."[19]

The Naming and Classification of Race in Colonial Mexico

Colonial Mexican society resembled that of Spain in some ways but differed significantly in others. Spanish immigrants attempted to replicate their own society in colonial Mexico and built on central organizing principles such as an estate hierarchy, patriarchy, honor and legitimacy, and devotion to the Catholic faith. While the socio-economic hierarchy that characterized early modern Spain whereby wealth and power were concentrated in the hands of a minority was transposed to colonial Mexico, it was also reshaped by new practices and categories that emerged in Mexico and in the New World in general. In the wake of the Spanish military conquest of the indigenous peoples of Mexico, the Spanish crown's early settlement policies in the sixteenth century sought to create and govern over two colonial polities—the *república de indios* (Indian republic) and the *república de españoles* (Spanish republic). The dislocation caused by catastrophic demographic decline of the indigenous peoples and the labor demands made upon them by the Spanish settlers, however, made any rigid separation impossible. To compensate for the decline in the indigenous population due to disease and violence, African slaves were imported to supplement the labor supply needed for the consolidation and growth of the colonial economy and society.[20] In addition, Filipinos, Chinese, Japanese, and other peoples from across Asia immigrated to Mexico beginning in the sixteenth century with the famous trading vessels, the Manila galleons, that traversed the Pacific. Numerically, the influx of Asians into Mexico was significantly smaller than that of Africans. Moreover, many Asians had converted to Christianity, adopted Spanish names, and were classified in colonial legislation as Indians, which has rendered their identification difficult.[21] The combination of the three major racial groups, Europeans, Amerindians, and Africans and a rapidly growing *casta* population—the result of miscegenation among these groups and to a lesser extent Asians—produced a complex and fluid multiracial and multicultural society. To be sure, Spaniards possessed previous experience of social and cultural heterogeneity and the marking of difference exemplified by the Jewish and Islamic communities in Spain, but the main difference in Mexican colonial society was the racializing of the socio-economic hierarchy and a proliferation of racial and ethnic distinctions.

While rank, privilege, power, and wealth were concentrated in the hands of the Spanish white settlers, their American-born descendants or Creoles acquired a distinct status of being-the-same-but-not-quite as their peninsular progenitors based on European beliefs that to be born in America resulted in inferior capabilities and qualities. *Castas* increasingly became equated with being illegitimate, a major stigma in Iberian society, and royal statutes and laws reinforced the hierarchical, corporate, and discriminatory aspects of the colonial social system. Many statutes permitted only Spaniards and Creoles to serve in political and ecclesiastical posts or to be masters of artisan guilds; they were also exempt from paying tribute while Indians and *castas* became the tribute-paying class of colonial society. Indians, however, were classified as wards of the crown and minors with an array of protective legislation, which blacks and *castas* did not enjoy.[22] Other legislation such as the Royal Pragmatic on Marriages (1778) permitted parents to oppose marriages of their children to "unequal" partners, by which was meant people of suspect hybrid background or blacks.[23] At the same time, "defects" in an individual's ancestry such as illegitimacy and dark skin could occasionally be "erased" through the dispensation of the Spanish monarch's privilege of *gracias al sacar*—literally, a "taking away" (for a fee, of course) of the perceived defect.[24] A proliferation of terms to describe and define racial mixtures and cultural categories such as *gente decente* (decent people), *gente de razón* (rational people), and *gente sin razón* (irrational people) emerged and constituted what Fredrick Cooper and Ann Laura Stoler have referred to as a "grammar of difference."[25] The essays in this volume by María Elena Martínez, Susan Deans-Smith, and Ilona Katzew address the formation, maturation, and subjective experience of this racial lexicon, as well as the historical relationship between colonialism and racial thinking and consciousness.

Martínez interrogates the central criterion of difference that emerged in early modern Spain—*limpieza de sangre* or purity of blood—and how its application to an emerging colonial society in New Spain was refashioned and transformed during three hundred years of Spanish rule. The importance and influence of Iberian concepts about purity of blood on the structuring of the *sistema de castas* in colonial Mexico has long been recognized. To date, however, there are few substantive studies that examine such influences and understandings of its vocabularies such as *casta* (caste) and *raza* (race). Why, Martínez asks, in the "language of social differentiation" that evolved in early modern Mexico, did *casta* emerge as the dominant term instead of *raza*? Based on a central organizing criterion of religion in fifteenth- and sixteenth-century Spain, the concept of *limpieza de sangre* marked individuals and families who could trace their untainted descent from Christians on both sides of the family for several generations, making them "Old Christians." Individuals and families whose lineages included Jewish and Muslim converts (*conversos* and *moriscos,* respectively) to Catholicism were marked with the status of "New Christians." In its application to colonial populations in Spanish America purity of blood was gradually transformed to emphasize descent based on African, Amerindian, and European ancestry in the creation of categories of difference and status and the evolution of the *sistema de castas*. Martínez emphasizes that by the late sixteenth century some of the main ordering principles of the *sistema de castas*, most notably that black blood corrupted Spanish lineages more than indigenous blood, and that the offspring and descendants of Spanish-Indian unions could, if they continued to reproduce with Spaniards, claim *limpieza de sangre*, were already being articulated. By the end of the seventeenth century concepts related to blood—*linaje* (lineage), *casta*, and *raza*—and a Spanish obsession with genealogy were reinforced and altered at the same time. With the significant expansion of mercantile capitalism the socio-racial hierarchies became more unstable. The language of blood began to merge with an embryonic language of class manifested in such categories as *calidad* (quality), *condición* (condition), and *clase* (class), while understandings of race and purity became secularized and increasingly separated from religion and lineage.

Recent scholarship on the *sistema de castas* in colonial Mexico has signaled a shift away from earlier approaches to the question of race from quantitative and demographic perspectives, which posited the declining importance of "race" in the eighteenth century and the increasing significance of "class" in determining an individual's position in society (the "caste versus class" debate).[26] Instead, scholars focus more on the importance of local contexts and community norms and the intersection of variables—race, religion, class, gender, and so forth—to shape particular articulations of racial thinking and labeling and determine status and position. The significance of racial categories therefore varied widely. As the historian Matthew Restall has recently argued: "Larger racial categories, such as 'Indian'. . . and 'black', were meaningless at the local community level, where self-identity tended to be rooted. Where such terms were not meaningless, they were ascribed a more local meaning than that intended by Europeans."[27] Matthew O'Hara and Andrew Fisher suggest, however, that despite a strong emphasis in recent scholarship on the limitations of the *sistema de castas* and the fluidity of racial categories, "[e]ven casual observers of Latin American history are struck by the pervasive and long-term use of vocabularies of social and cultural difference. Throughout the colonial era legal and social structures buttressed formal terms of difference, giving these categories practical meanings and material consequences."[28]

The relevance of the *sistema de castas* is analyzed by Susan Deans-Smith in her essay on the racializing of the painting profession in Mexico City as part of a broader effort by artists to improve their social status and gain control of their craft. For example, painters contributed to the creation of idealized colonial racial imaginaries through the production of series of *casta* paintings at the same time that they confronted, from their own perspective, a less than ideal situation with regard to their position in colonial society. Affecting their situation was a commonly held disdain for artisans who were often perceived to be *castas,* and public perceptions which were not always attuned to the difference between the mechanical and the liberal arts. Integral to their strategies to consolidate their social status and strengthen control of their profession was their self-fashioning that promoted painting as a liberal not a mechanical art, reform of a dysfunctional guild, the creation of the respectable space of an art academy, and attempts to restrict access to the profession of painting primarily to Spaniards or whites. In their efforts to exclude non-Spaniards from the practice of painting and to promote their Spanishness, painters, rather than challenging the social and cultural assumptions that underlay the *sistema de castas* of colonial Mexico, attempted to use them to their own advantage to improve their position in society. In this respect, the case of the painters of Mexico City provides insights into how prevailing socio-racial norms and structures were perpetuated and reproduced at least rhetorically since several prominent painters were known to be racially mixed. The painters' experience and strategies also demonstrate the importance of overlapping categories—race, class, honor, skill, and networks, for example—that fused to determine an individual's status expressed through the concept of *calidad* and, at the same time, illuminate the ambiguities of Spanishness-whiteness in early modern Mexico.

In her essay, Ilona Katzew discusses the racial marking of the Indian body in eighteenth-century Mexico. Since the European voyages of discovery in the fifteenth century and of the so-called fourth part of the world, the indigenous peoples of the New World became the subject of much debate. Katzew provides a threefold perspective of the debate by presenting the views of Spanish Catholic authors, northern Protestant thinkers, and eighteenth-century Creole patriots. A subject that was amply debated was the "origin" and "nature" of the Indians and whether they were capable of becoming true Christians. Both Spanish and Protestant writers described the indigenous peoples as a race arrested in an early state of development, a strategy that allowed them to naturalize their alleged inferiority and lay claim to the superiority of the European or white stock. In the case of the Spaniards, such opinions helped to justify the colonial enterprise. Creole authors—many of whom were priests—were fully cognizant of the disparaging observations about the population of the New World by European authors, leading them to provide their own accounts about their peoples and land. Some Creoles found it necessary to redeem the Indians' past in order to create a unique genealogy for their homeland—of which they were often perceived to be heirs—and were therefore compelled to trace their origin to biblical times. Others strove to defend contemporary Indians—commoners and nobles—by emphasizing their adherence to Christian doctrine, a trend that can be loosely described as proto-*indigenista*. This is also especially interesting vis-à-vis the large body of artistic works created in the viceroyalty of Mexico in the eighteenth century that celebrate the Indian nation. As Katzew notes, however, not all Creoles held the indigenous population in high regard and generally there was a great deal of ambivalence about this group. Nevertheless, as this essay shows, the Indian body remained a powerful emblem, an abstract category to wage philosophical debates and to articulate ideas of self-fashioning and nationhood that would take on an added dimension in the nineteenth and twentieth centuries.

"The Fifth Race": *Indigenismo, Mestizaje,* and the Making of Mexicans

In the politically tumultuous century after independence, political elites in Mexico faced the problem of forging and molding a viable modern nation-state and promoting capitalist economic development. If war and defense against foreign invaders over the decades contributed to a more homogeneous sense of *mexicanidad* and a national imaginary, internal conflict and revolution both exacerbated existing differences based on regional, corporate, and local interests and generated new ones.[29] The foundation of a strong, prosperous, and modern Mexican state depended in part on the creation of a unified patriotic and productive Mexican citizenry. In the nineteenth century Mexican liberals sought to secularize, modernize, and unify Mexico. To accomplish this, they embarked on the elimination and erosion of the institutions and privileges that had defined and maintained hierarchy and difference during the colonial period, particularly the Catholic Church, autonomous indigenous communities, and the military. Many of the mechanisms that supported and maintained socio-racial differences and classifications in colonial society such as the *sistema de castas* and its racial categories were diluted or eliminated through a succession of laws, constitutions, and constitutional amendments (a process that remains unfinished).[30] Although the insurgencies of Miguel Hidalgo y Costilla (1753–1811) and José María Morelos (1765–1815) ultimately failed in their calls to abolish slavery and create a merit-based social hierarchy, their efforts resonated in the reconstruction of an independent Mexico (1821) and its forms of government and laws. For example, a law of September 17, 1822, decreed that citizens of Mexico could not be classified in official documents according to their racial origin, and slavery was officially abolished in Mexico in 1829.[31]

In theory, then, the Spanish monarch's "subjects" were transformed in the nineteenth century into (ostensibly raceless) "citizens," equal before the law, able and willing to pursue their individual self-interests while redirecting their loyalties away from the localities and toward the emerging (abstract) Mexican nation-state. Mexican liberalism and its reformist agendas may have contributed to the erosion of a caste society and to shifts in racial thinking, but as the anthropologist Claudio Lomnitz has argued:

> The complex racial dynamics of the colonial period were simplified in the nineteenth century into a bipolar model (Indians/whites) with an intermediate class of "mestizos." . . . The passage from a caste to a class society therefore entailed a transformation—but not a complete elimination—of the old ethnic system . . . the implantation of liberalism as the official ideology had the net effect of discarding certain aspects of the colonial racial ideology while it built on others . . . some of the colonial racial ideas were simply revamped, especially those that referred to the brutishness of Indians and, generally, to the inferiority of dark skin. Moreover, the nineteenth century also retained the colonial ideology of whiteness as an attainable status to which many people aspired . . . with the abolition of slavery and with the end of legal forms of racial discrimination, the castas blurred into a single mass which came to be known racially as "mestizos."[32]

Although the liberal politician and lawyer José María Luis Mora (1794–1850) defined "Mexicans" as "the result of the intermingling of the ancient inhabitants, the dominant groups, and, in some places, the black slaves transported from Africa," the multiple racial categories, as Lomnitz points out, were effectively collapsed into Indians, "whites," and mestizos.[33] By virtue of the "assimilationist" work and racial alchemy performed by the emerging ideologies of *indigenismo* that advanced a positive view of the Indian and of *mestizaje* Mexico's "third root"—blacks and Afro-Mexican populations and specific categories of black-Spanish-Indian racial mixtures—virtually disappears, the black presence elided from the nascent national narratives and racial imaginaries.[34] The recognition of the importance of Mexico's indigenous peoples and their histories to the creation of a unique Mexican identity fused with the newly emerging narrative of *mestizaje,* which "promoted the idea of *la nación mestiza* (the mestizo nation)."[35] And it was within a broader national and international intellectual context which privileged "scientific racism" combined with the reassessment of race and racial ideologies generated by the Mexican Revolution (1910–1920) that the quasi-racial ideologies of *indigenismo* and *mestizaje* were molded.

Although a pro-indigenous stance originated in the colonial period, it was during the Mexican Revolution and its post-revolutionary regimes that a renewed valorization of Mexico's indigenous peoples as part of the country's productive assets and as a perdurable symbol of national identity emerged.[36] Not only did revolutionary thinkers confront the formidable task of rebuilding a country wracked by a decade of violent conflict, they faced the same problem as their liberal predecessors under the regime of president Porfirio Díaz (1876–1911): to forge a modern, republican, and secular nation out of a racially heterogeneous, largely Catholic, and regionally divided population. Shaped by the ambitious cultural revolution of the 1920s and 1930s and influenced by the ideas of the U.S. anthropologist Franz Boas (1858–1942), Manuel Gamio (1883–1960) emphasized the need to integrate the Indians into the new revolutionary state and nation.[37] In contrast to the hard-line coercive assimilation policies of Porfirio Díaz that derided indigenous cultures, Gamio stressed the importance of systematic anthropological, ethnographical, and linguistic research on native peoples.[38] Education provided the major vehicle for the "non-coercive" integration of the Indian (as with the population in general). Rural and Indian schools were created in the 1920s and 1930s, one of their primary objectives being to train bilingual Indian teachers.[39] During this time, Indian traditions such as music, dance, and other rituals, were appropriated and incorporated into an emerging folkloric nationalism, and government officials avidly commissioned artists to create public frescoes exalting the Indian nation.[40]

The appropriation of the pre-Hispanic Indian at a time when *what* constituted Mexico and being a Mexican was being formulated by nation-state builders is the focus of Jaime Cuadriello's essay. In his analysis of the figure of the Aztec king Moctezuma and his visual representations, Cuadriello demonstrates the various ideological shifts of *indigenismo* over time. Based on

Spanish accounts of the conquest, early images of the monarch depict him in the act of abdicating his imperial crown and scepter to symbolize his willing acceptance of the new Spanish regime and of the "true" Catholic faith. Such is the case of a painting believed to have once hung in the *tecpan* or indigenous government of Santiago Tlatelolco in Mexico City. As Cuadriello notes, this image which was in the possession of the indigenous nobility simultaneously symbolized the Indians' status as part of the Spanish kingdom and their own identity as a polity. Other images, such as a painting commissioned by the Creole savant Carlos de Sigüenza y Góngora (1645–1700) to send as a gift to Cosimo de Medici III (1642–1723), grand duke of Tuscany, portrayed the monarch dressed lavishly to embody the glorious past of pre-Hispanic rulers and therefore fulfilled a Creole patriotic agenda of creating an ancient genealogy for their homeland. After the Independence of Mexico and the establishment of the first federal republic in 1824, the image of Moctezuma acquired varying meanings: his submission to the Catholic prince was no longer seen as an act of pious self-sacrifice but as proof of the brutality of the Spaniards and their decimation of indigenous cultures, and later during the Mexican-American War as evidence of his cowardice for yielding to imperial powers. As time passed and nation builders resurrected the ancient past of the Indians, the image of Moctezuma was ambiguously fused with that of Cuauhtémoc, the last Aztec emperor who fiercely battled the Spaniards, becoming an emblem of the "bronze race" and of *mestizaje* that eventually found its way into mass culture. In his essay Cuadriello perceptively notes that while images played a significant role in the construction of historical memory in Mexico, the notion of a war of images whereby different groups of people could make claims through the creation and promotion of particular icons, or of a hybrid culture where different elements were simply combined more often than not, leads to reductive interpretations. Such views fail to take into account larger processes of acculturation and accommodation through which indigenous people and Creoles resort to sanctioned forms of expression to make their own corporate claims or *alegatos,* as exemplified by the mythical figure of Moctezuma.[41]

The resurrection of the Indian and the mestizo became a fundamental part of post-independence and revolutionary patriotic agendas.[42] *Mestizaje,* as seen in the case of Moctezuma, was not only "based on racial mixture, but also on the fusion of emblems from the indigenous remote past and the colonial heritage with representations of modernity."[43] The significant shift which occurred in perceptions of the mestizo from the colonial period to the nineteenth and twentieth centuries—that of the mestizo as "social pariah" to the foundation of the "national race"—are evident in the early articulations of *mestizaje*.[44] However, we should keep in mind that *mestizaje* encompassed varying assumptions about what the process meant with regard to racial mixture and its presumptions of assimilation and gradual disappearance of the cultural distinctiveness of the indigenous population and "others." If Porfirian thinkers—the *científicos* or men of science—such as Justo Sierra (1848–1912) tilted toward the rehabilitation of the mestizo, it was predicated on the need for a continual infusion of *European* blood which would "keep the level of civilization . . . from sinking, which would mean regression, not evolution."[45] In this powerful political fiction, Porfirian thinkers endorsed the superiority of the white European even as they lauded the "Mexican mestizo," and encouraged, although without much success, European immigration to Mexico. For the lawyer and sociologist, Andrés Molina Enríquez (1868–1940), however, the emergence of the mestizo as the basis of the Mexican nation could be explained in terms of adaptation to local environment and "a steady evolution through natural selection."[46] Regardless of the particular assumptions held by different constituencies about the racial makeup of mestizos, as the anthropologist Jorge Klor de Alva has keenly noted, it is important to remember the "problematic application of the concept of mestizaje as both a euphemism for the overwhelming presence of Western influences and as an excuse for eliding/dismissing that which is indigenous."[47]

The consolidation of the narrative of *indigenismo* and *mestizaje* by Mexican political elites and scientists was profoundly marked by the growing influence of eugenics and the "science" of improving a nation's population in order to prosper and advance. In 1883 the British scientist Francis Galton (1882–1911) coined the term "eugenics" to describe the process of better breeding of populations to improve the human race, a "science" purportedly based on new understandings of the laws of human heredity. While initially eugenics was advanced as a solution for social improvement, by the early twentieth century when it became widespread in numerous countries worldwide it was often used in structuring notions of inclusion and exclusion of various populations in the national body and in giving that body its racial identity. In other words, it became a means by which people deemed "unfit" would be identified and excluded from social reform projects. As the historian Nancy Leys Stepan has argued, "Groups self-identified as dominant marked off other groups as inferior, through the language that asserted difference and created boundaries.

These differences were presupposed to be fixed and natural (e.g., biological) and to limit each individual member to a fundamental "type."[48] In Mexico (as in the United States), the eugenics movement had a decisive impact. Changes in perceptions of the mestizo, from the colonial period to the nineteenth and twentieth centuries, were influenced in part by the reactions of the Mexican political elite and a group of scientists to the widespread notion in Europe that everybody in Latin America was a degenerate mongrel. European racial theories and Social Darwinism that emphasized the inherent degeneracy of mixed races and that only nations composed of "pure" races untainted by racial mixture could progress and thrive were vehemently (if contradictorily) contested.

In the heady atmosphere of the cultural revolution of the 1920s and 1930s, in addition to the anthropological and linguistic investigations to which Mexico's indigenous peoples were subjected, revolutionary elites also sought to improve the Mexican population in general—men, women, children, families, peasants, and workers—through a program of "behavioral modernization."[49] Scientists and intellectuals in Mexico looked to adapt European eugenic theories and models, even as they critiqued them, in order to map out policies to guide their social engineering of the Mexican population and to gain better understanding of social differences in populations.[50] The most influential, if somewhat bizarre, conceptualization of *mestizaje* was penned by José Vasconcelos who formulated the idea of the "Cosmic Race." A clear challenge and critique of the alleged degeneracy of hybrid races—particularly by Herbert Spencer (1820–1903), Gustave Le Bon (1841–1931), and Louis Agassiz (1807–1873)—Vasconcelos extolled the virtues of miscegenation.[51] Even though in his view, the mestizo represented "the fifth great race of humanity, forming a universal synthesis, a final blend of the peoples of Europe, Africa, Asia and America," the superiority of the mixture "resided in its spiritual creativity."[52] It is important to remember, however, that while Vasconcelos opposed the racist-eugenic norms of other countries, he still espoused many of the notions of the movement. In his view of the "cosmic race" of Mexico Indians and Spaniards—deemed superior—would naturally seek to mix among themselves and would voluntarily reject blacks as mates because they were inherently uglier. In this conceptualization of a voluntarily aesthetic eugenization, Vasconcelos's ideas were not unlike those advanced by the *sistema de castas*—the difference here being that instead of outlining the steps leading to the creation of a superior race of white Spaniards, he proposed a semi-official formula for the attainment of a fundamentally homogenous mestizo (Indian-European) nation.[53] Vasconcelos's conceptualization of a "cosmic" Mexican race was a popular and enduring one: it is still taught today in schools and is invoked by many Latin American politicians to prove that their nations are composed of racially diverse yet fully integrated groups of people.

In this volume, Alexandra Minna Stern explores aspects of Mexican social engineering through an analysis of the politics of eugenics, race, and classification in her comparative essay on Mexico and the United States from the late nineteenth century to the 1930s. She pays close attention to transnational exchanges and distinctive forms of racial thinking that emerged in Mexico and the United States despite the countries' common border. A telling example of divergent framing of racial ideologies focuses on the modifications made to the 1930 census which, as she notes, was "administered during the height of the eugenics movement worldwide."[54] In the United States, the category of "Mexican" was added to the U.S. census for the first time (subsequently removed in 1940) that effectively reclassified Mexicans as non-white. In comparison, in Mexico in the same year, 1930, all racial categories in the Mexican census were abolished, justified by the argument that it was impossible to provide accurate definitions of an individual's race or racial mixture. Questions about racial background in the Mexican census were replaced with questions about languages (culture) used by Mexico's many indigenous groups in order to map and quantify Mexico's population of monolingual and bilingual Spanish speakers.

Stern is attentive not only to the changes in understandings about "race" and racial classification systems which manifested themselves in the 1920s and 1930s but also to the continuities which illustrate how such classification systems "with genealogies reaching back to the sixteenth century were reinvigorated and reconfigured by the scientific racism of the early twentieth century." Scientists exhibited increasing distrust of external markers of an individual's racial makeup—somatic and phenotypic traits, clothing, and so forth—and privileged "invisible" markers located in the blood or germ plasm. She acknowledges, however, that in courts and in local communities (as Ian Haney López's essay in this volume confirms), perceptions of "race" based on skin color and other visible cultural markers did not entirely disappear. Stern also notes that despite key differences in racial thinking between the two countries, Mexico and the United States shared and expressed ambivalence and anxiety about racial mixing and the hybrid nature of the "mestizo" and its "biological instability." As she concludes, such ambivalence resulted in making "race" and racial categories "even more socially charged and potent." Overall, Stern's discussion reinforces arguments made by the historian Alan Knight and others that emphasize the resilience of racial and racist paradigms in Mexico. Although the formal incorporation of *mestizaje* and *indigenismo* into revolutionary ideology transformed official thinking on racial categorizations, it did not result in the erasure of "race" as a marker of difference; instead, it was displaced on to other "races" such as blacks and Asians who were deemed to disturb the racial "homeostasis" of the new nation. As Knight argues: "just as that nationalism sought to 'forge the nation' by integrating the Indian, so it also sought to cleanse the nation by expelling the Chinese . . . Sinophobia was the logical corollary of revolutionary *indigenismo*. And the outcome, in Mexico as in Europe, was discriminatory legislation, ghettoization, and expulsion."[55]

"The Third Space": Borderland Identities and Imaginaries

Mexican independence from Spain in 1821, the Mexican-American War (1846–1848), and the Gadsden Purchase (1853) reconfigured and redefined the territories and borders of the emergent nation-states of Mexico and the United States. The Treaty of Guadalupe Hidalgo (1848) allowed for the annexation of half of Mexico's territories (which included Texas and California); the Gadsden Purchase demarcated the Mexican border along Arizona and New Mexico. With each successive geo-political shift, Mexican populations in the far north found their citizenship, their identities, and their racial status in flux. In the first half of the nineteenth century in the case of Texas, for example, the Mexican-Texan population "went from [being] Spanish subjects, to Mexican citizens, to Texans, and wound up as Americans, in the short span of a lifetime."[56] Despite provision for the protection of the rights of Mexican citizens in the "new" American states, residents lost property and found their rights violated rather than protected. At the same time, as recent studies of the borderlands have argued, although residents of the northern frontier of the new Mexican "nation" were Mexican citizens, they were marginalized from Mexico and developed a distinctive identity occupying a "third space."[57] And it is within this "space" that a complex Mexican population composed of "former Mexican nationals, immigrant Mexican nationals, and U.S.-born Mexicans as settlers, resident aliens, and citizens of the United States" came into being and, indeed, continues to grow. With the steady flow of Mexican immigrants—legal, illegal, permanent, and temporary—throughout the nineteenth, twentieth, and now twenty-first centuries matched by aggressive Anglo expansionism, new racial and ethnic identities evolved, shaped by both subordinate and elite populations as well as by legal and administrative fiat.

In his essay, Ramón A. Gutiérrez surveys the history of racial and ethnic classification in the southwestern United States—the invention of "defensive ethnic identities"—from the region's colonial origins to the beginning of the twenty-first century. If Anglo settlers to the region began to define themselves as Anglos and Americans in relation to the ethnic Mexican populations, some Mexicans in New Mexico, for example, emphasized their Spanish origins and their "whiteness" in order to deflect the racist attitudes against racially mixed populations, and distance themselves from the increasing influx of lower class Mexican immigrants after 1848. The emergence of the Chicano/a as a political identity around 1969 at the height of the Movimiento Chicano or Chicano Civil Rights Movement privileged racial mixture between Spaniards and Indians as *la raza de bronce* (the bronze race) over any claims to white European Spanish ancestry.

Gutiérrez traces the gradual disappearance of the terms "Spanish American" and "Spanish speaking" and the increasing use of "Mexican" and "Mexican American" in California, New Mexico, and Arizona, while "Latino" became the preferred term in Texas. He also outlines both the survival over the centuries of racial labels from the *sistema de castas* such as *lobo* or wolf and *coyote*—which are still used today to refer to persons of Anglo and Mexican backgrounds—as well as the invention of an array of ethnic terms to describe Anglos including the ubiquitous term, *gringo*. He lucidly demonstrates the importance of region and space in shaping racial thinking and labels, but he also provides insights into both dominant and subordinate populations' understandings of racial classifications and discourses and how they participate in the creation of new ethnic and racial labeling.[58]

The question of how Mexicans were racialized, how they racialized themselves and the fluidity of Mexican-American identity in Texas in the mid-twentieth century is the focus of Ian Haney López's essay. He analyzes the disjuncture between legal racial categorizations and community norms and practices and its consequence—the undermining of the legal basis of equal rights. In his close reading of the most important civil rights case to date for Latinos in the United States, *Hernandez v. Texas,* he exposes the contested understandings of "Mexican." In 1954 the Supreme Court in a unanimous decision ruled the systematic practice in Texas of excluding Mexican Americans from jury service to be unconstitutional. Despite evidence of discrimination

Chief Justice Warren argued that the case was "about something *other* than race or color." In his analysis of the reasoning behind Justice Warren's argument that Mexican Americans were a "subordinated group" Haney López addresses the various constructions and understandings of whiteness; how Mexican Americans defined themselves racially; and how they were perceived by the broader community, and by the courts. Were they or were they not "white," who decides, and based on what criteria? As Haney López points out, what was "startling" in *Hernandez v. Texas* was that the lawyers for *both* sides—for Texas and for Pete Hernandez—argued that Mexican Americans were white under the laws of Texas, even if they were members of a non-Anglo "other white race." Regardless of legal "whiteness," however, Mexican Americans continued to experience discrimination and segregation in daily life. Equally at issue is the construction of identity by Mexican elites in the 1950s in the Southwest as "white," who lobbied to protect their interests through the League of United Latin American Citizens (LULAC).[59] As Haney López argues, "LULAC followed what it termed its 'other white' legal strategy, protesting not segregation itself, but the inappropriate segregation of Mexican Americans as a white racial group." LULAC's opposition to jury exclusion rested on what such exclusion symbolized: despite the legal whiteness of Mexicans, the possibility that Mexicans could judge whites suggested they were equal to Anglos, an ideal that clearly "violated Texas' racial caste system." Haney López concludes that *Hernandez v. Texas* exposes the relationship between categorization and subordination and that "race is ultimately a question of community norms and practices—that is, a matter of social domination."[60]

The widespread discriminatory practices against people of Mexican origin in the United States led to several social protests in the Southwest and Midwest that culminated in the Chicano Civil Rights Movement of the 1960s. This multilocal movement had a number of important leaders, including César Chávez in California who organized the United Farm Workers to stop the abuse of farmworkers; Reies López Tijerina in New Mexico who founded the Alianza de Pueblos Libres (The Alliance of Free Peoples) in 1963, and advocated the return of the Spanish land grants protected by the Treaty of Guadalupe Hidalgo (1848); and Rodolfo "Corky" Gonzales in Denver who founded the Chicano community-based organization Crusade for Justice, and later mobilized the Chicano student movement when he organized the first Chicano Youth Liberation Conference in March 1969. In "The Plan Espiritual de Aztlán" the organizers of the conference articulated in overt nationalistic terms that to be Chicano was to be Indian, a racial rhetoric designed to counter Anglo American racial discourse and to forge a new identity that privileged the "brown race." As Klor de Alva has noted: "Some particularly creative Chicanos, searching for common roots that could unite disparate communities identified Aztlán, the mythical point of origin of the Aztecs, with the U.S. Southwest and consequently—in the imagination of many in the barrios and schools—symbolically transformed all Chicanos (in spite of their distinct mestizo/ethnic heritage) into the most authentic Mexicans: the direct descendants of the original Aztecs."[61]

The question of what it means to be Chicano/a and the slippery slope language of race and its representation is addressed in Adriana Katzew's essay on the portrayal of Chicanos/as in film. In her comparative analysis of two films created by Chicanos/as—the classical *Zoot Suit* (1981) written and directed by Luis Valdez, and *Real Women Have Curves* (2002) based on the play by Josefina López—she analyzes the strategies for representing racial identity at two very different points in time. *Zoot Suit* was filmed after the Movimiento Chicano of the 1960s; its creator was a Chicano activist and founder of the Teatro Campesino (The Farmworkers' Theater), associated with César Chávez's United Farm Workers' movement. The first film created by a Chicano and focused on Chicano characters, *Zoot Suit* fuses two historical events in the 1940s that laid bare the institutional racism against people of Mexican origin—a time when paradoxically Chicanos were classified in the U.S. census as "whites." The first was the Sleepy Lagoon incident in 1942, when a gang of Mexican American youth called *pachucos* were wrongly accused of murdering a Mexican American man; the second was the Zoot Suit Riots in 1943, when thousands of Anglo soldiers, sailors, and civilians went into Mexican American communities to beat up and strip the *pachucos* of their zoot suits—a type of stylized clothing worn by young Mexican Americans. While the main characters of *Zoot Suit* are mestizos following the motto of the Chicano Movement "Brown is beautiful," there is one notable exception, a white *pachuco* who is embraced by the rest as such, and who conveys in a powerful way that race is socially constructed and not biologically determined. Nevertheless, while in the film Mexican Americans are represented as the outsider community that is not accepted by mainstream United States, it also exposes their profound desire to be part of broader society, futher complicating their identity.

Real Women Have Curves was filmed nearly thirty years after the Movimiento wound down, and its premise is radically different. This is fundamentally a coming-of-age film of a Mexican American young woman who finds herself negotiating between her traditional Mexican background and her urge to integrate into mainstream United States. As Katzew notes, the film includes a number of Mexican and Mexican American characters that span the phenotypical gamut, expressly subverting essentialist notions of what Chicano/a people should look like. There are significant differences between the two films: while *Zoot Suit* addresses the subject of institutional racism, *Real Women* is the personal story of a young woman trying to come into her own—part of the reason why the film resonated with a larger audience and became a Hollywood hit. Equally important is Katzew's observation that while Valdez came out of the Chicano Movement and therefore used film to address racial politics, when Josefina López was growing up she did not know the meaning of the word "Chicano" nor did she consider herself one. Such a comparison calls attention to the fact that there are different types of Chicanos/as and that class and privilege also determine their perceived identity and lived experience. Given the long-standing tradition in the United States of providing stereotyped images of Latinos in the media or of omitting them altogether, and the renewed wave of nativism and growing distrust of "foreigners," how, Katzew asks, are Chicanos supposed to react? Are Chicano artists expected to create works that "look" Chicano, and what does this mean? The comparative analysis of these two films show how strategies for self-representation have shifted over time, and concomitantly how racial categories continue to be relevant.

Indeed, the younger generation of Mexican American artists is ever more moving away from strictly identity-based work even when some continue to be labeled Chicano and operate under that rubric.[62] As people of Mexican origin increasingly partake of more than one culture and lifestyle, current systems of classification become more noticeable for their artificiality and as relentlessly awkward delimiters of self. As a kind of coda to this volume, performance artist Guillermo Gómez-Peña offers his perspective on what it means to be a Mexican/Chicano artist and activist in contemporary America. Born in Mexico, Gómez-Peña arrived in the United States in the late 1970s. Since then, he has explored cross-cultural issues through performance, multilingual poetry, journalism, video, radio, and installation art. In his conversation with Jennifer González, the artist reflects on the racial politics of his work over the past two decades, and how through his performance personas and using his body as a site of contestation he has become keenly aware of the mechanisms of identity construction—conscious and unconscious. In the late

1980s and 1990s Gómez-Peña was part of a generation of artists interested in deconstructing the "colonial gaze" or in what he calls "reverse anthropology": artists assumed fictional characters and exhibited themselves as human artifacts to push mainstream culture to the margins and treat *it* as exotic and unfamiliar. In his living dioramas, Gómez-Peña and his troupe La Pocha Nostra constantly question racial boundaries by assuming "extreme" personas to poke fun at them and simultaneously emphasize contemporary issues such as racism and sexism as expressed in global media, corporate multiculturalism, and tourist culture. His practice involves ethnic and gender bending and power inversions. In other words, he destabilizes expectations and categories which in turn bring into sharp relief the same reductive classificatory systems that he strives to debunk.

When González asks Gómez-Peña what the term *Chicano* means for him, he provides a broad definition—it is not a racial category that circumscribes people of Mexican origin, but more a way of being in the world, an "attitude [that] implies a certain border crossing fluidity, a capability to embrace syncretism and hybridity. It entails . . . knowledge of how to operate between two or more cultures and languages." In his view, *mestizaje* is no longer a useful term to refer to the mixture of people since inherited identities are somehow dysfunctional and useless.[63] Gómez-Peña's strategy is one of inclusion rather than exclusion. The choice of the term "pocha" to designate his artistic collective La Pocha Nostra is revealing; the neologism derives from the word *pocho*, a derogatory expression concocted by Mexicans to refer to those individuals who had abandoned national territory and are considered a type of "cultural bastard"—the contemporary version of the colonial "mestizo." By embracing people on the fringes of mainstream culture Gómez-Peña pushes them to the center. This act of resistance is of course limited to the realm of art (and is certainly not representative of all artistic practice) but it nonetheless represents a powerful critique of society's constant desire to categorize people and define who they are and who they can be. Through his work, Gómez-Peña creates a space for people—performers and their invented personas—to become, in the words of one critic, "what they had already been."[64]

The fluidity of transnational, transracial, and transgendered personas that Gómez-Peña invents and reinvents in his work sums up many of the issues highlighted in this volume. The desire to establish racial paradigms and fix notions of racial dominance and subordination has to a large extent structured the bound histories of Mexico and the United States. Marking the physical body of individuals is also about marking the body politic. When the French naval officer Jean de Monségur traveled to Mexico in 1707 under orders of the Spanish monarch, he proffered his opinion about the racial makeup of the place:

> In Mexico City, as in the rest of the Indies under Spanish rule one sees many races from various nations that form a mixture that is not pleasant nor sympathetic in the least, but rather very ugly and repugnant. When born, children are white, blond and of a beautiful complexion, but when they turn twelve, fifteen, and eighteen, they seldom if ever retain this color and instead most of them become brown and dark . . . With the exception of the race of Spaniards from Spain, the Creoles who descend directly from them, and the mestizos or children of Europeans and Indians, it can be said that all the other races are ugly, repulsive and even horrible to behold.[65]

Penned in the early eighteenth century, Monségur's description nevertheless embodies what gradually become central tenets of racial discourses over time that privileged (and continue to privilege) whiteness and, to a lesser degree, the Indians who made up the majority of Mexico's population. Colonial, liberal, and post-revolutionary rhetoric attempted to homogenize Amerindians and mestizos and cast them as paradigmatic proto-national and national symbols. Mexicans in the United States were equally color coded, leading Chicanos to redeploy this form of national rhetoric that extolled their Indian and mestizo past to proclaim their separateness within broader society and concurrently their right to be equal. The collection of essays in this volume show how the language of race and racial labeling and classification has operated in Greater Mexico over time, and how it continues to retain its power even when masked or clumsily pushed to the side. When the Spanish merchant and antiquarian Pedro Alonso O'Crouley (quoted at the beginning of this chapter) described racial mixing as a chemistry of purification, he was not entirely off the mark—the language and the living experience of race is always about unattainable distillations.

1 The Language, Genealogy, and Classification of "Race" in Colonial Mexico

María Elena Martínez

DURING THE PAST THREE DECADES, studies of race have tended to stress that the meanings and uses of the concept have varied across time, space, and cultures.[1] Indeed, the notion seems to derive some of its power from its very epistemological and historical instability, from what the historian Thomas C. Holt calls its chameleon-like and parasitic nature: "chameleon-like" because of its ability to transmute, "parasitic" because of its tendency to attach itself to other social phenomena.[2] Despite Holt's emphasis on the cultural and historical specificity of racial ideologies, he and a number of other scholars anchor modern notions of race in the sixteenth century, if not before.[3] During this period, the term began to appear with some frequency in the Romance languages and in English as European expansion to the Americas, the establishment of the transatlantic slave trade, and other "global" processes forged the Atlantic world—that metaphorical and physical space of cultural interactions and hybridity.[4] But if the emergence of modern notions of race and the rise of the Atlantic world went hand in hand, the racial ideologies that surfaced in that "world" also differed in significant ways due to the particularities of European colonizing projects and the ways in which they confronted local conditions, peoples, and change in the Americas. In certain regions of Spanish America, for example, these particularities produced a system of classification based on African, European, and Native American descent, the *sistema de castas,* some of the underlying principles of which were depicted in the eighteenth-century Mexican pictorial genre now known as *casta* painting.[5]

This essay focuses on three sets of questions that the *casta* pictorial genre raises about the nature and history of classification in New Spain and more generally about colonial Mexico's racial ideology. First, why is the language of social differentiation mainly one of *casta* (caste) and not *raza* (race)? What did these Castilian terms mean in the early modern period and how was their deployment linked to Spanish cultural-religious principles and notions of social order? Second, when and why did *casta* classifications emerge and in what institutional and social contexts were they used? Third, what implications did Hispanic definitions of "race" and "caste" have on central Mexican notions of *mestizaje* ("mixture")? Did these notions change in the eighteenth century and if so how? Addressing these three sets of questions will help provide an overview of Mexican colonial racial ideology and explain in part why the *casta* pictorial genre took the form that it did.

"Race" and "Caste" in the Early Modern Hispanic World, 1400–1700s

Although the origin of the Castilian word *raza* is uncertain, perhaps dating as far back as the thirteenth century, its use started to become prominent in the 1500s. As was the case with its equivalents in other European languages, it generally referred to lineage.[6] The strong belief in nobility as an essence transmitted by blood meant that the word was sometimes used to distinguish between nobles and commoners. This deployment did not necessarily contradict monogenesis, the potentially egalitarian idea of humanity's common descent. As the historian Paul Freedman has argued, medieval Europeans often explained inequality and in particular serfdom through biblical myths about past ancestors who had sinned (such as Noah's son Ham) or through more secular ones, in which, for example, the servile condition of a particular "national" or local group was attributed to descent from cowardly or conquered forefathers.[7] The division of humankind into different lineages was thus perfectly compatible with the doctrine of a common creation. That Spain's late medieval nobility was not a closed caste did not temper its belief in the superiority of its "blood" and its use of the concept of *raza* to distinguish itself from commoners. Indeed, some of Spain's military orders only granted habits to persons whose ancestors had been of noble blood and without the "race or mixture of commoners" ("*hijosdalgo de sangre, sin raza ni mezcla de villano*").[8]

Incubated in the estate system, the Castilian concept of race took a different direction in the sixteenth century as it attached itself, like a parasite, to religion and came to refer not so much to ancestry from *pecheros* (tax-payers) and *villanos* (commoners) but to descent from Jews, Muslims, and eventually other religious categories. This linguistic shift was largely the result of the *limpieza de sangre* statutes, requirements of "pure" Christian ancestry that various Spanish religious and secular institutions began to adopt in the mid 1400s.[9] Initially passed amid a climate of deep social and political tensions and rising anxieties over the "true" religious commitments of the Jews who had converted to Christianity, the *conversos* (also called New Christians), the statutes spread during the next one hundred years. Their spread therefore coincided with the establishment of the Inquisition in Spain, the rise of Protestantism, the expansion of the Ottoman Empire, and the Counter-Reformation, all of which, in different ways, heightened Spanish concerns with Catholic orthodoxy. By the end of the sixteenth century, the most important institutions with *limpieza* requirements—including the Inquisition, the three main military orders, and a number of university colleges and cathedral chapters—had extended the category of "impurity" to Muslim converts to Christianity, the *moriscos,* and developed genealogical procedures to distinguish "old" from "new" Christians. Furthermore, the term *raza,* whose meanings previously varied, had been displaced onto those who were considered impure and defined in unequivocally negative terms.[10] Hence, in the early seventeenth century the Castilian linguist Sebastián de Covarrubias Orozco wrote that when the term was used to refer to lineages, it had a pejorative connotation, "like having some Moorish or Jewish race."[11] For this reason, *cristianos viejos* (Old Christians) seldom applied it to themselves. Jews, Muslims, and even Protestants were marked through the concept of "race," but not the people with putatively long and unsullied ties to Christianity.

As the categories of "new" and "old" Christian imply, temporality was central to the concept of *limpieza de sangre.* Just as time produced vintage wine, generations of devotion to the faith seasoned and aged Christian lineages. Some of the first statutes stipulated that the "stains" of Jewish and Muslim ancestry were to be traced only to the four grandparents (the *cuatro costados,* or four corners), hence implying that it took three, sometimes four, generations for a convert's descendants to be considered Old Christians. But by the 1550s most of the key institutions with purity requirements did not place a limit on the investigations. The condition or status of *limpieza de sangre* thereafter referred to lineages that claimed to be Christian since "time immemorial," that is, for which there could be no memory of a different religious past. The more obscure one's ancestors, the better. The witnesses in the purity information of Pedro de Vega expressed this sense of religious genealogical time (made especially significant by the Peninsula's long struggle with Islam) when in 1585

they declared before an inquisitorial tribunal that he was pure because he derived from "simple, plain people, aged Old Christians" ("*gente boba, llana,
christianos viejos, ranciosos*").[12] That their Old Christian ancestry could imbue
peasants and common tax-payers with a sense of superiority over some nobles
seemed a "monstrous" situation to some of the proponents of reforming the
statutes. Spain was the only country in history, observed Diego Serrano de
Silva, an early seventeenth-century inquisitor and author of a memorial about
the statutes, to have produced not just a division between nobles and plebeians, but one based on *limpieza de sangre,* which he claimed was undermining
the prestige and privileges of the noble estate. The purity statutes, he claimed,
were placing aristocrats with converso ancestors in a lower social place than
peasants and people who practiced mechanical trades, and in general making Old Christian commoners believe that they were more important than
patricians.[13]

However, the growing importance of the concept of *limpieza de sangre*
did not destroy the more "feudal" or estate-based notion of purity of (noble)
blood, *nobleza de sangre.*[14] During the second half of the sixteenth century,
the traditional aristocracy, anxious to dispel the popular perception that in-
termarriages with converso families had made many noble lineages impure
as well as to enhance its exclusivity, made purity of blood a requirement for
noble status.[15] Helping to precipitate a "refeudalization" of Castilian society,
the merging of the two discourses of purity—one referring to the absence (or
remoteness) of commoner ancestry, the other to the lack of Jewish, Muslim,
or heretic ancestors—heightened the Spanish obsession with lineage.[16] By the
late seventeenth century, key Spanish institutions—including the Consejo de
Órdenes (Council of Orders)—tended to verify not only purity of religious
ancestry (*limpieza de sangre*) and of noble blood (*nobleza de sangre*), but of
occupation (*limpieza de oficios*). The multiplicity of *limpiezas* and *manchas*
(stains) enhanced the symbolic capital of genealogies, turning them into veritable fetishes.

Spanish society's obsession with genealogy was manifested not only in the
rise of the *linajudos,* experts in genealogies who devoted themselves to policing lineages for signs of "impure" ancestry (and to trying to profit from their
knowledge),[17] but in the pervasiveness of a language of blood that in the seventeenth century became increasingly baroque. Terms such as *sangre* (blood),
casta (breeding), *generación* (lineage), *raíz* (root), *tronco* (trunk), and *rama*
(branch) figured prominently in Castile's social and legal vocabulary and

continued to be important well into the eighteenth century.[18] For example, when members of the Calleja family of Placencia submitted proof of their purity and nobility, they included genealogical information for brothers and uncles, because they were all of the same "stock and trunk" (*cepa y tronco*).[19] The persistence of this vocabulary in the Iberian Peninsula was sustained by internal dynamics—by the refeudalization of Castilian society and spread of the *limpieza* statutes—but it was also influenced by events in Spanish America, which generated a plethora of transatlantic genealogical investigations for the secular and religious administration and which also produced a language of blood.[20] This language, however, was not fundamentally one of *raza* but of *casta*. How did the second term differ?

Both part of a lexicon of blood that had been influenced by common understandings of how reproduction functioned in the natural world (especially in the realm of horse breeding),[21] the terms *casta* and *raza* could refer to breed, species, and lineage. At times they were used interchangeably to describe groupings of animals, plants, or humans.[22] *Casta*, however, had a series of other connotations. If as a noun it was usually linked to lineage, as an adjective it could allude to chastity, nobility ("good breeding"), and legitimacy, and more generally to an uncorrupted sexual and genealogical history.[23] *Casta* was thereby able to give way to the term *castizo*, which referred to a person of notable ancestry and legitimate birth.[24] By implication the mother of a *castizo* would have been *casta*, virginal before marriage and faithful as a wife. When applied to humans, then, the sixteenth-century Spanish word *casta* and its various connotations were clearly alluding to a system of social order centered around procreation and biological parenthood, one in which reproducing the pure and noble group was mainly predicated on maintaining the chastity of its women. Whether in the "Old" or "New" World, notions of caste purity and their privileging of endogamic marriage and legitimate birth were never separate (because of women's role in reproduction) from discourses of gender and female sexuality, from a sexual economy constituted by gendered notions of familial honor.[25]

To make matters more complicated, Spaniards came up with new uses for the word *casta* in the Americas (to say nothing of the Portuguese in India). Some of its metropolitan connotations survived, but it quickly came to function, in the plural, as an umbrella term for the children of unions between members of the three main "trunks" of colonial society: Spaniards, Native Americans, and Africans. The *castas* were not the pure but "the very people who in endogamous India would be regarded as outside the system."[26] In New Spain, this deployment of the term began around the mid-sixteenth century, shortly after a nomenclature distinguishing people of mixed ancestry or lineages began to surface, its first and most enduring terms being *mestizo* and *mulato*. Hence, when in 1597 Diego de Simancas, the child of a Spanish-Indian union, was tried by the Mexican Inquisition for allegedly believing that Jesus was not the true son of God, he was asked to declare not his "race," but his "caste."[27]

Once the term *casta* was applied to people of mixed ancestry, it began to acquire negative connotations, but it remained distinct from, and more neutral than, the concept of *raza*, which as stressed earlier, became closely tied to religion, and in particular to Jewish and Muslim descent. Hence, mestizos, mulattoes, and in a general sense also Spaniards and Indians, were considered "castes," lineages, but not necessarily races. Or rather, not all of these categories were thought to have "race." As one scholar has argued, early modern Spain elaborated an exclusionary discourse of race within its peninsular borders, at the same time that it created a more inclusive system of caste in the Americas, one that allowed the different castes to claim to be connected through genealogical or symbolic kinship ties (which only contributed to the instability of categories).[28] Such a rigid distinction between the two systems of differentiation cannot be drawn, however. Not only did caste in the colonies become racialized over time, an increasingly naturalizing discourse, but as many *limpieza de sangre*-related documents from colonial Mexico demonstrate, notions of *raza* and impurity started to be used against persons of African ancestry as early as the beginning of seventeenth century, in some cases even before. For example, in 1599 Cristóbal Ruiz de Quiroz submitted his genealogical information to the Franciscan Order in Puebla, Mexico, to prove that he descended from "a clean caste and generation, without the race or mixture of Moors, mulattoes, blacks, Jews and the newly converted to the Holy Catholic Faith or of persons punished by the Holy office."[29]

The Spanish deployment of notions of impurity and race against Africans and their descendants can be attributed primarily to their association with slavery, an institution that in the sixteenth and seventeenth centuries had both economic and religious significance. For early modern Spaniards and other Europeans, the condition of enslavement was not just one of debasement, the antithesis or negation of *nobleza de sangre* or nobility of blood, but a function of religious infidelity or ancestral sin. When the transatlantic slave trade began in earnest and it became less and less feasible to contend that bondage was a tool to convert infidels, the enslavement of Africans as well as their darker skin color was increasingly attributed in Portugal, Spain, and other European countries to their being the cursed descendants of Ham. Previously harnessed to explain serfdom and other oppressive conditions, the Hammitic myth was marshaled to explain both "blackness" and slavery during the seventeenth-century plantation revolution, manifesting the rise, in Robin Blackburn's words, of a "Christian, European, or 'white' racial consciousness."[30] The emergence of this consciousness is perhaps what compelled Spanish thinkers to equate the perpetuity of the stain of slavery with the intractability of the "blemishes" of Jewish and Muslim ancestry.[31] In their mental universe, black blood emanated from slaves and therefore could not be completely absorbed into Old Christian lineages, purified, redeemed. This religious-cum-racial construction of blackness as ineffaceable strongly influenced the *sistema de castas* and its main classifications.

The Rise, Categories, and Development of the *Sistema de Castas*

New Spain's *sistema de castas,* based on a dual-descent model of classification, started to surface in the second half of the sixteenth century, in the context of a rapidly expanding and largely illegitimate population of mixed ancestry, a rise in the number of imported African slaves, a dwindling of the spoils of conquest as more and more Spanish immigrants (including women) arrived, and increasing anxieties about the conversion project. Its first categories were thus intimately tied to the heightened colonial concern with restricting the political and economic claims of non-Spaniards—indeed, with delimiting who could claim to be a "Spaniard." More generally, the classifications were part of the establishment of the institutional and ideological mechanisms intended to reproduce colonial hierarchies of rule, among which lineage would play a prominent role.[32] The *sistema de castas* was influenced by political and economic factors, including the government's interest in dividing the colonial population and in creating a free wage-labor force in order to meet the growing labor demands (aggravated by the decline of the native population) of urban economies and hacienda and mining complexes.[33] But it was also strongly shaped by Castilian cultural-religious principles, their adaptation to colonial dynamics and in particular by the different ways in which they were applied to the native and black populations.

These differences are reflected in the *sistema*'s very nomenclature. For example, the term *mestizo*, which surfaced in the 1530s and by the next decade had become almost synonymous with illegitimacy, simply meant "mixed" and had been used in Spain mainly to refer to the offspring produced by the mating of animals of different species.[34] The category of *mulato*, which in the Spanish colonies only appeared on a regular basis as of 1549, referred to the children of Spaniards and blacks and in general to anyone with partial African ancestry. In both Mexico and Peru it was initially applied to persons of either black-Spanish or black-native descent, but in the seventeenth century a separate, though sporadically used, category for the latter was created, that of *zambahigo* (*zambo* in Peru).[35] According to the seventeenth-century jurist Juan de Solórzano y Pereira, the term *mulato* was used to describe the offspring of Spaniards and blacks because they were considered an "uglier" and more unique mixture than mestizos and because the word conveyed the idea that their nature was akin to that of mules.[36] The rise of the category and its connotations of infertility—which simultaneously eased Spanish anxieties about the uncontrolled growth of populations descending from slaves and sanctioned the continued sexual exploitation of enslaved women by their masters—was inextricably linked to the institution of slavery's gendered and racialized social and reproductive relations, as well as to incipient Western notions of beauty and race.[37]

Since both *mestizo* and *mulato* derived from a zoological vocabulary and implied crossbreeding, neither appellation was exactly flattering. But as Solórzano y Pereira suggested, their use marked an important difference in Spanish attitudes towards reproduction with blacks and indigenous people. This difference becomes even more evident in the next two *casta* categories that surfaced in central Mexico: *castizo* and *morisco*. These terms for the most part did not appear in sixteenth-century parish registers but were used in some colonial administrative and Inquisition documents. The first, which emerged in the last third of the sixteenth century, referred to the child of a Spaniard and a mestizo or someone who was only one-quarter Indian.[38] The second was at first more ambiguous for it was associated with blacks, Islam, or both.[39] In New Spain it continued to be applied to people who were accused of practicing Islam, but by the beginning of the seventeenth century it started to be used in reference to the children of Spaniards and mulattos.[40] Needless to say, the terms *castizo* and *morisco* carried significantly different cultural baggage. In Spain, the first alluded to a person of "good lineage and caste" while the second referred to Muslim converts to Christianity. It is true that when Mexican Holy Office officials first explained the meaning of *castizo* they did not associate the category with any redeeming qualities. In a 1576 letter to the Supreme Council of the Inquisition (which was based in Spain) they wrote that "the descendants of *indios mestizos,* or *castizos,* as they are called here, in general are regarded as vile and despicable, restless and vicious, liars and unable to keep secrets."[41] The inquisitors then added that the "white skin" of some *castizos* allowed them to deceive Spaniards regarding their "true descent" to enter religious orders, which not only suggests that phenotype was already playing an important role in colonial relations, but that exclusions based on ancestry were operating in certain institutions—some informally. These exclusions would become more formal precisely as appearance became an unreliable measure of descent.

Despite the Holy Office's disparaging remarks about *castizos,* the displacement of a word that in Castile mainly had positive connotations onto the children of mestizos and Spaniards was no linguistic accident. It not only acknowledged the aristocratic bloodlines of some *castizos,* descendants of Spanish conquerors and noble native women, but also signaled the construction of a colonial ideology that recognized the purity, or potential purity, of native lineages (especially if they were noble) and hence allowed for their complete assimilation into Spanish Old Christian ones. Indeed, in the last decades of the sixteenth century royal policies began to privilege *castizos* over other *castas*—among other things, by making them eligible for the priesthood and (like mestizos) exempt from paying tribute—and the Holy Office considered them eligible for the status of purity of blood.[42] Notwithstanding their approximation to "whiteness," *moriscos* were generally not allowed to claim a status that corresponded with their ancestry. The *moriscos'* real or imagined connection to slaves not only associated them with infidelity and sin, but also limited their ability to make genealogical claims, particularly about the longevity of their ties to Christianity. According to Castilian legal formulas, descendants of slaves could not establish the history and depth of their loyalty to the faith because slavery implied the severing of kinship ties (in ascending and descending generations) and because they could not prove that their ancestors had converted to Christianity voluntarily. In other words, the discourse of purity of blood and its emphasis on the construction of a certain familial and religious past—on the invention of a particular genealogical memory—made it virtually impossible for persons of African parentage to be considered "aged

Old Christians." Spanish religious cosmologies, the early modern obsession with genealogy, and the transatlantic slave trade thus colluded to extend notions of "impurity" and "race" to black ancestry.[43]

The growing importance of lineage for determining identities, rights, privileges, and obligations at the end of the sixteenth century made the establishment of parish records a crucial component of the Spanish colonial project. Indeed, at the same time that certain colonial institutions started to undertake *limpieza* investigations, the state and church began to create an archival infrastructure that would enable the production and reproduction of "caste." Signaling the rise of the ethnographic state and archival "technologies of power" tied to the production of colonial knowledge, royal and ecclesiastical decrees ordered parishes to maintain separate birth, marriage, and death records for *españoles, indios,* and *castas.*[44] Not all did and there were certainly variations in parish record-keeping practices, but by the mid-seventeenth century many central Mexican churches followed the crown's orders, a trend that for some scholars represented the crystallization of the *sistema de castas.*[45]

The process of recording caste classifications in parish archives was fraught with complications. For example, ancestral information provided at the time of a birth or marriage was not always trustworthy, and parish priests were sometimes less than rigorous in their use of categories. These and other factors lessened the reliability of parish records. Nonetheless, these records were extremely important within Mexican colonial society for they were sometimes used for fiscal purposes (among other things to determine tributary status), for the establishment of the jurisdiction of the Inquisition and other tribunals that were not allowed to try native people, and for "proving" purity of blood. By the second half of the seventeenth century few *probanzas* (certificates) of purity of blood in central New Spain did not include a notarized copy of an individual's birth record, which was supplied and signed by the appropriate parish priest. Despite their unreliability, colonial archives were thus strongly implicated in the production and reproduction of *casta* categories and the discourse of caste. This discourse not only continued to operate throughout the colonial period, but gained prominence during the last century of Spanish rule.

Raza, Casta, and *Clase:* The *Sistema* in the Late Seventeenth and Eighteenth Centuries

Even though the number of lineage categories used in central New Spain gradually increased, only some of the classifications recorded in the *casta* paintings appeared in colonial records such as parish registers, tax lists, and censuses.

These classifications mainly include "Spaniard," "Indian," "black," "*mestizo,*" "*mulato,*" "*castizo,*" "*morisco,*" and "*zambaigo,*" and in the eighteenth century also "*lobo,*" "*coyote,*" "*pardo,*" "*moreno,*" and occasionally "*chino.*" That a relatively small number of terms figure in legal records does not mean, however, that others were not in everyday use. As documents containing petitions or witness testimonies indicate, categories such as *mestiza coyota, mulato lobo,* and *coyote mestizo* circulated among the population, and composite zoological names became increasingly common in the eighteenth century.[46] But the appearance and relevance of certain terms varied by region and period. The system of classification was not as rigid in the northern Mexican frontier, for example, as it was in central Mexico.[47] Even within the same region, their use was often inconsistent and influenced by a number of subjective and situational factors.[48] In short, although the use of *casta* categories in official records tended to follow certain genealogical rules in that they were supposed to be determined according to proportions of Spanish, Native, and African ancestries, in practice the uses of the classifications tended to be anything but systematic.

In fact, central Mexico's *sistema de castas* became more unstable as it "crystallized" in official records. This instability was largely the result of the greater complexity of colonial society, which witnessed a dramatic surge in the population of mixed ancestry, the beginnings of a working-class culture (especially in the northern mining towns and in Mexico City and Puebla), and greater social mobility due to the expansion of mercantile capitalism. Mobility went in both directions. Thanks in large part to its silver mines in Guanajuato, Taxco, Pachuca, and Zacatecas, eighteenth-century Mexico experienced modest but steady economic growth rates. This expansion, however, did not lead to noticeable structural and institutional changes or to a significant increase in wages. Economic growth in Bourbon Mexico was accompanied not just by an unparalleled rise in taxation that diverted an important percentage of the viceroyalty's income to the Spanish crown, but also by an acutely uneven distribution of income; between the start and the end of the century various segments of the population, including Creoles, underwent some downward mobility.[49] Eighteenth-century central New Spain also experienced important changes in marriage patterns, especially in the capital. At the start of the century, legitimacy rates among the *casta* population were rising and Spanish women were beginning to wed men from other groups in significant numbers.[50] All of these socioeconomic and demographic shifts helped make the relationship between "race" and "class"—or rather descent and economic standing—more complicated and gave credence to the notion that wealth and personal achievement were more important than blood and lineage.[51]

Colonial elites, particularly the Creole aristocracy that claimed to have ancient roots in the land, responded by attempting to make colonial institutions more exclusive. Some establishments, including the Inquisition and certain religious orders, town councils, colleges, and seminaries, implemented requirements of purity of blood, nobility, and/or occupation (*oficio*). The exclusionary trend is evident in the records of the Franciscan Order in central Mexico. Starting in the mid-seventeenth century, candidates for the novitiate normally had to provide proof not only that they did not descend from Jews, Muslims, and heretics but also that they did not have any "stains of vulgar infamies" (*mancha de infamia vulgar*) in their past; that no one in their family was or had been associated with "vile" occupations.[52] *Probanzas* produced by the Inquisition also reflect an increasing emphasis on establishing that candidates for *familiaturas* (titles for Holy Office's *familiares* or lay informants) and posts did not have relatives who had exercised *oficios viles* (vile occupations).[53] During the eighteenth century a wider array of institutions (including town councils, guilds, academies, colleges, and seminaries) were establishing, formalizing, or enforcing purity policies than in previous centuries.[54] Combined with the identification of more "stains," the proliferation of *limpieza* requirements exacerbated central Mexican concerns with lineage and encouraged the production of memorials and reports containing genealogical and historical information.

Although the preoccupation with lineage was by no means exclusive to one group, some of the most elaborate genealogical histories were produced by members of the Creole aristocracy. For example, in 1730, don Antonio Joaquín de Rivadeneyra y Barrientos competed for a *prebenda* (a stipend or income from a position, usually ecclesiastical) in Mexico City's Colegio de Todos Santos, for which he submitted proof of his purity of blood, nobility, and "respectable behavior" (*buenas costumbres*). In his *relación* (report) he stressed that all of his ancestors from both bloodlines had been "Old Christians, clean of all bad race, and notable gentlemen and hidalgos" ("*cristianos viejos, limpios de toda mala raza, caballeros hijosdalgo notorios*") and that his parents and grandparents had held honorific posts in Mexico City and Puebla. Don Rivadeneyra y Barrientos, who would later serve as a lawyer in Mexico City's *audiencia* (high court) and for the Inquisition's prisoners and eventually as a judge in Guadalajara's *audiencia,* also provided extensive information regarding his ancestors from his mother's side. He claimed that his maternal ancestors had belonged to some of the most illustrious Spanish families, dating back at least to King Alfonso VI (1066), and had participated in the wars against the "Moors" as well as in the conquest of New Spain.[55] Like other genealogical histories produced in eighteenth-century Mexico, Rivadeneyra y Barrientos's report demonstrates not only the survival of a historical conscience that linked the *Reconquista* or Christian "reconquest" of the Iberian Peninsula to the conquest of Mexico, but also the continued importance of providential or religious conceptions of time in Creole discourses of blood. Pure lineages were those that had for many generations rendered services on behalf of the faith.

As had occurred in seventeenth-century Spain, the proliferation of *limpiezas* and concomitant obsession with lineage led to the fetishization of genealogies and made the language of blood increasingly baroque. Thus, when Francisco Antonio de Medina y Torres applied to be the Holy Office's *alguacil mayor* (constable) in 1767, he claimed to descend from "Old Christians, entirely clean of the bad race of Jews and Moors, and from noble people, notable gentlemen and hidalgos" (*"cristianos viejos, limpios de toda mala raza de Judios y Moros, y personas nobles, caballeros hijos dalgos notorios"*). Just a decade earlier one of his relatives, a secretary in Mexico's *audiencia* who tried to have his purity and nobility certified, claimed to be able to produce genealogical proof for thirty-eight of his ancestors.[56] At least among the traditional aristocracy, the *hidalgo-cristiano viejo* cultural paradigm—promoted centuries earlier by the state and church—was alive and well in late colonial New Spain.

Despite the endurance of this paradigm, the period's socioeconomic realignments—namely, the acceleration of mercantile capitalism and greater possibilities of social mobility that it generated—together with the growing acceptance of individual achievement and other principles of enlightened rationalism (especially popular among the Jesuits) increasingly peppered the language of purity of blood with concepts related to "class" or social status (such as *calidad, condición,* and *clase*).[57] The ancient regime's lexicon of blood essentially merged with "bourgeois" concepts of diligence, work, integrity, education, and utility to the public good. An example of this merging is provided in a 1752 opinion that don José Tembra (also spelled Tenebra), a cleric from the diocese of Tlaxcala, sent to the crown regarding the role of the church in cases of parental opposition to marriages between "unequals"—a subject of much debate among Spanish secular and religious authorities in the mid-eighteenth century and subsequent decades. He wrote that although the common practice in New Spain had been for priests or ecclesiastical judges deciding on prenuptial disputes to be most concerned with safeguarding or restoring a woman's honor, it was time to consider the negative implications that such thinking could have on the social order. Dr. Tembra argued that protecting female honor, even in cases of rape, should be less important than upholding the differences in *condición* between the bride and groom and the damage that would be inflicted on the male's family if, for example, he was of noble or notable ancestry and she were a *mulata, china,* or *coyota,* or the daughter of an executioner (*verdugo*), butcher, tanner, and so forth. His main point was that marriages between honorable men and women who lacked the three *limpiezas* (of nobility, caste, and occupation) were to be avoided in order to ensure the public good. Citing the Roman emperor Justinian, Dr. Tembra added that traditional practices—here referring to the Spanish church's propensity to support the principle of free marriage choice even if it meant undermining parental wishes—should be changed when they were no longer useful for the republic.[58]

Anticipating some of the arguments behind the issuance of the Real Pragmática or Royal Pragmatic of 1776 and the new vision of state and society held by advisors to Charles III (1759–1788) and enlightened Creoles, Dr. Tembra implied that the crown, not the church, was to assume the main role in controlling the population, reproduction, and the social body in general.[59] The transition which in Foucauldian terms would be called a shift from a "symbolics of blood" to an "analytics of sexuality"—from a regime of power centered on kinship ties, marriage, and the transmission of property and names to one in which social life was regulated through normalization and a "technology of sex" aiming to discipline the body as well as to control and expand populations—retained the family as a crucial site for engineering the social order.[60] It also did not destroy traditional notions of lineage and blood but rather recast them in a partly new secular idiom.

Indeed, in addition to incorporating concepts that gained currency with the expansion of mercantile capitalism, the Spanish concept of *limpieza de sangre* began to be secularized. If the declarations of people who testified in genealogical investigations are a good indication, the notion started to become more distanced from the issue of religious practices and antecedents and more related to a visual discourse about the body, and particularly about skin color. The change was already perceptible at the beginning of the eighteenth century. For example, when the authorities of a Franciscan convent in Querétaro, Mexico, interrogated community elders regarding the ancestry of two brothers who were suspected of having "the bad race of mulattoes," many reported that they knew or suspected that they were not pure of blood because of the skin color and hair texture of their mother and some of their grandparents.[61] Several witnesses also referred to the brothers' skin color and physiognomy, a concept that derived from Greek and Roman texts and referred to a "technique that diagnosed a person's interior disposition or character through a visual examination of the body's external appearances."[62] The body was thus read as a system of signs, external appearances taken to reflect moral and ethical inclinations.

As the century unfolded and natural explanations (especially environmental ones) for human variation became more prominent than theological ones, the colonial body became the main text through which the issue of purity of blood was framed. The *casta* paintings, many of which depict people with plants and animals and other elements of the "natural" environment of the Americas, are in a sense a testament to the increasingly dominant place of natural history and other "scientific" approaches to human difference and hence also the gradual secularization of notions about race in New Spain. However, the paintings also betray the weight that medieval notions of inheritance and traditional Spanish concepts of mixture derived from the religiously based discourse of purity of blood continued to have in New Spain. As just about every known series of *casta* painting suggests, the idea that it took three or four generations for new Christians to become Old Christians and for the descendants of a Spanish-Indian union to claim *limpieza,* had by the eighteenth century given way to similar formulas for "whitening." But again, the possibility of complete "redemption" through progressive infusions of Spanish blood was not allowed for the descendants of blacks, at least not in New Spain.[63] As Mexican Inquisition officials affirmed in 1773, African-descended people could not be recognized as pure because "as is popularly believed, blackened blood (*sangre denegrida*) never disappears, because experience shows that by the third, fourth, or fifth generation it pullulates, so that two whites produce a black, called *tornatrás* (return backwards) or *saltatrás* (jump backwards) (fig. 1.1).[64] Categories such as *tornatrás* as well as the obsessive attention to skin color might have been new, but eighteenth-century discourses

Figure 1.1. Miguel Cabrera, *7. De español y albina, torna atrás* (7. From Spaniard and Albina, Return Backwards), 1763, oil on canvas, 132 × 101 cm. Private Collection.

of difference were grafted onto older ones. As the chameleonic and parasitic notion of race transmuted yet again in the context of capitalist expansion and Enlightenment thought, its older meanings strongly informed its new ones.

Conclusion

The system of classification represented in the *casta* paintings was not simply a product of the Enlightenment's taxonomic impulse or the late colonial Creole imagination. Although it might only have been in the eighteenth century that the caste categorizations were conceived of as a system, made visual, and explicitly linked to natural history—and in that regard the scientific spirit of the times did have an influence—Spaniards began to deploy some of the classifications and to place them in hierarchies as early as the late 1500s. It was also then that they started to articulate some of the *sistema*'s main ordering principles—including the notions that reproduction between different *castas* produced new *castas,* that black blood was more damaging to Spanish lineages than native blood, and that the descendants of Spanish-Indian unions could, if they continued to reproduce with Spaniards, claim *limpieza de sangre.* From that moment on, Spaniards deployed the concept of *raza*—more essentializing than that of *casta* because of its presumption of immutability—much more frequently against people of African ancestry than against other castes.

When the Castilian concept of purity of blood extended to colonial categories, it happened during a time of heightened anxieties over conversion and was initially framed, as in Spain, in religious and temporal terms. According to some of the first discussions of the *limpieza* status of different American populations, the native people were unsullied but were new to the faith and therefore had to wait several generations, usually three or four, before they could be considered Old Christians. Because blood was thought to be a vehicle for the transmission of not only physical but moral and spiritual qualities, "mixture" with "pure" Spaniards could accelerate the process. These temporal and genealogical ideas could have been applied to blacks as well because they too were relatively recent converts. However, their association (direct or indirect) with slavery and infidelity, not only marked them as impure, but undermined their ability to make genealogical claims. Castilian religious cosmologies, popular conceptions of reproduction, and the different legal-theological status of native people and blacks within the Spanish colonial order strongly shaped New Spain's discourse of *limpieza de sangre* and the *sistema de castas,* both of which "raced" and gendered the two groups differently.

Emanating from the early modern Spanish obsession with genealogy, Mexico's lexicon of blood—of *linaje, casta,* and *raza*—was reinforced and altered in the latter half of the colonial period. As mercantile capitalism expanded and colonial hierarchies became unstable, some colonial institutions adopted requirements of purity, nobility, and occupation, thus both reflecting and exacerbating the elite preoccupation with lineage. The period's socio-economic realignments, however, made the ancient regime's language of blood merge with an incipient idiom of class that featured the concepts of *calidad, condición,* and *clase.* Furthermore, notions of purity and race became increasingly secularized, gradually detached from religion, kinship, and lineage and inserted more into pseudoscientific and visual discourses of the body. By the mid-eighteenth century, the notion that three generations had to pass before new converts became Old Christians had been replaced by the idea that it took three generations for the descendants of an Indian-Spanish union (provided they continued to reproduce with Spaniards), to become "Spaniards." Nonetheless, central Mexico's *sistema de castas* continued to be supported by some of the main principles that had given it life in the late sixteenth century—principles that allowed native blood to be "redeemed" but which deemed that of blacks to be a corruptive force on "pure" lineages and the social body as a whole. The Spanish concept of race itself had both new and old connotations. Transmuting in the context of the Enlightenment and rapid social change, it did not entirely shed its old skin.

2 "Dishonor in the Hands of Indians, Spaniards, and Blacks"

The (Racial) Politics of Painting in Early Modern Mexico

Susan Deans-Smith

IN 1789, THIRTEEN PAINTERS, "professors of painting and sculpture" resident in Mexico City protested the city council's order that they contribute to the costs of the *jura* (swearing of the oath of loyalty) to the new monarch Charles IV (1788–1808), a demand made of all guild members. In their appeal to the president of the newly founded Royal Academy of San Carlos they claimed that "it is well known that these two noble arts have never been organized as guilds."[1] After a lengthy discussion defending their claim, the artists requested that the president of the academy declare them to be exempt from the required contribution now and in the future on the grounds that they were not members of a guild but subject only to the Royal Academy.[2] Ten years later, in 1799, the painters complained again to the president of the Royal Academy about the "intruders and offenders" ("*intrusos y ofensores*") who painted and sold paintings and sculptures to the public but who had neither formal training nor had been examined by the academy.[3] The painters expressed the negative consequences of such practices: "We see nothing less than our own dishonor in the hands of Indians, Spaniards, and blacks who attempt, without rules or fundamentals, to imitate the most holy of objects."[4] They concluded that if efforts were not made to eradicate such practices, the damage to the Academy would be irrevocable.[5]

The painters' complaints about untrained and unexamined artists and peddlers who, they argued, reflected poorly on their own status and on their profession were not new. In many ways such objections constituted a continuation of and connection with those of several generations of ambitious painters, who, beginning in the mid-seventeenth century, attempted to redefine their own status and that of the painting profession in colonial Mexican society. What is striking, however, about the painters' complaint of 1789 was their assertion that they had never been constituted as a guild, when in fact, both painting and sculpture had been organized as guilds since the mid-sixteenth century. The deliberate denial that painters had ever functioned as a guild captures not only how they sought to redefine their status and the institutional organization of the painting profession but also how such representation of their status was a continual rather than a fixed process. It is precisely this question of how painters sought to define their profession and their status during the decades between 1670 until the official opening of the Royal Academy of San Carlos in 1785 that I will explore in this essay. Their case offers a useful vantage point from which to examine broader questions related to the construction of status and identity among artisans in early modern Mexico, particularly how such identities could become racially inflected, and how artists conceived of themselves in relation to other sectors of the population.[6]

Although the reactions of Spanish-dominated guilds to the increase of the *casta* or caste population in seventeenth-century Mexico is often noted, the process is only superficially understood.[7] As the historian Ruth Mackay argues: "As in Spain, the prestige of a craft seemed to demand the absence of certain racial groups . . . guilds showed new interest in the eighteenth century in delimiting their territory, often using markers of ancestry or race, to ensure that their prestige was greater than that of their competitors."[8] Yet, in one of the few substantive contemporary studies of the painters' guild and confraternity, the Mexican art historian Rogelio Ruiz Gomar argues that the profession of painting remained "open to all," unlike many other guilds where one had to be Spanish in order to become a master.[9] Ruiz Gomar is correct in noting that the painters' guild had no such prohibition as articulated in its original ordinances of 1557.[10] Such an argument, however, does not consider the social anxieties exhibited among ambitious painters in their attempts to elevate the status of their profession and distance themselves from an artisan population increasingly perceived to be dominated by racially mixed people and thus associated with a debased *calidad* (literally "quality"). While other artisans shared the painters' concerns and attempted to restrict their guild membership or the positions of master artisans to Spaniards, the painters' case is especially suggestive for assessing the relevance of the *sistema de castas* or caste system to their daily lives and position in colonial society. Some of the most prominent painters of the eighteenth century—Juan Rodríguez Juárez

(1675–1728), José de Ibarra (1685–1756), Miguel Cabrera (1695?–1768), Juan Patricio Morlete Ruiz (1713–c. 1772), and José de Alcíbar (1725/30–1803)—contributed to the production of the colonial imaginary with its objectified and idealized socio-racial hierarchies represented in their individual series of *casta* paintings. But, as Ilona Katzew has emphasized in her work on the *casta* genre, unlike the traveler-artists of Great Britain who produced representations of imperial subjects as temporary residents in the colonies and who returned home to England, the artists who painted *casta* series were permanent residents of Mexico.[11] As such, the socio-racial hierarchies the painters represented in *casta* painting were far from abstract or irrelevant to their own lives, status, and ambitions.

In the first part of this essay, I provide a brief overview of the socio-economic backgrounds of the painters prominent in efforts to reform and redefine the painting profession. The second part examines strategies employed by painters to elevate their status and regulate the profession. Recent studies have emphasized how painters sought to project an image of their profession that emphasized its rigorous training, intellectual foundations, and affinities with other liberal arts such as poetry and to disassociate it from the mechanical arts (low-status occupations).[12] Based on this research and the uncovering of new documentation, I suggest the following. First, in the context of a society where the socio-racial hierarchy and its boundaries had become increasingly porous, the painters' ambitions to improve the prestige of the painting profession became closely linked to their efforts to associate the profession with Spanishness through the marginalization and/or exclusion of indigenous and *casta* artisans. These attempts at imposing racially restrictive policies, however, cannot be understood as being only about a person's "race." In targeting Indians and *castas,* the painters were also targeting untrained and unlicensed craftsmen and vendors whom they perceived to be the source of the sale of low quality artworks and illicit production. Low quality work detracted from the painters' ambitions to defend their image as educated and learned practitioners. In fact, by the mid-eighteenth century, Spaniards were not immune from the painters' efforts to exert control over illicit production of artworks. Second, if the painters' attempts to redefine their status and defend painting as a liberal art received support from secular and ecclesiastical authorities, their efforts to reform their guild and to control both the production of and commerce in artworks proved less successful. Despite evidence of their enhanced status, demonstrated by the acclaim and prestige achieved by some individual painters in their own lifetimes and increasing acknowledgment that painters possessed special expertise, colonial authorities remained ambivalent toward their collective ambitions, thus limiting the painters' corporate power.[13]

The Painters

By the mid-seventeenth century, painters in Mexico City comprised a heterogeneous group. At one extreme, self-taught and poorly trained craftsmen produced low quality and cheap work, their activities facilitated by a virtually moribund guild. At the other extreme, a group of ambitious and learned painters in Mexico City sought to protect and reform the practice of their craft. Similar to the situation among painters in Spain for the same period, these ambitious individuals constituted, as the Spanish art historian Javier Portús Pérez has noted, "a small group of relatively cultured men, who, conscious of the dignity of their art stood apart from the majority of painters."[14] In New Spain the painting dynasties of the Echave and Juárez families provided the driving force behind this "small group of relatively cultured men."[15] Both families shaped several generations of painters in Mexico City through father-son and master-apprentice relationships and formed the founding members of the Mexican school, many of whom became active in the painters' reform efforts.[16] Nicolás Rodríguez Juárez (1667–1734) and his brother Juan Rodríguez Juárez (1675–1728) (the great-grandsons of Luis Juárez [1590?–1639?], and grandsons of José Juárez [1617–1661]), both supported the foundation of an art academy. Their father (son-in-law and pupil of José Juárez) Antonio Rodríguez (1636–1691) became prominent in the demand for reform of the painters' guild. Other master painters who supported reform of the profession and who trained within these circles included Cristóbal de Villalpando (c. 1649–1714) and Juan Correa (c. 1645–1716), both possibly trained by Baltasar de Echave Rioja (1632–1682).[17] José de Ibarra (1685–1756), a pupil of Juan Correa, in turn, may have been Miguel Cabrera's master.[18] Juan Patricio Morlete Ruiz (1713–c. 1772) apprenticed in Ibarra's workshop.[19] Villalpando, Correa, and Juan Rodríguez Carnero (c. 1650–1725) all had sons who became painters.[20] In addition to master-apprentice and professional relationships, marriage, godparenthood (*compadrazgo*), personal friendships, and confraternity memberships provided the foundational basis for networks forged by the painters among themselves. These networks and relationships also provided links among successive generations of painters, which allowed for the transmission from generation to generation of not only the secrets and skills of the craft but also of the histories of painters and painting.[21]

The majority of painters involved in the reform of their profession were Spanish or "passed" as Spanish; some could lay claim to high status, as in the case of Indian *caciques* (hereditary Indian nobles). Antonio Rodríguez, Nicolás and Juan Rodríguez Juárez, Villalpando, and Francisco Antonio Vallejo (1722–1785) were all Creoles (Spaniards born in the Americas); Pedro Quintana (active 1753–1771), Cabrera's son-in-law, was a peninsular; Manuel Osorio (b. 1703; active 1753) was described as a Spaniard ("español"), but whether a Creole or peninsular is unclear; Carlos Clemente López (1725?–1790?) and Mateo Gómez (active 1669–1723) were Indian *caciques*.[22] Miguel Cabrera's racial background is unclear, though he tended to describe himself as a Spaniard.[23] Racially mixed painters included Ibarra (*moreno;* offspring of *morisco* and *mulato*), Morlete Ruiz (*mestizo;* offspring of Spanish and Indian), and Correa (*mulato;* offspring of Spanish and black).[24] Although Ruiz Gomar points to the presence of *castas* in the painters' guild (primarily Correa) as evidence of its openness, it is important to note that Ibarra, Morlete Ruiz, and Cabrera, subsequently identified themselves as Spaniards, a point to which I will return later.

The corporate power of the painters (or lack thereof) as a guild, and their socio-economic backgrounds and networks reveal ambiguities in their position and status in colonial society that undoubtedly influenced their attempts to consolidate the social respectability of their profession and improve control over its commercial aspects. Unlike the silversmiths, painters as a corporation did not appear to wield much power or influence. The painters' confraternity, founded in the late seventeenth century, was not wealthy.[25] Their guild ordinances, originally issued in 1557, fell into disuse by the early seventeenth century, although the daily practice of their craft followed standard guild methods of working in workshops (*talleres*) with assistants, and training of apprentices.[26] Some master painters such as Correa, Villalpando, Juan Rodríguez Juárez, Ibarra, and Cabrera achieved significant fame and success in their own lifetimes. Occupational and family networks, moreover, provided painters with access to the colonial elite, and to powerful secular and ecclesiastical authorities. Many painters used the honorific term *don* and are described in various documents as respectable citizens (*vecinos*).[27] Some painters—such as Cabrera—became affluent, but did so only after a lifetime of hard work and in spite of penurious beginnings. Others such as Francisco Martínez (active 1717–1757) and Rodríguez Carnero experienced cycles of prosperity and deep debt. Evidence from probate, property, and commercial transactions suggests that the most affluent painters not only engaged in income-producing activities related to their art, such as appraisals and the sale of artworks, but also in real estate dealings and commerce.[28] Such diversification suggests the painters' need for additional sources of income to supplement that received from the commissions and sale of their work.[29] It also explains why many of their complaints and reform objectives focused on increased control over the production and trade in artworks and of who could and should carry out appraisals.

It is not surprising, therefore, that painters who supported reform of the painting profession tended to be the most successful in their careers or were in the process of building a reputation. Artists may have moved within the world of the wealthy and powerful, but they were not of that world.[30] In fact, there is little evidence to suggest that their success translated into social acceptability within elite circles. The painters' social position placed them in the situation of what the historian James Amelang has described as "both belonging and exclusion, of being simultaneously inside and outside the structures of authority and respectability."[31] This liminal position undoubtedly contributed to the painters' efforts to assert the respectability and professionalism of their craft.

Projecting the Image of the Painter

In seventeenth-century Spain, artists attempted to defend painting as a liberal art through petitions to the treasury (primarily seeking exemption from the payment of the sales tax or *alcabala*), the writing of treatises on the theory and practice of painting, the establishment of art academies, and disassociation from guild structures and related bodies such as confraternities.[32] They found support from writers and intellectuals who incorporated the theme of painting as a noble and liberal art into their writings and who portrayed painters as cultured, literate individuals.[33] Painters in Mexico City engaged in similar strategies, such as their self-fashioning as practitioners of a noble art and their attempts to found painting academies. A major difference, however, consisted in their attempts to reform their guild as a way to improve standards of painting, which suggests that they did not necessarily view the guild as antithetical to their ambitions and status, at least not the generation of painters active in the late seventeenth century such as Correa, Villalpando, and Antonio Rodríguez.[34] In addition, whereas removing the social stigma of paying the *alcabala* loomed large on the painters' agenda in Spain, painters appeared to be less concerned with this issue in Mexico.[35] Their main complaints were directed toward untrained and unqualified painters and sellers of art-works, particularly Indians and *castas,* but by the mid-eighteenth century also toward Spaniards.

In their efforts to distinguish themselves from artisans employed in the mechanical arts, painters engaged in various self-fashionings, which empha-sized their social respectability, training, expertise, and devoutness.[36] Aside from laying claim to their elevated status through the use of the honorific "don," painters made deliberate use of the terms "noble" and/or "liberal art of painting" and of "professor" in preference to "master."[37] A particularly re-vealing example of such self-designation appears in a notarized deposition by a group of painters to grant power of attorney to Luis Bertucat in 1768.[38] At the beginning of the document the painters refer to themselves as "professors of the Very Noble Arts of Painting and Sculpture." Further in the document, "master" appears before Bertucat's name but is crossed out and replaced by "professor." The correction is suggestive. Whatever else it may indicate about customary and continued use of "master," it reveals a highly self-conscious act of correction by the painters and determination to control their social designations.[39]

Painters attempted to project the dignified, intellectual and theoretical di-mensions of their work through association with the literati of Mexico City, and through an emphasis on the relationship between the sister arts of poetry and painting, epitomized by the formula *ut pictura poesis* ("as is painting so is poetry").[40] In 1742 Ibarra composed several verses collectively titled *Quejas de la Agua Dulce.*[41] Subsequently, in his opinion on the Virgin of Guadalupe published in Cabrera's well-known treatise titled *Maravilla americana* (1756), Ibarra discussed the relationship between poetry and painting.[42] Painters also drew attention to the relationship between poetry and painting in its perfor-mative dimensions in the construction of ephemeral architecture for public celebrations such as triumphal arches. From the actual conception of an arch to its construction, painters presented themselves as literate professionals in their collaboration with poets and writers. Such a relationship is made clear in contracts for these works. For example, in the contract to erect a triumphal arch to welcome Viceroy Melchor Portocarrero y Lasso de la Vega, conde de la Monclova (1686–88) in 1686, Villalpando stipulated in one of the clauses that before beginning to paint the arch, he would provide a design of what was to be painted "to the Poet or person in order to perfect its history."[43] But the re-lationship also played out in public as the painters and writers consulted with one another during the physical construction, decoration, and creation of paintings for the triumphal arches.[44] Public ceremonies and fiestas also provided opportunities for the painters as a corporation to express the elevated nature of their art.[45] A telling example is an elaborate triumphal arch that they erected in front of the Royal Palace in the *Plaza mayor* or main square on the occasion of the swearing of the oath of loyalty to Ferdinand VI in 1747. The painters projected their view of the genius and honor inherent in their art, typical of painters in general, by their association with the most revered artists from antiquity such as Timanthes and Apelles—what Joan Stack has described as the "historical brotherhood of painters."[46]

As artists in Spain found support in their quest for the recognition of painting from some of the most important writers and intellectuals of the period, so too did painters in Mexico.[47] Their claims for the special nature of painting and their professional expertise were nurtured by an increasing tendency for colonial authorities to seek artists' opinions in the authentication of art works, the most well-known being inspections of the image of the Virgin of Guadalupe in 1666 and 1751.[48] Writers reinforced the artists' claims about the nobility of painting and lauded their achievements in their printed descriptions of the ceremonial life of Mexico manifested in public festivals, *juras,* processions, funerals, and other commemorations. The Creole author Cayetano Cabrera y Quintero (c. 1695–1778), for example, refers to "the Very Noble Art of Painting" in his description of the statutes of the painters' confraternity in 1733.[49] References to specific painters appeared in issues of the *Gazetas de México* and acknowledged their talents with laudatory comments such as "the strong hand of the celebrated Ibarra."[50] The trope of *ut pictura poesis* appears in writings such as Pedro Abarca's *El Sol en León . . .* (1748), where in his description of the painters' triumphal arch erected for the swearing of the oath of loyalty to Ferdinand VI in 1747 he reflects on the sisterly arts of painting and poetry.[51] Writers, like the painters themselves, drew favorable comparisons between New Spanish painters and a classical artistic pantheon. The Augustinian Fray Matías de Escobar in his *Americana Thebaida* (1729) declared Antonio Rodríguez to be "the Titian of this New World," while the Carmelite Fray Andrés de San Miguel described Juan Rodríguez Juárez as "the Apelles of our America."[52] Fray Agustín de Castro, probably a Creole Jesuit, in his description of a triumphal arch designed by Miguel Cabrera to honor king Charles III (1716–1788) lauds it as "the most sublime triumphal arch" that any courts ever had, and very pointedly declared the arch to be a

Figure 2.1. Attributed to Juan Rodríguez Juárez,
Self Portrait, c. 1719, oil on canvas, 66 × 54 cm.
Museo Nacional de Arte, CONACULTA, INBA,
Mexico City.

work worthy of the Royal Academy of San Fernando.[53] In so doing, De Castro places Cabrera's talents on an equal footing with the academicians of the fine arts academy in Madrid.

Painters forged images of their status and the prestige of their profession, collective and individual, through portraits, with their signatures, through their emphasis on the intellectual foundations of painting, and through visual representations of the "noble" art of painting. All of these different forms of representations could also articulate a painter's particular association with other corporations and groups within colonial Mexican society.[54] Portraits provide evidence of the growing consciousness of artists as individual masters and of their appropriation of the symbols of status, as in the examples of Juan Rodríguez Juárez and Ibarra (figs. 2.1 and 2.2).[55] In the unfinished self-portrait attributed to Rodríguez Juárez, he is represented holding what appears to be a paintbrush. Evidence, however, of physical labor—the tools

Figure 2.2. Attributed to José de Ibarra, *Self Portrait*, first half of the eighteenth century, oil on canvas, 57 × 42 cm. Museo Nacional de Arte, CONACULTA, INBA, Mexico City.

and accoutrements of a painter's workshop—are virtually absent. Ibarra's half-length portrait is a much more explicit depiction of the artist at his easel, although he too is represented in a moment of reflection rather than actually painting—his brush is motionless. Both appear in dignified and sober dress. It is difficult to say more about these portraits without knowing where they would have been placed—in public or private spaces—and in association with what other images and contexts. In both instances, however, the portraits project "a fiction of individual, unique, and unassisted production—the artist's *ingenium* visualized" and thus emphasize the intellectual dimensions of painting.[56]

Variations on the standard signature of a painter's name with the colophon *fecit* ("made by"), *faciebat* ("was making"), and *pinxit* ("painted by"), in full or abbreviated form, also express the specific status and associations of artists. Nicolás Rodríguez Juárez, for example, included his position as a priest in his signatures, as in *"Nicolas Rodriguez Xuarez, Presbytero faciebat."*[57] Cabrera included his title as court painter (*"pintor de cámara"*) to the archbishop of Mexico Manuel José Rubio y Salinas (1748–65) on at least two paintings, thus making clear his explicit association with the archbishop.[58] He also provided additional information about his individual identity as an *American* painter. On a painting of Saint Joseph, he signed himself "Michl. Cabrera *americanus* pinxiebat" [my emphasis].[59] As the art historian Clara Bargellini has noted, the way of signing and the specific placement of signatures convey not only authorships. The particular location of a signature and its form can also be indicative of the intellectual process involved in such placement, as well as a painter's desire to be associated with a certain person, corporation, or devotion.[60] In his portrait of the viceroy Pedro de Cebrián y Agustín, Conde de Fuenclara (1742–46), for example, José de Ibarra inserts his signature on a document that the viceroy holds in his hand, prominent and visible to the viewer, and identifies himself as "José de Ibarra, professor of the very noble art of painting" (*"Joseph de Ibarra, profesor de la nobilissima arte de la pintura"*) (fig. 2.3).

Visual representations of the art of painting by God himself, as the art historian Jaime Cuadriello and others have argued, also provide eloquent testimony about the painters' engagement with the theoretical and practical foundations of their art, and particularly their desire to represent it as a socially acceptable profession by association with the divine and as an act of the intellect. One particularly compelling example is an anonymous canvas depicting God in the act of rendering the Virgin of Guadalupe (fig. 2.4); the work not only portrays God as divine artist and creator of the sacred image of Guadalupe, but also as a divine artist in his workshop.[61] The canvas includes two cherub artists grinding pigments and practicing drawing as they perfect their skill in copying various facial features—eyes, mouths, and noses. Both scenes call attention to the intellectual and practical formation of the painter.

Specific evidence of the "liberal nature" of painting and its intellectual foundations could be found in art treatises that addressed the theory, practice, and defense of painting. The central purpose of such works was to present a "new conception of the artist as a learned individual who had made a serious study of his art."[62] Although it appears that painters in Mexico City did not compose treatises comparable to those by artists in Spain such as Vicente Carducho (1576–1638) and Francisco Pacheco (1564–1644), other evidence—visual and textual—illustrates their engagement with the intellectual and theoretical

Figure 2.3. José de Ibarra, *Portrait of Viceroy Pedro Cebrián y Agustín,* 1743, Oil on canvas, 94 × 74 cm. Museo Nacional de Historia, CONACULTA, INAH, Mexico.

Figure 2.4. Unknown artist, *God the Father Painting the Virgin of Guadalupe,* second half of the eighteenth century, oil on canvas, 85.5 × 64 cm. Museo de la Basílica de Guadalupe, Mexico City.

foundations of painting. Miguel Cabrera's *Maravilla americana* (1756)—an assessment of the "miraculous origins" of the Virgin of Guadalupe—provides an example of a published work in which questions of perspective, technique, and materials are explicitly discussed. Cabrera also included, in addition to his own evaluation, six professional "opinions" by expert painters. The text emphasizes the "noble" qualities of painting and draws favorable comparisons between Cabrera and famous European masters.[63] The partial Spanish translation of a discourse on the rules, technique, and practice of painting from the Italian *L'Arte Maestra* (1670) penned by the Jesuit Francesco Lana Terzi (1631–1687) may also have been used and consulted by a group of painters in New Spain. As the art historian Paula Mues Orts has recently argued, one possible candidate for work on the translation (perhaps in collaboration with Cayetano de Cabrera y Quintero) is Ibarra, one of the painters whose "opinion" Cabrera had included in his *Maravilla americana*.[64] Also revealing of the painters' familiarity with and use of art treatises is Cabrera's depiction of Sor Juana Inés de la Cruz (1750), based on a portrait by Juan de Miranda (active 1660?–1714). In his rendition Cabrera enlarges the space for Sor Juana's library, where among the books represented are two volumes on painting with the easily readable titles of *Gloria del Pintor* and *Arte de la Pintura*.[65] With this deliberate placement, Cabrera not only depicts works that represent the aesthetic and theoretical basis of painting but associates them with one of Mexico's most acclaimed intellectuals and poets.

Integral also to the projection of the theoretical and intellectual foundations of painting is the use of the term *inventor* by some painters such as Cabrera, Ibarra, Juan Rodríguez Juárez, and Villalpando to connote the originality of their compositions. In the lower left-hand corner of an engraving based on a design by Ibarra included in Cabrera y Quintero's *Escudo de Armas de México* (1746), for example, is the inscription "José de Ibarra inventor." Although not all that common a practice among painters in Mexico City, as Clara Bargellini argues, "The better-informed inhabitants of New Spain, artists and patrons among them, could not but know that imagination and invention were considered the hallmarks of the most highly appreciated achievements in the art of their time."[66]

Grappling with the theoretical problems of invention, of pictorial representation, and of understandings of sight and its broader relationship to knowledge may also be seen in two of Cabrera's *casta* paintings. The first is his well-known *casta* painting of 1763, *From Spaniard and Indian Woman, Mestiza* (fig. 2.5).[67] Because Cabrera positions the Spanish man with his back to the viewer, his face and expression cannot be seen. Decipherment of his identity—that he is, in fact, a Spaniard—must rely on the markers of his clothing style and the inscription of the figure as an "español." Not being able to "see" the individual's face induces a degree of uncertainty as to the Spaniard's identity despite a categorical statement that he is an "español." Cabrera may have been working through questions about the "reliability of sight" and of the relationship between "seeing" and "knowing" a person's *calidad*.[68] This particular composition may also be interpreted as evidence of Cabrera's explicit desire to convey his knowledge, use, and interpretation of European pictorial sources within the specific locale of Mexico. The painting is, in fact, signed "painted by Miguel Cabrera, Mexico." In another of his *casta* paintings, which depicts a tobacconist and his family in their shop, hanging on the back wall is a Flemish print.[69] The inclusion of this engraving may be

Figure 2.5. Miguel Cabrera, *1. De español y de india, mestiza* (1. From Spaniard and Indian, Mestiza), 1763, oil on canvas, 132 × 101 cm. Private Collection.

interpreted as Cabrera's deliberate intention to display not only his knowledge of Flemish genre scenes but to locate them within the frame of a distinctive New Spanish genre, that of *casta* painting, thus articulating the originality of his own invention.

The Revitalization of the Painters' Guild and the Limits of Reform

By the mid-seventeenth century the painters' guild in Mexico City had become virtually dysfunctional. Those officials responsible for enforcement of guild regulations—the guild inspectors—had ceased to be elected by the beginning of the seventeenth century. The inability to enforce guild regulations resulted in unwelcome competition on the one hand, and the production and sale of "bad" paintings by unlicensed and untrained craftsmen on the other, practices that brought (or so the painters argued) disrepute to painters and their profession.[70] In 1681 master painters lamented "the great irreverence which afflicts sacred images made by Indians and other people who have not learned the said arts [of painting and gilding], and not knowing anything about them they do great harm."[71] Integral to the painters' attempts to elevate their profession was their criticism of the quality of painting in Mexico City in general, its structures of production, and the mechanisms for the distribution of artworks.[72] In so doing, they justified the need for increased regulation over the everyday practice of painting and its pedagogical foundations.

The question of the subjection of Indian craftsmen to guild regulations compounded the painters' problems of a lack of control over the production and sale of artworks. As the historian Charles Gibson argued:

> [T]he exclusion of such Indian craft groups from the Spanish guilds was a policy expressed in several viceregal and guild statements, to the effect that none of the specified regulations for manufacture was to apply to Indian craftsmen. The point was made regarding . . . the painters' and gilders' guild in 1589 . . . and it was surely implied in a number of other guild regulations for it followed a general order of the crown.[73]

Indians were not subject, for example, to the guild regulations of related crafts such as those of the carpenters, carvers, joiners, and viol makers (*carpinteros, entalladores, ensambladores y violeros*) (1568), or of the sculptors and carvers (*escultores y entalladores*) (1589).[74] In addition to these rulings, by the 1640s the Indians were ascribed a special legal status as poor and miserable (*pobres miserables*), "as disadvantaged [people] . . . who deserved public compassion and protection."[75] Moreover, by the late seventeenth century, there is evidence that prominent sculptors and joiners (*ensambladores*) began to subcontract with unlicensed painters and gilders, many of whom were Indian craftsmen, for the fabrication of *retablos* (altar ensembles).[76] The elaboration of a *retablo* theoretically was the product of a complex interdependence among several different craftsmen and their assistants. They generally included a carpenter, a woodcarver, a joiner, a gilder, and a painter.[77] Contracts were often given to one master craftsman who was then responsible for contracting masters from each related craft in accordance with the respective guild specifications. The new (and illegal) practices of the *ensambladores,* however, bypassed the master painters and created increased competition.

Painters also expressed their concern over what they perceived to be the widespread practice of the sale of artworks by *trapaleros* (unlicensed vendors, possibly secondhand clothes or rag dealers, who sold paintings and sculptures as part of their inventories).[78] Cristóbal de Villalpando complained about vendors who sold images in the "arcades, squares, open air markets . . . and at public auction," who were "only concerned with the money which they can earn from such sales . . . [and] are ignorant of, or do not care about the representations in their pictures."[79] Edicts issued by the Inquisition targeted a thriving market in popular folk art, although with little success.[80] In addition, merchants' imports of paintings and prints from Spain and the Low Countries may have also provided competition, although the question of the volume and distribution of imported paintings requires much greater scrutiny.[81]

In 1674, thirteen master painters (including Antonio Rodríguez and Juan Correa) of Mexico City granted power of attorney to two of their colleagues, the master painters Sebastián López Dávalos and Cristóbal Caballero, to represent them in "all matters and affairs related to painting and its defense."[82] While the specific circumstances of the petition are unknown and what precisely they meant by "defense" is not expressly articulated, the painters had undoubtedly become frustrated by the problems outlined previously. It is in 1681, however, that on behalf of a group of master painters in Mexico City, Antonio Rodríguez and José Rodríguez Carnero granted power to the *procurador del número* (attorney) of the *audiencia* (high court of appeals), Juan López de Pareja to present their request for the adoption of a set of revised guild ordinances to the Mexico City council.[83] They argued that such revisions were necessary because "for a long time now [the old ones] have not been used."[84] As a consequence, untrained individuals practiced painting and gilding with the result that the kingdom was full of "bad paintings."[85]

The revised ordinances (sixteen in total) submitted by the painters covered technique and administration, defined who could and who could not practice painting and gilding, and who could legally appraise and sell artworks. They deleted clauses that had become obsolete to their profession and sought to add new ones to address their current concerns. Central to the painters' aspirations was the exclusion from the painting profession and prosecution of untrained individuals and unlicensed craftsmen, the enforcement and maintenance of rigorous standards of training, and control over sales of artworks. Punishments for violation of the ordinances were clearly stated. Major emphasis was placed on the election of guild inspectors, regular inspection of artists' workshops, and the importance of the guild examination.[86] The painters also demonstrated their determination to use the guild examination as a vehicle through which to establish the importance of the theoretical foundations of painting and to defend it as a liberal art.[87] They attempted to eradicate the sale of poorly made images that caused (or so the painters argued) "irreverence and lack of devotion." As an added form of control, ordinance six required that all painters must sign their works. Ordinance seven stipulated that anyone who engaged in the resale of sculptures or paintings whether in a shop, the street, or an outdoor market, would be fined 50 pesos. Ordinance thirteen ordered that no one other than master painters and gilders who had passed the guild exam could conduct evaluations (*tasaciones*) in matters related to painting and gilding, the violation of which incurred a 10-peso fine for the first offence, and double for the second.

Ordinances that targeted craftsmen involved in the making of *retablos,* particularly the *ensambladores,* demonstrate the painters' efforts to demarcate and enforce the professional boundaries between painting and gilding, on the one hand and crafts such as joinery, carpentry, woodworking, and stonecarving, on the other.[88] Significant in this regard is ordinance two, which authorized guild inspectors to examine not only the workshops of painters and gilders but also those of *ensambladores.* Ordinance twelve specifically prohibited sculptors, joiners, woodcarvers, and carpenters from accepting any work that would require them to paint and/or gild, subject to a 30-peso fine for the first violation, and a 60-peso fine and ten days in jail for the second. Conversely, painters and gilders could not accept or contract for any works that required them to carry out woodcarving.[89] By way of a pre-emptive strike, ordinance sixteen specified that those master *ensambladores* who currently owned painting and gilding workshops would request "to be examined in the said arts in order to keep their workshops open but should be prohibited from doing so." Carpenters, joiners, and woodcarvers could not apply to be examined in the arts of painting and gilding.

Efforts to implement clauses that sought to limit indigenous participation are represented in two instances. Clause eight stipulated that Indians could work freely on the lesser painting genres of landscapes, flowers, fruits, animals, and birds. In order to produce religious paintings, however (the bulk of painting and commissions in the colonial period), Indians would have to pass the guild examination in conformity with the requirements of Spanish painters. A new clause, number fifteen, proposed that once the reformed clauses became effective no master painter could agree to train and accept apprentices who were not Spanish. Although other than the term *español,* no specific racial categories were used in this instance, the all-encompassing "not Spanish" extended the exclusionary clause to blacks and *castas* as well as Indians.[90]

There is little documentation that sheds further light on the authorship of the revised ordinances and the discussions that produced them, especially the insertion of the racially exclusive apprenticeship clause. The painters framed their objectives as synonymous with those of Church and Crown: their intended objective of eliminating erroneous and bad paintings and images could only work to the public good. In accord with the logic and rationale of guilds in the polity, therefore, they conveyed the guild's contribution to the maintenance of order, social hierarchy, orthodoxy, and morality. The restriction of apprenticeships to Spaniards provided one mechanism by which to protect social respectability and ensure that future masters—and thus the future of the painting profession—would be the preserve of Spaniards, effectively whitening the guild.[91] At the same time, the proposed ordinance revisions designed to enforce the boundaries among allied crafts and control over sale of artworks indicate the painters' growing concerns about competition.

In response to legal advice that to subject Indians to the guild's new ordinances would cause too many "inconveniences," viceroy Melchor Portocarrero Lasso y de la Vega refused to approve the clauses that would have restricted apprenticeships to those of Spanish blood, and that prevented anyone who was not a master painter or gilder from participation in the public auction of paintings.[92] Thus, the painters found their claims to expanded privileges counteracted by the invocation of the Indians' special status as *pobres miserables*. The rest of the ordinances received approval on 17 October 1686, but were not announced publicly until six months later, on 28 April 1687.[93] The process to reform and reimplement the guild ordinances had taken approximately six years to complete.

The implementation of the revised ordinances in 1687 demonstrates a renewed, albeit short-lived ability of the painters to enforce guild regulations. Following the promulgation of the ordinances, guild inspectors were elected and examinations administered. Some of Mexico City's most promising and prominent painters were elected (and re-elected) as *veedores* (inspectors) of the guild such as Antonio de Arellano (active 1693–1711), Nicolas Rodríguez Juárez, Antonio Rodríguez, Correa, and Villalpando.[94] Newly elected guild officials provided what had been lacking until the late seventeenth century: the policing of their profession and inspection of workshops. Between 1687 and 1717 the *alcaldes* (supervisors) and *veedores* embraced their regulatory positions and, emboldened by the new ordinances, carried out inspections of artists' workshops in Mexico City, Tlatelolco, and Xochimilco (two Indian sections of town).[95]

Evidence of the erosion of the painters' guild's ability to enforce its ordinances in the early eighteenth century is provided by its prosecution in

1717 of two well-known master *entalladores* and *ensambladores,* Salvador de Ocampo and Juan de Rojas. In considering the sculptors' appeal against such prosecution, the *fiscal,* or prosecutor, faced the problem of whether they should be held accountable for violation of the painters' guild regulations. Rojas and Ocampo testified that it had been "the custom for sixteen or eighteen years" to gild works without intervention from the painters' guild. If this was indeed the case, then their testimony suggests that by 1700, the painters' guild was unable once again to enforce its regulations on a regular basis.[96] As a result of the case against Rojas and Ocampo, an order was issued for the painters' guild's ordinances to be publicly announced again "so that people cannot plead ignorance of their existence." And so they were, in three different places in Mexico City on July 24, 1717, though I have yet to find evidence that indicates the re-announcement of the painters' guild ordinances resulted in another surge of inspections, elections of inspectors, and enforcement of guild examinations.[97]

Petitions in the Defense of Painting and Painting Academies

Faced with the weakening of the painters' guild's regulatory powers, some master painters looked to the creation of societies or academies to facilitate the teaching of painting, development of pictorial style and techniques, and to provide an institutional expression of their ambitions in a respectable space.[98] Such attempts may have been influenced by knowledge of painters' initiatives in Spain, such as Bartolomé Esteban Murillo's foundation of an art academy in Seville (1664–1675) and Francisco Antonio Meléndez' (1682–1752) efforts (albeit unsuccessful) to found an academy in Madrid (1726) modelled on those active in Rome, Paris, and Florence. The creation of the Royal Academy of San Fernando in Madrid in 1752 clearly influenced the initiatives of Mexican painters who invoked its foundation to justify their own ambitions to establish a similar academy in Mexico City.[99] Efforts to dictate the terms of eligibility to become a painter's apprentice—and who could and who could not paint what and where—also accompanied the painters' initiatives in the first half of the eighteenth century. Such efforts and the discourse that accompanied them suggests a steady and continuing racializing of the painters' targets—the unlicensed and untrained painters and vendors of Mexico City.

Evidence of the existence of an "academy" appears in the contract for a triumphal arch commissioned by the Mexico City council in 1722 to receive viceroy Juan de Acuña y Bejarano, Marqués de Casafuerte (1722–34). Eleven painters belonged to the academy, including Nicolás and Juan Rodríguez Juárez (both described as "correctors" of the academy), Ibarra, Br. José Rodríguez, and two Indian *caciques,* Clemente López and Mateo Gómez.[100] Little else is known about this academy. Its relationship to the guild is unclear, as is its actual legal status or even its physical location. It is probable that this academy functioned as a series of informal gatherings of the painters in their homes and workshops.

Six years later, in 1728, nine painters (including four signatories active in the aforementioned academy, Nicolas Rodríguez Juárez, Br. José Rodríguez, Nicolás Enríquez, and Clemente López) granted power of attorney to Clemente del Campo to present their case before the king, the Council of the Indies, and "all relevant tribunals in Spain."[101] They requested that the king grant them as "professors of the art of painting" a special prerogative and privilege that would allow them to restrict apprenticeships to young men of Spanish birth and Indians who could prove they were *caciques* or descendants of *caciques.*[102] The petitioners also stated that those individuals currently serving apprenticeships who were neither Spanish nor descendants of *caciques,* "even though they are of inferior *calidad,*" might continue with their apprenticeships so as not to cause any harm. They proposed that in the future Indians who were not *caciques* be permitted to paint "in their pueblos, republics, and barrios but not in the court, cities, towns, or places of the Spanish."[103] Their petition may have been part of a formal request to establish an academy, but without additional evidence no firm conclusion can be drawn. The petition is significant, however, since it provides insights into the painters' strategies and priorities in the definition and organization of their profession. First, the painters' intention to limit apprenticeships to young Spanish males and Indian nobles, and to restrict plebeian Indian craftsmen to their own towns and villages, suggests a reinforced determination to impose restrictive recruitment statutes which grappled with both racial and estate categories. Second, the painters' experience of the colonial authorities' (*ayuntamiento, audiencia,* and viceroy) ambiguous support for enforcement of the guild's regulations may have forced them to modify their position on the exclusion of non-Spanish apprentices from the profession. Their inclusion of a grandfather clause that would have permitted those who were neither Spanish nor Indian *caciques* or their descendants to continue with their apprenticeships is revealing. It suggests that the painters recognized the need to frame their proposal in such a

way that colonial authorities would not interpret it as harmful to the population in general. At the same time, they evidently decided to bypass colonial
authorities in Mexico City and directed their petition to the highest possible
authority—the king.

Although there is no evidence of any official response to the painters' petition of 1728, a subsequent petition submitted some twenty-five years later
in 1753 suggests that little had changed during the intervening years in the
painters' ability to regulate their profession. José de Ibarra and "other professors of the Liberal Art of *Pincel y Buril*" ("Brush and Burin") reiterated in their
petition to the viceroy, in a clear and pointed manner, concerns expressed in
previous requests to colonial authorities.[104] Three major themes dominated
the petition: complaints about the vexed presence of the *tratantes,* unlicensed
and untrained individuals who operated workshops as painters and engravers, and engaged in the selling of artworks; the need to exclude individuals
of inferior *calidad* from the profession; and the importance of recognizing
painting as a liberal art. The petitioners expressed their dismay about "mulatto professors and some Spaniards who although they are not painters,
own workshops in order to earn their living," and requested the exclusion
of those of "inferior *calidad*" from apprenticeships in painting and engraving. In direct connection to the objectives of the 1681 ordinances, Ibarra's
petition also emphasized the need to shut down workshops run by anyone
(including Spaniards) who was not trained as a painter or engraver.[105] Finally,
the petition demonstrates a strong familiarity with the traditional arguments
made in defense of painting by authors such as Carducho and Pacheco and of
the painters' situation in Spain. Ibarra mentions specifically the peninsular
painters' privileges such as exemptions from the *alcabala* and other taxes, and
royal approval and financing of the recently founded Real Academia de San
Fernando in Madrid. In a new line of argument, however, Ibarra attempted to
legitimate the painters' demands for the exclusion of individuals of "inferior
calidad" from the profession by noting similar prohibitions against admission to the Royal University of Mexico City.[106]

Again, there is no record of any response from the Mexico City council but
several months later in 1754, Ibarra along with twenty-three other painters
and the architect Miguel Espinosa de los Monteros (active 1740–1760) formulated a petition to seek royal approval for an academy of painting in Mexico
City.[107] Several artists provided continuity with previous petitions and/or association with an academy including Ibarra, Fray Miguel de Herrera, Clemente

López, Cabrera, Vallejo, Morlete Ruiz, and Espinosa de los Monteros. Also included in this initiative were five of the six painters whose opinions on the image of the Virgin of Guadalupe were included by Cabrera in his *Maravilla americana*—Ibarra, Morlete Ruiz, Alcíbar, Osorio, and Vallejo.[108] It is surely no coincidence that a major push to establish a Mexican academy occurred within the context of the inspection of the Virgin of Guadalupe in 1751, the creation of the Royal Academy of San Fernando of Madrid in 1753, and the publication of Cabrera's *Maravilla Americana* in 1756.[109]

When the painters met on March 13, 1754, before the notary don Andrés Bermúdez de Castro the academy for which they sought royal approval seemed to be already functioning. They declared that they had "been working for some time to form an academy or society or company which has been and is meeting twice a week."[110] On March 23, 1754 they granted power of attorney to a merchant, don José Vázquez, to appear "before his Catholic Majesty and request his patronage and royal support and that he confirm the painters in all the *fueros* and privileges that he has bestowed on this art [painting] . . . and especially those he has conferred and granted to the said Academy or Society of Painters in Madrid."[111]

The academy's faculty included a president (Ibarra), an expert in mathematics or "*corrector de matemáticas*" (Espinosa de los Monteros), and several other experts in painting or "*correctores*" (Miguel de Rudecindo de Contreras, Cabrera, Morlete Ruiz, and Vallejo).[112] Its main purpose was to provide instruction in painting and drawing. The painters emphasized the importance of such training, as it would ensure the production of paintings conducive to "the veneration and respect of images."[113] As in the case of the petition submitted in 1728, the painters reiterated that the academy would not harm any interests.[114] In this respect, they continued to rehearse their contributions to preserving morality, orthodoxy, and order.

The Mexican writer José Bernardo de Couto (1803–1862) in his *Diálogo sobre la historia de la pintura en México* (1872) described the academy as providing drawing lessons, the study of the live model, and holding annual competitions.[115] Despite mention of the academy's statutes (*Estatutos o constituciones que deberá observar y guardar la Academia de la muy noble e inmemorial arte de la Pintura*), Couto quotes only one (number nine) which excluded everyone except Spaniards from taking lessons in the academy. The statute stipulated that "No one may accept pupils of "*color quebrado*" (literally "broken color"); anyone who does will be expelled from the Academy."

Before academy members could accept students they must prove that they were "Spanish and of good habits." The secretary "will verify from the baptismal papers which the student brings with him whether he is of the *calidad* he says . . . and only in this way will pupils be received and in no other way."[116] What is significant here in combination with Ibarra's 1753 petition is the painters' increasing sensitivity to the *casta* population and an apparent shift in emphasis from targeting Indians, as in the painters' 1681 ordinances and 1728 petition, to the construction of a more generalized category of "*color quebrado*" as a social marker of inferior *calidad*.

The painters' subsequent action suggests that after ten months they had yet to receive a response to their petition. On January 21, 1755, they granted another power of attorney to Bartolomé Solano, *procurador* (attorney) of the high court to represent the painters in "all the complaints, petitions, lawsuits and transactions pertinent to the art of painting now and in the future in both civil and criminal cases." They did so as members of "a society or academy of painting," which suggests that the institution whatever its nature still operated.[117] What remains unclear, as in the case of the painters' previous proposals, is the nature of the formal relationship between the proposed academy and the guild (if indeed the guild remained functional by the mid-eighteenth century) and its physical location. The documentation suggests that the painters' rationale for establishing an academy may have been to provide a supplement to the daily training provided in painters' workshops as opposed to replacing it, and to improve the quality of training through the inculcation of the proper precepts of art by a group of "professors" of painting. The ninth clause of the academy's statutes, suggests, moreover, the painters' continued determination to make painting a "Spanish" occupation by restricting admission to the academy to Spaniards.

There is some evidence that the "academy" may have functioned for several years. The petitions indicate that Ibarra acted as president for at least a year beginning in 1754, possibly earlier. Moreover, the statutes described by Couto suggest the evolution of the academy's structure from one which included a president (Ibarra), a corrector of mathematics, and several correctors of painting specified in the petitions of 1754 and 1755, to those specified in the *Estatutos,* a president (Cabrera), five directors, and a secretary.[118] Alcíbar also refers to the existence of this academy, prior to the establishment of the Royal Academy of San Carlos in Mexico City, and in which he "served from my earliest years and . . . [of which] I was named director . . . "[119] It is also worth noting that only six out of twenty-one master painters listed in the 1753 census signed at least one of the petitions submitted in 1754 and 1755 in support of an academy of painting. Whether the lack of participation of the remaining fifteen master painters may be read as opposition, indifference, or exclusion remains to be clarified. The attempts to establish an academy undoubtedly signified for a select and ambitious group of painters the opportunity to reclaim meaningful control over the painting profession, which had been eroded as demonstrated by the short-lived success of their guild reforms.[120]

Failure to receive royal approval and patronage of an academy did not seem to prevent master painters from achieving individual success, as I argued at the beginning of this essay. Individual success, however, could not substitute for the consolidation of the painters' improved status collectively or the effective regulation of the painting profession.[121] In 1768, the year Cabrera died and a year after the expulsion of the Jesuits from Mexico, a group of master painters and sculptors granted power to Bertucat, to negotiate once again "the most effective and opportune measures to protect our interests, and that these be conducive toward the establishment of an Academy of Painting and Sculpture, and the establishment of rules and ordinances for its most formal conservation and arrangement."[122] Of twelve signatories to this petition, five appear in the petitions of 1754 or 1755 to establish an academy—Morlete Ruiz, Vallejo, Manuel Carcanio (active 1731–1782), Quintana, and Clemente López. As with previous requests, the lack of additional documentation makes it difficult to know whether any serious discussion of their petition ever occurred. When the Royal Academy of San Carlos opened its doors in Mexico City in 1785, its origins were to be found not in the initiatives of local artists but in the interests of the Spanish monarchy.

Looked at collectively, the painters' petitions for the defense of painting, reform of their guild, and projects for painting academies (1674, 1681, 1722, 1728, 1753, 1754, 1755, and 1768) exhibit concern with two central issues: first, improved control over the training, production, and commerce of artworks; second, the elevation of the status of their profession to entail emphasis on painting as a liberal art and also as fundamentally a "Spanish" profession. One strategy to achieve these goals was to not only crack down on unlicensed and untrained craftsmen but in the process to racialize this population by targeting Indians and *castas*. Yet the roles played by some *casta* painters in the various reform efforts and the prominence they achieved reveals a certain disjuncture between the painters' racialized rhetoric that marked the inclusionary and exclusionary boundaries of their profession. In other words, what the painters said and what they did were not quite the same. Ibarra and Morlete Ruiz (and possibly Cabrera) provide examples of painters of mixed race who chose to redefine themselves as Spaniards. Correa, as a mulatto, however, is an interesting case because there appears to be no evidence that he described himself or was described in racial terms as anything other than a *mulato* or *pardo* (mulatto). Moreover, none of the extant documentation suggests that Correa was ever addressed with the honorific "don" yet he became one of the most prominent painters of the late seventeenth century whose work was in great demand, and who was widely esteemed by his colleagues.[123] Clearly, his categorization as racially mixed did not seem to affect his career or standing in the painters' guild. In all of these cases the acceptance of mixed-race painters by their colleagues and patrons undoubtedly depended upon other attributes such as their talent and reputation as artists. As R. Douglas Cope observed in his classic study of race in colonial Mexico: "as we move from the racial label-ling of strangers to the racial labelling of friends and acquaintances, physical traits become less important, and the pull of other criteria grows stronger."[124] It is important to note, however, that all of these *casta* painters supported in-creasingly restrictive recruitment regulations intended to privilege Spaniards. The painters' public projection of painting as a "Spanish" profession—both discursively and institutionally—and their private practice of accepting some mixed race apprentices reflected on a smaller scale the slippage that occurred between the ideals of the *sistema de castas* and their practical relevance to the population of colonial Mexican society. Not only does the painters' case point to the continuing importance of race in mid-eighteenth century Mexico City, it also demonstrates how the fluidity of the racial hierarchy worked not to un-dermine its relevance but to perpetuate its functioning and power.[125]

Concluding Thoughts

The founding of the Royal Academy of San Carlos in 1785 represented a major step forward in the consolidation of the status of artists in colonial Mexico. As the painters' complaints in 1789 and 1799 described at the beginning of this essay indicate, however, not all problems faced by artists were solved with the establishment of the Royal Academy of San Carlos. To deal with the prob-lem of illicit production and sale of artworks, the painters requested that the Academy appoint inspectors to identify all individuals engaged in such ac-tivities and order their workshops to be closed down.[126] The directors of the

Royal Academy agreed and recommended that no one should be permitted to maintain a painting or engraving workshop without first having undergone a rigorous examination by the Royal Academy.[127] The request was forwarded to the *fiscal protector de indios* (chief legal counsel for Indian affairs). In response to the directors' suggestion, the *fiscal* described the hardships that Indian craftsmen would suffer if their workshops were shut down since they had no other source of income. He recommended that all painters examined by the Academy should affix a distinctive sign on their houses or workshops which indicated their academic affiliation and training so that "the public would not be defrauded." The *fiscal* also advised that a list of all painters in New Spain who had been examined, especially those based in Mexico City, should be compiled, and invited further discussion about the "intruder artisans" (*"oficiales intrusos"*).[128] A century had passed since the painters' attempts to reform their guild in 1681 and their successors' complaints about untrained and unlicensed craftsmen in 1799. Not only did "academic" painters continue to confront the enduring problem of illicit production of artworks but such activity compromised their status as they perceived their "dishonor [to be] in the hands of Indians, blacks, and Spaniards."

There are two images that provide compelling evidence for the continuing efforts of the painters to define and defend their profession even as the establishment of the Royal Academy of San Carlos symbolized the prestige of the fine arts. An anonymous *casta* painting of the last quarter of the eighteenth century, depicts a well-dressed Spanish painter in his studio with a female sitter (an *albina*, presumably his wife), their *torna atrás* (return-backwards) child, probably an apprentice of his father, and an assistant with no race specified who appears to be at work grinding pigments (fig. 2.6).[129] The artist's workshop represents the Spanish painter as "theorist and educator" by the presence of neoclassical sculptures, paintings, and prints of different genres hanging on the walls, and by the practice of sketches of the young *torna atrás* apprentice. The second image from an anonymous series portrays a gilder— gilders, as mentioned earlier, were also members of the painters' guild, and gilding was also commonly practiced by painters (fig. 2.7). In stark contrast to the image of the Spanish painter in his prosperous workshop, the very dark-skinned *casta* gilder (a *zambaigo*) appears in impoverished surroundings. At work on gilding a frame, seated on a simple stool, he is barefoot, and his clothes are torn and stained. His wife (a *loba* or wolf) also modestly dressed and barefoot, spins thread helped by her son, a *grifo*. There is little in this

Figure 2.6. Unknown artist, *De albina y español, nace torna atrás* (From Albina and Spaniard, a Return-Backwards is Born) c. 1785–90, oil on canvas, 62.6 × 83.2 cm. Private Collection.

image that suggests the accoutrements of a well-equipped and respectable workshop or of an artisan who has been trained in his craft. These are among the only extant representations of artists in over one hundred extant series of the *casta* genre. We do not know why and on whose initiative these particular representations were introduced—the painter's, the patron's, or both—into what had become a fairly standard repertoire of occupational representations in the *casta* genre.

The appearance of the first image (an anomaly in the entire *castas* corpus) in the 1780s is probably not accidental given that the Royal Academy of San Carlos was functioning by 1781 (at least in its provisional form) and fully established by 1785. It may reflect the painters' growing confidence in the consolidation of their respectable status physically embodied in an academy buttressed by royal patronage, a status sufficiently well defined to withstand confusion or conflation with other occupations and racial mixtures represented in the *casta* series. Conversely, the image of the *zambaigo* gilder may also represent a subtle critique of the ongoing problem for the painters of the "intruders and offenders" despite the academy's foundation. The academy may have provided painters with privileges and prestige but it could not eradicate the illicit production and sale of artworks by unexamined and untrained craftsmen. The fact that prior to the mid-eighteenth century there is a complete absence of images of painters and artists in the *casta* corpus suggests a deliberate act of elision by painters. Such an elision may reflect the painters' ongoing attempts to distance themselves from an unlicensed, untrained, racialized "Other" who threatened their status and claims to be practitioners of one of the most "noble" and "liberal" of arts.

The case of the painters points to a much wider trend, not only in eighteenth-century colonial Mexico, but also within the Spanish empire: anxiety about social status and the development of strategies to shape and protect such status. As Ruth Mackay asserts: "two sets of exclusionary practices gained importance: limits placed by guilds on membership, and limits placed by other arenas (social, political, or religious) on access by practitioners of certain

Figure 2.7. Unknown artist, *N. 15 De zambaigo y loba nace grifo* (N. 15 From Zambaigo and Wolf a Grifo is Born), c. 1780, oil on copper, 31.8 × 41 cm. Private Collection.

crafts. Together, they add up to the category of *limpieza de oficios.* Social status and impurity now were linked." Yet much more research is required on how different guilds and artisans framed such limits or, indeed, became the targets of them, and on the slippage between discourse and practice.[130] Even the language employed by different groups of artisans in the construction of such exclusionary practices, for example, seems to have varied. Rarely did the painters employ the term *limpieza de sangre* (purity of blood). Rather, they exhibited a preference for the term *calidad,* even though the practice of requiring a birth certificate for admission to study at the "academy" established in 1753 suggests that they in fact upheld the principle of *limpieza de sangre.* The silversmiths of Mexico City, however, increasingly emphasized, well into the early nineteenth century, the importance of *limpieza de sangre.* Not only did the silversmiths' guild require proof of *limpieza de sangre* as a requirement of applicants who wished to sit the guild exam in order to qualify as a master but also that they must swear on oath not to accept any apprentices who could not prove their legitimacy and purity of blood.[131] Finally, regional variations not only within Mexico but also throughout the Spanish empire require much more detailed reconstruction and comparison in order to avoid erroneous homogenization of artists' and artisans' experiences. Only then will we gain a more nuanced understanding of both the universal and local practices, laws, and discourses that shaped the lives and identities of artists during the colonial period.[132]

"That This Should Be Published and Again in the Age of the Enlightenment?"

Eighteenth-Century Debates About the Indian Body in Colonial Mexico

Ilona Katzew

DEBATES ABOUT THE NATURE OF AMERINDIANS have a long history that harks back to the beginning of Spanish colonization. Even though the Pope declared the Indians to be fully human in a Bull of 1537, and in the sixteenth century the Spanish crown determined that they were Christian neophytes who deserved its protection, discussions about their rational capabilities and their ability to become true Christians extended over the next three centuries.[1] This essay addresses the debate about the origin, nature, and place of Amerindians in the eighteenth century. To understand the nuances and complexities of this debate, I first explain how many of these issues form part of a discursive continuum that began practically since colonization. Crucial in assessing the renewed fervency of the subject in the eighteenth century is to consider the different social groups or actors who generated the debates and their reasons for doing so. As we will see through the close reading of a number of texts (some unpublished and largely unknown), Spaniards, northern Protestant, Creoles, and the indigenous communities themselves, all had different interests at stake, and were largely responsible for producing and reproducing various epistemologies which have had an enduring effect until today.

While most early descriptions about the Americas and its inhabitants were written by Spanish authors, in the eighteenth century a new trend emerged in Europe, whereby northern philosophers positioned themselves as the legitimate producers of New World narratives. Since the sixteenth century Spain had zealously guarded its American colonies, prohibiting official travel by foreigners. Spain's obsession with restricting access to information about the colonies and their administration was legendary. "Spain, with an excess of caution, has uniformly thrown a veil over her transactions with America. From strangers they are concealed with peculiar solicitude," noted the Scottish enlightened thinker William Robertson (1721–1793) in 1777.[2] This lack of information coupled with the growing desire to learn about the promise of riches of the last discovered continent—a topos in writings about the New World—led authors from France, Scotland, and Great Britain among other places to publish a number of widely read accounts.

Most authors had never set foot in the Americas, eliciting the impassioned response of Creole patriots—the American-born descendants of the Spaniards. It is important to note, however, that not all Creole responses were the same nor did they further the same agenda. Because Europeans frequently considered Creoles a degraded race due to their transference to the New World and their "dangerous" proximity to Amerindians (and blacks), some emphasized the grandeur of Mexico's precolonial past as a way to give the country a classical pedigree comparable to that of the Greeks and Romans in Europe. Others, particularly Creole clerics (American-born priests) who were more familiar with the indigenous communities and their ways of life, offered lengthy theological justifications of the natives' adherence to the Christian faith to demonstrate the spiritual maturity of the colony. These were strategies that served to counter the largely iniquitous view of Europeans regarding the New World and its inhabitants. In this essay, I explore how Amerindians were at the center of many of these debates, and how they were racialized and used to contest sovereign notions of dominance and subordination. On a broader level, this essay addresses the competing factions—Spanish, northern European, and Creole—and their contestation of knowledge production about the New World during the Enlightenment.

The Origin of the Indians: "A Sea of So Many Literary Storms"

The origin of the Indians was a subject amply debated beginning in the sixteenth century and continued to the end of the colonial period. Since all the people of the world had to be accounted for, their ancestry had to be traced to recognized biblical lines; the debate therefore centered on the following set of questions: Where do the Indians come from? When and how did they arrive in the New World? A milestone in the debate was the Spanish Jesuit José de Acosta's popular *Historia natural y moral de las Indias*. In his tract (published in Seville in 1590, and reprinted several times and translated into the most important European languages), Acosta provides the reader with a description of the origin of the inhabitants of the New World and a concise history of the Inca and Aztec empires prior to the arrival of the Spaniards. He suggests that the first men to arrive in the New World came by land rather than by sea, crossing from Asia in the northeastern corner of the hemisphere. According to Acosta, on their arrival these men were still savages who traveled in small bands and slowly spread to the rest of the continent; their Asian origin was clear by the similarity of their physical appearance and because he believed that the many languages that the Indians spoke had a common source in East Asia. Because his was a providential account, Acosta held to the biblical notion that after the Deluge people and animals were distributed over the face of the earth, and that the existence of identical species of animals in the Old World and New World proved that they, too, had crossed over by land.[3]

Acosta's theory was enormously influential; it was tied to his larger idea about the division of "barbarians" (understood as people who neither subscribed to European religious views nor lived according to European social norms) into three categories: (1) those who most resembled Europeans and possessed stable republics, civil laws, fortified cities, and rulers, and above all systems of writing, such as the Chinese, Japanese, and certain nations in India; (2) those situated in an immediately preliterate state, and who were also organized into polities and had some form of religious cult, such as the Inca and the Aztec; (3) those "savage" and nomadic men who lived outside of the norms of civil organization, and were thus considered to be at the bottom of the human scale. According to Acosta, all men had at one point passed through one of these three stages of "barbarism" prior to being converted to Christianity and becoming fully civilized. His theory of a steady evolutionism helped him account for the concurrent existence of all three types of Indians in the Americas. If the Inca and the Aztec were somewhat more civilized than the majority of Indian nations, it was because they had migrated at a much later stage and therefore retained more of their ancestral cultures.[4] The idea, of course, was that the Indians were "perfectible" humans, and that once they had passed through all stages of development they would become fully civilized Christian citizens, an issue that we will see was at the core of many eighteenth-century debates.

The repository of many of the theories and myths regarding the origin of the Indians was the Spanish Dominican Gregorio García's *Origen de los indios del Nuevo Mundo,* first published in Valencia in 1607. The impact of this publication cannot possibly be overestimated. In the seventeenth and eighteenth centuries virtually every author who wrote about the New World—

Spanish, Creole, and indigenous—ventured a theory or attempted to grapple with those described in García's book.[5] A key issue in the debate was whether the Indians had descended from Adam and Eve, and thus if they were fully human. As a priest, García was compelled to begin his treatise with a set of unassailable provisions: the first and most important, derived from Genesis, argued that all human beings from the beginning of time descended from Adam and Eve and therefore from Noah and his sons who survived the Deluge; the second provision contended that since the New World was the last continent to be discovered, its inhabitants could only have migrated from one of the three previously known ones—Europe, Asia, or Africa. In other words, the biblical origin of the natives of the New World was irrefutable. The theory of monogenesis was essential not only to prove that the Indians were human but also to justify the evangelizing mission of the Spanish crown. If the Indians were not descended from Adam and Eve, as some polygenetic theories argued, it followed that they were not human and were therefore devoid of a soul.[6] How, then, could their conversion be justified?

Based on alleged commonalities of language, architecture, forms of literacy, customs, dress, temperament, and physical traits among other characteristics, García's theories included those claiming that the Indians descended from the Carthaginians, from Solomon's Ophir (an unidentified region mentioned in the Bible), The Ten Lost Tribes of Israel, the Atlantis, Africans, Phoenicians, the Huns, Tartars and Chinese, and every imaginable nation in Europe.[7] The section of García's treatise devoted to the opinion that they descended from the Hebrews is particularly revealing.[8] This was a widespread opinion, and García admits devoting more time to it than to any other in the book. According to this idea, the Ten Lost Tribes of Israel migrated first to Tartar and Mongolia and then crossed over to Mexico and Peru by land through the so-called Strait of Anian (part of the legendary Northwest passage that linked the Atlantic and Pacific oceans). García also suggests that they could have crossed from China, which would account for the many similarities among the Indians and the Chinese.[9] Resorting to the worst form of racial typing that goes back to the Middle Ages and before, García explains that those connecting the Indians with the Jews noted similar physical traits (such as their big noses and hair styles); their disbelief in Christ and their supposed role in his death; their penchant for idolatry; and their dress and customs. One of the objections that García raises was a purported difference in intelligence, manners, and beauty among the two groups. He notes that some people credited the Jews with being the most intelligent and handsome people on earth, which explained why they were chosen by God. The Indians, on the other hand: "lack all of this, because they are unpolished and slow of learning, with ugly bodies and faces, and in my opinion they are the least esteemed nation in the world; even the blacks, that among us are little valued because they are slaves and natural servants, are of a better caste and stronger nature; this is accepted by the Indians themselves who refer to a black person as *señor* [master], and because Indian women prefer to marry black men, seldom or never marrying an Indian, which is more prevalent in New Spain."[10] García also noted that Indians were weak and effeminate. This sort of description which derives from Hippocratic-Galenic medicine argued that climate had the power to shape the bodies, minds, and moral inclinations of people.[11] The climate of the Americas, a region that was often referred to as the torrid zone (*zona tórrida*) and once thought by the ancients to be uninhabitable, was found to be rather temperate and excessively moist; the dampness of the continent made the natives' bodies humid and feeble like those of women, and also accounted for their "innate" slothfulness and diminished intellectual abilities.[12]

García lived twelve years in Mexico and Peru, which allowed him to pepper his account with first-hand observations and opinions of this kind. But making such overt disparaging remarks about the nature of the Indians carried deep semantic implications. What did this mean for mestizos, the offspring of Indians and Spaniards? García's way out of the conundrum was to create a line dividing the Jews responsible for the death of Christ, and those who descended from the Ten Lost Tribes of Israel, believed to have arrived in the New World before this cataclysmic event in the history of Christianity. In addition, he stressed that the Spanish side of mestizos carried more weight, which explained why mestizos adopted Spanish names and surnames, lived among Spaniards in the *república de españoles* or Spanish polity, and were awarded honorable posts and occupations. The underlying principle was that because Spanish men tended to mix with Indian women, their blood had the ability to shape the character of their progeny. This notion which derives from Aristotelian theories regarding heredity also largely informed Spanish juridical-cum-religious notions of genealogy and nobility. Because the male seed was the most potent of the generative fluids and women were seen as passive and malleable, men ultimately determined the proclivities of their children. However, the transformative process of *mestizaje* also harbored the possibility of racial mending. Through the right pattern of successive mixtures with Spaniards, Indians and mestizos could eventually become a vigorous race of Spaniards on the third generation—an idea that became most visible in the eighteenth-century pictorial genre of *casta* paintings (see Introduction, fig. I.1). This is also why García urged his readers not to disdain or offend mestizos for being part Indian, and was prompt to add that this theory was simply a matter of opinion and not of science; if it did not suit certain people, namely mestizos, they were free to ignore it and espouse another of their liking. And there were plenty of options from which to draw in García's compilation.[13]

The final section of García's book is devoted to the Indians' own account of their origin. Although García appears to give agency to indigenous peoples, he dismissed their pictographic traditions—codices in the case of Mexico—and *quipus*—a mnemonic cord with knots used by the Inca for record keeping in Peru—as unreliable and filled with fables, relying instead on early chronicles by Spanish authors. The subject of the Indians' lack of a clear recollection of their past had plagued European accounts since the encounter and extended well into the nineteenth century; it was a way of stressing their inferior state of civilization when compared to Europeans and ultimately of justifying Europe's expansionist efforts. In the end, García's assessment of the origin of the Indians was as elusive as the many theories that he exposed. The natives, he noted, could have descended from just about anyone—the same way that the Spanish nation was a mixture of various cultures over time. To bring this notion to the present, he concluded in one sweeping remark:

> What I have been saying is most evident in our Indies, where there are Castilians, Indians, Portuguese, Galician, Basques, Catalans, Valencians, French, Italians, Greeks, blacks, and even *moriscos* [people of Moorish descent] and gypsies who are either covert or retain a shred and piece of this caste; and there is no lack of descendants of Jews: all of whom living in the same provinces, are compelled to mix through marriage or illicit sex.[14]

Even if García was reluctant to favor any theory in particular, his opinion about the meekness of the Indians due to their excessive body humidity remained unchallenged. The environment and unique constellation of the continent had transformed the original traits of the natives' ancestors—wherever they migrated from—and eventually became "fixed." In other words, people and animals that crossed over from the Old World to the Americas degenerated. This was not the case of contemporary Spaniards—like García himself—

and their children, as they were better suited to preserve their "nature," in part because of their diet based on European staples. But despite García's best intention to temper his argument, this was a paradox that he could not fully resolve.[15]

In the eighteenth century, the origin of the Indians remained as vexing and hotly debated as in the two preceding centuries. It is no coincidence that García's book was reprinted in 1729 and that it was often referenced by contemporary writers—clerical and secular.[16] In a short tract about the life and manners of the Indians in Mexico of 1762, for example, an anonymous Spanish author begins by acknowledging the difficulty of determining the origin of Amerindians; he dismissed the idea that they descended from the Jews and argued instead that they came indistinctly from China or Ophir. Citing the work of García, he noted that after laboring intensively on various theories García rebuffed them all, "leaving the issue in much greater doubt."[17] Lorenzo Boturini Benaducci (1702–1753), the illustrious Italian antiquarian who lived in Mexico from 1736 to 1743 also attempted to grapple with the issue of the Indians' origin. During his stay in Mexico he amassed an impressive collection of indigenous codices and antiquities. These materials were eventually confiscated by Spanish royal authorities in Mexico, forcing Boturini to write a book on the Mesoamerican past largely from memory and based on published sources. Despite some of the shortcomings of his *Idea de una nueva historia general de la America septentrional* (1746), Boturini was well aware of the disparate theories regarding the origin of the Indians, which he described as "a sea of so many literary storms" (*un mar de tantas literarias tormentas*).[18] As he noted, "Many, including celebrated historians, have tired in discovering the origin of our Indians, and some have devoted entire books to this matter, such as friar Gregorio García, a Dominican, whose investigations and efforts, even though entirely praiseworthy, have never appeased my little understanding, nor that sea of conjectures satisfied my curiosity."[19]

For Boturini the method of establishing analogies between the Indians and other idolatrous cultures based on language, forms of government, and customs was far from adequate, as similarities were often simply the result of chance.[20] Boturini stated that the Indians came from Asia by sea, as their codices, maps, and songs showed that they had a clear memory of Babylon. In other words, they were part of the human dispersion after the Flood and the Tower of Babel when the division of tongues occurred, and therefore were connected to the biblical world.[21] To further stress their ancestry and prove that they were part of the Christian brotherhood, Boturini noted that prior to the arrival of the Spaniards the apostle Saint Thomas had arrived in Mexico and Peru to preach Christianity. This was an old idea that the Italian antiquarian trotted out to prove that the Indians (though lapsed) had been exposed to Christianity early in their history and that they were far from being barbarians. García himself devoted an entire book to the evangelizing mission of the apostle in the New World prior to Columbus's world-changing voyage; the book, however, was quickly banned, presumably because it lessened the role of the Spaniards as the first to set foot in the New World.[22]

Another book that became hugely prominent in eighteenth century debates about the origin of Amerindians was Isaac de la Peyrère's (1596–1676) *Prae-Adamitae*. In this explosive text published in Amsterdam in 1655, the French Huguenot hypothesized that God created two groups of men: the first produced the gentiles that spread over the world, including America; the second group were descendants of Adam, the father of the Jews. Because the human race was in such a state of disarray, a war of all against all, God created Adam, the first Jew, as a means of saving humanity. According to La Peyrère, this theory explained why people could recall ancient pagan cultures, as well as some of the incongruities in the Bible; it also meant that the Flood destroyed only the Hebrews but did not reach the New World. More pointedly, the dual thesis implied that there were two "species" of man, an idea that went against Scripture and elicited a widespread commotion among theologians and thinkers of the time (La Peyrère was forced to retract, convert to Catholicism, and his books were burned in public).[23]

La Peyrère's radical views struck a deep chord in various writers of the Spanish-speaking world. Eighteenth-century authors charged the French author with being a heretic Calvinist. The enlightened Spanish Benedict friar Benito Jerónimo Feijoo (1676–1764) accused him of "vomiting a most pernicious error."[24] Others referred to La Peyrère's theories as "insolent absurdities" (*desvaríos insolentes*), and devoted numerous pages to proving that the Flood had reached the New World, and that the Indians recorded this watershed event in their pictographs, *quipus*, and songs.[25] For example, in 1763 the Mexican Jesuit Francisco Xavier Alejo published a short tract about the subject to do away with the "ridiculous opinion of the Pre-Adamites . . . a malicious arrow shot to tarnish the origin of the Americans."[26] The purpose of the book was to restore the honor of the inhabitants of the Americas—especially Creoles—as La Peyrère and others had "attempted to exile us Americans, or deny us the Father that according to Holy Scripture is that of all of mankind."[27] Although Alejo agreed with Feijoo, he was disappointed that the influential Spanish enlightened thinker had not taken a stronger stance in what he called "a thorny problem" (*un ruidoso problema*). In Alejo's opinion, the Flood was universal, and people had crossed over from the Old World to the New World both by sea and land: by sea, because there was ample proof that ancient peoples were dexterous navigators; and by land because the continents, contrary to what the Pre-Adamites postulated, were once linked. He went as far as to note that the Indians' rites, customs, and lowly spirit, made them descendants from Ham, Noah's son whom according to the Bible the patriarch condemned to perpetual servitude after he exposed his nakedness to his brothers Shem and Japheth. (Traditionally, Japhet was believed to have populated Europe, Shem Asia, and Ham Africa.) By stating that the Indians descended from Ham via Africa, Alejo did not intend to extol their character (in fact, he hardly mentions the Indians at all), but he was giving the original inhabitants of the New World a biblical origin.[28] However, it was one thing to argue for the biblical origin of the Indians, and a very different one to suggest that they were the same as Creoles. After all, the notion that all people descended from Adam and Eve did not preclude a hierarchical ranking of humankind: Spaniards and their American-born descendants were clearly situated at the top.

This is a key point in the response generated by Creoles, who were willing to defend the natives insofar as they were often perceived to be connected to them by European authors. Since the sixteenth century, Europeans offered negative characterizations of Spaniards and Creoles, suggesting that their transference to the New World transformed them, almost by virtue of alchemy, into Amerindians, that is, into equally pusillanimous and effete beings. This tradition derived from Greco-Roman geopolitics that divided the world into three main zones. Pliny the Elder, for example, argued that the coldest regions of the world gave rise to fair-skinned people who were fierce but unwise and therefore unable to govern (e.g., Boreal peoples); the hottest latitudes engendered dark-skinned peoples who were wise but cowardly and equally ill-equipped to rule (e.g., Ethiopians); and the temperate areas begat people of medium complexion who were inherently suited to govern (e.g., people from the Mediterranean). The New World, located in the belt of the tropics, was viewed by early explorers as extremely hot and humid, a combination that accounted for the hyperproductivity of the land, but also for the quick ripening of plants, animals, and peoples—in other words, for their de-generation.[29] As one Creole friar noted: "If in general people consider the tal-ent of the Indies to be great, [they also claim] that it does not last long because in a few years its fruits wither given the climate of the place."[30] The notion that the inhabitants of the New World, as well as Europeans who transferred there ripened and "spoiled" quickly, persisted well into the end of the colonial period. In the seventeenth century, Creoles increasingly looked to extol their land and defend themselves from such negative views. Some went to great lengths to prove that the temperate climate of the Americas meant that it was the original location of paradise, and contrived various patriotic theories to prove that the properties of a place could not be judged by the quality of its inhabitants.[31] Based on Hippocratic-Galenic physiology, and the Aristotelian notion that peoples of warmer climates were more intelligent than those of colder ones, many learned Creoles sought to prove that once transplanted to the New World, Spaniards and their children did not degenerate but instead became more intelligent. To prevent people from drawing the wrong conclu-sions, however, Creoles stressed that because the constitution of Amerindi-ans, Spaniards, and blacks was intrinsically different, the temperate climate of the Americas affected their bodies differently and could never change their innate disposition. The idea was that certain elements or conditions operated differently upon diverse matter depending on the material's base quality. Pen-insulars who emigrated to the Indies and their offspring enjoyed better con-stitutions because they had moved from colder to more temperate climates; blacks born in the Americas were of a much better condition than those of Africa; and the Amerindians of New Spain, for example, were more civilized than those of the Caribbean and Florida. Yet, because of their "natural" dif-ferences, Amerindians, blacks, and Spaniards could never be homologized.[32]

Enlightenment Thinkers: The Noble Savage and the Savage Spaniard

If the subject of the origin of the Indians remained elusive in the eighteenth century, their state of development also continued to be the subject of pro-tracted debates. Since the sixteenth century, European authors devoted hun-dreds of pages to describing the newly discovered land of America and its inhabitants. While some accounts were partially based on firsthand observa-tion, particularly those by Spanish authors who had witnessed the conquest, many repeated and altered previous accounts, giving rise to a flurry of texts that often contained inaccurate and biased descriptions. By the eighteenth century, northwestern Protestant philosophers bent on questioning the accuracy of Spanish accounts developed their own narratives.[33] Most authors never traveled to the New World and based their texts on earlier sources or on purely fabricated facts. Nevertheless, these texts had a wide readership and greatly contributed to creating a picture of the New World that neither Spaniards nor Creoles, for different reasons, were keen to accept. Engraved images sometimes enhanced these accounts and blatantly cast the Spaniards as cruel savages trampling indigenous peoples.

In 1770, the French abbot Guillaume Thomas François Raynal (1713–1796) published his account *Histoire philosophique et politique des établissements et du commerce des Européens dans les deux Indes,* the fifth best seller on the New World, and the first to chart the European expansion to the West and East Indies. Raynal's massive compilation was reprinted and revised three times and translated into a host of languages. The book, now generally acknowledged to be the work of several enlightened authors, underscores the rapaciousness of the Spaniards and their overall negative effect on the development of a peaceful global economy—a major topic of the book.[34] "Tell me reader," Raynal asks rhetorically, "whether these [the Spaniards] were civilized people landing among savages, or savages among civilized people?"[35]

Though Raynal is quick to provide a negative image of the Spaniards as intolerant, uncultured, and greedy slayers of Indians (a trend known as Hispanophobia), he did not mince words either in describing the limitations of the indigenous populations of Mexico and Peru. He believed in the equality of man and found slavery and the commerce of human beings abominable, yet he also upheld the notion that not all mankind had reached the same degree of evolution. While Raynal describes the Aztec and Inca courts in hyperbolic terms, he argues that neither had attained a degree of civilization comparable to that of European nations. The fine arts and writing were the "spring and support of every civilized nation," argued Raynal, but neither the art nor architecture of these formidable empires, or what was left of them following their destruction by the Spaniards, could be "considered a monument of genius." Furthermore, the codices of the Mexicans had remained indecipherable and therefore unreliable as sources of information, and it was impossible to assert that the Peruvian *quipus* "could ever merit much confidence."[36] All in all, the natural indolence of native people coupled with the unjust and avaricious Spanish administration had greatly retarded the prosperity of that celebrated region. According to Raynal, colonization had also given rise to mixed, ostentatious, and highly corrupt societies, where the ignorant Catholic clergy encouraged superstition, and where the hot climate led to the degeneration of both animals and people. Further, it was the lasciviousness of women and the little attention that their own men paid to them—a tacit allusion to the preponderance of homosexual tendencies—that paved the way for colonization: "This furious attachment of the American women for the Spaniards, may be reckoned among the causes that contributed to the conquest of the New World."[37]

While there is no denying that Raynal's work was highly complex, particularly with regard to his defense of humanity and his proposition that a more gentle form of commerce could counter the ills of colonization, it is not difficult to see why his often incendiary tone alarmed the Spaniards and offended the colonial intellectual elite. Aside from portraying the Spaniards as savages, Raynal also introduced comments forecasting the independence of the colonies:

> It [colonization] hath procured to some empires vast domains, which have given splendour, power, and wealth, to the states which have founded them. But what expenses have not been lavished to clear, to govern, or to defend these distant possessions? When these colonies shall have acquired that degree of culture, knowledge, and population, which is suitable for them, will they not detach themselves from a country which hath founded their splendour upon their prosperity?[38]

Any attentive Spanish reader could not fail to realize the danger of Raynal's rhetoric and looked to strengthen the interests of the motherland; Creole patriots in turn sought to erase the false image of their history and population, even when compelled to admit their place within the Spanish empire to avoid being considered insurgent.[39]

Another major work of the time that both Spanish and Creole authors referenced is the Scotsman William Robertson's *The History of America* (1777). Robertson based much of his descriptions on travelogues and the work of other European philosophers, as well as primary sources that he was able to obtain through personal connections.[40] Like Raynal, he praised the Aztecs and the Incas for being more advanced than most of the rude tribes that populated the continent, but also claimed that their progress could never compare to that of ancient Europe. Natives were largely indolent and had no clear recollection of their past: "It is not surprising . . . that the unlettered inhabitants of America, who have no solicitude about futurity, and little curiosity concerning what is past, should be altogether unacquainted with their own original." As to their origin, Robertson admits that all humankind had one common source, yet determining where the Indians migrated from was no simple task. "The theories and speculations of ingenious men with respect to this subject, would fill many volumes; but are often so wild and chimerical . . . We may lay it down as a certain principle in this inquiry, that America was not peopled by any nation of the ancient continent, which had made considerable progress in civilization."[41] Even when Robertson condemns the Spaniards for their cruelty and the ruthlessness of their administration, the naturalization of the Indians' inferiority served to account for the success of the colonial enterprise as a whole.

Robertson was also of the opinion that the hot climate of the Americas was the reason why people and animals degenerated there. Citing the celebrated French naturalist George-Louis Leclerc, Comte de Buffon (1707–1788), and his immensely popular multi-volume *Histoire naturelle, génerale et particulière* (1748–1804), Robertson stated that the climate explained the less vigorous nature of the place. For instance, in describing the birds of the Americas as "decked in plumages, which dazzle the eye with the vivid beauty of their colors," he added that "nature, satisfied with clothing them in this gay dress has denied most of them the melody of sound, and variety of notes, which catches the delight of the ear."[42] The idea of the pan-degeneration of the Americas, as mentioned earlier, was rooted in classical antiquity, and was widespread among many enlightened thinkers. Creoles were especially targeted for their purported diminished intellectual faculties: "by the enervating influence of a sultry climate, by the rigor of a jealous government, and by their despair in attaining that distinction of which mankind naturally aspires, the vigor of their minds is so entirely broken, that a great part of them waste their life in luxurious indulgences, mingled with an illiberal superstition still more debasing."[43]

Though hardly the only ones, the examples of Raynal and Robertson, two of the most widely read authors of the time, illustrate the enormous interest of European authors in learning and writing about the Americas. There was a huge hunger for news about the continent largely motivated by economic interests. As mentioned in the introduction, the Spanish crown was famous for concealing information about the colonies from foreigners. As a result, authors tended to combine information deriving from disparate sources; they cited indistinctly sixteenth- and seventeenth-century sources to describe eighteenth-century society and occurrences, thereby perpetuating a range of notions about the New World that originated practically since the beginning of colonization. Although most northern European authors had never traveled to the New World, it did not prevent them from elaborating popular narratives about the region. The Indian was often at the center of these discussions, becoming a malleable, abstract category in the intellectual battlefield of knowledge production in the eighteenth-century world.

The pervasive skepticism about Spanish historiography, which contributed in part to the increase of texts by northern authors, eventually led the Spanish crown to commission a new history of the Indies.[44] In 1779 Juan Bautista Muñoz (1745–1799) was appointed to write the new history of Spanish America, a project that was originally to comprise several volumes but which yielded only one published in 1793. In his preface, Muñoz explained the great effort it took to collect the materials used to write his treatise because they were scattered in archives throughout Spain and the colonies. Though he proclaims wanting to do away with the "charlatanism" (*charlatanería*) of previous texts, he, like many contemporary northern European authors, describes the pre-Hispanic Amerindians as arrested in an earlier state of development and as a nation that could never compare to the pagan cultures of ancient Europe. "None appear to have ever achieved an adequate number of abstract and universal ideas," he claimed, "nor to have sustained peaceful empires long enough to have brought them out from the abyss of darkness to the true light of civilization." According to Muñoz, the Indians were so primitive that they only had a vague recollection of the Universal Deluge and no memory of their origin. All in all, it was thanks to Spain's intervention that the barbarians of the Americas were ultimately redeemed. Justifying the Spanish intervention in the New World is not surprising, nor is Muñoz's claim as a Spaniard to be the only one in the position to write the "true" history of the Americas.[45] After all, his was a project commissioned by the Spanish crown to wipe clean the nation's image as retrograde but also to proclaim its continued right to be the arbiter of knowledge about the New World. If Spain was to sustain its power over the New World, the natives could only be cast as "imperfect" souls.

Good Colts and Bad Horses (*Buenos potros y malos caballos*): The Creole Invective

A strong sense of Creole pride developed in Mexico in the late sixteenth and early seventeenth centuries. The eradication of the *encomienda* system (a grant of Indian labor given to the conquerors and early settlers in perpetuity) resulted in the loss of social standing of Creoles. Unhappy with the crown's failure to protect their interests in the New World, the American-born descendants of Spanish peninsulars took other measures to sustain their power and prestige. Many went on to occupy important positions in the church (which they eventually dominated) and the university—two major platforms from which they were able to voice their strong sense of belonging to the land and their desire to be part of the Spanish monarchy but in their own right.[46] Motivated by the insults and arrogance that Europeans continued to exhibit toward them, Creoles sought to establish an identity for themselves by extolling their country and its inhabitants. New Spain (like Peru), however, was a hierarchical society composed of various castes and riddled with its own internal conflicts. That the Indians made up the majority of the population of New Spain was indisputable. The Indians' juridical status as new Christians and their *limpieza de sangre* (that is, the absence of Jewish, Muslim, or black blood) made this group an appropriate symbol of the providential destiny of Mexico and its grandeur. In addition, many local intellectuals descended from the Mesoamerican nobility, with whom they sometimes shared cultural codes and values.[47]

The strong sense of *criollismo*, which was cemented in the second half of the seventeenth century, was foregrounded by several authors in the second half of the eighteenth century. The attack of the dean of Alicante, Manuel Martí (1663–1737), on the population of the Americas is well known. When he responded to a student inquiring about the advantages of studying in the New World, he suggested that he move to Rome instead, citing the lack of significant writers and libraries in Mexico. Reactions among the intellectual elite of New Spain were vehement. One of the best-known responses is that of Juan José de Eguiara y Eguren (1699–1763), professor and rector of the University of Mexico, who published a vast bio-bibliography of all known Mexican writers titled *Biblioteca Mexicana* (1755). In the preface of his massive compilation, Eguiara y Eguren boasts of the many accomplishments of the Indians: "If [Martí] had paid careful attention to the works of our predecessors and only leafed through the chronicles written by foreigners, surely he would have not concluded that the Indians of Mexico are ignorant."[48]

In 1695 a Peruvian cleric described in similar indignant terms the little esteem in which Europeans regarded the people of the Americas:

> It is held as truth among many that the subjects of the Indies turn out to be *good colts and bad horses* (*buenos potros y malos caballos*), a metaphor with

which they intend to say that they are of such feeble nature, that until the age of forty they stand out for their intelligence, but after that, they decline and become indolent . . . I confess that sometimes it takes much patience to ignore this indignant piece of nonsense.[49]

The old canard that Creoles degenerated in the Americas due to the climate was spread by Spaniards and absorbed by Protestant writers. Furthermore, the New World was seen as a land where miscegenation was rampant, promoting Europeans to constantly question the degree of purity of Creoles and to profess that their mixing with Indians and blacks had contributed to their racial degradation. The noted Spanish scientist and royal bureaucrat Antonio de Ulloa (1716–1795), for example, described Creoles as vain people who abhorred the Spaniards; they were not only idle and full of bad habits but, as he noted "rare is the family where there is no mixture of blood."[50] The origin of Creoles, their suspect sexual moralities, ostentatious lifestyles, and cultural hybrid affiliations were all notions that reinforced the discourse about who was fit to rule.

This mischaracterization of Creoles led some sympathetic Spaniards who resided in Mexico to defend the Indians and the Creoles from European attacks. In his work *Tardes Americanas* (1778), the Spanish friar José Joaquín Granados y Gálvez resorted to an alleged dialogue between a Spaniard and an Indian—a literary device designed to make the subject more entertaining—to provide numerous examples of the Indians' elevated condition. He counters enlightened philosophers like Raynal and Roberston and their "custom" of belittling the Indians, and noted that in pre-Hispanic times the natives had attained a high degree of civilization comparable to the Greeks and Romans. Their pictographic tradition alone exemplified their sophistication, and their advances in the arts and sciences were sufficient proof of their talents. He also noted that just as in Europe one would distinguish between the nobility and the plebe, the same applied to Mexico; if the plebe was rustic it was not due to a lack of intelligence or willpower, but to its overall lack of education. Because the intellectual capacity of people resided in the individual, he argued that the Indians were as qualified as the Spaniards to become priests and that many had excelled in this role. As he noted, "everybody has the same soul, nature, and potential, and are affected equally by the same climate and stars."[51]

While the Spanish friar acknowledged that the Indians had been idolatrous before the arrival of the Spaniards, he also argued that so had every nation of the ancient world prior to the coming of Christ. With Catholicism viewed as the supreme marker of civilization, Granados y Gálvez hastened to note that Mexico boasted of a flurry of miraculous images, including the famous Virgin of Guadalupe who had appeared to a common Indian vassal. Following his discussion of the natives of New Spain, Granados y Gálvez set out to defend the Creoles. "To God, the beautiful influence of the stars, and the mildness of the climate," noted the author, "they owe their rare intelligence, natural acuteness, clarity of purpose, and fast wit with which nature has so adorned them."[52] Even though the relationship of Creoles to the indigenous population of New Spain was contradictory at best, several families boasted of their mestizo origin when the union was among equals (that is, among the Mesoamerican ruling class and noble Spanish conquistadors).[53] Given the tendency of European authors to equate the Indians with the Creoles, Granados y Gálvez found it necessary to extol both groups by connecting them historically but also by clearly noting their different rank within the colonial social order. In addition, the Spanish author was careful to inscribe his discussion within a patriotic framework that celebrated Spain and its role in converting and protecting the Indians. In other words, he emphasized the loyalty of Mexico to Spain and to the Catholic prince.

The same patriotic sentiment led the Spanish Benedict friar Benito María de Moxó (1763–1816) to write his *Cartas mejicanas* (1804–05).[54] Moxó traveled to Mexico in 1804 where he lived nearly two years. An avid reader and collector of antiquities, Moxó was fully immersed in the new age of philosophical thought. The reason for writing his text was twofold: to rebuff European thinkers like Raynal and Robertson and to justify the Spanish conquest and its sustained presence in the New World. Moxó's stay in Mexico, even if short, put him in an ideal position to proclaim his authority. While he acknowledged the value of the Spanish historiography of Mexico, he also admits that a complete history of the viceroyalty was still lacking. His rebuttal of northern European thinkers focused primarily on Mexico's eminent past. Contrary to what Robertson had claimed, the Indians were perfectly suited to form abstract ideas and concepts as their pictographs and codices showed: they contained not only signs but symbols—characters that embodied a complex process of abstraction whereby one thing was represented through another. Moreover, their antiquities demonstrated that they had achieved a high degree of sophistication; many of their finely carved idols could scarcely be distinguished from those created in Egypt, Greece, and Rome. Moxó admitted that before traveling to Mexico, he shared the low opinion of many of his fellow countrymen about the artistic talent and ability of the Indians, but that in seeing some of their idols he was quickly persuaded otherwise. "In what I say," Moxó noted, "there is no exaggeration. This is not a theory or a conjecture, but a fact."[55]

Such stark declarations were meant to stress the conclusive veracity of his opinions and to separate him from northern philosophers prone to deceiving their readers. In 1768, for example, the renegade Dutch cleric Corneille de Pauw (1739–1799) published in Berlin his *Recherches philosophiques sur les Américains,* a short and highly provocative book that proved immensely popular, in which the author sternly announced that the climate of the New World led to the degeneration of both people and animals. To Pauw's contention that the cold temperament of the Indians accounted for their baldness and superabundance of milk—even in the breasts of men—Moxó noted that this "could not but elicit the laughter of readers." If Moxó engaged in responding to such drivel, it was because of Pauw's undue influence on certain credulous philosophers incapable of discerning the truth.[56]

Even though this sort of refutation conformed to those advanced by Creole patriots, Moxó adhered more strongly to the imperial tradition that justified morally the presence of the Spaniards in the New World. For one, the Indians were sunken in the most debased type of behavior due to their alleged cannibalism in pre-Hispanic times. In fact, Moxó devotes several chapters to the Indians' purported anthropophagic tendencies, and stresses that if Spaniards had not arrived in the New World that abhorrent custom would have never ceased. To explain how despite such depravity the Indians had the potential to become civilized, Moxó compared precolonial Indians with the behavior exhibited by Roman gladiators. The idolatry of Amerindians was another persistent problem with which the Spaniards had to contend. Because contemporary Indians were "stupid" and "slothful," given to adoring idols and to debauchery, they deserved the protection of the Spanish crown. The recrudescence of the Spanish imperial tradition that Moxó espouses is in part why he counters the famous Spanish defender of the Indians Bartolomé de Las Casas, accusing him of providing a distorted picture of the conquest and blaming the Spaniards for their excessive cruelty. "Without so many exaggerations and hyperboles, the short book by Friar Bartolomé would have never made it across the Pyrenees and the Alps, and would have ended up like so many others gathering dust and moths in some dark corner of one of our libraries."[57]

Though Moxó condemns Las Casas—an author repeatedly cited by European authors to attack Spain and its inhumanity toward the Indians—and defends Sepúlveda's view of the natives' natural serfdom, he also states that

Figure 3.1. Conversion of the Indians, from
Barón de Julas Reales, *Entretenimientos de un
prisionero* (1828). Private Collection.

it was thanks to the benevolence of the missionaries that so many Indians
were and continued to be brought closer to the faith. In other words, Moxó
does not subscribe to the opinion that the natives were fundamentally incapable of becoming good Christians, but he underscores the ongoing need
to educate them, thereby establishing a continuum between precolonial and
colonial natives to validate Spanish intervention. An engraving inserted in
another book based on Moxo's work illustrates the great charity and zeal of
the missionaries. Conceived as a Christian version of the Greek god Orpheus,
the missionaries are shown successfully coaxing the Indians into submission
with their music and singing (fig. 3.1).[58] In his discussion of the conflicting
view of Indians by priests in the eighteenth century, the historian William B.
Taylor has stated that the terms used to describe the Indians centered "around
two inconsistent notions: Indians as simple, timid, obedient, and perhaps
stupid innocents; and Indians as deceitful, malicious, cunningly disobedient
subjects—children of the Seven Cardinal Sins." As Taylor has noted, many

of these terms were rooted in sixteenth-century "encounter" vocabulary. In explaining the recurrence of the term *miserable* and other expressions used to describe the lowly spirit of the Indians, Taylor has perceptively noted: "In this lexicon, one term led to another, but not in endless variations or particular complex ways. *Miserable* and its elaborations and extensions toward fear, shamelessness, ignorance, rusticity, laziness, and the rest led back to the idea that Indians were incomplete humans, lacking in willpower and reason."[59] For Granados y Gálvez and Moxó, the Indians were not the debased creatures that northern Europeans authors tried to make them, but they were clearly far from attaining the religious perfection that would render the colonial bureaucratic engine superfluous.

The Mexican Enlightenment:
Against a Recalcitrant Rhetoric

Although some of the texts discussed above were written by long-term European residents in the Indies, in the eighteenth century Mexican enlightened thinkers formulated their own responses to the profusion of European texts about the Americas. There is, however, one important and highly strategic distinction to keep in mind: their desire to inscribe the colony's future within that of the Spanish empire as a whole. Like Granados y Gálvez and Moxó, the secular priest José Antonio de Alzate y Ramírez (1737–1799), one of the most noted representatives of the Mexican Enlightenment, was careful to assert his loyalty to Spain. This was important for reasons that go beyond a mere deployment of pro-Spanish sentiments; it was essential to avoid being considered insubordinate, particularly given the looming independence of the United States from Great Britain in 1776 and the famous Túpac Amaru revolt in Peru in 1781 that threatened to overthrow the Spaniards. Furthermore, part of Alzate's mission was to position Mexico's destiny as part of Spain's— a clever way of disarming Spanish authors who bought into a recalcitrant imperial rhetoric that diminished the value of Indians and Creoles alike.[60]

Deeply interested in astronomy, natural history, and science in general, Alzate kept abreast with much of the literature that was being generated in Europe, particularly when it referenced the Americas. He was a corresponding member of several scientific societies in Europe and established various periodicals in Mexico that served as his mouthpiece. Between 1788 and 1795 Alzate published the *Gazetas de literatura de México*. Conceived as a miscellany of current and useful information about science, natural history, commerce, and so forth, the journal also served as a platform for Alzate to demystify the information about the New World that circulated in European travelogues and natural histories. His remarks against the work of the French abbot Joseph de Laporte (1713–1799) and his multivolume work *Le voyageur François, ou la connaissance de l'ancien et du nouveau monde* (1765–1795) are a case in point. For example, he observed that despite the fact that Thomas Gage (1602–1656), the English Dominican friar who traveled to Mexico in 1626 had penned his famous *A New Survey of the West Indies* in 1648—almost a century and a half earlier—"some authors who are enemies of the glories of Spain [including De Laporte] insist in copying it, continuing his bloody satire." Among the harmful errors contained in De Laporte's text were his assertions of the alleged ignorance, superstition, and crude customs of the people of New Spain, as was his flawed account of the natural history of the place. De Laporte also provided fraudulent descriptions of Mexican society, as when he stated that there were more than 4,000 coaches in Mexico City alone that were made of solid gold and silver and adorned with precious stones, which clearly derived from Gage's preposterous descriptions about the ostentation and conspicuous consumption by the inhabitants of New Spain. Such statements enraged Alzate, leading him to question the usefulness of so-called enlightened texts and to ask rhetorically: "That this should be published and again in the age of the Enlightenment?" (*¿Que esto se imprima, se reimprima en el siglo de las luces?*).[61] As he noted, this type of compilation was often teeming with paradoxical information. Even Buffon who was widely regarded as the modern Pliny had filled his descriptions with falsehoods in his desire to picture the Americas as a new continent where ignorant Indians could never become entirely good Christians.[62]

In both the *Gazetas de literatura* and in subsequent works, Alzate attempted to combat the notion that precolonial Amerindians had been rustic and uncultured. In his work *Descripción de las antigüedades de Xochicalco* (1791) published as a supplement to his *Gazetas de literatura,* he argued that the ancient people of Mexico had been highly civilized and that their monuments were as masterful as those created by the Egyptians and Greeks. The fact that contemporary Indians were downtrodden did not reflect the grandeur of their past; in other words, commoners should not be equated with the Mesoamerican ruling elite just as the plebe in Europe would not be compared to the nobility. In response to the allegation that the Spaniards—who were least in number—succeeded in conquering the Aztecs because the Indians were meek, he remarked that such misleading information derived from Antonio Solís's widely read book about the conquest of Mexico, *Historia de la conquista de México* (1648). If the Spaniards had succeeded it was because of the alliances they forged with other native polities desirous to rid themselves of the tyranny of the Aztecs. Similarly, while acknowledging the human sacrifices of the Aztecs (of which most people had an exaggerated sense through plays they saw performed all over Europe), he observed that prior to the arrival of the Spaniards the Indians had not yet been guided by the true religion, and that all nations at similar points in their history had been equally idolatrous. In short, he dismissed the pejorative statements of foreigners like Raynal and Buffon as he looked to provide a more nuanced picture—a picture from *within*—of the natives of his homeland. "The various ways that the Mexican Indians are still described today, the excessive contempt with which some, even among our own, tend to see them, and especially the black and vile colors with which foreign authors have painted them, [have] led me . . . to explore their origin, uses and customs, and generally everything related to their arts, sciences, etc."[63]

Because precolonial writing was often seen as an unreliable measure of culture, Alzate described various Mesoamerican ruins to attest to the degree of civilization of Amerindians. His *Descripción de las antiguedades de Xochicalco* describes a fortified castle in Xochicalco (present-day state of Morelos), its architectural and engineering complexity, as well as its elaborate decorative program. "The architectural monuments from ancient cultures that have survived despite the abuse of time are a great resource to learn about the nature of those who fabricated them whenever there is a lack of contemporary authors and also to replace the omission or bad faith of historians. A building manifests the nature and culture of people because it is true that civilization or barbarity is manifest in the progress that nations make in the sciences and arts."[64] Alzate also commissioned a set of engravings to enhance his account, which was a way of strengthening the written word, often seen as polysemic and highly ambiguous (fig. 3.2). One image describes on one side an Indian man being devoured by an eagle, which Alzate interpreted as the defeat of a southern polity by the Aztecs, and on the other the reconstruction of a pyramidal structure based on the ruins found in the site, a structure analogous to that of ancient Egypt. As the historian Jorge Cañizares-Esguerra has keenly noted, Alzate played the northern European philosophers at their own game by using an alternative, nonliterary form of evidence to prove the critics wrong when it came to describing the past of the Indians.[65] It is important to keep in mind, however, that Alzate draws from a long tradition of Creole

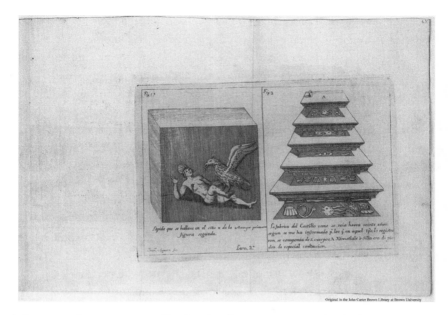

Figure 3.2. Reconstruction of Xochicalco, from José Antonio de Alzate y Ramírez, *Descripción de las antigüedades de Xochicalco . . .* (1791). Courtesy John Carter Brown Library at Brown University.

patriots that goes back to the seventeenth century with the likes of Carlos de Sigüenza y Góngora (1645–1700) and Agustín de Vetancurt (1620–1700) among others. In the first issue of his *Gazetas de literatura,* Alzate expressed his intention to provide new information about the antiquities of the Indians, but clearly aligned himself with this long line of Creole intellectuals and polymaths who in their effort to create a grand past for their country drew on native histories.[66]

In addition to his archaeological pursuits, Alzate, tried to demonstrate his more thorough knowledge of indigenous cultures by distinguishing between various polities and describing their customs, such as Nahuas and Otomí. He found the popular adage "That who has seen one Indian has seen them all" (*Quien ha visto a un indio los ha visto a todos*) deplorable.[67] Yet, drawing on the learned tradition of sixteenth- and seventeenth-century authors such as Juan de Cárdenas (1563–1609) and Enrico Martínez (d. 1632) he also asserted that the Indians' constitution was radically different from that of Europeans, Asians, and Africans. Were it not for the Bible that stated that man had a common origin, it would be easy to infer that the Indians were of a different species altogether. Climate, therefore, was responsible for their phenotypical difference, even if he could not exactly explain why.[68] Put another way, Alzate supported the widespread idea that since its inception humankind had been white, but a set of inexplicable circumstances including climate created a gradation of colors that became fixed and would only be altered through the right pattern of *mestizaje* or racial mixing with whites.[69]

In a fascinating note published in his journal *Observaciones sobre la física, historia natural y artes útiles* (1787), for example, Alzate grappled with the origin of the color black. While he acknowledged that philosophers could hardly agree on the subject, he was baffled by the opinion of an "anti-religious" author who claimed that blacks had a different origin—a notion that he found reprehensible as it went against the Judeo-Christian account of creation. Alzate argued that just as a white person who mixed with a black would beget a mulatto, if a mulatto continued to mix with whites in time that person's black traits would entirely disappear. He then related the peculiar case of a group of people in the vicinity of the Jorullo volcano (present-day state of Michoacán) who had dark spots on their bodies that continued to spread, and which Alzate surmised would turn the townspeople fully black in four or five generations. He was skeptical of the townspeople's explanation that, after an Apache woman had intercourse with a cattle ranch worker, the stains of the animals were impressed on her progeny, and continued to pass from generation to generation.[70] Although Alzate was at a loss to explain this phenomenon, he suggested that nature (i.e., nutrition) and the excessive heat of the region could have had an effect on "this sort of depravation of humors." Ancient medicine argued that the human body was composed of four humors corresponding to the four elements of the cosmos—fire, air, water, and earth—each of which possessed distinctive qualities that, when out of balance, could yield "monstrous" results.[71] As with the Indians, Alzate believed that climate could be responsible for the mutation of the color and appearance of people, pulling them away from the innate whiteness of biblical exegesis.[72] What Alzate did not seem to question is that Amerindian bodies could mutate into darker or fully black ones without sexual contact with blacks. This sort of environmental determinism that posited that under certain conditions bodies could be transmuted into a different race is precisely the notion that Creoles had fought so tirelessly to undermine when it came to their own bodies turning into Amerindian. This is one instance of the type of contradiction that characterizes Alzate's descriptions. As a Creole patriot he assumed the voice of authority to counter European authors, but the Indian body did not entirely cease to be an abstract category to wage philosophical debates and to articulate ideas of self-fashioning and nationhood. In his case, it was the ancient past of Amerindians that merited being vindicated as it granted Mexico a classical pedigree comparable to that of the Greeks and Romans in Europe. The common Indian of his time was a different matter altogether.

A similar patriotic intent is present in the work of the Creole scientist and antiquarian Antonio León y Gama (1735–1802), who in 1792 published a treatise on two pre-Hispanic monoliths discovered in the main plaza of the viceroyalty's capital. The expert opinion (*parecer*) of Friar José Rafael Olmedo at the beginning of the book is highly revealing of this double-directed Creole discourse. He noted that the text was published to dissipate the "gross errors" about the Americas spread by Raynal, Robertson, Buffon, and Pauw, who were intent on damaging the Spaniards. León y Gama himself reminded the reader of King Charles III's (1759–1788) archaeological interests and his role in the 1738 excavations of Pompeii and Herculaneum in Italy, and how it inspired him to write his own account to show to the entire literary community the great artistic and scientific achievements of pre-Hispanic Indians. Part of his intention was also to prove how the natives were falsely accused of being "irrational" and "simple" by the enemies of Spain, whose sole goal was to tarnish the empire's image and diminish the glory of the conquest.[73] Comments like these turned the Spanish imperial rhetoric inside out. Now the Indian body—of which Creoles were often perceived to be an extension—was an inalienable part of the Spanish empire; it was incumbent upon Spain to uphold a positive view of the natives in order to combat the common enemy of the crown. In other words, to present a unified image of empire, contemporary Indians and their past needed to be woven into the fabric of Spanish patriotic rhetoric.

Another key text from the Mexican enlightenment is Francisco Javier Clavijero's (1731–1787), monumental *Storia antica de Messico* (1780–1781), which he penned during his exile in Italy following the expulsion of the Jesuits in 1767. He framed his text with a description of the natural history of Mexico at the behest of some of his friends given the popularity of the genre. But part of the reason for annexing this section of his work dedicated to Mexico's precolonial past was also to refute European descriptions of America and its native population. He cites, for example, Gage of whom he states that there "is no author about America who lies with more impudence."[74] Among the modern authors he lists Raynal and Robertson, and blames their work—and others—for including images and information that were more the product of their fantasy than reality: "Some authors, unhappy with corrupting their books about the history of Mexico with errors, nonsense, and lies, have altered them even more with their deceptive images and engraved figures."[75] Clavijero also provides a description of the contemporary Indians of Mexico, which he claims to have based on firsthand knowledge, and states that his intention was to provide a true semblance untainted by patriotic sentiments.[76] In his opinion, the Indians like every nation had some positive and negative traits. Their penchant for drinking, for example, was undeniable and the cause of many problems. Among their positive qualities was their rational capacity and inventiveness: "Their souls are irrefutably like those of the rest of mankind and they are endowed with the same faculties. Nowhere have Europeans erred more than when they questioned the rational capacity of Americans."[77] He further notes that superstition was a trait that defined ignorant people in general, and stated that the Indians' "alleged adherence to idolatry is an unfounded supposition created by the wild imagination of a few stubborn people."[78] Clavijero went as far as to propose the creation of a mestizo nation, as when he observed that politically the Spaniards would have stood to gain much more had they married solely into the indigenous nobility and refrained from bringing women from Europe and African slaves. Such alliance, he argued, would have not only benefited Mexico but the entire Spanish kingdom. In other words, Clavijero tacitly likens the Spaniards to the Indian nobility, but reproves their extensive mixture with blacks and the ensuing disruption of the social order.[79] To be sure, this was an audacious statement, one that in all likelihood precluded the publication of his work in Spain. Clavijero's work, however, was immensely popular among northern intellectuals, largely due to the fact that it was written by someone who could actually claim to be from Mexico.[80] His firsthand experience granted him immediate *autorictas,* allowing him to counteract the information supplied by authors like Robertson and Raynal and rendering his account more believable in European circles.[81]

The Indians as Good Christians:
The Case of José Mariano Díaz de la Vega

One of the underlying issues in the debate about the nature of the Indians in the eighteenth century was their ability to become good Christians. A deliberate pro-Indian stance or what we can loosely term *proto indigenismo* is no better illustrated than in the unpublished manuscript by the Franciscan friar José Mariano Díaz de la Vega titled "Memorias piadosas de la nación yndiana recogidas de varios autores" (1782).[82] Not much is known about Díaz de la

Vega, except that he was from Huichapan (present-day state of Hidalgo), that he entered the Franciscan order in Mexico City in 1736, and that he studied theology at the convent of Tlaxcala in 1740.[83] Like Clavijero, Díaz de la Vega was a Creole clerical author who strove to vindicate the Indians. But instead of focusing on their precolonial past, Díaz de la Vega concentrated on the religious fervor of contemporary Indians by compiling a group of widely known texts about the subject written in Mexico and based on his own experience. Given that the text is virtually unknown to specialists, it is worth turning our attention to it in some detail.

When Díaz de la Vega wrote his apologetic text, he was responding to the increasing hostility toward contemporary Indians by northern European and Spanish authors, as well as to the flurry of texts dealing with their origin such as that by Gregorio García. "Despite the fact that many authors have spilled a great deal of ink in describing the native inhabitants of the Americas," the friar declared, "they have all treated them as a single group, assigning them different origins according to their own conjectures, or based on what they have read, claiming indistinctly that they descend from the Hebrews, Jews, Ham . . . and even Judas . . . Oh, wretched nation! How far can your misery extend, when all that remains is that they make your ancestors and progenitors into satyrs, minotaurs, lions, and tigers!"[84]

Accounts of the ability of Amerindians to become true Christians began to be codified in earnest in the seventeenth century. Díaz de la Vega culled many examples from Juan de Torquemada's *Monarquía Indiana* (1615), Sigüenza y Góngora's *Parayso Occidental* (1684), and Agustín de Vetancurt's *Teatro mexicano* (1698). The examples mostly refer to miracles that occurred to the Indians soon after the "encounter" and their natural susceptibility, as descendants of Adam, to partake of the sacraments. Others describe the mysterious origin of devotional images namely as sculptures of Christ that were allegedly delivered to various sanctuaries by angels dressed as Indians.[85] The author also transcribes two short accounts describing the lives of two virtuous Indian women—one *ladina* or hispanicized and the other heathen.

The first book narrated the life of the Otomí Indian Salvadora de los Santos, derived from a text by the Jesuit Juan Antonio de Paredes of 1762.[86] Written as an edifying letter (*carta edificante*), Paredes's text conforms closely to established hagiographic models. Otomí referred to the various indigenous groups that inhabited areas west and north of the Valley of Mexico since pre-Hispanic times. Although they aided the Spaniards in the conquest, they were often described as downtrodden and uncultured by colonial authorities. Salvadora's life was meant to tell a different story and prove that even the most rustic Indians could be redeemed and attain glory. The "saint," as she is often referred to in the text (though she was never canonized), was born in 1701 in the mining town of Fresnillo of noble Indian parents. When she turned twelve the family moved to San Juan del Río (her mother's hometown), where they lived poorly cultivating the land, taking care of a few sheep, and serving the Spaniards. From an early age Salvadora proved to be very obedient; she helped her parents on the ranch and opted for a life of utmost austerity, solitude, and penance. She also prayed constantly and devoted herself to weaving. Animals (especially birds) gravitated to her, and members of the important Spanish families of the region sought her company. Her innate piety led her to learn to read and write on her own to study the life of the saints. While visiting Querétaro one Christmas Eve, she saw a nativity scene that a group of Carmelite *beatas* (pious women) had lovingly set up; enraptured by the figure of Christ, she asked to be admitted in their company, where she made vows of celibacy. For twenty-six years she served the *beatas* with utmost diligence and patience and collected alms for their subsistence. Her kindness, hard work, and healing abilities made her famous in the region. In 1762 she fell sick during an epidemic that killed many natives and died at the age of sixty-one. She was buried with great solemnity, and her portrait was immediately commissioned to be placed in the convent's parlor (*locutorio*).[87]

The second hagiographic text that Díaz de la Vega cites is that of Catherine Tekakwitha, an Iroquois of the Mohawk nation born in 1656 in what is today northern New York. Composed by the Jesuit missionary in Montreal Pierre Cholenec in 1717, the life of Tekakwitha became known to Spanish audiences through a translation by the Jesuit Juan de Urtassumm titled *La gracia triunfante en la vida de Catharina Tegakovita: India iroquesa* (1724).[88] The Iroquois were known for their fierceness and unwillingness to be pacified, but in the 1670s the Jesuits succeeded in converting several Mohawks and moving them into mission settlements near Montreal. The book describes Tekakwitha's natural inclination to follow the path of God, and the vicissitudes she endured until she arrived at a mission where she renounced sex and followed a life of religious perfection. Her penances (fasting, self-flagellation, sleep deprivation, and so forth) were particularly severe. She died in 1680 at the age of twenty-four, and almost immediately after her death she became the object of a cult among native and French Canadian Catholics. The book describes the lengths that Tekakwitha went to abandon her tribe and live among Christians, her enormous piety, virtues, and early death; it also dramatizes the case of several other Iroquois who embraced the faith, and their persecution and horrid martyrdoms at the hands of their own tribesmen who saw their conversion as betrayal.

Urtassumm added a chapter to his translation listing several examples of virtuous Indian women in New Spain. Some examples were based on first-hand knowledge, but most derived from earlier texts by Creole intellectuals and clerics such as Sigüenza y Góngora and the Jesuit Francisco de Florencia (1620–1695). Drawing on the work of the most reputed intellectuals of the colony allowed Urtassumm to establish a type of pious genealogy that lent further credence to his account.[89] The annexation of this chapter was particularly relevant since, at that time, discussions about the spiritual potential of the natives was at the fore in the capital of New Spain. In fact, it is no coincidence that Tekakwitha's text was translated precisely when the city's elite and clergy were debating the establishments of Corpus Christi in 1724, the first convent destined exclusively for Indian women of noble background. Equally important is the inclusion of a lengthy opinion and apologetic examination (*parecer y punto apologético*) by Juan Ignacio de Castorena y Ursúa (1668–1733), where he justifies the establishment of the convent. This is not surprising, given that among Castorena y Ursúa's many public charges, he was vicar-general (*provisor*) of the Indians of the Archbishopric of Mexico. His *punto apologético* is a philosophical argument and fervent defense of the rational capabilities of the Indians and their ability to be good Christians. "If other species that were unknown, once transplanted in the Indies gave such copious fruit that if they do not exceed at least compete with those of the motherland," he stated, "are we not to expect that once religious virtues are transplanted in the native women of this land they not yield similar and copious abundance of religious perfection?"[90] The parallelism between the natural abundance of the land—a trope of the time enacted by Creole patriots—and the spiritual riches of the colony could not be more explicitly drawn. To assess the relevance of establishing the convent, the high court (*audiencia*) conducted an investigation and interviewed members of several religious orders. Even though no consensus was reached among the various factions, Corpus Christi (as well as other similar institutions devoted to the education and religious training of Amerindians) was ultimately established. As Allan Greer has noted, the debate was as much about race as gender. White consecrated virgins were charged with the role of safeguarding the city through their purity; Indian women were deemed not only racially inferior but incapable of being chaste.[91]

The tale of Tekakwitha, an "exotic" Indian from a remote land was sure to grab the attention of the readers and convey the idea that even the most heathen of nations could become good Christians. In the case of Salvadora, her biographer went as far as emphasizing that poor, uneducated Indian women could be more pious than many Spanish noblewomen who preferred worldly pleasures than to follow the path of God.[92] Significantly, Paredes's book about the life of Salvadora was reprinted in 1784 at the behest of the indigenous *parcialidades* (large sections of a town) of Santiago and San Juan in Mexico City. Dedicated by the Indian governors Miguel de la Mota and Juan Ignacio de S. Roque Martínez to the viceroy of Mexico Matías Gálvez (1783–84), the book was designed to instill a sense of pride in their community and prove their loyalty to the king. "The reprint of this *edifying letter*," noted the governors, "has the advisable goal of providing the schools and groups where our children are educated with a type of *cartilla* (reading primer), so as they learn to read they also learn to imitate Christian virtues by seeing them practiced in such a sweet, powerful, and naturally appealing way by a person of their own condition."[93] The stories of Salvadora and Tekakwitha, as Díaz de la Vega knew well, were potent examples that proved the power of God's grace to effect perfection even within this sector of humanity.

To emphasize the religious virtue and innate intellectual capacity of Amerindians, Díaz de la Vega also offers a detailed description of a series of portraits of illustrious Indian men, a number of them priests.[94] The ordination of Indians as priests was highly contested throughout the colonial period.[95] In keeping with the hyperbolic tone of his manuscript, Díaz de la Vega states that many Indians attained important ecclesiastical positions in the viceroyalty and "that to attempt to count them would be like trying to count the stars of the firmament."[96] Interestingly, Díaz de la Vega relies directly on images to construct his argument. He describes four portraits that he claims to have seen many times at the Colegio de Indias, a school for Indian girls in Mexico City. Known also as the Colegio de Guadalupe, the school was established in 1753 by the Jesuit father Antonio de Herdoñana.[97] According to Díaz de la Vega, the full-length portraits were placed in the *cuarto chocolatero,* a room next to the church's sacristy where hot chocolate was served. Each portrait bore a detailed inscription that described the figure's name, place of origin, major literary works, and posts. The portraits represented distinguished ecclesiastical figures identified as Indian, including Francisco de Siles, Don Juan Merlo de la Fuente, Nicolás del Puerto, and Don Juan Espinoza y Medrano (El Lunarejo).

Díaz de la Vega tells that the four paintings were commissioned by a priest from the oratory of San Felipe Neri in Mexico City—whom he knew—from an indigenous artist.[98] He also mentions a portrait of Antonio Valeriano at the entrance hall of the school. A native of Azcapotzalco, Valeriano was an Indian governor and Latinist, said to be related to Moctezuma II. In the sixteenth century he had been one of the first students of the Franciscan college of Santa Cruz de Tlatelolco, where he later taught. A governor of the Nahua *parcialidades* of Santiago and San Juan, he instructed some of the early missionaries in Nahuatl, including Bernardino de Sahagún, Juan Bautista, and Torquemada. He was also reputed to be the author of an account of the apparitions of the Virgin of Guadalupe written in Nahuatl sometime in the mid- to late sixteenth century.[99]

The cases of Francisco de Siles and Juan de Espinoza y Medrano (El Lunarejo) also deserve some attention given their prominent place in colonial society. Siles was a member of the cathedral chapter, professor of theology at the university, and enthusiastic champion of the cult of Our Lady of Guadalupe. He wrote a laudatory letter that accompanied Miguel Sánchez's *Imagen de la Virgen Maria* (the first published account of Guadalupe, 1648), and fought tirelessly to secure a feast day and proper mass for the Virgin. As part of the necessary canonical investigations ordered by Rome, Siles instigated the 1666 examination of the image by a group of prominent painters and clerics who corroborated her miraculous origin.[100]

Born in Cuzco, Juan de Espinoza y Medrano (El Lunarejo) (1628/30?–1688) was variously described as an Indian, a mestizo and a Creole; he received his nickname because of the beauty marks (*lunares*) on his face. El Lunarejo became canon preacher at the cathedral chapter in Cuzco in 1683, and his fame as one of Peru's most talented literary figures, linguists, and preachers extended well beyond the Andes.[101] Including his portrait in the Colegio de Indias was a way of establishing a bridge—all the way from the north to the very southern tip of the hemisphere—between the natives of the Americas, and of stressing the talent of the original inhabitants. The Colegio hosted a veritable gallery of indigenous portraits meant to instill pride in the indigenous community. However, the school was visited by a much broader spectrum of people. From the time of its establishment, it had served as a refuge for single men, students, clergymen, widows, and foreigners of all social backgrounds who stopped by to grab an inexpensive bite to eat or purchase sweets and other foods. Its portrait gallery must have been well known; it is not surprising that Díaz de la Vega would single it out to praise the Indian nation.[102]

The bulk of Díaz de la Vega's manuscript addresses the significance of Amerindians in the apparition stories of some of New Spain's most celebrated religious icons: the Virgins of Guadalupe, Remedios, Ocotlán, and San Miguel del Milagro. In each case the holy figure appeared to or was found by a *ladino* Indian.[103] The Virgins of Guadalupe and Remedios were the divine bastions of the viceroyalty's capital who protected the city during floods and droughts, respectively; the Virgin of Ocotlán and San Miguel are associated with Tlaxcala, a city granted special status for aiding the Spaniards during the conquest and being the first to embrace the faith. These devotions became intertwined with a sense of local pride: they not only demonstrated that New Spain was a chosen land for divine interventions but offered proof of the Indians' readiness to receive a host of apparitions. Although Díaz de la Vega's manuscript is a compilation of excerpts from the most widely read texts about the images, its value resides in his choice of subjects and the way he interrelates them to emphasize the role of Amerindians.

The section devoted to the Virgin of Guadalupe draws on the work of the Jesuit Francisco de Florencia (who has been largely credited with fixing the tradition of these images and creating a coherent narrative of local devotions) as well as the short treatise by the Nahuatl expert and priest Luis Becerrra Tanco (1603–1672), titled *Felicidad de México* (1675).[104] The cult of the Virgin of Guadalupe appears to go back to the second half of the sixteenth century, although efforts to codify her origins only occurred in the mid-seventeenth, when a strong sense of Creole identity crystallized in New Spain. The story of her four apparitions to the pious Indian Juan Diego in 1531 are well known, as is the stubborn disbelief of Bishop Juan de Zumárraga (1528–47) until proof was brought in the form of Juan Diego's cloak filled with extraordinary flowers that, once emptied out, revealed the image of the Virgin imprinted on his mantle. The apparition and dramatic unfolding of the cloak captured the attention of devotees, and also became the element of the story most often represented (fig. 3.3).[105]

The story of the Virgin of Remedios was documented in 1621 by the Mercedarian Luis de Cisneros and later added to Florencia's corpus; Díaz de la Vega cites both sources.[106] Like Guadalupe's, the tale of Our Lady of Remedios originated after the conquest but was preserved mostly in oral form. According

Figure 3.3. Attributed to Miguel Cabrera,
Portrait of Juan Diego, c. 1755, oil on canvas,
107 × 82 cm. Museo Regional de Querétaro,
CONACULTA, INAH, Mexico.

to tradition, the Virgin of Remedios was a tiny sculpture brought to the New
World by Juan Rodríguez de Villafuente, one of Hernán Cortés's soldiers.
After razing the idols of the Aztecs' main altar, Cortés had the image placed
at the top of the shrine. The Virgin is said to have produced many miracles
and to have aided the Spaniards during the *Noche triste* (the bitter night when
they were forced to retreat to the hill of Otoncalpulco) by casting dust in the
eyes of the Indians. That evening Cortés's soldier hid the sculpture under a
maguey plant. It was found some twenty years later by the *cacique* (noble) Indian Juan Ceteutil, who had witnessed her apparition during the *Noche triste*
and several times thereafter.

Juan first took the image to his house, where he lovingly cared for it, but in
seeing that the Virgin would constantly return to the place where he originally
found her at the hill of Totolotepec, he eventually erected a small sanctuary

at the site. From that point on, Remedios became one of the most important devotions in New Spain, especially after she was backed by the city council (*cabildo*) in 1564 and a more spacious sanctuary was built in 1575.[107] She was often brought out in processions to Mexico City during droughts, plagues, and other calamities and had a wide following among all sectors of society (natives, Spaniards, and blacks).[108] As Díaz de la Vega reports, she remained closely associated with the Otomí communities of Tacuba until the late eighteenth century: the descendants of Juan Ceteutil continued to care for the house where Juan originally took in the image, which was well known in the region as *"la casita de la Virgen"* (the Virgin's little house).[109] By the eighteenth century the visual representation of Remedios began to be codified; surviving images frequently show the tiny sculpture hidden in a maguey plant at the moment when Juan Ceteutil discovers her, an apt way of dramatizing the story and highlighting the Indian as protagonist (fig. 3.4).

The significance of devotional images in Tlaxcala should be considered in relation to those of Mexico City. As the city that first swore obedience to the Spaniards, Tlaxcala claimed a glory unlike any other region of the viceroyalty.[110] The cults of San Miguel del Milagro and the Virgin of Ocotlán were late occurrences that can be linked in part to the fame attained by Guadalupe and Remedios in the capital as the two cities vied for icons. The archangel Saint Michael is said to have appeared in Tlaxcala in 1631, but the cult was only documented in earnest by Florencia in 1690, from where Díaz de la Vega extracts his account.[111] Tradition here affirmed that the archangel appeared to the Indian Diego Lázaro in a religious procession in the town of San Bernabé in the jurisdiction of Nativitas. He informed Diego Lázaro of a well with healing waters and asked that he publicize the miracle, but afraid that he would be met with disbelief, the Indian ignored the command. Saint Michael punished him with a grave illness and appeared to him a second time, when he miraculously transported him to the site of the well. A brilliant ray of heavenly light illuminated the spring, and Saint Michael demanded again that Diego Lázaro publicize the event or risk punishment. Eventually Diego Lázaro visited the bishop of Puebla, Gutierre Bernardo de Quirós, who upon seeing the healing effects of the water, and aware that Guadalupe and Remedios had also appeared to Indians, conducted a formal investigation (1631).[112]

Meanwhile devotion to the well and to San Miguel del Milagro grew. The bishop sanctioned the apparition, and a tiny sanctuary was erected around the well. A few years later (1643) the bishop Juan de Palafox y Mendoza (r. 1640

Figure 3.4. Unknown artist, *The Discovery of the
Sculpture of the Virgin of Remedios,* c. 1750, oil on
canvas, 141 × 64 cm. Pinacoteca del Templo de
San Felipe Neri "La Profesa," Mexico City.

to 1654) of Puebla visited the site, and, after fully embracing the cult, ordered another investigation and the building of a larger sanctuary (a third investigation took place in 1675). Following the erection of the small shrine in the 1630s, narrative paintings commemorating the apparitions were placed inside.[113] By the eighteenth century the scene of the archangel revealing the spring of healing water to Diego Lázaro had become canonical in paintings and prints in the regions of Puebla and Tlaxcala, as well as Mexico City (figs. 3.5 and 3.6).

The history of the Virgin of Ocotlán, the most venerated image of Tlaxcala, was only recorded in 1745 by the sanctuary's third chaplain (*capellán*), Manuel Loayzaga—the source cited by Díaz de la Vega.[114] According to tradition, soon after the conquest there was a terrible epidemic. One evening an Indian (also named Juan Diego) went to the river Sahuapan in the outskirts of Tlaxcala to fetch water to heal the sick and saw an apparition of the Virgin at the hill of Ocotlán. She led him to a mountain stream nearby filled with *ocotes* (local pine trees), where she showed him a spring of healing waters, and explained that an image in her likeness could be found there and that he should alert the Franciscans. Seeing the healing effects of the water, the friars set out to look for the image and found a small sculpture inside a burning *ocote*. The image was then taken in a great procession to the Franciscan convent and placed in the center of the main altarpiece, where it replaced an image of Saint Lawrence. At night, the displeased sacristan removed the image of the Virgin and returned Saint Lawrence's, but the next morning he found that the statue of the Virgin had reappeared on the altarpiece. He attempted to remove the Virgin's image several more times, even taking the statue to his house and later to the sacristy, where he locked it inside a trunk and slept over it to prevent it from escaping. His attempts met with no success, as the Virgin continued to return to the altarpiece. From this point on the Virgin of Ocotlán attained great fame, and a sanctuary was erected for her. Backed by Bishop Pantaleón Álvarez Abreu of Puebla (1743–65), she was sworn a patroness of Tlaxcala in 1755, just a year after Guadalupe's official feast day was approved by the Pope. As the cult of Ocotlán spread so did her images showing the encounter of the Virgin and the Indian Juan Diego (fig. 3.7).

Probably following Loayzaga's cue, Díaz de la Vega also devotes two chapters to the martyrdom of three recent converts in Tlaxcala after the conquest: Cristobalito, Antonio, and Juan.[115] The story of these boys was legendary since the sixteenth century and was also represented in art and performed in plays.[116] Cristobalito, a pious Tlaxcalan Indian who studied with the Franciscans,

Figure 3.5. Unknown artist, *The Apparition of San Miguel del Milagro to Diego Lázaro,* first half of the eighteenth century, Oil on canvas, 170.5 × 118 cm, Museo Universitario de la Benemérita Universidad Autónoma de Puebla, Mexico. Photo: Archivo Fotográfico Manuel Toussaint del Instituto de Investigaciones Estéticas, UNAM.

Figure 3.6. Francisco Silverio, *The Apparition of San Miguel del Milagro to Diego Lázaro*, c. 1760. Real Academia de la Historia, Madrid.

begged his father to embrace the Christian faith, but was brutally killed by him when he destroyed his idols and smashed his *pulque*-filled jars. Led by the Franciscan friars, Antonio and Juan set out on a mission to find and destroy all pagan idols in the region, but were caught by the owners and viciously murdered. The story of these three martyrs was especially appropriate as it proved their willingness to die in the name of the faith and the special status conferred on the city of Tlaxcala. There was no higher honor than to die defending the faith. To stress the spiritual capacity of the Indians, Díaz de la Vega also tells the story of Querétaro's prodigious stone cross (*cruz de piedra*), much publicized in the eighteenth century by the Franciscans.[117] After the conquest, the Spaniards and Otomí Indians—led by the *cacique* Nicolás de San Luis Montañez—joined forces against the Chichimec, considered the most indomitable Indians of New Spain. Suddenly, during the battle, a resplendent light appeared in the sky, giving way to an image of a cross and the

Figure 3.7. Unknown artist, *The Apparition of the Virgin of Ocotlán to the Indian Juan Diego,* second half of the eighteenth century, oil on canvas and beads. 29.5 × 24 cm. Museo Soumaya, Mexico City.

apostle Santiago. The vision prompted some heathens to flee in terror and the rest to convert to the faith. A great cult of the cross ensued and was connected to the founding of the city, and portraits of the knighted Indian leader set against the miraculous scene were painted (fig. 3.8). As the historian Antonio Rubial has argued, the tradition was a Franciscan invention, but it was widely accepted, particularly by the indigenous nobility, as it allowed them to broadcast their role in the establishment of the city and claim privileges and land.[118] Because of the Indians' alleged participation in the foundation of Querétaro, for Díaz de la Vega the cross was a further mark of their honor.

Díaz de la Vega attempts to create a veritable cartography of Indian spirituality by mapping various cardinal points within the viceroyalty. In a real tour de force of apologia, the friar states:

> Of what importance is it that the Indian nation should be generally derided by men, when the Indian nation is extolled by Heaven and favored and exalted

Figure 3.8. Unknown artist, *Portrait of Diego Nicolás Montañez,* c. 1750, oil on canvas, 187 × 117 cm. Museo de la ciudad de Querétaro, CONACULTA, INAH, Mexico. Photo: Archivo Fotográfico Manuel Toussaint del Instituto de Investigaciones Estéticas, UNAM.

by God and his most Holy Mother? The incredulous should come to Mexico and inquire to whom the most Holy Empress Mary appeared so many times, to whom she spoke in a soft voice, and on whose mantle she impressed her miraculous image of Guadalupe. And he will learn that no other was elected by the Holy Virgin for such glorious enterprise than a poor, humble, and miserable Indian. Go to Tlaxcala and find out who was the subject to whom the Queen of Angels visibly appeared on the hill on the way to the river? Whom she led to that forest? To whom she offered the healing waters that she miraculously produced there? And to whom she promised her sacred image that today is known as Ocotlán? And they will be told to another Indian of the same class as the previous one. Go back to Mexico and approach the hill of Otoncalpulco to learn about the invention of the extraordinary image of Our Lady of Remedios, and you will find out that the inventor was an Otomí Indian. Go a second time to the province of Tlaxcala, and ask who the archangel Saint Michael favored with various apparitions? Who was miraculously healed with the spring of healing waters that is today venerated in the archangel's sanctuary known as San Miguel del Milagro? And you will be told an Indian like those mentioned above . . . Continue to the city of Querétaro and find out about the miraculous stone cross that is venerated there . . . and you will realize . . . that it was all in favor of the Chichimec Indians who inhabit that land. And after you have been fully informed of all this, then you can tell me if the Indians have made no happy progresses in Christendom, if they have not been favored by God and his most Holy Mother, and finally if this nation deserves to be abandoned, disparaged, and deemed irrational.[119]

This is clearly apology at its best, and creating a catalogue of the benefits brought to the Indians served many purposes beyond extolling the viceroyalty. In connecting the devotions of Guadalupe, Remedios, and San Miguel del Milagro, Florencia, for example, had noted in passing that the Indians were the recipients of the apparitions despite being the most downtrodden nation in the colony.[120] But Florencia's fundamental aim, like that of many leading patriotic intellectuals of the seventeenth century was to place New Spain at the center of a unique Christian cosmography—not necessarily to redeem contemporary Indians. Since the natives composed the majority of the population, Florencia's impetus was to prove their status as Christians rather than catalogue their accomplishments. The Jesuit's association of these devotions, however, had an impact among the clergy and on the visual arts, particularly in the eighteenth century. The main altarpiece of the church of the Merced de las Huertas in Mexico City, for instance, comprises a set of canvases by Miguel Cabrera of the Virgins of Guadalupe and Remedios and San Miguel del Milagro (fig. 3.9).[121] It is no coincidence that this altarpiece that brings together these three devotions was in the jurisdiction of Tacuba, a native town near the sanctuary of Remedios. The ensemble must have instilled a great sense of pride in the local parishioners, for the association of these devotions extolled the Indian nation and their role in the sanctity of the viceroyalty and fostered an indigenous consciousness.

The significance of Díaz de la Vega's compilation lies in his direct reinterpretation of a classic Creole agenda and his exaltation of the Indian side of things. There is little doubt that the stories that Díaz de la Vega so carefully culled were preached in Indian towns to instill a sense of ethnic pride and promote devotion, and that this type of narrative resulted in the commission of significant artistic programs.[122] Equally significant is Díaz de la Vega's emphasis on certain groups of Indians, such as the Tlaxcalans and the Otomí. If the Tlaxcalans were the first to embrace the faith and aid the Spaniards in the conquest, the Otomí surrendered to the Spaniards not because they were cowardly, but because as fully rational beings they recognized the new Christian religion as superior.[123] A similar desire to prove that the Indians were no longer "barbarians" in the Acostan tradition, but that they had progressed into fully civilized Christians, may account for the large body of artistic works created in Mexico in the eighteenth century—some illustrated here—that celebrate the Indian nation. Although the reasons for the commission of images is complex and tied to individual as well as corporate interests, I propose that the increasing number of images devoted to Amerindians in the eighteenth century can be seen as part of a larger indigenous and Creole movement to proclaim the spiritual maturity of the colony.[124]

Where Díaz de la Vega's manuscript ended up is as revealing as his overt proposition of a fully Christian Indian nation. This topic brings us back to the broader subject of the essay as to who could write an authoritative account of the New World. In the 1780s and 1790s the Bourbon regime repeatedly requested that the materials confiscated from Boturini be shipped to Spain in their efforts to centralize information about their overseas domains, and to assist them in re-writing the history of the New World; this was an enormous task that, as mentioned before, fell on the Royal Chronicler of the Indies Juan Bautista Muñoz, who prepared the requests. Disappointingly for the Spanish crown and in keeping with the colonial bureaucratic dictum *obedezco pero no cumplo* (I obey but do not comply), their petitions went largely unanswered.[125]

Figure 3.9. Altarpiece, Capilla Merced de las Huertas, Tacuba, Mexico City, with paintings by Miguel Cabrera of the *Virgin of Guadalupe,* the *Apparition of San Miguel del Milagro to Diego Lázaro,* and the *Discovery of the Virgin of Remedios by Juan Ceteutil;* eighteenth century. Photo: Fito Pardo.

When the Italian Alejandro Malaspina (1754–1810) traveled to Mexico as the leader of the largest Spanish expedition around the world (1789–94), he was again charged with bringing back Boturini's documents. Although Creole clerics such as Alzate tried to dissuade him of their usefulness noting that the indigenous sources were unreliable, as the historian Cañizares-Esguerra has convincingly argued, this was in all likelihood a Creole ploy—what he aptly refers to as a "Creole conspiracy" to keep Mexican codices in New Spain. In the end, in response to a royal decree from February 21, 1790, the Franciscans collated thirty-two volumes to send back to Spain with Malaspina. Nevertheless, the friars circumvented the original request by deliberately excluding original codices and sources in indigenous languages.[126] In his preface to the collection, father Francisco García Figueroa stated that after sifting through hundreds of documents, they discarded what was not useful and selected only the materials that they deemed most significant.[127]

Díaz de las Vega's text was included as part of this thirty-two-volume collection titled "Colección de Memorias de Nueva España" sent to Madrid.[128] In the preface of the volume with Díaz de la Vega's text, the Franciscan scribe stated that he included the manuscript despite being a miscellany of some of the best known texts, because "such matters, though common, together and focused on a single subject honor the Indian nation, and also because of other important news that are still not well known, and are the result of the curiosity of the author, of his unique understanding of the Otomí language, and his constant application to safeguarding good manuscripts from antiquity."[129] In other words, the selection of the text was designed to spread specific information, and aid in the construction of a particular historical memory across the Atlantic. Díaz de la Vega's knowledge of Indian cultures and his role as a custodian of important old manuscripts could satisfy, even if at one remove, the Bourbons' request for information about the ancient past of the Indians. More importantly, the patriotic tone of the manuscript was a way of rebuking Spanish authorities who insisted on naturalizing the inferiority of contemporary Indians by citing their purported paganism. The tacit implication was, of course, that the days when the Spaniards could justify their intervention based on the alleged barbarity of the natives had long since passed. In this sense, Díaz de la Vega's manuscript (along with the Franciscans' decision to ship it to Spain) can be interpreted as a discourse of resistance, even when framed within sanctioned forms of expression—those of the writings of the Church.[130]

Concluding Remarks

In his preface to the manuscript collection sent to Spain which included Díaz de la Vega's text, father García Figueroa crafted a clever explanation for his selection. "[In choosing the documents] we tried to follow the precautions taught by Criticism, fleeing from credulity and incredulity, two extremes which tend to imperil the truth. Joyous the one who is able to move forth without falling prey to either trap!"[131] This was an apt methodological warning to Spanish bureaucrats who were in the midst of amassing documentation to write their version of the history of the New World. Moxó had expressed similar concerns when he stated that: "Most people, who read a book of history or philosophy, get more carried away by their imagination than reason; a satire when spicy and even peppered with a degree of refinement and delicacy is a most delicious tidbit for certain palates."[132] Although Moxó was responding to the texts by northern Protestant writers, the comments of both authors are predicated on the same skepticism regarding enlightened philosophical tracts and how knowledge remained elliptical and only partially explained.

As this essay shows, many of the issues foregrounded by early chroniclers in the aftermath of the conquest were rooted in classical antiquity and continued into the eighteenth century. Spanish authors and early explorers had preconceived ideas of what they would encounter in the New World based on the tripartite division of the world. Located under the belt of the tropics, the alleged moisture and heat of the Americas gave rise to a nature—animals, plants, and humans—that degenerated quickly. Amerindians were seen as pusillanimous and effeminate, and destined to be governed by the Spaniards. The irony, of course, was that once Spaniards were transplanted to the New World, they and their children—Creoles—were said to acquire the qualities of the place and become "Indian-like." While it was peninsular Spaniards who largely spread this type of negative characterization, it was subsequently absorbed by northern Protestant writers who insisted on describing the Indians as arrested in an earlier state of civilization, and who emphasized the diminished vigor of Creoles. The twist here is that if the Americas was unable to achieve maturation it was largely due to the cruelty of the Spaniards and their inadequate rule. Comments like this were politically motivated, as northern countries had an equal desire in partaking of the legendary riches of the New World and lay claim to the region.

To the European invectives against the native and Creole body, Creole intellectuals responded in a variety of ways. The land, yes, was temperate and prolific but it did not turn Creoles into Amerindians; instead, it accentuated their natural intelligence and talent. Given the tendency to connect the Indians and the Creoles, some Creoles found it necessary to redeem the Indians' pre-Hispanic past in order to establish a unique genealogy for their homeland, and were compelled to trace their origin to biblical times. In general, however, there was a great deal of ambivalence about the actual indigenous peoples who made up the majority of the colony's population and who were deemed to be less than a pale reflection of their glorious ancestors. Alzate, for example, was careful to distinguish between nobles and plebeians, thus establishing a parallelism with Spain's own social order. Further, he had no qualms in applying the same line of reasoning that argued that Spaniards could become Indians based on climate, to natives becoming blacks—the most undesired social caste. Enraged by the flurry of so-called enlightened texts, Alzate also contrived a clever form of resistance whereby he positioned the history of Mexico as part of Spain's; in other words, he merged metropole and colonial history to provide a unified vision of empire that conjoined their destiny. This was not an active form of resistance that clashed head-on with peninsular rule, but it was an important strategy that allowed the colonial elite to lay claim to its own history and the way it was told. For Spain to maintain its power in the face of challenging political circumstances, it needed to gain consciousness of New Spain's intrinsic grandeur.

In the case of Díaz de la Vega, the Franciscan priest concentrated on contemporary Indians—commoners and nobles—by emphasizing their adherence to Christian doctrine. If the colony's indigenous subjects had matured into a fully Christian nation (following Acosta's model of a steady evolutionism), what was the reason for the sustained presence of the Spaniards? The question is not explicitly stated in his manuscript, but it is a thoroughly implied one through the act of writing the text and the subsequent decision of the Franciscans to ship it to Spain. Spaniards, northern philosophers, Creoles, and the native communities themselves, all had a stake in the construction of particular historical memories that would allot them a rightful place within the imperial social body. In this sense, it is important to keep in mind that race is not a discourse only forged by those in power, but also a counter-narrative espoused by those contesting sovereign notions of supremacy and rule.

4 Moctezuma Through the Centuries

Jaime Cuadriello

I WAS BROUGHT UP WITH THE IDEA that colonial societies had existed in perpetual tension, the result of a dichotomy between imposition and resistance. The possibilities of alternative responses by different social groups involved either minor transgressions of order and political stability or a challenge to the statutes of the Catholic king. The latter inevitably led transgressors to the legendary dungeons of San Juan de Ulúa in Veracruz, to the cells of the Inquisition, or to a fugitive and thus silenced life in the Maroon forest. Such was the legacy of a free and obligatory textbook that was still under the spell of liberal and post-revolutionary nationalist thought. This official pedagogy posited a polarizing vision of history that contrasted the evil religious fanaticism of the Spaniards with an idyllic vision of ancient Mexico and the cosmovision of its indigenous peoples. As schoolchildren, we celebrated October 12 not to commemorate the arrival of Columbus's ships but to honor the "Día de la Raza," albeit without knowing for sure, as mestizos, on which side of the racial equation between Indian and Spaniard we would fall. In keeping with this euphemism, in the 1940s the Mexican state went so far as to erect an improbable Monumento a la Raza, a massive pyramidal structure crowned by an eagle and decorated with reliefs of the indigenous leaders who resisted the Spanish invasion. To be sure, the "coward" Moctezuma was altogether absent from the decorative scheme. It is important to understand that post–World War II Mexico, a refuge for so many, was not immune to the passions and phobias awakened by the totalitarianism politics of Europe, which manifested themselves with considerable belligerence in the domestic political arena, even if only through journalistic anathemas that were more rhetorical than real. The fears about a power whose control would be based on genetic laws involved irreconcilable radicalisms. The state needed to project alternative responses that would at least serve to conceal the existence of an internally discriminatory subculture.

The figure of the emperor Moctezuma is an exceptional prism through which to examine the ideological trajectory and construction of *indigenismo* in Mexico, at least in its symbolic manifestations. The ruler embodies the many tensions implicit in the fabrication of an official version of history. Moctezuma's indigenous background and his political status made him the ideal symbol for legitimizing the aspirations and demands of indigenous peoples during the colonial period, the more so for having been the "providential" means for the establishment of the kingdom of New Spain, as we will see later in this essay. Furthermore, in the first independent republic of Mexico, Moctezuma was appropriated as a foundational icon by Creole Freemasons. During the nineteenth century, however, foreign invasions transformed him into a somewhat problematic figure, largely because of his alleged collaboration with Spanish imperialists and his failure to resist them. Without denying altogether his racial and political status, Moctezuma was by turns, and rather ambiguously, relegated to the folk imaginary and to the world of advertising; yet he retained sufficient power to endure as a foundational icon. In this essay, I will explore some of these ideological transmutations and underscore the role played by the racial identity of one of the last Aztec rulers. The various manipulations of his image over time function as a historical and political barometer of the construction of identity in Mexico, an identity that was often considered essentialist and immutable in official twentieth-century post-revolutionary thought.

Like every society that has undergone a continuously changing process of encounters and miscommunications, New Spain's ruling elite was able to create a space that allowed for the expression of various discursive forms. By alluding to the memory of the victor or to the legal status of the Catholic monarchy, non-Spaniards were able to make corporate claims—the real historical agent of social change in colonial Mexico. The pictorial image was certainly an arena of controversy and a resource that helped to attenuate social tensions—at least symbolically—among the groups that needed to stress (if only rhetorically) their loyalty to the Catholic king. This was especially important in a multicultural society such as New Spain, where the loyalty of its subjects was constantly questioned. But I doubt that the belligerence and the forcefulness of the images, which were rarely explicit, would allow us to claim that a "war" of images was unleashed against "colonial domination," or that the production, emission, and circulation of these images resulted from a top-down imposition on colonial society.

In fact, one of the most effective ways to make the voices of competing groups heard was—as with all processes of acculturation—through the appropriation of sanctioned forms of expression. By using the same visual language employed within the dominant sphere of power, different groups could articulate their rhetorical "demands"—even if the meaning of the images they employed would be ultimately subverted. The ambiguity and allegorical content of public festivals, for example, which were fundamentally juridically motivated, gave rise to visual artifacts that were endowed with a degree of agency (e.g., paintings). In other words, these objects serve as "devices of negotiation" whereby different groups could make a public display of their virtues and loyalty to the King—known at the time as *representación de méritos* (representation of merits). In these public festivals, the culture of dissimulation and duplicity, so integral to Creoles and the indigenous nobility, found its most effective form of expression to make corporate claims.[1] "Saying something else," as a metonymic resource, denoted literally and precisely the function of the allegorical trope. This was in keeping with the political idea that life was governed by a regime of pacts between kingdoms—in this case, the *república de españoles* (Spanish polity) and the *república de Indios* (Indian polity)—although the de facto practices of domination and exaction clashed with this desired de jure or legal status.

If the concept of a war of images seems inadequate as a historical explanation of images, so does the notion of "hybrid culture." This is partly because of the awkward and unpredictable contamination of a score of colonial identities with the memory of the ancient past. Perhaps the phrase "hybrid culture" is only useful in distinguishing its visual formulation, as if it were a matter of a graft received and recycled into a system of representation that is otherwise highly eclectic; with every change in power, the content of images shifted according to each region, group, or demand, as did the degree of intentionality that was carefully planned in advance. I believe there are indigenous, even Creole, societies on the brink of extinction, whose future is uncertain, but we must ask ourselves under what circumstances do they change, and at what moment do the alliances between different groups that were once opposed to one another become a convenient strategy to prove their adherence to the dominant sphere of power? There is a need to deepen our understanding of the contradictory behaviors that characterize mobile cultures such New Spain's, and to consider the idiosyncrasies of its political culture—such as the aforementioned practices of dissimulation, self-indulgence, and complicities among its members—especially the use of historical memory and its foundational and legitimizing claims. Essentially, there is a need to examine how these societies resorted to the past in order to make contemporary political claims.

Until recently, the dispute over history was the true ideological driving force of a society of contrasts; however, and predictably, the dispute did not possess a systematic path that would fully resolve the numerous contradictions encountered along the way. This is particularly true when a political model is proposed, a model which is almost invariably based on the historical imaginary of the competing factions but rarely rooted in the diversity of society itself. For this reason, it is important to pay close attention to an example in which the construction of identities does not always follow a predictable course, and where the appropriation of visual means and discourses appears to contradict the more traditional rhetoric of victors and vanquished, or the idea that the racial ordering of society is a sign of imposition or exclusion. It is also important to be aware of the directionality of the message: from the Creoles, who formulated their own idea of Mexico's ancient past, to those indigenous peoples who made use of a Western juridical and symbolic language to make their demands more effective. All community identity is an imagined act, "a continuous process of differentiation" that moves from the primary racial condition of a group toward its—rejected or shared—multicultural existence. As a consequence, the meaning of its visual productions becomes transitory and changing.[2]

As an art-historical problem, the fabricated persona of Emperor Moctezuma is particularly conspicuous as a kind of transhistorical icon, ideologized since the consolidation of Charles V's empire (1516–1556) through the emergence and decline of our current concepts of nationhood. The figure of Moctezuma is more than a case study of the social function of images, however, because it exemplifies the ways in which visual representations could acquire different levels of meaning over time. Beginning in the nineteenth century, Moctezuma's image and its "life" as an agent was indeed predicated on the possibility of its very reproducibility.

I will analyze a portrait of Moctezuma that has been consistently reactivated as a *raison d'état* (reason of state) by different political regimes. In the history of the image's appropriations across the centuries, it was remade and deprived of its original meaning, transformed into an "intelligent artifact," and used for political rites completely unrelated to those for which it had been originally created.[3] The survival and manipulation of the visual artifact, which acquires the status of an active agent, compels us to reconsider the notion that the life of images extends beyond their initial manifestation, that they are in fact directed toward a "negotiating" purpose, and that their transformations, or what the art historian Ernst Gombrich calls "open implications," can be unpredictable.[4] In addition, the portrait of Moctezuma is one of the few colonial images that, once resignified, unexpectedly survived the national imaginary of the first federal republic (1824–1837) and the years of triumphalist liberalism during the restored republic (1867–1872). These two historical periods configured a somewhat credible portrayal of Moctezuma between history and legend, a portrayal that, even if shrouded in mystery, lived and continues to inhabit the arena of historiographical polemic.[5] Paradoxically, for better or for worse, this image has also survived as a historical source of legitimacy and transcendence, whether it be to establish a monarchy, to consolidate the empire, or to restore, after three centuries, the Mexican republic of today. Moctezuma's image also validates something far more audacious in its metahistorical projection: the figure of the *tlatoani* (king) was, undoubtedly, a mythical, racial, and foundational archetype of the Mexican state for all time. By tracing the shifting meanings of this portrait of Moctezuma, one of the best known and most widely reproduced, I will demonstrate that the image was as compelling as it was fabricated, and that it was also an indispensable device of social representation.

A Dramatic Profile

There is a highly dramatic event in the conquest of Mexico, which is given particular emphasis by the chroniclers of the times of Hernán Cortés which is also depicted in painting and evoked in plays and dance during baroque festivals. When Moctezuma, sunk in "bewilderment and sorrow," consented to become Cortés's vassal, the conquistador became the true "successor to the Aztec god Quetzalcóatl and the lord and master of the Empire"—this in keeping with the ancient myths that identified Quetzalcóatl with one of Christ's apostles.[6] As the new ruler and captain-general of Moctezuma's armies,

Cortés ordered Moctezuma to send him his crown, scepter, and medals. This was much more than a ceding of power: it was essentially an exemplary act whereby the groundwork was laid for the construction of a new political body of New Spain.[7] In fact, Moctezuma's nobles and subjects would recognize in this act of *exemplum virtutis* the imposition of a tribute that corresponded to a new sovereign and in which they saw themselves as in the rising sun. Thus, the Aztec monarch "would have been the first to strip himself of the Dignity he possessed by laying the Crown at his [Cortés's] Feet either to leave it to his absolute disposal, or to receive it again from his Hand."[8] Cortés accepted the royal dowry as a provisional trustee of this renunciation and, to that end, appointed a notary to witness this transcendent deed, even when he suspected that "Moctezuma's tears and the distress with which he pronounced the terms of his vassalage" were merely a ploy to drive the Spaniards from his court.[9] In his *Historia de la conquista de México* (1684), the Spanish chronicler Antonio de Solís emphasizes that, from that precise moment, the Spanish emperor was acknowledged as the rightful lord of the Mexican empire, as he was "being indeed destined by Heaven to a more real Possession of that Crown." Later in the *Historia,* Solís highlights the value of this gesture of submission to protocol: "Upon this resolution a Public Instrument was formed, with all necessary solemnities, according to the method they used of paying Homage to their Kings."[10] The precious symbols of authority placed in Cortés's care, who was a surrogate for Emperor Charles V, sealed this ritual of submission, because these gifts were "those he used about his own person, and others that were kept for Grandeur, and served for ostentation."[11]

Cortés immediately named a bookkeeper and treasurer to formalize Moctezuma's subordination, and he distributed to each of his followers a "ransom" according to their services. This act constituted the first juridical instrument by which the newly founded polity of New Spain was born into political life, even if over time it would give rise to bitter disputes, lawsuits, and Cortés's return to Spain to defend himself before the king.[12] It is important to remember that a few days earlier, as a kind of prelude to his abdication, Moctezuma had been captured and imprisoned on the direct order of Cortés, who had uncovered an indigenous conspiracy. It is precisely this controversial subject, with which royal chroniclers found it so difficult to contend, that became prevalent in visual representations celebrating the triumph of Cortés's allies, the Tlaxcalteca. In plate 20 of the *Descripción de la ciudad y provincia de Tlaxcala* (c. 1580) by the mestizo chronicler Diego Muñoz Camargo (c. 1529–1599), Moctezuma serves as an obedient squire to the noble

Figure 4.1. *Hernán Cortés, The Personification of New Spain, and Moctezuma,* from Diego Muñoz Camargo, *Descripción de la ciudad y provincia de Tlaxcala* (c. 1580), ink on paper. Hunterian Museum Library, Glasgow University, Scotland.

Cortés; he is depicted "shackled at the feet," while the royal crown, the club, and an idol lay shattered, trampled beneath the hooves of a steed bearing the conquistador (fig. 4.1). Cortés is represented not only as a skilled horseman attacking his opponent but also as captain-general of his armies, returning victorious from his campaigns and parading in a lordly fashion reminiscent of books of chivalry, or triumphal entrances into a captured city.[13] Despite his humiliation, Moctezuma still preserves two of the royal and sacred insignias with which he was originally invested: the facial perforation evident on the ear pieces, and the emerald labret, or lip ornament.

The few surviving portraits of Emperor Moctezuma, along with the iconography of exceedingly rare dynastic paintings such as those of the Inca kings of Peru, seem to corroborate the triumph of the historiographical version of the "voluntary vassalage" and the official acceptance of the tribute in

Figure 4.2. Miguel and Juan González, *The Visit of Cortés to Moctezuma*, 1698, oil on board with inlaid mother-of-pearl, 97 × 53 cm. Museo de América, Madrid.

gold as the condition sine qua non for the political creation of New Spain, and consequently its existence in historical memory.[14] A set of *enconchados* (inlaid mother-of-pearl paintings) from the second half of the seventeenth century is very explicit: in one of the most accomplished panels, Moctezuma is shown welcoming Cortés to his reception hall as he points to two empty thrones (already reserved for the Habsburg monarchs?) situated beneath the Mexican coat of arms and the portraits of the eight previous kings of Mexico (fig. 4.2). The genealogy of the ancient kings of Mexico was so emblematic of New Spain's glorious past that the famous Creole polymath Don Carlos de Sigüenza y Góngora (1645–1700) included it as an example of "political virtue" in a triumphal arch erected to welcome the viceroy Tomás Antonio de la Cerda y Aragón, conde de Paredes and marqués de la Laguna (r. 1680–86); in 1680, he also wrote a book explaining the symbolism of the arch.[15] There is nothing here to imply that Moctezuma's willing abdication was an act of madness or cowardice; rather, it was a legitimatizing political choice. Furthermore, writers with a Creole sensibility saw in Moctezuma's captivity and renunciation a theological premise that was eminently moral and consistent with a divine summons: the pagan ruler's confusion and distress were necessary before he could be led to his own enlightenment and ultimate destiny. It is worth recalling that the role of a sacred king was to maintain "cosmic harmony" in the name of his "mystical marriage" to the people, and to attract God's "favor" with his virtue.

Through a sublime gesture, this imaginary Moctezuma set himself apart from the barbarian and irrational Turks and Tatar satraps, and thus he was initially portrayed as an "illustrious man" despite such abominable sins as cannibalism and idolatry, which were thought to result from the intervention of the devil rather than from his personal inclinations.[16] In other words, Moctezuma's "historical" and now eminently spiritual persona was an instrument of divine providence, a characterization that, by observing the omens and shrouding them in mystery, ultimately paved the way for the universal redemption of his subjects. In this regard, the construction of the figure of a "propitiatory" Moctezuma seemed to follow the ancient medieval tradition of "sacred royalty," whereby authority was conferred upon the sovereign by divine grace and his actions ruled by providential designs. The monarch was anointed and invested with the highest authority so that "political power would be subjected to the rule of the Holy Spirit."[17] The Spanish chronicler Francisco Cervantes de Salazar (1515–1575) even declared that, although Moctezuma was not a *natural* king but a *despotic* one, "in majesty and grandeur . . . few if any princes were his equals." He further assured his readers that "had he [Moctezuma] died a Christian, [he would have been] one of the greatest and most notable princes of all nations."[18]

Moctezuma's Juridical and Theological Persona

In a powerful full-length portrait, which can be dated to the late seventeenth–early eighteenth century and is associated with the pictorial style of the Arellano family, Moctezuma appears overwhelmed with sadness and confusion (fig. 4.3).[19] The pathos of the figure is emphasized by his languid limbs. These traits, as well as the position of the feet, which are slanted in an almost choreographic twist or a reverential gesture, evoke a persona that is quite different from those seen in most royal portraiture. Typically, the subject would be portrayed in heroic and vigorous *contrapposto,* with arms akimbo to express dominance, a convention in the visual arts that is associated with principles of *elocutio* and *dispositio.* Moctezuma's portrait also contrasts with the more

Figure 4.3. Unknown artist, *Moctezuma*, last quarter of the seventeenth century, oil on canvas, 185 × 100 cm. Private Collection.

austere and hieratic portraits of the nobility of New Spain. Although this is a historical painting, it nonetheless follows some of the basic conventions of court portraiture: the figure is set against a backdrop revealed under creased crimson curtains flecked with gold; the line of the horizon is placed lower than three-quarter level; and the interior is dark, typical of palatial settings.

The courtly appearance is further emphasized by Moctezuma's royal gilded insignia and the overt "Roman style" of his imperial finery. His Roman general's breastplate is encrusted with precious stones, crossed with gold chains, and decorated with "flowers and teardrops" on its borders. The sash and clasps fastening his *paludamentum* (red Roman military cape) are emphatically one of the most striking examples of baroque jewelry represented in New Spanish painting. He also wears richly decorated gold sandals, which the Roman emperors called *caligae*. There are, however, some features that were considered typical of his royal Mexica garb, which distinguished him from the rest of his princes: his pleated and flowing *faldellín* (short skirt) is made of feathers, and while his bladed club is mounted like a Roman sword with an eagle hilt, it is in the style of the obsidian *macquahuitl*. The portrayal of Moctezuma as a Roman emperor was not fortuitous; what may initially seem a "failure" to adhere to New Spanish conventions of portraiture, was by no means the result of ignorance or inexperience.

One of the most outstanding details (which can hardly be called "ethnographic") is the large, filigreed headdress that Moctezuma wears instead of his original *xihuitzolli* (plumed royal crown). This attribute identifies Moctezuma as a legitimate ruler, owner by virtue of his majesty and head of his *regnum* (kingdom) that was established since antiquity. What is striking is the inclusion on the front of the symbol of the Habsburg monarchy, the two-headed eagle, to signify Moctezuma's willing consent to the juridical principle of *traslatio imperii* (transfer of rule). The portrait might appear to be no more than an elegy to vanished glory if it did not also convey the act of imperial transference, which is the culmination of the message. Moctezuma is clearly placing the scepter on a tray that already holds his crown. Atop the crown is an eagle perched on a cactus, the coat of arms of Mexico and a symbol of the throne that he had recently occupied as ninth ruler of Mexico. This gesture is a declaration in itself: it gives us reason to think that the emperor's dejected mood, his downcast gaze, and his hand on his chest are signs not only of his consent and oath-swearing but also of the grief caused by having to relinquish his scepter. The nobility of Moctezuma's action, however, also alludes to the "official" Creole historiographical tradition that emphasized his renunciation of the throne for higher and loftier purposes. The transfer of his symbols of power to a silver tray—the crown as locus of *auctoritas* (authority), and the distinctive scepter as the repository of his *potestas* (power)—is not an act of fatalism or cowardice.[20] The truly transcendent nature of this act for both Spanish and Creole chroniclers (especially Creole authors from Cervantes de Salazar to Francisco Javier Clavijero [1731–1787]), was decidedly theological and therefore immune from any historical critique. Moctezuma, "the inspired one" according to the historian Guy Rozat, was not only a central actor but also a witness and executor "of the prophecy of destruction, [of] the necessary and inescapable catastrophe" that would forecast the advent of a new Jerusalem-Tenochtitlan. Its ruins will be the theater of a new alliance, which would rebuild itself as a holy city dedicated to the true God.

Royal sovereignty follows the concept of sacred kingship, in which a "celestial mandate" promotes unity, harmony, peace, justice, and the material and spiritual common good of God's people. Thus, the king is the visible body of the guiding divinity and the unifier and conserver of order, by means of his two arms or swords.[21] This portrait of Moctezuma "in sacred form" is also a representation of the medieval theological doctrine of the "two swords" and the corresponding notions of spiritual *auctoritas* and temporal *potestas* evident in his regalia or insignias of command. He no longer exercises his *imperium* (ultimate power of the state), symbolized by the surrender of his scepter. At the same time, Moctezuma renounces false idolatry, symbolized by the placement of his crown on a tray. He still wears a royal headdress, although emblazoned with the eagles of the Habsburg coat of arms, signifying his continued membership in New Spain's aristocracy. Despite Moctezuma's loss of the two forms of power, he maintains—and through his descendants, continues to maintain—his membership in a royal lineage or house.

Indeed, it appears that in this painting, Moctezuma is not abdicating his throne in the presence of the astute and Machiavellian Cortés; rather, he is in the sacred presence of Jehovah transfigured into light—which, though absent in visual terms, is immanent in his afflicted royal spirit, overwhelmed with sadness but transformed by his repentance. This element of "illumination" endows the painting with an undertone of a "mystic vision," which betrays a conceptual intentionality that is neither innocent nor capricious. To be sure, Moctezuma is a biblical king who has entered the sanctum sanctorum, the holy of holies of the tabernacle, to receive the message of revelation. He is a prudent and Christian king who has recognized the majesty of the true King of Kings and whose pact and covenant with the people resides in the tabernacle, the sign of a new alliance.[22]

Moctezuma's lost gaze, eyes dilated and welling with tears, and furrowed brow all indicate that the once powerful and tyrannical *tlatoani* is also, ambiguously, a repentant sinner, a Magdalene who has been purified and is submissive to the wisdom of the divine teacher. However, following the tradition of *vanitas* paintings, Moctezuma remains surrounded by the gold and finery typical of courtly pageantry. The Word has transformed the monarch's inner being: more than a defeated general, he is a tragic hero, conscious of a destiny that cannot be renounced, that is inscrutable to him yet utterly transcendent. Perhaps for this reason, this image of Moctezuma evokes the moving figure of Christ, who has placed his hand on his chest to show his disciples his wounds. It was not accidental that the Franciscan friar Juan de Torquemada (c. 1562–1624) wrote that when Moctezuma was a young man, "he was so serious and judicious that even before becoming king he was greatly feared and the gods spoke to him."[23] However, as he grew to adulthood, his character began to "show [signs] of the grandeur of his heart." When Torquemada wrote his massive compilation on the history of New Spain, he based it on two clearly programmatic political premises: to emphasize the crown's providential role in evangelizing the indigenous peoples by eradicating idolatry and any signs of the devil; and to defend the foundational role of the mendicant orders in spreading the Christian faith.[24]

Moctezuma's lavish attire, crown, and scepter are not merely devices to elicit wonder and prove the fame of his treasure-laden rooms. Rather, they are elements that serve as moral contrasts, because they exemplify the degree of selflessness attained by this pagan king upon renouncing all those trappings of material wealth and power. He has been swayed not by Emperor Charles V or his legionaries such as Cortés, but by reverential fear, by God's true majesty. He is a man who has seen the light, and who realizes that the legitimacy and sovereignty of a *rex sacrorum* (holy king) exercising temporal power derived from heaven-bestowed grace, and that he must be attentive to his creator's plans. We need only recall that Moctezuma's willingness to obey originates in a message that was already ciphered in the ancient myths of his people. This message, revealed to him through various oracles on the eve of Cortés's landing, led to a predicament: Moctezuma could either confront the Spaniards, or he could relinquish his power and accept that he was the vehicle for the establishment of a new law. The Spanish chronicler Francisco López de Gómara (1511–c. 1562) places in the "wise" mouth of Moctezuma a grave and solemn piece of oratory, worthy of moral philosophy, in which "with tears and sobs" he conveys the fulfillment of the prophecies to his allied kings, recognizing that he and his ancestors had governed in the name of an omnipotent God that until then had remained unknown to them, and therefore that their rule was transient: "We are not natives of this land, nor is our kingdom a lasting one."[25]

Personification of the Kingdom

Where could this image of the "inspired" Moctezuma, which carried such emotional and ceremonial weight, have been displayed? Who commissioned the painting, and under what circumstances was it shown? I believe that this is the same portrait referred to in 1846 by Don Isidro Rafael Gondra (1768– 1861), the director of the former Museo Nacional de México, which he declared to be the property of the nobility of Tlatelolco, one of the indigenous *parcialidades* (separate sections of a town) of the capital of New Spain. That would mean it is the same painting that once hung in the main chamber of the *tecpan* (indigenous royal house) of Santiago Tlatelolco.[26] If true, the painting would have been displayed during sessions in the "reception hall" of the indigenous governors and noblemen of this jurisdiction. For the painting to have been exhibited in a royal house or palace—the seat of the civil power of the indigenous council, of tribute-collecting officials and magistrates who oversaw the enforcement of the law and justice for the indigenous peoples—is especially significant. All matters regarding internal questions and minor and criminal infractions within the locality were resolved in the *tecpan*. In addition, the *caciques* (ruling indigenous nobility) lived on the premises, and the *tecpan*—as an institution of royally mandated exceptions and privileges—was responsible only to the viceroy and the royal *audiencia* (high court). This refuge of the remaining vestiges of the Aztec nobility, whose first colonial governor had been the last Aztec emperor Cuauhtémoc, was comparable, although on a different scale, to the viceroy's palace: it was the physical residence of the indigenous nobility and the seat of power for its judges and elders, a microcosmic version of the viceregal palace that embodied indigenous *civitas*.

At the turn of the seventeenth century, when the names Alvarado Moctezuma and Cortés Moctezuma succeeded each other rather frequently in the rotation of the post of Indian governors of Tlatelolco and Tenochtitlan— including the *parcialidades* of San Juan, San Pablo, San Sebastián, and Santa María—various key events informed the "pactist" discourse of this pictorial commission. First was the indigenous uprising of 1692, in which a large part

of the viceregal palace was destroyed and which called into question the loyalty of *caciques*. Second was the arrival in 1696 of viceroy José Sarmiento y
Valladares, count of Moctezuma (r. 1696–1701), who brought renewed interest
to the subject of the conquest and its pictorial representation. This interest
was motivated in part by his desire to exalt his wife's genealogy—she was a direct descendant of Moctezuma—and to establish ties with the Creole nobility,
who had already begun to draw on Mexico's ancient past to create a patriotic
epistemology. Third was a dynastic change and the War of Spanish Succession (1701–1714), which created two parties in support of either the Austrian
Hapsburg claim or that of the French Bourbons.[27] Equally relevant was the
bicentenary of the conquest of Mexico in 1721, which underscored the di-
minishing power of the indigenous nobility. As the historian Charles Gibson
noted, in the seventeen and eighteenth centuries everything changed: "Cere-
mony lost some of its Indian character and became mandatory under Spanish
direction, as in 1721 when the gobernadores of Tenochtitlan and Tlatelolco
were requested to participate in the bicentennial of the "felicitous conquest"
and to celebrate the "singular benefits" that the Indians had received under
church and state."[28]

It is difficult to ascertain when and under whose patronage the portrait of
Moctezuma was displayed in the *tecpan*—if this is indeed, the same painting
once hung on its walls, as I propose. What is certain is that the painting was
created during a period of great instability and crisis among the indigenous
nobility; a time when the Spanish government demanded proof of both their
nobility and of their loyalty to the Spanish king. The opportunity that this
moment presented for the creation of a markedly concessionary and humble
image was not lost on the indigenous nobility.

Given the precarious political situation of the indigenous nobility, the
image of Moctezuma that was expressly "fabricated" for the ruler's descendants is quite different from the erudite painting created under the patronage of Don Carlos de Sigüenza y Góngora to be sent to Cosimo de Medici III,
grand duke of Tuscany (1642–1723) (fig. 4.4).[29] In this work, which was possibly painted by Antonio Rodríguez (1636–c. 1691), Moctezuma more resembles
a European prince. The painting enjoyed great popularity among European
printers, and it was used to illustrate the two Venetian editions of Antonio de
Solís's *Historia de la conquista de México* (1704 and 1712), among others.[30] It is
interesting that for a courtly European audience, hungry for concrete American "realities" to collect in their *Kunstkammern* (art cabinets, or cabinets of
curiosities), Sigüenza y Góngora should have sent an image of Moctezuma

Figure 4.4. Attributed to Antonio Rodríguez, *Moctezuma*, 1680–91, oil on canvas, 182 × 106.5 cm. Museo degli Argenti, Palazzo Pitti, Polo Museale Fiorentino, Florence.

that not only was much more accurate in its ethnographic details and based on the pictographs that he himself possessed (e.g., the Codex Ixtlilxóchitl) but was also endowed with greater dignity in its perceptible majesty and warrior-like grandeur.[31] Dressed in military garb, Moctezuma is presented as a great captain-general of his armies, ready to leave for the battlefield, as he holds his spear and looks directly at the viewer. He is depicted as a partially nude middle-aged man, the way he was often described by early chroniclers. This type of depiction is in keeping with the tradition of courtly portraiture, as seen, for example, in the paintings by the Italian artist and treatise writer Vicente Carducho (1576–1638) for the Palacio del Buen Retiro in Madrid, who in an effort to create a Spanish genealogy as ancient as possible included the Gothic kings.

For Creole intellectuals familiar with pre-Hispanic antiquities, as well as the few learned travelers who visited Mexico such as Giovanni Francesco Gemelli Careri (1651–1725), traces of historical verisimilitude were valued over discursive sophistication: for instance, Gemelli Careri's series of engravings of Mexican kings that he included in his book *Giro del mondo* (1699–1700).[32] This was also true of the advisors who counseled the indigenous nobility on how to claim their rights of succession and privileges, including, for example, the *representación de méritos* and *probanzas* (proofs). One of the most representative examples is the painting of the Mendoza Moctezuma y Austria family, which was rendered as a genealogical tree and attached to a written document attesting to the family's royal lineage.[33] The tradition of creating so-called faithful images of the past seems to have been widely practiced, but it was not encouraged as a formal legal and public device. Although the reasons for this lack of encouragement are not clear, it may have been because the discursive efficacy of the images was lessened if they failed to allude to the pact of vassalage or the "theological" motives of domination—as they often did. The pride and pompousness evident in the exquisite portrait of Moctezuma sent to Cosimo de Medici III was probably deemed unsuitable for local audiences, especially since the Indian leaders themselves preferred to view their own political reality in sublime and allegorical images. For example, there is the even more stereotypical series of the "wise tetrarchy" of Tlaxcala. The tetrarchy of Tlaxcala was a sui generis provincial institution, in which the four joint rulers were fully enlightened as to their historic destiny and their providential calling to collaborate with Cortés during the conquest. Surviving iconography represents the four kings of Tlaxcala racially as Indians and wearing their quetzal-plumed headdresses, but with the honor of being attired in the garb of "European" princes. This type of depiction was a means of demonstrating the unique form of government of Tlaxcala: four rulers with equal power, a tetrarchy that since ancient times was opposed to the rulers of Mexico/Tenochtitlan—and whose present-day intellectuals continue to voice their resentment of "Aztec imperialism."[34]

Despite the inaccuracy of the Western attributes of power introduced in the portrait of the Tlatelolcan Moctezuma—in my opinion, deliberately employed to connect this American prince to his biblical and European equivalents—one can argue that there is an undeniable element of "public relations" at work. The depiction of Moctezuma was probably necessary to guarantee the survival of the indigenous nobility and of all those who considered themselves familial and political descendants of the royal house of Mexico. Herein lies the image's function as a "device of negotiation," which goes beyond the invention of the image as a mere banner of identity.[35]

In his *México pintoresco* (1880–83), the historian Manuel Rivera Cambas (1840–1917) notes that, in the first half of the nineteenth century, the largest and most famous festival of Santiago Tlatelolco—Corpus Christi—was still held in the plaza or main square. It was the most anticipated celebration of the year, because the Indians of the *tecpan,* following the tradition of their ancestors, danced in royal costumes, led by Moctezuma and Malinche (the king and kingdom personified), to praise the universal majesty of the institution of the Eucharist (fig. 4.5).[36] Was it not perhaps better to mask indigenous politics

Figure 4.5. *Dance of Moctezuma,* from Joaquín Antonio de Basarás, "Origen, costumbres y estado presente de mexicanos y philipinos" (1763). Hispanic Society of America, New York.

through these highly theatrical characters, who amply attested to the historical motives of their existence, rather than to argue for the lawful respect of their privileges? What else could be pleaded in this allegorical manifestation if not the "legitimacy" of a sublime memory in the face of what for the indigenous people was becoming an increasingly oppressive existence under Spanish rule?

A Figure of National History

The impact of the liberal laws issued by the Cádiz Cortes (1812–1820), which refused to recognize the Indians' communal property and, ultimately, the representative nature of the indigenous corporate bodies, broke up the already weakened native town councils.[37] Although the *tecpan,* as a token "municipal" institution, survived the first years of the republic, it was ultimately absorbed by the administration of Mexico's federal district in 1833. The tripartite theory of the state promoted by Montesquieu and North American federalist constitutionalism influenced the creation of an abstract profile of the Mexican citizen, making a tabula rasa of his condition and his past, particularly without distinction of nobility, ethnic affiliation, or race. Indigenous communities quickly found themselves in a disadvantageous situation that displayed the paradoxes of a theory and a practice that ignored all previous covenants.[38] For example, the property and archives that once belonged to the *tecpan* were transferred to the Creole constitutional town councils. It was at this point, if not before, that the pilgrimage of that "Roman-style," dejected, and lachrymose Moctezuma began. There was yet another expropriation by the "Creole republicans" of the old political and legislative privileges of the Indians, a race now vanquished for a second time and left without the possibility of ethnic representation. Moreover, from this point on, the image of Moctezuma is reformulated into that of an active agent, whose meaning varied according to Mexico's shifting politics.

As paradoxical as it may seem, the first Mexican federal republic of 1824 brought with it the symbolic resurrection of Emperor Moctezuma. He was appropriated as a legitimizing figure of sovereignty, largely due to the efforts of an emerging group of Creole Freemasons, and became elevated to the condition of martyr to Spanish brutality and iniquity. Hispanophobia, and consequently the eradication of Cortés—the old founding figure of the kingdom—as the "Indian Moses," found in Moctezuma instead of Cuauhtémoc its historical nemesis. Moctezuma acquired a new status as the venerable grandfather of the country. It is no accident that the Italian carbonaro revolutionary

Figure 4.6. Claudio Linati, *Moctezuma,*
1828. Archivo Fotográfico Manuel
Toussaint del Instituto de Investigaciones
Estéticas, UNAM.

and printer Claudio Linati (1790–1832) began his lithographic series of Mexican historic figures (printed in Paris in 1828) with a bust of Emperor Moctezuma.[39] Here, the portrait of Moctezuma serves as a fictive bridge between the three centuries extending from the end of the Aztec empire to the beginning of the Mexican republic embodied by its first president, Guadalupe Victoria (1786–1843) (fig. 4.6). It was obvious, and to a certain degree convenient, that one symbolic device of the new state to affirm its identity was the repeated use of a foundational fiction: the existence of a presumed Aztec state, whose resurrection appeared to be assured once the chains of Spanish domination were broken. The constant references to an Anáhuac confederation, as one of the names for the nascent national state, was no mere accident of the moment. (Anáhuac was an ancient name used to designate an Aztec area located in the Valley of Mexico.)[40] Linati resorted to the same mechanism of imagination and fabrication by rendering the portrait of Moctezuma that he had surely seen. Now, however, the Aztec king is depicted as an impassive, muscular man, his former shame and despair due to his theological destiny removed: the scepter, no longer a token of surrender, has returned to its position of command.

The first minister plenipotentiary of the United States, Joel R. Poinsett (1779–1851), employed the painting of Moctezuma with a similar purpose, without concealing his overt manipulation of the image. During a banquet at the embassy, Poinsett proposed a toast in front of his sympathizers and turned toward the portrait of the dethroned Moctezuma that presided over the room, hailing him as the legitimate founder of the political order he sought to restore. In effect, the Yankee ambassador taught a class in national history to a select group of Mexicans from the Yorkist party, which included none other than President Guadalupe Victoria.[41] Through this statement, the practice of history as ideological battlefield, or ritualistic enactment, once again unfolded, as did the practice of historical amnesia.

News of this event reached the ears of the impassioned patriot Don Carlos María de Bustamante (1774–1848), a historian and champion of insurgent nationalism. In his *Diario histórico de México* (1825), Bustamante assumed that the painting in the embassy was possibly the same one that had previously belonged to the Andrade *mayorazgo* (estate), a remnant of the indigenous hereditary nobility linked to Moctezuma. The painting had been sold at public auction for twenty-five pesos, and apparently no Mexican patriots showed any interest in its purchase. Now, however, Bustamante asserted, the painting was being admired by the new generation of politicians, and "it received the applause denied it for three hundred years, and from a foreign nation [the Yankees]."[42] Once again, Poinsett's vaunted Machiavellian wiles were demonstrated: he gave agency to a disparaged and unclaimed relic in order to legitimize a power embodied by his Spanish adversary, thus exercising all the interventionist power he was surreptitiously building.

Although Bustamante describes the subject of the portrait as being portrayed full-length and richly attired, it is difficult to ascertain whether it is the same work that we have been discussing, "or one very much like it," as Don Isidro Rafael Gondra, the director of the former Museo Nacional de México in Mexico City, would have said. Around the same time that Gondra resurrected the image once more by including an illustration of it in the Spanish edition of William Prescott's *Historia antigua de México y la de su conquista* (1846),[43] the portrait of Moctezuma appeared in other publications, including the 1844 Paris edition of Solís's *Historia de la conquista de México* (published by J. Baudry). The inside cover of the latter includes an engraving by

Figure 4.7. *Moctezuma*, from William H. Prescott, *Historia antigua de México y la de su conquista* (1846). Archivo Fotográfico Manuel Toussaint del Instituto de Investigaciones Estéticas, UNAM.

Figure 4.8. Amadée Varin, *Portraits of Antonio de Solís, Hernán Cortés, and Moctezuma,* from Antonio de Solís, *Historia de la conquista de México* (Paris, 1844). Private Collection. Photo: Courtesy of Jaime Cuadriello.

Amédée Varin in which Moctezuma forms a triad with portraits of Solís and Cortés (figs. 4.7 and 4.8).[44]

In contrast to the image of Moctezuma sent by Sigüenza y Góngora to Cosimo de Medici III, which later lay forgotten in the galleries of the Palazzo Pitti in Florence, the romantic taste of the nineteenth century was fascinated by this "exotic" image. Now believed to be of considerable antiquity and to date back to the time of the Spanish invasion, the image was rendered even more effective by its dramatic, almost operatic composition. Henceforth, this image was reproduced in virtually every history book published in Mexico and abroad. For example, the Catalan lithographer who illustrated Niceto de Zamacois's (1820–1885) monumental multivolume edition of the *Historia de México* (1876–82) created another interpretation based on Moctezuma's costume: a portrait, also "in Roman style" (Carthaginian or Moorish?), of his nephew Cuauhtémoc. The lithographer may have created the portrait as a moral pendant between the mature, reflective statesman and the dashing, reckless youth (figs. 4.9 and 4.10). By then, Cuauhtémoc was already hailed as a hero who resisted the Spaniards, and his reputation overshadowed that of Moctezuma. Cuauhtémoc's fierce, anti-interventionist determination— comparable to that of the mestizo *caudillo,* or leaders, of the restored republic (1867–1872)—made him the perfect racial archetype of the Mexican people. Since the times of President Porfirio Díaz (1876–1911), and still today, the image of the warrior-like Cuauhtémoc published by Zamacois—which imitated and recycled that of the melancholic Moctezuma—has been subjected to the ploys of the marketing world. If we look closely, we see that the image is also reproduced on the Cerveza Indio label (fittingly, a dark beer, similar to the skin color of the bronze race that mostly consumes it today) (fig. 4.11).

Although these visual variants attempted to follow their pictorial models, two iconographic novelties were introduced that reflected the political climate

Figure 4.9. *Moctezuma,* from Niceto de Zamacois, *Historia de México* (1878), Private Collection. Photo: Courtesy of Jaime Cuadriello.

Figure 4.10. *Cuauhtémoc,* from Niceto de Zamacois, *Historia de México* (1878). Private Collection. Photo: Courtesy of Jaime Cuadriello.

Figure 4.11. Label of the "Cerveza Indio," Cervecería Cuauhtémoc, S.A. de C.V. Photo: Courtesy of Jaime Cuadriello.

of the first federal republic and the constant threats against those in power. In the prints discussed previously, the scepter remains clutched in Moctezuma's fist, although it now dangles delicately from his hand. His hand is placed on his chest, recalling religious prints of a Mater Dolorosa or the Sacred Heart of Jesus and attesting to the figure's willingness to be sacrificed. If his *potestas* is symbolized through this gesture, the double-headed Habsburg eagle has disappeared altogether from his royal headdress, replaced by the Mexican eagle of the national coat of arms, with its wings outstretched. Through this sort of representation, Moctezuma might as well embody the immortal phrase, "The Mexican state begins with me." In addition, the features of the formerly sorrowful Moctezuma have softened, and he takes on the appearance of a handsome young man with mestizo traits, right down to the very Mexican cut of his mustache. Once again, the bronze race appears as the protagonist of the liberal reform period (1850–1910), of which the essayist and first Mexican theorist of *mestizaje* Andrés Molina Enríquez (1868–1940) was so proud; he

Figure 4.12. *Moctezuma,* from Vicente
Riva Palacio, *México a través de los siglos*
(1887–89). Private Collection. Photo:
Courtesy of Jaime Cuadriello.

also did not hesitate to attribute the country's historical transformations to
mestizo men, "the vigorous heroes of our revolutions."[45] Using the idea advanced by the liberal polymath Vicente Riva Palacio (1832–1896), in which he
posited the superiority of the indigenous race based on its lack of facial hair
and back molars, as well as its adaptability and resistance to hostility, Molina
Enríquez developed a nationalist strain of positivism.[46] He situated the mestizo not only as a fortunate genetic specimen but also as the repository of all
the virtues—already somewhat essentialist—of so-called Mexicanness. In the
monumental *México a través de los siglos* (1887–89) edited by Riva Palacio and
reprinted several times, this already emblematic icon of the construction of
the national state—the mestizo—was truly reactivated as a foundational and
permanent artifact, one that would endure "through the centuries." Its inclusion is not surprising given that the original painting on which the image is
based once belonged to the editor's own father, the politician Don Mariano
Riva Palacio (fig. 4.12).[47]

Spokesman for "Eternal Mexico" . . . or in the Trash

In the early years of the postwar period, the art historian Fritz Saxl stated that "the study of the genesis, continuity, and variation of images [was] a fascinating and gratifying subject," but one that above all presupposed a historical problem inscribed within the sphere of power. By virtue of its very vitality or magnetism, the "changing" image belongs to the consciousness of humankind; if not, it risks death, becoming simply an object of archeological but not historical interest.[48] Today we consider that the function of an image depends on its discursive efficacy and its capacity to move into the field of reception. Art historians pay special attention to the phenomena of reception, to the various factors that shape our perception of images—and our ideas of the past—and to the responses we have to our own culture as well as others. In the words of the art historian Michael Baxandall, we move between our own understanding as a "participant" or "observer" of a culture; however, to gain access to the slippages or shifts of meaning, we are also required to approximate the perspective of the "Other."[49] This is why art historians increasingly venture into the realm of marketing and consumerism, especially now, when we are all part of a global economy where images become dysfunctional, literarily ending up in the trash.

A review of the different incarnations of the image of Moctezuma throughout the twentieth century falls outside the scope of this essay; suffice it to say that his image is far from disappearing as a politically useful tool. (I myself became acquainted with the ruler's icon in high-school textbooks published by Editorial Jus in Mexico City.) The acclaim of the portrait of the once mournful Moctezuma has apparently not subsided; it continues to be reproduced in the most current revisionist historiography on this fascinating figure (see, for example, the psychedelic cover of Hugh Thomas's biography of Moctezuma, which purports to examine the person behind the myth) (fig. 4.13).[50] Between the massive consumption of Indio beer in Mexico, and the ongoing attempts by pro-indigenous groups to force the Austrian Ethnographic Museum in Vienna to return the alleged feathered headdress of Moctezuma as a means of reclaiming national dignity (according to legend, Moctezuma offered the headdress to Emperor Charles V), lie the two categories of a popular imaginary that will continue to resonate throughout the twenty-first century. Although there is no proof that the headdress ever belonged to Moctezuma, it has acquired a highly symbolic value as a political and juridical artifact, to the extent of engaging Mexican diplomats in international claims to have it

Figure 4.13. *Moctezuma II,* book cover from Hugh Thomas, *Yo, Moctezuma, Emperador de los Aztecas* (1995). Private Collection. Photo: Courtesy of Jaime Cuadriello.

restored to Mexico. In both cases—one media driven (the marketing of beer) and the other politicized (indigenous activist politics)—the issue continues to be the maintenance of a primordial racial identity, without which the Mexican state cannot be fully legitimized: *indigenismo* as historical and social capital. But even here, we witness the survival of a rhetoric of disguises that masks the real existence of the "Other," discriminated against or victimized, the last Indian bastion who from time to time appears in the newspapers, engaged in acts of active or passive resistance. As the anthropologist Guillermo Bonfil Batalla asserts, somewhat ominously, as long as the racial and social category of the Indian continues to exist, the problem will not disappear.[51]

By way of a coda, it is important to note that a truly unusual fate awaited this portrait, which prevented it from being incorporated into the monotonous and calcifying discourse of the Museo Nacional de Historia in Mexico (where historians-turned-curators have sought to pass off these fictions as

truths preserved in display cases). In the mid-1940s, this fabricated Moctezuma, divested of his birthplace and lineage, was in a private gallery in cosmo-
politan Paris, part of the assortment of objects that the surrealists had taken
back with them from Mexico.[52] Like Diego Velázquez's (1599–1660) portraits
of lunatics and court jesters, their faces disfigured by grimaces, who parade
before the viewer with equal degrees of obsequiousness and reverence, this
downtrodden Moctezuma of the *tecpan*, "racked by madness," surely must
have amazed André Breton's "courtly" and fantastical sensibility. (Breton, as
is well known, was quite taken by the magical substrate of "primitive" art.)
Seen from this perspective, Moctezuma could pass for a shamanistic artist, an
initiate, a grand master of the "marvelous," or a mirror of oneiric revelations:
the finest emblem of the unconscious.

   In official speeches or in school-assembly oratory in Mexico, it is still common to resort to a social, patrimonial metaphor to describe the indigenous
peoples as *la raza de Moctezuma* (the race of Moctezuma). As with Abraham
and his descendants, this type of patronymic has not only homogenized the
ethnic diversity of people but has also apparently resolved the pitfalls of finding a common source for them. But "the race of Moctezuma" also implies a
very specific set of moral and behavioral codes: the impassiveness, strength,
and stoicism of the vanquished Indians, which is diametrically opposed to
the vulnerability exhibited by the white tourists who visit Mexico. It is a retal-
iatory act that every foreigner, particularly Spaniards, must endure, and which
is meant as a historical apology to the figure of the dethroned Moctezuma.
It is well known that "Moctezuma's revenge" applies not only to a gastro-
intestinal malady caused by consuming food and water in Mexico but also to
a symbolic vengeance that—even momentarily—renders the dominant race
helpless. However, it is no accident that, to compensate for this reprisal, which
makes any *gachupín* (the pejorative term for Spaniards) or *gabacho* (the derogatory term for Americans) pay dearly, another expression is used to express both hospitality and camaraderie. This expression captures a foreigner's
complete integration into the local Mexican scene, especially those who have
successfully learned to break the rules: "*Finalmente se puso el penacho de
Moctezuma*" ("He finally donned Moctezuma's crown").

   As we have seen, Moctezuma is much more than a historical figure elevated to the status of an icon. He retains his ability to epitomize political and
social aspects of a rather complex culture. Therefore, the repatriation of the
painting of the "sorrowful" Moctezuma, along with its exhibition and study in
recent years, is certain to open a new chapter in the trajectory of the Tenochca

ruler's image. It could well be, for example, that the archeologists devoted to studying the iconography of the former official party of Mexico—the Partido Revolucionario Institucional (PRI)—could discover in this Moctezuma the prototype of the subculture of underhanded deals, corruption, dissimulation, and complacency, of the antihero repeatedly mocked in comic books and adopted by the PRI: the *agachado* (downtrodden panhandler) as political constituent (fig. 4.14). This peasant subculture partakes in the game of dissimulation and conceit to satisfy its most basic needs, and sells its vote without second thought to the highest bidder. Its members "bow" respectfully to the *cacique,* or chief—similar to how it was forbidden to raise one's eyes in the sacred presence of the *tlatoani*—who compensates them accordingly. This is the same kind of description repeatedly offered by political analysts of a similarly *Aztequizado* (Aztec-like regime) of the PRI that resorted to Moctezuma as a symbol of its own extreme form of presidential power. Every six years during Mexico's presidential change, Mr. President, the high priest of the people and of the official mega-party, is presented as a model of the inexorable statesman backed by the illusion of foundational myths. Likewise, his power was centralist, inspired "reverential fear," and existed by means of a legislative *agachón* (loosely translated as reverential nod). The PRI's monolithic political culture constituted its most splendid throne of legitimacy and, in ontological terms, the pre-Hispanic past served as its immutable mirror of identity. Even the presidencies of the "modernizers," Carlos Salinas de Gortari (1988–1994) and Ernesto Zedillo (1994–2000), continued to disseminate through national and international exhibitions the idea that, after *Mexico: Splendors of Thirty Centuries* (organized by the Metropolitan Museum of Art, New York, 1990), the Mexican state was a perennial reality named *Eternal Mexico* (presented at the Museo Nacional de Bellas Artes, Mexico City, 1999) and "located in the infinite." However, like every teleological invention of history taken as "destiny," this imagined country continued to be populated by ghosts and all sorts of unspoken truths.[53] What happened to Moctezuma also happened to great monoliths such as the Aztec calendar and the goddess Coatlicue (both uncovered in the capital of New Spain at the end of the eighteenth century), which functioned as iconic repositories of a primordial identity, as immovable emblems of a purported essentialist Mexican space and time. And although there are no pre-Hispanic stone sculptures of Moctezuma to elicit fervid cult, his figure, due to his primeval racial and historical legitimacy, continues to represent the enduring institution of the modern state, especially its centralism. Such is the discourse implied by every exhibition organized in Mexico and

Figure 4.14. Attributed to Jesús Martínez Carreón, "Four more years" (Porfirio Díaz blesses the reelection of Teodoro Dehesa as governor of Veracruz), illustrated in *El Colmillo Público,* no. 67 (México, December 18, 1904). Biblioteca de Arte de Ricardo Pérez Escamilla, Mexico City.

Figure 4.15. Wrapping of the *Tostadas Emperador,* Mexico, 2001. Photo: Courtesy of Jaime Cuadriello.

abroad that singles out—like the Museo Nacional de Antropología in Mexico City—Aztec civilization as the culminating point of the tour. The great sculptures of the Museo Nacional de Antropología form a kind of primordial altar on which a civic liturgy unfolds and in whose presence almost every president of the country has had his portrait taken.

The Moctezuma portrait sent to Cosimo de Medici III in Florence—the pompous and belligerent counterpart (created to satisfy the Creole gaze) to the more submissive and "cowardly" Moctezuma (produced as an indigenous strategy) who ended his days selling Indio beer, even if disguised as Cuauhtémoc—had a better fate. After the two portraits were displayed together for the first time in 1999 at the Museo Nacional de Arte in Mexico City, as part of an exhibition of history paintings, the NAFTA publicity machinery rediscovered the muscular, healthy warrior of the Florentine portrait, an image that is sure to become the most eloquent icon of the new planetary and globalized bronze race (even though this type of imagery has been a staple of Chicano border culture and calendar art since the 1960s).[54]

In the packaging of toasted bread made for the United States export market, consumers are promised that "Tostadas Emperador will conquer your taste" (fig. 4.15). A corncob replaces Moctezuma's spear, and the product sets out to conquer new markets by reclaiming a primal identity, one which, after race, stems from the most elementary cultural unifier: a corn-based diet. It is not fortuitous that Moctezuma has been the oracle of the entire Mexican nation through the centuries, and that his image has been able to speak and to sell, as the case may be, in the language of the times: whether dramatized through the "virtue" of dissimulation or through his investiture as a sublime device of negotiation.

5 Eugenics and Racial Classification in Modern Mexican America

Alexandra Minna Stern

IN 1930, A NEW CATEGORY—"Mexican"—was added to the U.S. census, and enumerators were instructed to count all persons "born in Mexico, or having parents born in Mexico, who were not definitely white, Negro, Indian, Chinese, or Japanese" as Mexicans.[1] Purged from the category of "white," which they had previously inhabited, Mexicans were now explicitly labeled as nonwhite and foreign. Moreover, "Mexican" functioned as a mixed-race category not unlike mulatto, which had been included in the census from 1850 to 1920 and was only dropped definitively in 1930.[2] In a seeming irony, that same year architects of the Mexican census chose to eliminate all racial categories, explaining that because it was impossible to ascertain with any certainty a person's "race" or degree of "race-mixing" (*mestizaje*), it was futile and absurd to attempt to gather such data. Rejecting racial categories and what they called the "concept of race," the formulators of the Mexican census instead expanded questions about the use of language that aimed to distinguish among the country's many indigenous groups and determine the percentages of monolingual and bilingual speakers.[3]

If in the United States, the addition of "Mexican" was part and parcel of an ever-ramifying list of exclusionary racial categories, all counterposed to white, in Mexico, the submergence of "race" reflected the inclusionary sentiment of the post-revolutionary state. This chapter traces the countervailing politics of racial classification in the United States and Mexico, emphasizing the different meanings and manifestations of science and society in each country. It situates this comparative history in the context of the growing popularity of eugenics among scientific experts involved in formulating national policies related to immigration, demography, and the census. From 1900 to 1950, eugenics—the theory that individuals and populations could be improved through biological selection and control—gained a great deal of currency worldwide. In nations as diverse as Japan, Argentina, India, and France, eugenics proponents founded organizations, published voluminous periodicals and books, and put their beliefs into practice through the passage of laws aimed to regulate human heredity and reproduction.[4]

This chapter explores how eugenicists and eugenic ideas informed the architecture of racial classification systems in two countries that share an international border; legacies of warfare, invasion, and imperialism; and Mexican-origin peoples.[5] I argue that, even given critical differences, similar ideas about the virtues and dangers of race-mixing held sway in both countries, and how racial classification systems with genealogies reaching back to the sixteenth century were reinvigorated and reconfigured by the scientific racism of the early twentieth century. Both Mexico and the United States were states that relied heavily on racial categorization, as informed by prevailing theories of biology and heredity, to draft a blueprint for national identity.[6] Ambivalence existed in both countries about racial hybridity and the significance of the term *mestizo,* which in either instance required expert classificatory management. Anxieties over the putative biological instability and failure to define the mestizo in particular and mixed-race categories in general were rife on both sides of the border. Rather than indicating the irrelevance of "race," this anxious ambivalence demonstrates how such fluidity and imprecision worked to make "race" and racial categories even more socially charged and potent.[7]

One important distinction between the time period that I explore and earlier eras is the extent to which reading "race" off the body and its external markers—such as skin color, phenotypic traits, clothing, and personal accessories—began to be distrusted by experts. Even more distant were the days in which persons of African ancestry in Mexico could purchase legal "whiteness" with a *gracias al sacar* certificate (a decree of legitimation that translates literally as "thanks for removal"), or fair-hued Spanish descendants in the United States could lay claim to "whiteness" without much scrutiny.[8] By the 1910s and 1920s, eugenicists in Mexico and the United States were successfully instituting racial classification systems that placed the highest truth value on what was hidden under the skin, usually in the blood or germ plasm, and determinable only through the retrospective or prospective mapping of genetic ancestry.[9]

Armed with knowledge of plant and animal heredity, inheritance patterns, and concerned with tracing family lineages, U.S. and Mexican eugenicists devised new techniques and nomenclatures to measure and codify "race." In Mexico, this translated into the cult of the mestizo of the 1920s, which, by the 1940s, had been supplanted by a nagging preoccupation with ethnic and racial disparities.[10] In the United States, heightened attention to racial classification in the 1920s resulted in the passage of stringent immigration laws and quotas based on census figures, a solidification of most ethnic Europeans into the "melting pot" of "white," and the concomitant extrusion of Asians and Mexicans to the domain of racial otherness.[11] For Mexican-origin peoples in the postcolonial borderlands of Mexican America this meant traversing a slippery terrain where Mexicans could simultaneously occupy the amorphous and enigmatic category of mestizo, the selectively contractive category of white, the bio-national category of *Mexican,* and a variety of in-between hybrid positions. Coupled with expanding immigration laws and requirements, the variability of their racial status made Mexicans in the United States—whether citizens, visa holders, or undocumented migrants—more, not less, vulnerable to deportation, segregation, and mistreatment at the hands of authorities.

Eugenics and Classification

We are surrounded and interpellated constantly by classification systems, which constitute crucial components of the scaffolding of our everyday existence. For example, the buildings we inhabit and the roads we drive on are fabricated according to specifications contained in classification systems. These dictate permissible types of construction materials, allowable size dimensions, paint color, safety requirements, and so on. In establishing the parameters for our lived world, classifications are also cognitive systems of organization that segment peoples, objects, and concepts along spatial, temporal, and spatio-temporal lines.[12] As Geoffrey Bowker and Susan Leigh Star explain, a classification system "is a set of boxes (metaphorical or literal) into which things can be put to then do some kind of work—bureaucratic or knowledge production."[13] To function well, classification systems must possess a logical form of ordering (e.g., alphabetical or numerical), mutually exclusive categories (e.g., adult/child), and be coherent and complete (i.e., a newly found plant species can be named with relative ease). When they operate smoothly, classification systems remain largely imperceptible and unquestioned; when they encounter material roadblocks or conceptual snags, contestation and struggle often ensue. Given that social, cultural, and moral values are embedded in classification systems and their accompanying technologies, it is not surprising that there is usually conflict at some point over their workings. In the early 1970s, heated confrontations occurred at the annual meetings of the American Psychiatric Association when gay activists and their allies demanded that "homosexuality" be removed from the list of deviant disorders. And indeed, "homosexuality" was expunged as a disease from the *Diagnostic and Statistical Manual* after a divisive internal vote in 1973.[14] Similar discontent also erupted around the 2000 U.S. census, which, due in large part to the pressure of persons who self-identify as mixed race, included the category of "multiracial" for the first time.[15]

Classification systems have long been the bread and butter of race scientists. As authors in this volume show, Europeans brought racial typologies and theologically inspired notions of racial purity (*pureza de sangre*) with them to the New World in the sixteenth century.[16] Two centuries later, the ordering fervor of the Enlightenment, as embodied by the development of Linnaean taxonomies of flora and fauna, spurred the social and technical extension of classification systems. The production of *casta* paintings, which date back to the 1710s, reached a zenith between the 1760s and 1780s, just as the burgeoning field of statistics was becoming central to the administration of nation-states and contemporary racial nomenclatures began to congeal.[17] In the 1790s, based on craniometrical comparisons, the German physical anthropologist Johann Blumenbach divided the world's human types into five races: *Mongolian, Ethiopian, American, Malay,* and *Caucasian,* proclaiming the latter the most beautiful of them all.[18] Over time, these categories and their geographical or colorized variants—such as *African, Polynesian, black,* and *yellow*—entered the scientific and popular lexicons. Significantly, they were integrated into that quintessential modern classification tool, the census, which was created to comprehensively enumerate an entire territorial population on a regular basis and generate publicly accessible data at the individual, household, and aggregate level.

During the eighteenth century, newly formed nation-states interested in gathering demographic information on their citizens, began to conduct censuses on a periodic basis. In 1790, the United States inaugurated the world's first decennial census, instituting what would become a ritual of statecraft every ten years.[19] Initially, this instrument sought to determine the numbers of slave versus free (which overlapped with black versus white) peoples in the country for the purposes of apportionment and political representation in the southern and northern states. As Melissa Nobles has argued, race science began to exert a strong influence on the census in the nineteenth century, as statisticians and legislators acquired (and often helped to produce) quantitative data that would in turn attest to the physical and mental inferiority of blacks.[20] With growing disquiet about miscegenation and a desire to track the offspring of mixed-race progeny, census designers added the category of mulatto in 1850 and decennially incremented the roster of racial categories according to national affiliation and putative blood quantum. The 1850 census, for instance, included black, mulatto, and white (as the default category); the 1870 census white, black, mulatto, Chinese, and Indian; and the 1890 census white, black, mulatto, quadroon, octoroon, Chinese, Japanese, and Indian, not to mention foreign nationals.[21] As fluid categories influenced by political priorities, evolving scientific theories, and changing demographic patterns, racial labels varied from census to census. Nevertheless, what almost always remained constant was the hierarchical structure underpinning racial classification systems, characterized by European-origin types (e.g., white, Caucasian) on the top, African-origin types (e.g., black, Ethiopian) on the bottom, and colored hybrids placed somewhere on the mid-rungs of the ladder, as determined by a variety of social, demographic, and cultural factors.

During the nineteenth century, Mexico also witnessed the development of racialized statistics, in large part due to the Ministry of Development, which launched a series of major statistical surveys. Under the aegis of this Ministry, Antonio García Cubas undertook four interlinked studies between 1861 and 1872 that resulted in *The Republic of Mexico in 1876: A Political Ethnographic Division of the Population, Character, Habits, Customs and Vocations of its Inhabitants,* which was translated into English in order to reach Anglophone U.S. and European audiences.[22] Despite García Cubas's aim to produce a detailed inventory of all things Mexican, he did not perpetuate the multiplicity of racial types portrayed in the *casta* paintings of the preceding century. Rather, he asserted that the country's human resources could be distilled down to the three base groups of white, mestizo, and Indian, tersely dismissing the presence of "negroes and mulattos" as "limited" to the country's coastal regions.[23] This reorientation symbolized the yearning of liberal elites and the positivist *científicos* (scientists) who succeeded them to return to the intellectual drawing board to reconceptualize *mestizaje* and racial classification

on behalf of modern nation building. Indeed, García Cubas did not characterize mestizos as degenerate or backwards, but instead as "vigorous," "tena-
cious and strenuous" types without which independence from Spain would
not have been won.[24]

By concentrating on the three human ingredients of *mestizaje,* scientific elites such as García Cubas brought categories with New World origins
in sync with European racial categories such as Caucasian (white or European), American (red or Indian)—and to a lesser extent, Ethiopian (black or
African)—that were then being fortified by various strands of evolutionary
thought. Notably, the tripartite schema of white, mestizo, and Indian was
included in the three censuses conducted during the regime of the Mexican
president Porfirio Díaz (1876–1910), and in the 1921 census administered in
the immediate aftermath of the revolution.[25]

The preferred methods of nineteenth-century race science were craniometry, anthropometry, and visual registers of racial ascription. The twentieth
century, however, was set apart by a growing interest in determining racial
type through invisible human traits and tracking racial descent (or ascent)
into the past and attempting to manage it in the future.[26] In part, this new
optic was ushered by the rise of bacteriology and the germ theory, which postulated that illness was not caused by foul air nor could it be diagnosed principally based on clinical symptoms. On the contrary, microscopic pathogens
were the culprits of disease and these germs could only be properly detected
and identified by magnification and penetrative imaging modalities. Furthermore, as Martin Pernick has astutely observed, during this era there was often
little distinction between *germs* and *genes,* a semantic and conceptual overlap encapsulated in the widespread phrase "germ plasm," invoked to describe
one element or the whole of a person's biological makeup.[27] Without doubt, in
some popular and legal arenas such as courts and among local communities,
perceptions of "race" based on phenotype, physiognomy, and cultural behavior did not disappear during these decades and in some instances prevailed.[28]
If anything, oscillation between the primacy of external versus internal criteria worked, even if in a convoluted fashion, to widen the ideological ground of
race-marking and race-making.[29]

The transition to "germ plasm" and the impossibility of visually discerning race was inextricably linked to the emergence of eugenics at the turn of
the nineteenth century. Eugenicists pioneered and mastered human classification based on the unseen, inferred, and abstracted, even as they frequently

assumed and strove to demonstrate with a perversely circular logic the superiority of whites, Anglo-Saxons, or Nordics. Sir Francis Galton (1882–1911), a
cousin of Charles Darwin, coined the term *eugenics* in 1883, eventually defining it as "the science which deals with all influences that improve the inborn
qualities of a race; also with those that develop them to the utmost advantage."[30] Galton was a seasoned statistician whose initial project was to develop
biometric techniques to measure and correlate the physical, psychological,
and physiological traits of a wide cross section of British families. He hoped
that his data would confirm that musical, intellectual, and other desirous
traits were innate—not learned—and, further, predominated in aristocratic
families. Toward this end, Galton manned an anthropometric booth at the
1884 International Health Exhibition in London. After several months in his
temporary laboratory, he had calculated the height, weight, and respiratory
capacity of about 9,000 parents and children in order to determine hereditary
patterns.[31] Plotting these variables, Galton stratified individuals and groups
into subnormal, normal, and gifted, a method that furthered the abstracted
visualization of human functioning through the use of "normal distribution"
or Bell curves.

Due to a confluence of factors—including Galton's promotion of eugenics
in the Anglophone countries, the rediscovery of the inheritance laws of the
Austrian monk Gregor Mendel (derived from his pea plant experiments), and
the broad acceptance of Darwinian evolution—eugenics caught on across the
world in the 1900s.[32] Elites keen to implement scientific theories of heredity
and evolution in order to diagnose and treat what they perceived to be dire social problems formed eugenics organizations. Concerned with profiling and
improving the hereditary "health" of their national population, eugenicists
seized upon a panoply of classificatory technologies in order to measure, rank,
label, and correlate—all with the expressed purpose of biopolitical inventory-
ing and management. Indeed, it was often eugenicists, affiliated with nascent
state bureaucracies of health and welfare, who invented such instruments and
oversaw their utilization.[33]

In both Mexico and the United States, eugenicists were some of the most
prominent classifiers attached to the state: they helped to determine categories for immigration policy, the census, and demographic surveys. Sometimes
their classification schemas functioned seamlessly; other times they engendered discord, confusion, or outright opposition. On one hand, classification systems often encountered resistance over time, as their epistemological

underpinnings clashed with maturing and eventually accepted scientific theories. On the other hand, spatial dislocations could also disrupt the transparency of classification systems, for instance, when home-grown national taxonomies and their underlying assumptions entered the transnational stage. This was certainly the case with the category of mestizo, which Mexican and U.S. eugenicists alike agreed was a hybrid characterized by particular characteristics. They disagreed, however, on whether this race-mixture was viable, advantageous, and capable of biological improvement over time. In terms of people's lived experiences of racialization, other social variables, such as class and gender, played a critical role in how they were racially labeled and perceived. The following two sections focus on how Mexican and U.S. eugenicists influenced each nation's racial classification systems, paying particular attention to the 1930 census, which was administered during the height of the eugenics movement worldwide.

The Paradoxes of Hybrid Homogeneity

The marriage of eugenics and racial classification affected Mexico in two key but not always compatible ways in the first half of the twentieth century: the promotion of state demography and of mestizo nationalism. At the beginning of the twentieth century there were many scientists who wanted to continue the statistical inquiries launched by García Cubas in the late 1800s. But the close of the armed phase of the Mexican Revolution (1910–1917), the signing of a revamped Constitution (1917), and the installation of a fairly unified cadre of national leaders intent on creating a post-revolutionary polity and citizenry imbued this task with fresh urgency. For example, in 1923, José Joaquín Izquierdo, a preeminent physiologist who had attended the Second International Congress of Eugenics held in New York City two years prior, delivered a lecture at the Second Mexican Congress of the Child. Speaking as the president of the eugenics section, Izquierdo expounded on the need for the state to take demographic stock of its inhabitants. Using the term *Creole* synonymously with European-origin types, Izquierdo recommended that a public health agency embark on a "serious study of the distribution of the great Mexican family, to determine the characteristics of the Indian, the Creole, and the mestizo, and to precisely ascertain the results of their unions in order to finally determine how to exalt the qualities of the Mexican and discard his defects."[34] Izquierdo's call was reiterated during the 1920s and 1930s by other eugenically minded scientists such as Dr. Rafael Carrillo, who in a

1932 article focused on race-crossing stated that, "given the genuine mosaic of races which make up the inhabitants of our territory, it is necessary that the eugenicist, in order to become oriented, immediately begin to study all of the anthropometric traits which distinguish the races from one another."[35] This classificatory impulse quickly gained intellectual and technocractic currency, promoted by a wide circle of Mexican post-revolutionaries and incorporated into state knowledge and projects.

In the 1930s, Gilberto Loyo, an economist who had trained in fascist Italy under Corrado Gini, an internationally known statistician at the University of Rome, founded the Mexican Committee for the Study of Population Problems and then joined forces with the Mexican Eugenics Society to advance the gathering of demographic intelligence.[36] Convinced of the great need to encourage *mestizaje* in order to demographically reorganize and synthesize Mexican society as a whole, Loyo promoted a quantitative increase in the nation's population through the acceleration of natural human growth. Largely due to Loyo, the goal of intensifying population density was codified into the 1936 Population Law, which moreover touted the "fusion of all the nation's ethnic groups," and "the general protection, conservation, and improvement of the species."[37] Akin to other "Latin" countries, such as Italy and France, during the 1930s the official Mexican position on demography, reproduction, and race was simultaneously organist and eugenic in orientation, reflecting neo-fascist elements. Yet, unlike Germany and the United States, where laws aimed to stringently regulate reproduction (for example, through sterilization laws) and control immigration, Mexico's approach focused on improving quality and quantity, largely through policies aimed at inclusion and increase rather than exclusion and decrease. For the most part, Mexican eugenicists sanguinely assumed that their country would eventually become a nation of mestizos and thus usually avoided mentioning racialized groups, such as blacks and Asians, that might disrupt this harmonious vision of the future.

In the 1920s and 1930s Mexican eugenics was principally framed by a neo-Lamarckian understanding of human heredity, which posited that characteristics acquired from environmental interactions could be inherited and morph from generation to generation down the family line. This was in contradistinction to the United States and Germany where Mendelian theories of heredity predominated and encouraged the idea that genes were passed unaltered (although in varied reassortments and recombinations) from parent to child. According to the stricter Mendelian version of eugenics, it was futile to attempt to influence heredity through social or medical interventions such as public health or personal hygiene campaigns. Following this scientific logic, the most effective way to better society was through policies, such as immigration restriction and forced sterilization of the "unfit," that would prevent the introduction or reproduction of bad heredity.

In countries such as France, Italy, and Brazil, "Latin" eugenicists eschewed Mendelianism, instead believing that individuals and populations could be improved through programs of social amelioration, such as public health efforts or expanded maternal and infant care, or, alternately, would deteriorate due to vices such as alcoholism or prostitution (which ostensibly led to higher incidences of venereal diseases and related immoral behavior).[38] For this reason, Mexican eugenicists worried about the long-term consequences of "racial poisons" such as syphilis, tuberculosis, and alcoholism, which could wreak havoc over several generations, and waged their fiercest battles against these destructive foes. At the same time, they saw the possibilities for a national utopia realized through the vigilant eugenic supervision of breeding and race-mixing. By requiring marriage certificates, blood tests, and sponsoring prenatal and maternity programs, Mexican eugenicists believed they could steer the body politic down the path of biological enhancement. The motto of the Mexican Eugenics Society—"For the Improvement of the Race" ("*Para el Mejoramiento de la Raza*")—fittingly captured this attitude. And when it came to "race," Mexican eugenicists found their prototype in the mestizo, which they championed as the vehicle for the simultaneous improvement and homogenization of the Mexican stock.

This position, while revitalized by neo-Lamarckian eugenics, was neither novel nor surprising. Mestizophilia was a socio-scientific phenomenon that stretched back to preceding generations of intellectuals who had evinced bitter dissatisfaction with European raciology and its ramifications. In the late 1800s, several of the positivist *científicos* allied with Porfirio Díaz's regime (including García Cubas, mentioned previously) began to challenge the belief then commonplace in Europe and the Americas that racial hybrids in general and mestizos in particular were inherently degenerate. Drawing from theories that emphasized the benefits of plant and animal hybridization and cross-fertilization, *científicos* countered that the mestizo was a virile hybrid that melded the vigor of the European-origin type (alternately referred to as *europeo, blanco, criollo,* or *hispano*) and the Indian and carried enormous biological potential. Andrés Molina Enríquez, who published the widely read *Los grandes problemas nacionales* in 1909, cemented this revisionist view, proposing what historian Agustín Basave Benítez has termed "mestizophilia" as an alternative doctrine of nation-building.[39] This optimistic reinterpretation took root in Mexico, and flourished in the 1920s and 1930s. An appealing and invigorating vision of racial amalgamation that resonated well with the ideals of (post)revolutionary nationalism, mestizophilia was a problematic construction that could never fully escape the premises of racial purity and hybridity on which it was built. This tension—between hybridity and homogeneity—lent the mestizo icon a malleability that enabled it to fulfill many roles, especially in aesthetic and cultural realms.[40] Nevertheless, the fact that it was comprised of two mutually exclusive categories made the mestizo an awkward and unstable creature of racial classification.

The approaches of two leading Mexican thinkers, Manuel Gamio and José Vasconcelos, to the mestizo and *mestizaje* illustrate the complications of enshrining a hybrid during an era in which hybridity could only be defined against a more stable pole of purity. Gamio, who studied with the noted anthropologist Franz Boas at Columbia University, held high-level positions during the first half of the twentieth century. These included the directorship of the Department of Anthropology of the Ministry of Agriculture and Development in the 1910s, Undersecretary of the Ministry of Public Education in the 1920s, and director of the Inter-American Indigenist Institute in the 1940s.[41] Vasconcelos, who penned the classic *The Cosmic Race* (*La raza cósmica*) in 1925, served as Minister of Education from 1921 to 1924 and was the most recognized advocate of what Ana María Alonso has called the "mythohistory of mestizaje."[42] Influenced by eugenic ideas about the biological optimization of populations and products of the post-revolutionary moment, both Gamio and Vasconcelos seized upon the mestizo as the harbinger of homogenization and national cohesion. Each, however, maneuvered the hybridity-purity dilemma in a distinct manner. Following the teachings of Boas, Gamio rejected doctrines of white supremacy, a stance that left him little option but to infuse the mestizo with biological purity by linking his (and the mestizo was definitively a masculine metonym) genesis to the noble Indian, chiefly the Aztec and Maya.[43] Gamio laid out this vision in the immensely popular *Forjando Patria* (1916), which countenanced broad-based anthropological investigations, and in *Ethnos,* the journal he edited in the 1920s that was "dedicated to the study and betterment of Mexico's indigenous population" ("Revista dedicada al estudio y mejoría de la población indígena de México").[44] Gamio's veneration of the Indian as a desirable and pure racial type mirrored the contemporaneous idolization of the Aryan volk in Germany. Yet, the irony, of course, was that

Gamio's proposed incorporation of the Indian into the mestizo body politic necessarily implied a loss of the primordial purity of the Indian. These contradictions stood at the heart of the politics of racial classification in Mexico, as experts like Gamio sought to apply imperial theories of biological superiority and improvement to racially mixed populations.

If the Indian was the centerpiece of Gamio's *mestizaje,* then the Creole or Hispanic carried more weight for Vasconcelos. Like Gamio, Vasconcelos exhibited a tendency to romanticize the Indian, whose culture he compared to the wondrous and lost civilization of Atlantis.[45] Yet Vasconcelos was less interested in looking back at the Indian past than in looking forward to Mexico's future; which from his perspective, needed a narrative of national rebirth that simultaneously denounced Anglo materialism and imperialism and celebrated the icon of the mestizo. In *The Cosmic Race,* Vasconcelos, an eclectic philosopher indifferent to the terminology of state demography, creatively interwove elegiac prose with catchphrases of Mendelian genetics to assert, with no tinge of irony, that only a "mysterious eugenics of aesthetic taste," not "scientific eugenics" could produce an ideal hybrid "race" that merged the superior traits not just of Indians and whites but also of blacks and Asians.[46] Vasconcelos put forward a total inversion of the doctrine of pure "races" that had kept Mexican intellectuals trapped within European frameworks and reliant on constrictive European racial categories. He forcefully challenged imperial assertions about "the inferiority of the mestizo, the hopelessness of the Indian, the condemnation of the black, and the irreparable decadence of the oriental."[47] Overlooking the logical inconsistencies of relying on Mendelianism to debunk "scientific eugenics," Vasconcelos expressed exultation about the prospects of the coming of a "cosmic" or fifth race that would transcend the limitations of the original four. As with Gamio, however, the issue of racial purity disrupted Vasconcelos's plan of *mestizaje,* which, in the final analysis, contained much doubt about the ability of distinct types to propitiously combine.[48] Notably, in the prologue to the 1948 edition of *The Cosmic Race,* Vasconcelos clarified the not so veiled paradox of his thesis and rejected the idea that all four races were on equal footing. Instead, he stated that the European race was one of a few "relatively pure races" and that the mixture of distant types "as in the case of Spaniards and American Indians, has questionable results."[49]

Until the 1940s mestizophilia was sturdy enough to placate these contradictions and to stimulate a climate in which the designers of the 1930 census

could unambiguously jettison racial categories.[50] In effect, mestizo nationalism reigned in the 1920s and 1930s. As such, Mexican eugenicists rarely endorsed plans for national cohesion that were based on the overt exclusion of
groups labeled as "undesirable" such as the Chinese, Africans, Syrians, Jews,
and gypsies. A virulent Sinophobia replete with ugly stereotypes drawn from
degenerationism was a crucial facet of nation-building in the 1920s and 1930s
(especially on the northern frontier) but eugenicists in Mexico did not partake
in anti-Chinese or anti-Semitic agitation.[51] Typically Mexican eugenicists simply optimistically endorsed the icon of the mestizo without reference to any
other racial group. Commonplace was the viewpoint of Dr. Alfredo Correa,
who founded the Mexican Eugenics Society with Dr. Alfredo Saavedra. In
the mid-1930s, Correa wrote that *mestizaje* "is the problem and at the same
time the solution. It is the problem because we are investigating the methods
to achieve it and to some extent accelerate it. It is the answer because once
realized, the national race will be one, a model that we have seen in other
countries whose result is growth and progress in addition to collective well-
being."[52] To a great extent, the mestizo presence-absence expressed the unspoken wish of eugenicists that the inexorable outcome of race-mixing would
be the demise of the process of *mestizaje* and the eventual ascendance of the
European type and his qualities. In this sense, full-fledged eugenicists such
as Correa and Saavedra were decidedly less interested in overt discussions of
racial mixing than Vasconcelos and Gamio, figures of much greater national
prominence who borrowed heavily from theories of heredity but nevertheless
never became central actors in the Mexican Eugenics Society. Given the slippery terrain of paradoxes on which Mexican eugenicists developed their ideas
about race-mixing, it is not surprising that the terms they used to describe
Europeans varied, regularly ranging from Creole (*criollo*) to white (*blanco*) to
European (*europeo*). Whether consciously or unconsciously, Mexican eugenicists tended to avoid the confusion of this fluid terminology and circumvent
some of the contradictions of their racialized formulas by referring to either
an explicitly unraced subject or the generic mestizo.

Furthermore, like Vasconcelos, when they engaged "race" head on, Mexican
eugenicists tended to believe that only proximate, not distant, races could mix
well. In his 1934 *Eugenics and Social Medicine,* Saavedra, the long-term president of the Mexican Eugenics Society, explained "not all races mix compatibly;
from the biological or social point of view not all can amalgamate and produce
a desirable mixing; there are families that degenerate by mixing or crossing,

while others improve through *mestizaje*."[53] Yet in the heyday of hybridity, it was difficult to justify (not to mention finance) the kinds of massive statistical surveys that could accurately reveal patterns of race-mixing across the country; to do so would expose deep-seated ethnoracial, cultural, and socioeconomic variation and spoil the master plan of mestizo homogenization.

Paradoxically, eugenicists helped to create the conditions for the mestizophilia of the 1920s and 1930s, which by definition, militated against some of the objectives of state demography to distinguish groups and types through racial classification. Beset by these pressures, by the 1940s mestizo nationalism was beginning to erode. Increased worries among eugenicists and other scientific experts that race-mixing in Mexico ultimately might not produce a superlative biological product, widespread awareness of the uneven assimilation and cultural resistance of indigenous groups, and the realization that neo-Lamarckian theories of acquired inheritance had been severely discredited by recent discoveries in genetics, prompted new approaches to racial classification. Although the mestizo never completely lost his luster, eugenicists turned away from optimistic plans for national homogenization toward the mapping of human differentiation through the science of biotypology, which sought to classify people not as races but as universal biotypes (such as ectomorph/endomorph and long type/short type) with complex correlations of constitutional and cultural traits.[54] Freed from the constraints of mestizophilia, eugenic classification exploded in the 1940s and 1950s, as biotypologists traveled the country measuring and categorizing students, soldiers, proletarians, professionals, and Indians. In the end, however, the underlying biases of biotypology, which always ranked Mexican groups against independent controls made up entirely of middle-class European and U.S. males, made this alternative classificatory science nearly as troublesome as mestizophilia.

Mexican for a Decade

One of the first things that Charles B. Davenport did after founding the Eugenics Record Office (ERO) in Cold Spring Harbor, New York, in 1910 was to publish *The Trait Book*.[55] The objective of this manual was to classify "every human trait by a numbering scheme akin to the Dewey Decimal System."[56] It contained hundreds of entries, including—just to name a few—organizing ability, cysts and tumors, wanderlust, and convulsions, as well as a long list of opposing temperamental and personality traits (e.g., honesty v. dishonesty).[57] As a classification system, *The Trait Book* represented the dominance in the

United States of Mendelian theories of heredity, which posited that virtually every human trait was a discrete "unit character" that was passed intact from progenitor to offspring. Beholden to Mendelianism, the majority of U.S. eugenicists affiliated with institutions such as the ERO, the American Eugenics Society (formed in 1925), and the Human Betterment Foundation (formed in 1928), disdained neo-Lamarckian pretensions of biological improvement through medical or social intervention. Rather, they believed that the only viable way to create a hereditarily superior population was to ensure that the "fit" propagate in much higher numbers and to curtail the reproduction of the "unfit." Accordingly, eugenicists needed to obtain a comprehensive genetic profile of the population. They viewed this task with great urgency, both because they were convinced that "race suicide" was killing off "fit" Americans and that many genetic characteristics, especially negative recessive ones, were not readily visible to the human eye and had to be identified through family pedigree charting. *The Trait Book* was a critical tool for this enterprise and in the 1910s and 1920s the ERO prepared hundreds of eugenic field-workers to take this classificatory instrument into communities across the country to survey Americans from various walks of life. As Garland E. Allen has pointed out, by January 1918 the ERO had amassed close to 540,000 three-inch by five-inch cards that decimally cross-referenced traits by family name, entry number, and geographic location.[58]

Given their preoccupation with classification, U.S. eugenicists were exceedingly interested in the format and organization of the census. As mentioned, race science began to shape the U.S. census in earnest in the mid-nineteenth century. The advent of eugenics, however, added another dimension to this dynamic. Many U.S. eugenicists saw the census as a ready-made technology that could be merged with or transformed into a eugenic registry. John Harvey Kellogg, the head of the Race Betterment Foundation (formed in 1906), proposed his plan for a eugenic registry, which garnered ample support from his colleagues, at the Second National Conference of Race Betterment held in San Francisco in 1915.[59] At the ERO's annual meeting the following year, a recommendation drafted by Alexander Graham Bell and unanimously adopted by his fellow board members, asked the U.S. Bureau of the Census to make all enumeration records "available for genealogical and family-pedigree studies."[60] As Harry H. Laughlin explained, the 1920 census and all subsequent censuses could thus foster "race betterment in the United States" by requiring an entry for the racial ancestry of the respondent's mother and father.[61]

One reason why U.S. eugenicists cared so much about the census was because its body counts played a deciding role in immigration policy. In a manner comparable to their understanding of specific human traits as "unit characters" transmitted in the "germ plasm," most eugenicists, at least until the 1930s, viewed ethnic and racial groups as discrete biological types with intrinsic attributes. Hence, U.S. eugenicists frequently referred to the Anglo-Saxon stock or the Jewish or Italian "germ plasm."[62] Eugenic ideologies certainly attracted a wide range of adherents in the early twentieth century, including the African American educator W. E. B. DuBois and birth control crusader Margaret Sanger.[63] For the most part, however, official eugenics organizations such as the ERO and the American Eugenics Society were the exclusive province of wealthy and educated men (and some women) whose ancestors hailed from the Anglo, Nordic, or Germanic countries of Europe. When this privileged and pale-skinned segment of American society looked around them in the early 1900s, especially in the densely packed cities of the East Coast, they did not perceive others of their ilk but impoverished hordes of swarthy newcomers from the ostensibly less civilized European countries of Poland, Russia, and Italy. Cognizant of the fact that these "new" immigrants were reproducing at a faster rate than the "old" immigrants with which they identified, U.S. eugenicists concluded that the "unfit" were overtaking the "fit" and that a massive influx of defective "germ plasm" was threatening to contaminate and destroy the America's superior racial stock. When they consulted the censuses of 1890, 1910, and 1920, eugenicists felt that their worst fears were confirmed: over those three decades approximately 25 million immigrants had entered the United States, the bulk from Eastern and Southern Europe (fig. 5.1).[64]

Based on a simplistic application of Mendelian laws, extrapolated from plant and animal species to historically and culturally complex ethnoracial groups of human beings, eugenicists managed with a fair amount of success to shape U.S. immigration law in the 1910s and 1920s. In the context of extant strands of nativism, above all Sinophobia, and in a country that maintained a system of racial apartheid vis-à-vis African Americans, eugenic appeals to severely restrict the number of immigrants based on national origin were met with a great deal of success.[65] It helped that several members of the American Eugenics Society, notably Albert Johnson of Washington and John C. Box of Texas, were well-placed congressmen. For instance, during his chairmanship of the House Committee on Immigration and Naturalization in the early

Figure 5.1. Photograph included with article W. A. Plecker, "Race Mixture and the Next Census," *Eugenics: A Journal of Race Betterment* 2:3 (March 1929), 3–7. This issue of *Eugenics* devoted a section to the census, explaining its importance as a eugenic tool to track and increase the Anglo-Saxon element in the U.S. population. Image in public domain.

1920s, Johnson appointed Laughlin to be the "Expert Eugenics Agent," a position Laughlin relished as he strove to convince with statistics derived from the census that the foreign-born drastically outnumbered the native-born in prisons and reformatories.[66] In 1924 the U.S. Congress, manifestly influenced by eugenic nativism and racism, passed the Johnson-Reed Immigration Act. This law established a system in which immigration to the United States was capped at 2 percent per group as defined by national origin and as tallied in the 1890 census, a formula that dramatically reduced the number of admissible "new" immigrants. In addition, this act replaced the preexisting piecemeal restriction of specific Asian nationals with a total ban on all entrants from Asia.[67]

The stringency of the Johnson-Reed Immigration Act would seem to suggest that eugenicists and their nativist allies had accomplished their goal of impeding the pollution of American "germ plasm" by undesirable foreign stock. Yet, from the perspective of Laughlin, Johnson, and Box, one major crisis remained: "the Mexican problem." Since the start of the Mexican Revolution and with the demand for workers in factories and fields sparked by World War I, Mexicans had come to the United States in growing numbers in the 1910s and 1920s, becoming more visible in the Southwest and in major cities of the North such as Chicago and Detroit.[68] Their entry was facilitated by the fact that the only part of the world where the 2 percent quota did not apply was the Western hemisphere, due mostly to the political and economic pull of a formidable lobby of growers and industrialists. In the late 1920s, eugenicists made extensive efforts to overturn this forced compromise between restrictionists and agribusiness. To some extent, the creation of the Border Patrol in 1924, which was folded into the passage of the Johnson-Reed Immigration Act, compensated for a lack of quotas with increased surveillance and deportations. But for eugenicists eager to attain racial purity through immigration law, the boundary line policing Mexicans did not suffice. Thus, between 1926 and 1930, Box and Johnson held numerous hearings in an attempt to persuade Congress to implement Mexican quotas.[69] The debates that took place during these sessions reveal why eugenicists were so perturbed by "the Mexican problem." In short, they viewed Mexicans, with most emphasis on working-class Mexican laborers, as degenerate hybrids who carried the worst elements of intermixed stocks. For example, in a 1928 hearing, Box explained why legislation had to be revised to bar Mexicans: "another purpose of the immigration law is the protection of American racial stock from further degradation or change through mongrelization. The Mexican peon is a mixture of Mediterranean-blooded Spanish peasant with low-grade Indians who did not fight to extinction but submitted and multiplied as serfs. Into that was fused much of Negro slave blood."[70] Such disparagements, which emphasized the supposed biological inferiority of Mexicans, were commonplace in the legislatures, courts, newspapers, and mainstream American culture in the 1920s and 1930s. During this period, eugenic racism and the popularization of negative stereotypes worked hand in hand to help delimit "Mexican" as a separate racial category defined as volatile, hybrid, and foreign.

This was the environment in which "Mexican" was added to the 1930 census. Census designers were frustrated that it was so tricky to count Mexicans precisely, a situation exacerbated by Mexicans' ambiguous legal status in a land many called home, even decades after the United States had seized close to one-half of Mexico's territory in the mid-nineteenth century. Should seasonal laborers, day commuters, long-term residents without documentation, and naturalized citizens all be enumerated as Mexicans? The transcript of the 1928 hearings of the House Committee on the Census, which debated these issues in anticipation of the upcoming decennial census, indicates that while mainly classed as a national type, Mexicans were also viewed as a classificatory enigma.[71] For this reason, and because at least some Mexicans had been able to straddle and occasionally occupy the category of "white" or "Caucasian," defining "Mexican" as the racial other became integral to defining "white" as the racial insider. Thus, in 1928, Laughlin returned to the House to offer his opinion on naturalization, which since the passage of the Fourteenth Amendment in 1870, had applied solely to those of white or African ancestry.[72] In cooperation with Box and Johnson, Laughlin spent much of the late 1920s agitating for the institution of Mexican quotas and harsher border controls. Nevertheless, before the House Committee Laughlin stated that the quotas were not sufficient because they still allowed "some white-Indian-black Mexicans" to enter the United States, a breach he hoped to remedy by replacing national origins with "the white naturalization standard."[73] Following this standard, only white persons—individuals with virtually all "ancestors of Caucasian stocks"—would be admitted to the United States.[74] True to the Mendelian idea of discrete racial "unit characters," Laughlin suggested that the fractions of either 15/16ths or 31/32nds Caucasian be employed in order to ensure that this criteria was enforced and racial purity defended for generations to come. While Laughlin's proposals were never codified into law, they illustrate the pervasive influence of eugenics and its peculiar optics of racial detection and labeling on immigration and census classifications in the early twentieth century (fig. 5.2).

As Neil Foley has argued, the dilemma of the classification of Mexicans in the United States in the 1920s and 1930s was as much about demarcating the outer limits of whiteness as it was about managing the unwieldiness of perceived biological hybridity.[75] Laughlin's and Johnson's clamors to add entries for the racial descent of the mother and father of census respondents need to be situated not just in the overall context of eugenic racism but as integral to the heated deliberations about the census box, if any, in which "Mexicans" belonged.[76] In other words, debates over the classificatory boundaries of "Mexican" were as much, if not more, about delimiting whiteness than about formulating an exact definition of "Mexican." Given this, and in part due to the pressure of the League of United Latin American Citizens (formed in 1929), whose members backed placing quotas on Mexicans and were eager to

TABLE 4.—TOTAL POPULATION BY COLOR OR RACE, FOR THE UNITED STATES: 1790 TO 1930

[Figures are given under each class for all census years for which data are available. Per cent not shown where less than 0.1]

CENSUS YEAR	POPULATION									PER CENT OF TOTAL POPULATION					
	Total	White	Negro	Mexican	Indian	Chinese	Japanese	Filipino	All other	White	Negro	Mexican	Indian	Chinese	Japanese
1930	122,775,046	108,864,207	11,891,143	1,422,533	332,397	74,954	138,834	45,208	[1]5,770	88.7	9.7	1.2	0.3	0.1	0.1
1920	105,710,620	[2]94,820,915	10,463,131	[1]700,541	244,437	61,639	111,010	5,603	[3]3,885	[2]80.7	9.9	0.7	0.2	0.1	0.1
1910	91,972,266	[2]81,731,957	9,827,763	[1]367,510	265,683	71,531	72,157	160	[4]3,015	[2]88.9	10.7	0.4	0.3	0.1	0.1
1900	75,994,575	66,809,196	8,833,994		237,196	89,863	24,326			87.9	11.6				
1890	62,947,714	55,101,258	7,488,676		248,253	107,488	2,039			87.5	11.9				
1880	50,155,783	43,402,970	6,580,793		[5]66,407	105,465	148			86.5	13.1		0.1	0.2	
1870	38,558,371	33,589,377	4,880,009		[5]25,731	63,199	55			87.1	12.7		0.1	0.2	
1870 [6]	39,818,449	34,337,292	5,392,172		[5]25,731	63,199	55			86.2	13.5		0.1	0.2	
1860	31,443,321	26,922,537	4,441,830		[5]44,021	34,933				85.6	14.1		0.1		
1850	23,191,876	19,553,068	3,638,808							84.3	15.7				
1840	17,069,453	14,195,805	2,873,648							83.2	16.8				
1830	12,866,020	10,537,378	2,328,642							81.9	18.1				
1820	9,638,453	7,866,797	1,771,656							81.6	18.4				
1810	7,239,881	5,862,073	1,377,808							81.0	19.0				
1800	5,308,483	4,306,446	1,002,037							81.1	18.9				
1790	3,929,214	3,172,006	757,208							80.7	19.3				

[1] Comprises 3,130 Hindus, 1,860 Koreans, 660 Hawaiians, 18 Siamese, and 6 Samoans.
[2] The white population as classified in 1920 and 1910 included 700,541 and 367,510 persons, respectively (estimated), who would have been classified as Mexican in 1930. If the figures are adjusted by deducting these estimates, the number of white persons in 1920 becomes 94,120,374, or 89.9 per cent of the total, and in 1910, 81,364,447, or 88.5 per cent of the total.
[3] Comprises 2,807 Hindus, 1,224 Koreans, 110 Hawaiians, 19 Malays, 17 Siamese, 6 Samoans, and 2 Maoris.
[4] Comprises 2,545 Hindus, 462 Koreans, and 8 Maoris.
[5] Exclusive of Indians in Indian Territory and on Indian reservations, not enumerated at censuses prior to 1890.
[6] Estimated corrected figures. See explanation in text.

Figure 5.2. This image shows Mexicans counted in the 1930 census for the first time. The entries for 1910 and 1920 were italicized to indicate that these figures were estimates of the number of Mexicans classified under "white" in the two previous decennial censuses. The table is from the U.S. Department of Commerce, Bureau of the Census, *Fifteenth Census of the United States: 1930*, X, Volume II: General Report, Statistics by Subject (Washington, D.C.: Government Printing Office, 1931), p. 32.

avoid dilution of their assimilated middle-class hold on whiteness, "Mexican" was removed from the 1940 census.[77] This action, however, did not tidily nor radically transform the politics of Mexican racial classification; since then the Mexican diaspora in the United States has continued to straddle and confound designations of white and black and negotiate the internally and externally imposed ethnic labels of Hispanic (added in the 1980 census), Latino, and Chicano.[78]

Conclusion

In Mexico and the United States, concerns over the composition and potential of the mestizo as a racial type were crucial to nation-building and played a key role in shaping the architecture of racial classification systems. Although their motivations for and techniques of measuring and determining "race" varied, Mexican and U.S. eugenicists shared the categorizing mission, which they hoped would lead to an enhancement of national biological capacity. There were, however, significant differences between the doctrines of mestizo nationalism and exclusionary whiteness. These were thrown into stark relief in 1927 when eugenicists from across the Americas gathered in Havana,

Cuba, for the First Pan American Conference on Eugenics and Homiculture. The delegates assembled to discuss maternal welfare, the feasibility of prenuptial medical exams, immigration restriction, and the criteria for biological classification.[79] Representing the imperious role of the United States, which sought to impose policies and regulations inspired by Mendelianism, not neo-Lamarckism, throughout the Americas, Davenport delivered the keynote address. He outlined a schema for classifying the many human hybrids populating the globe and informed his audience that virtually all mixed-race offspring were overwhelmingly "disharmonious" and "incompatible." Even if it intermittently produced favorable results, Davenport contended that miscegenation was to be avoided: it was highly unpredictable and, its results—mestizos and mulattos—were almost always undesirable.[80] On another occasion at the conference, Davenport linked his assessment of hybridity to the urgency of stringent immigration restriction. He applauded the Johnson-Reed Immigration Act, which he believed was enabling the United States to achieve racial homogeneity. He reasoned that "a population of fairly uniform type is, on the whole, to be preferred to one made up of a mixture of racial types, just as a population of purebred sheep dogs and a population of pure bred fox terriers are generally more useful for a particular purpose than a population of hybrids between them."[81]

Of all the delegates who scoffed at Davenport's assertions, the Mexican physician Rafael Santamarina responded with the most vehemence. The Director of the newly established (1925) Department of Psychopedagogy and Hygiene at the Mexican Ministry of Public Education, Santamarina denounced Davenport's speech as "a hysterical exposition of the development of immigration laws in the United States."[82] He rebuked Davenport's statements about superior and inferior types, and noted that one of the most commonly used methods in the United States to measure the fitness of individuals and racial groups—mental testing—was biased and inadequate. Santamarina was particularly incensed that Mexican schoolchildren in the Southwest and California were being tested exclusively with culturally insensitive and monolingual English instruments. Clearly aware of recent studies that ranked the I.Q. of Mexican children between 65 and 85 (an average of 15 points below their Anglo counterparts) Santamarina inveighed against those "preeminent psychologists who have had no scruples in classifying Mexican children as mentally inferior, something that is completely false."[83] Furthermore, in a brief evening lecture, Santamarina glorified the mestizo, which he described as a hale combination of the "indomitable courage of the ancestral peoples [of Mexico] and the quixoticism and gallantry of the Spanish race."[84] To prove his point, Santamarina referred to the psychometric tests being administered at the Casa del Estudiante Indígena in Mexico City, which he claimed were demonstrating beyond a doubt the "striking adaptability" of "pure" Indians to civilization and the duties of citizenship and, furthermore, patently undermined the "humiliating idea that the indigenous race was an inferior race" incapable of betterment or change.[85]

The confrontation between Santamarina and Davenport at the First Pan American Conference on Eugenics and Homiculture illustrates how eugenicists who shared the objective of the biological improvement of national populations could clash dramatically in their understandings of the virtues and detriments of race-mixing. Santamarina, reflecting the confident outlook of the Mexican cult of the mestizo during the decade of its zenith, heralded the coming of a "cosmic race" (a la Vasconcelos) via the intertwined processes of assimilation, education, and eugenic regulation. Conversely, Davenport viewed race-mixing as anathema to human betterment and its prohibition as a eugenic imperative. Their disagreement pivoted around the politics of racial classification in their respective countries, as each man expounded on the intrinsic qualities of specific racial types and arrived at divergent conclusions about the prospects for propitious race-crossings.

On a broader level, the heated exchange between Davenport and Santamarina encapsulated the interplay of race, eugenics, and classification in and between the United States and Mexico in the 1920s and 1930s, an era in which eugenicists held key posts in the federal government and shaped national policy in immigration and demography. It is no coincidence that eugenicists on both sides of the border sought to influence the formulation and usage of racial categories. Ultimately, Mexican and U.S. eugenicists alike played a role in the elaboration of their respective 1930 censuses, although with diametrically opposing results: the Mexican schedule was purged of racial categories in the name of mestizophilia, despite the inherent paradoxes of such a model, as we have seen, while the U.S. schedule added the confounding label of "Mexican," which was abandoned for various reasons in the next decennial census.

Indeed, it was not until after World War II, as social scientists worldwide began to shift from a biological to a cultural explanatory model and geneticists began to demonstrate that human inheritance was polygenic and complex, that the ideological fractures between U.S. and Mexican eugenics gradually gave way to resemblances. In the 1940s and 1950s, Mexican and U.S. eugenicists (and many of their counterparts in other countries) turned to biotypology and theories of constitutional medicine, which allowed a much wider role for environmental factors (including health care, social programs, and personal hygiene) without relinquishing the primacy of heredity. Nevertheless, the racially charged decades examined in this chapter, during which organized eugenics movements and policies thrived in both countries, left a lasting imprint, above all, on the racial label of the mestizo, which carried and has continued to carry remnants of its eugenic baggage into the twentieth and twentieth-first centuries.

For example, in Mexico, the longevity of mestizo as a category with eugenic infections is demonstrated by the announcement in 2005 of the launching of a race-based genome project, led by the National Genomic Medicine Institute of Mexico (Instituto Nacional de Medicina Genómica) in collaboration with several U.S. biotech entities. According to its director Gerardo Jiménez, one of the project's initial goals is to sample the genotypes of individuals in six remote regions of the country in order to identify "a consensus genetic map that fits the entire Mexican mestizo population." Soon after learning about this project, a bioethicist at the National Autonomous University of Mexico (Universidad Nacional Autónoma de México) questioned its rationale: "attempting to prove there is a 'mestizo genome' will fail if it pretends to correlate race and disease. Mestizo is a label, not a race."[86] As this example shows, even if the historical actors and many aspects of society, culture, and science have changed over the past century, the politics of eugenics, race, and classification will continue to play out in different forms in Mexico and the United States in today's genomic era. Historical familiarity with this dimension of Mexican America from 1900 to the 1940s can help to illuminate some of today's pressing bioethical dilemmas.

6 Hispanic Identities in the Southwestern United States

Ramón A. Gutiérrez

THERE IS A POPULAR STORY of recent vintage that circulates in folklore along the Mexico/United States border. It tells of an act of miscommunication, born of a mistranslation between a Mexican migrant traveling north and an officer of the U.S. Border Patrol trying to stem that immigrant flow. The migrant is a woman named Molly who is waiting in line to cross the border to the American side. After waiting many hours, her interview moment with the U.S. Border Patrol agent finally arrives. In a gruff and raspy voice the officer asks, "Are you Latina?" "*No, no, no señor,*" she replies. "*Yo no soy la Tina. Yo soy la Molly. La Tina ya cruzó.*" "No, no, no sir. I am not Tina. I am Molly. Tina already crossed." The border agent was asking the woman about her ethnic identity as a Latina. The woman, clearly unfamiliar with this specific U.S.-based identity interpreted the question as best she could. She heard Latina not as one word but as two discrete words—*la* and *Tina*—and interpreting "*la,*" which mean "the," and "*Tina*" as her friend's name. Indeed her name was not Tina; she was Molly.

This story of miscommunication across national borders frequently provokes nervous laughter when heard by Spanish/English bilingual speakers in the southwestern United States. It shows not only how the racial and ethnic labels that operate in one national space often make no sense when transported just a few miles north or south and illustrates the ways in which national regimes monitor and surveil populations through the very act of defining them. In these matters of state, language clearly matters, for ethnic and racial insults hurled in one language, if not understood or lost in translation, hardly hurt or wound their intended victim. Yet the power of the state to impose classification and statuses clearly remains.

Racially and ethnically subordinated groups have always resisted and defied the easy classifications of their oppressors and have generated their own forms of identity rooted in ethnic and religious conceptions of personhood, kinship, and community. Institutions such as the Catholic Church, professional guilds, even merchants hoping to capture specific markets for ethnic foods and goods, have also long had a vested interest in generating racial and ethnic identities. My goal in this essay is to survey the history of racial and ethnic classification in what is now the southwestern United States, looking simultaneously at self-generated identities as well as those imposed from without, paying particular attention to the role that language plays in issues of dominance, subordination, and resistance.

The presence of Spaniards in what is now the United States has a long and complicated history that began several decades before Jamestown (1607) was founded and the Pilgrims landed at Plymouth Rock. Spain's citizens had already established permanent settlement on American soil in Saint Augustine in Florida (1565) and began colonizing the Kingdom of New Mexico in 1598, which then encompassed roughly the current states of New Mexico and Arizona. Texas's first Spanish settlements date from 1691. The settlement of Alta California began with the founding of San Diego in 1769. The Kingdoms of New Mexico, Texas, and Alta California were all situated at the northern edge of Spain's empire, isolated from each other, surrounded on all sides by hostile indigenous groups, and too distant from the major centers of Spanish culture in central Mexico for frequent communication. What developed in each of these provinces over the centuries were distinct regional subcultures that were Spanish in name and form, but thoroughly hybrid in content due to prolonged contact with local indigenous cultures.

National consciousness, by which is meant identity as a citizen of a particular nation-state, was weakly developed among the colonists Spain initially dispatched to settle the Southwest. What common identity they did share was religious; they were Christians first and foremost. The fervor of their religious sentiment had been forged during Spain's reconquest, those years of warfare between AD 711 and 1492 when the Moors occupied the Iberian Peninsula. In these years the Christian monarchs rallied their populations behind the standard of the cross to push the forces of Islam back into Africa. What victories they won were in the name of Christianity and so it was only logical for women and men to think of themselves as Christians first and foremost even in the New World. Gradually an even sharper distinction would be drawn to differentiate *cristianos viejos,* or old Christians who defended the faith from infidels and heretics, and *cristianos nuevos,* or New Christians, which in Spain included Moors, Jews, and in the New World recent converts to the faith such as the Indians.[1]

Next in importance to the identity of these colonists was the *patria chica,* the "small fatherland," or the region of origin. Each of Spain's kingdoms had a well-developed *conciencia de sí,* or self-consciousness by the sixteenth century. After men and women proclaimed themselves Christians, they boasted of being Aragonese, Catalans, Leonese, Galicians, and Castilians. Indeed the word the Indians of the southwestern United States first used to describe their Spanish overlords was *Castillas,* meaning a person from the Spanish province of Castile. Though initially the Indians understood very little of what Spain's soldiers told them, they did repeatedly hear the soldiers call themselves *castellanos,* announce that the Indians were subjects of *Castilla,* and that a king in *Castilla* was their new lord. Gaspar Peréz de Villagrá, who participated in the 1598 conquest of New Mexico and in 1610 commemorated the feats in his book *Historia de la Nueva México,* writes that the Indians at Acoma Pueblo "called to me, crying, Castilian! Castilian! . . . Zutacapan [their chief] asked me if more Castilians followed me and how long before they would arrive."[2]

Identification with Spain's various regions was gradually lost in the Southwest, but the habit of identifying with one's locality lived on. By the beginning of the nineteenth century residents of the Kingdom of New Mexico were calling themselves *nuevo mexicanos* or *neomexicanos,* those in California were referring to themselves as *californios,* and those in Texas as *tejanos.*

The Spanish conquest of the Americas brought together men from different regions, and through their common experiences of conquest they shaped new identities for themselves. Men who in 1598 had never before thought of themselves as Spaniards on the Iberian Peninsula, both because a unitary national identity had only recently emerged at the end of the fifteenth century with the unification of the kingdoms of Aragón and Castile forged through the marriage of King Ferdinand and Queen Isabella, and because they were more deeply invested in their regional loyalties, in the Americas came to think of themselves as Spaniards, particularly when confronting indigenous peoples as overlords. By calling themselves Spaniards or *españoles* the colonists in the Southwest acknowledged that their culture and social institutions were of Iberian origin and thus quite different from those Native Americans they called *indios* or Indians. Three hundred years of contact between these two groups through intermarriage and cohabitation would radically transform what it meant to be *español* and *indio,* but that story is beyond this essay's scope.[3]

What does deserve mention here is the role the term *indio* would play historically in the subordination of native peoples. In 1491, on the eve of the Columbian voyages, there were some 123 distinct indigenous language families spoken in the Americas, with over 260 different languages in Mexico alone. In the Valley of Mexico itself perhaps as many as 20 million people lived in a complexly stratified theocracy.[4] But there were then no Indians in Mexico. Christopher Columbus invented them in 1492 by mistakenly believing he had reached India, thus calling them *indios.* Inventing Indians was to serve an important imperial end for Spain, for by calling the natives *indios,* the Spaniards erased and leveled the diverse and complex indigenous political and religious hierarchies they found. Where once there had been native lords, warriors, craftsmen, hunters, and farmers, the power of the conquering Spanish armies was not only to vanquish but to define, reducing such peoples as the mighty Aztecs to a monolithic defeated Indian class that bore the pain of subjugation as racialized subjects.

The *españoles* of the Southwest were extremely conscious of their status and viewed society hierarchically, as ordered by a number of ascriptive categories based on religion, citizenship, property ownership, occupation, race, and legitimacy of birth. Whenever anyone came before a legal tribunal, whether civil or ecclesiastical, the first fact always recorded in court dockets was a person's *calidad* or social status, because punishment was meted out differentially according to one's standing in society. These statements were always rather formulaic in the sixteenth and seventeenth centuries. Petitions, denunciations, even routine investigations always began with a statement such as the following: Pedro López *"es de calidad mestizo, obrero, hijo legítimo de tal y tal y cristiano nuevo,"* or Pedro López's social status is mestizo, a laborer, the legitimate son of so and so, and a New Christian.

From 1600 to 1760 in the Southwest the principal identities recognized in law were based on religion, property ownership, occupation, and race, with the last category usually limited to a differentiation between Spaniards and Indians. But starting in the 1760s, and stretching into the 1820s, racial classification took on a greater importance to the legal order, and increasingly a precise legal color code known as the *sistema de castas* was broadly invoked both by the church and the state. Access to marital partners and honorific posts, to desirable occupations, and even the Roman Catholic priesthood, was based on one's ability to prove one's genealogical racial purity by the categories of the code.[5]

The *sistema de castas* precisely defined every possible biological mixture that could occur when Spaniards, Indians, and Africans mated and reproduced. A Spaniard and an Indian produced a mestizo. A mestizo and a Spanish woman begot a *castizo*. The mating of a Spanish man and a mulatto woman produced a *morisco,* and so on. The legal color code was spelled out for several generations of descent from an original set of ancestors, yielding categories that were quite difficult for individuals, much less for the church and state to keep track of through personal declarations or the observations of officials, priests, and scribes. Theoretically, this classificatory system visually fused notions of blood, ancestry, and lineage so that without reference to baptismal certificates, family histories, or personal genealogies one could quickly glance at a person's physique and just as rapidly conclude if a person was of pure blood, of gentle birth, and of an honorable past. In Spain even remotely impure blood derived from Jews, Moors, and other heretics disqualified a person from high honorific posts. In America contact with Indians and black slaves was deemed equally undesirable. Physical color, what we today call phenotype, became the basis on which the state and the church, and all of their functionaries praised and reviled their subjects and privileged and punished society's inferior racial groups.

The Spanish in the Southwest in the 1760s began to imagine colonial society in much more complicated ways than the original conquest dichotomy between Spaniards and Indians allowed, precisely because the *sistema de castas* provided them with a lexicon of racial difference. The reality on the ground after several generations of miscegenation was that only at the polar extremes of the classification system did the categories actually fit any visible physical types. The color regime put into place was intended to protect the privileges of local nobilities, as the quickening of the economy spurred on by the Bourbon Reforms in the second half of the eighteenth century led to the rise of statuses based on enterprise and personal achievement, which began to displace notions of aristocracy, particularly after the Spanish crown began selling writs of whiteness, known as *gracias al sacar,* to anyone who could afford them.[6]

Racial status was of grand importance because it was intimately associated with one's legitimacy or illegitimacy at birth. The legal scholar Juan de Solórzano y Pereira in his *Política Indiana* (1648) maintained that illegitimates were: "Those born of adulterous or other illicit and punishable unions, because there are few Spaniards of honor who marry Indian or negro women; this defect of birth makes them infamous, at least *infama facti,* according to the weighty and common opinion of serious scholars; they carry the stain of different colors and other vices."[7] Throughout the colonial period, illegitimacy was deemed an indecent and shameful mark because of its association with mixed racial unions.

Two additional categories were widely circulated in local affairs in the eighteenth century. To differentiate Christians of peninsular origin from those recently converted to the faith, the categories "Old Christian" and "New Christian" were widely used in ecclesiastical affairs. To call someone a "New Christian" was to recognize indigenous ancestry, his or her infamy and low standing in the status hierarchy. Whether one worked with one's hands or not was similarly regarded an important distinction. The assumption was that blacks toiled because of the infamy of their slavery. Indians worked because of their conquest and vanquishment.

The multiple categories that defined a person's *calidad* were intricately tied to each other. Indeed, a person's reputation was a summation of these various measures of social standing. This was particularly clear in social action. The fiercest fighting words one could utter were slurs that impugned a person's total social personality—their race, their ancestry, and their position in the division of labor. On June 3, 1765, for example, a fight occurred in Albuquerque, New Mexico, between Eusebio Chávez and his father-in-law Andrés Martín. Chávez beat Martín with a large stick and dragged him by his hair, leaving Martín's arm badly bruised, his chest covered with black-and-blue welts, his scalp swollen out of shape, and his hair completely tangled and caked in blood. The reason was Martín had called Chávez a *"perro mulato hijo de puta"* (a mixed-blood dog son of a bitch). One insult, perhaps, would have been enough; but by calling Chávez a dog, Martín implied that he was less than human, a habit well understood by Spaniards who often referred to the Indians as dogs. He added that Chávez was of mixed blood, and if truly a son of a bitch, he was undoubtedly illegitimate. Martín had thus combined three statuses to insult Chávez.[8]

The Catholic Church usually invoked the same identities that the Spanish state generated. One exception that deserves mention because it was widely used in the Southwest during the colonial period, particularly in California, was *gente de razón,* literally "people of reason," or rational beings. The category is best understood through its dichotomous opposite, or *gente sin razón,* "people lacking reason," as irrational persons. The Holy Office of the Inquisition concocted this legal distinction to protect the Indians from prosecution for heretical ideas. They reasoned that the Indians were *gente sin razón,* mere children lacking the rational faculties to understand the dogmas of faith. Everyone else was a rational person punishable by the Inquisition for acts judged heretical. With the demise of the Inquisition in the early 1800s, the term *gente de razón* remained in circulation in the Southwest as a way of differentiating individuals who were culturally "Spanish" from those who lived by their more traditional "Indian" ways.

Indian slavery was a significant social institution in the Southwest, particularly in New Mexico and Arizona, and accordingly generated a stigmatized identity that was known by the word *genízaro.* The category appeared in New Mexico at the beginning of the eighteenth century and from there spread outward to Texas and California. The *genízaros* were primarily Apache and Navajo Indians, occasionally Utes and Comanches, enslaved during Spanish raids provoked to facilitate what would become a very lucrative trade in captives. In time Pueblo Indian foundlings abandoned by their indigenous mothers as well as adults exiled from Indian towns because of some transgression also held this status. Approximately four thousand *genízaros* entered New Mexican society during the eighteenth century and by the 1750s composed about one-third of New Mexican society. They were considered marginal because of their slave, ex-slave, or outcast status.[9] *Genízaros* did not own land, spoke a distinctive broken form of Spanish, were residentially segregated, married endogamously, and shared a corporate identity, living together, said Fray Carlos Delgado in 1744, in great unity *"como si fueran una nación"* (as if they were a nation).[10] Fray Atanasio Domínguez described the *genízaros* he met in New Mexico in 1776 as "weak, gamblers, liars, cheats, and petty thieves." This caricature survived for centuries. Mischievous and unruly children are still ridiculed in the Southwest with the saying: *"genízaro, genízaro, puro indio de rescate"* (*genízaro, genízaro,* pure bartered Indian). When New Mexicans today say *"no seas genízaro,"* or "don't be a *genízaro,"* they mean "don't be a liar." Anthropologist Florence Hawley Ellis was told by the villagers of Tomé in the 1950s that the *genízaro* residents in the adjacent village of Belén were "semi-slave, low class, and without ability." The anthropologist Frances Swadesh encountered the same issue in the 1970s in northern New Mexico. When someone was referred to as *genízaro* there, it meant crude, low class, and "indiado" (Indian-like).[11]

Some folk classifications still in use in the Southwest were derived from the *sistema de castas.* In the colonial period, Spaniards did not hesitate to dehumanize Indians and people they called "half-breeds" (mixed race) by barking the epithet "dog" at them, usually in combination with some other expletive: dirty dog, Indian dog, half-breed dog. Half-breeds were thus frequently called *lobos* and *coyotes,* denoting an unspecific mixture between a Spaniard and an Indian. With both of these identities, the mixed-blood individual was portrayed as a low species close to an animal. *Lobo* and *coyote* still remain in common parlance and are used to refer to persons of any racial mix between Anglo and Mexican.

The native peoples the Spaniards conquered and dominated had a linguistic arsenal of their own to describe their oppressors. The search for this lexicon has yielded only modest results. The Pueblo, the Yaqui, and the Mayo Indians all seemed to have caricatured the Spanish as closely tied to the sacrament of baptism. Among the Pueblo Indians the Spaniards were called "wet-heads" because of the water poured on a person's head at baptism. For similar reasons the Yaqui and Mayo Indians called the Spaniards "water-fathers."[12]

As Mexican independence approached in 1821, other identities displaced those that had been established at the time of the conquest and came into more prominent use in the Southwest. Residents did at times employ *peninsular* (person born in Spain) and *criollo* (persons of Spanish origin born in Mexico) to differentiate *españoles* from *españoles mexicanos.* At the beginning of the nineteenth century the only persons in the Southwest who could genuinely claim peninsular Spanish origin were the priests, and it is among them that one sees conflicts over these identities and the privileges they conferred most viciously waged. For the rest of the population of New Mexico, Texas, and California, little seems to have changed as a result of Mexico's independence from Spain. One does not find a rapid increase in people calling themselves *mexicanos* or Mexicans. This identity appears in the 1830s but is used by a very small number of people. In New Mexico, for example, only about 5 percent of all individuals who married legally between 1830 and 1839 claimed they were *mexicanos.* The rest still preferred to call themselves *españoles* and increasingly *vecinos,* or propertied male citizens.[13]

Forces of change operating in the Southwest and beyond began radically transforming the nature of social identities after 1821. Locally, the increased level of economic activity, fostered by the Bourbon Reforms of the 1760s and 1770s, worked to spur economic growth, safeguard the area, and integrate it into the larger market economy in northern Mexico, quickly shattering the traditional bonds of society. With the rise of wage labor and the increase of a large landless peasant class, identities based on ascription slowly gave way to those based on enterprise and achievement. International rivalries, large-scale migration, and other political events accelerated the rate of change. In 1836 Anglo Texans and Mexican *tejanos* united in revolution to win their independence from Mexico for the Republic of Texas. A decade later, ownership of the rest of the Southwest was the cause of war between Mexico and the United States. At the end of the Mexican-American War in 1848 a new political order was established. As people moved back and forth across the Rio Grande and west across the Great Plains, a new conception of society emerged. Just as when colonists from various parts of Spain first arrived in the Southwest, abandoned their local and regional identities, and defined themselves culturally as Spaniards vis-à-vis the Indians, so too after 1848 settlers from various parts of the United States began to define themselves as Anglos and Americans when they confronted Mexicans and Indians as conquered classes.

From the moment *americanos* entered the Southwest, the ethnic Mexican population residing there concocted a variety of ethnic terms for their invaders. These were names that primarily brought attention to the peculiarities of their skin, eye, and hair color, and to the size of their feet. Accordingly we find in folklore *canosos* (gray-haired), *colorado* (red-faced), *cara de pan crudo* (bread-dough face), *ojos de gato* (cat eyes), and *patón* (big foot). Other Mexican ethnic labels for the Americans were the result of difficulties with and misunderstandings of the English language. The word *gringo,* for example, comes from a linguistic corruption of a song the Mexican soldiers heard the Texas rebels singing at the Alamo. The first two words of the prairie song, "Green grow the lilacs," were heard by Mexicans and corrupted as *gringos.* Because the *americanos* allegedly loved cabbage, or at least those of Irish origin, they were called *repolleros.* And because of their penchant for chewing tobacco they became known as *masca tabacos.* Some of the negative stereotypes used to describe the Americans originated in central Mexico as terms first used to describe nineteenth-century French invaders. Such was the case with the derogatory terms *gabacho* and *güero* (blond).[14]

The Anglo Americans who arrived in the Southwest after 1848 were equally adept at name-calling. The Mexican diet seems to have been the source of much of their inspiration, starting with "greaser," both because of the lard that Mexicans used for cooking as well as their oily skin. Subsequently came "grease-ball," "goo-goo," "pepper-belly," "taco-choker," "frijole guzzler," "chili picker," and for women, "hot tamale." From a linguistic corruption of the word "Mexican," came such slurs as "mex," "meskin," "skin," and "skindiver."[15]

When Anglo Americans began entering the Southwest as conquerors after 1848, they reacted to the ethnic landscape much as the Spaniards had in 1598; they saw few cultural distinctions. Certainly long-standing cleavages and status differentiation on the basis of race, occupation, legitimacy, and property ownership existed. In addition, the long-established Spanish residents of the area clearly saw themselves as superior and different from the Mexican immigrants that started to cross the border in large numbers after 1848, and particularly after 1880. But to the conquerors of the land, people were quite simply Americans, Mexicans, or Indians. Through American eyes the residents of the area all looked alike, dressed alike, spoke Spanish, and were fanatical Catholics. They were all Mexicans. The deep-seated racial prejudice among some *americanos* toward blacks was easily transferred to persons of Spanish origin due to their swarthy skin color.[16]

To call someone a Mexican in 1850 was an insult because it signified a dominated population, stigmatized by defeat and subordination. To counter the tendency of Americans referring to all the Spanish-origin population as Mexican, the resident population began employing old ethnic categories in new ways. Those who had lived in the Southwest since before 1848 wanted to clearly differentiate themselves from the constant flow of what they perceived as lower-class Mexican immigrants. In addition, they wanted to clearly establish that they were descendants of Spaniards, of white European ancestry and not of racial mixes with inferior indigenous peoples.

Because the massive influx of immigrants into California after the 1848 discovery of gold radically transformed the ethnic mix of the state, let us begin here with our discussion of these ethnic and racial dynamics: the *californios,* the colonists who settled the area first under Spain's control, then after 1821 under Mexican rule, and after 1848 under American rule. Individuals from many Latin American nations arrived in California, but particularly Mexicans who were especially adept at mining and wanted to strike it rich. The *californios* referred to these immigrants as *mexicanos* when speaking among themselves in Spanish, because they were indeed Mexican nationals. Anglos, however, saw no apparent physical or cultural differences between the *californios* and the *mexicanos,* and referred to both as Mexicans. To counter their being stereotyped as a conquered population, to insist that they were unlike the recent Mexican immigrants, *californios* began referring to themselves as Spaniards and as the Spanish-speaking people of California, insisting that other English speakers do the same. This tendency was particularly strong at the old Spanish pueblos at Santa Barbara, San Fernando, Los Angeles, and San Francisco.[17]

The sheer number of Mexican immigrants entering California after 1848 quickly reduced the numeric and political importance of the *californios*. The first good statistics on Mexican immigration to the United States start with the decade 1911–1920. Mexican immigration then totaled 219,000, representing approximately 20 percent of all immigrants entering the United States. From 1921 to 1930, the official number more than doubled, reaching 459,287. In this decade Mexicans were the largest national group and represented close to 10 percent of the total number of immigrants entering the United States. Most of these immigrants went to California and so increasingly after the 1920s the terms "Mexican" and "Mexican American" became prominent, and "Spanish American" and "Spanish-speaking" totally disappeared. Ethnic Mexicans were indeed a subordinated class, living in poverty, marginalized in politics, and relegated to menial work.

Ethnic identity in New Mexico was shaped by similar population movements, but here the process did not begin until after World War I. Unlike California where the *californios* were quickly outnumbered by Mexican immigrants, in New Mexico the long-term residents clung to their identities as *españoles* or Spaniards much longer. When faced with the arrival of Mexican immigrants in the 1920s and 1930s, they referred to themselves as Spaniards, Spanish Americans, and gradually even "Hispanos," a term first put into circulation in New Mexico by U.S. Department of Agriculture specialists interested in rural poverty in the state. Some New Mexicans went so far as to claim that they were the direct descendants of conquistadors who had colonized the region in 1598 and that over the centuries they had maintained their bloodlines free of any taint with inferior races. Of course, this was more fiction that fact. Most of the people who settled New Mexico were racially mestizos, and few, if any, after three hundred years of miscegenation could claim pure Spanish aristocratic blood. Whatever the accuracy of the ideology it nevertheless functioned well to resist being called Mexicans, presumed to be of racial mixture, and therefore assumed to be inferior.

If we examine the linguistic context in which ethnicity was defined, we can better understand the logic of this defensive ethnic ideology. When linguist Arthur L. Campa asked longtime residents of New Mexico in the 1950s what their ethnicity was, most responded, "*soy mexicano*" (I am Mexican). When he asked the same individuals what they liked to be called in English, they responded, "Spanish American." Campa then asked in Spanish, "What do you call a person from Mexico?" "*mexicano de México*" (Mexican from México). One informant remarked that in English such a person was simply a Mexican because "Mexican . . . is the most used when someone is being rude . . . Example—dirty Mexican." Another echoed these sentiments, "I'd rather not be called Mexican because of the stereotype remarks that are associated with it. Such as lazy, dirty greaser, etc."[18]

Part of the New Mexicans' hostility to the term "Mexican" stemmed from its association with Mexico and with Mexican nationals. New Mexico was always marginal to Spain's imperial project and just as isolated from Mexico City. This fact prompted one man to state: "My identity has always been closer to Spanish as an ethnic group and for that reason I consider myself Spanish . . . being from northern New Mexico the only connection I have with anything Mexican is as a tourist and not as my national origin."[19] Novelist Erna Fergusson has argued that Spanish American came into popular use as an ethnic identity in New Mexico after World War I to counter the Anglo American perception that soldiers who called themselves in Spanish *mexicanos* were aliens from another county. According to the anthropologist Nancie González, the term "Spanish American" emerged in response to an upsurge of prejudice and discrimination against Spanish speakers during the 1920s.[20]

Arizona too had a native core of settlers that had been residing there since the 1680s who considered themselves Spaniards. In the 1920s a similar tension between Spanish and Mexican identities emerged there when confronted with massive Mexican immigration. One of the first civil rights organizations in Arizona was the Spanish American Alliance of Tucson, founded in the 1920s. The rapid influx of Mexicans into the area with the development of irrigation agriculture meant that Mexican and Mexican American identities quickly gained ascendancy, and Spanish identity disappeared from public discourse.[21]

The ethnic categories of self-reference employed by *tejanos* or Texans of Spanish and Mexican origin are more difficult to explain. One would assume that, as with the *californios* and *nuevo mexicanos,* they too would have called themselves Spanish or Spanish Americans when differentiating themselves from the Mexican immigrants in the 1920s and 1930s. They did not. Instead they called themselves *latinos* and Latin Americans. Historical events offer some, but not all, of the explanation. When the *tejanos* joined forces with the American settlers of Texas to form their own independent republic in 1836, they decisively rejected their Mexican identity. Faced with the same discrimination and prejudice that Mexican immigrants suffered in the 1920s, the *tejanos* insisted on being called Latin Americans in polite English-speaking company. Obviously they did not want to be called Mexicans or Mexican Americans. In 1929 when the first major civil rights organization in the United States among ethnic Mexican was established, they called it the League of United Latin American Citizens (LULAC).[22]

As should be obvious from these examples of defensive ethnic identities fashioned in New Mexico, Texas, California, and Arizona in response to both Anglo American conquest and massive Mexican immigration, the local populations proclaimed themselves white, asserted their European origins as Spaniards, and doggedly resisted being labeled colored and thus presumed of equal status to African Americans. Whenever Anglo Americans have wanted to depict the Spanish origin and ethnic Mexican population in the United States in a positive light, they have been called Spanish, Spanish Americans, or Spanish speakers as they wished, and by so doing declaring them heirs of European civilization and whiteness. Identifying someone as Spanish immediately signaled a set of identities: Christian, romance language speaker, a culture and ancestry that originated in Rome, European legal institutions, and a Caucasian racial origin. This tradition is often called Hispanofilia and when operating in the English-speaking world, ethnic Mexicans sought this status as a sign of respect and superiority over Mexicans.[23]

Throughout much of the twentieth century and also now into the twenty-first, the categories, depictions, and stereotypes of ethnic Mexicans that Anglo Americans have constructed have vacillated between Hispanofilia and Hispanophobia. For centuries, fear of things Hispanic has been expressed specifically as a disdain for Mexicans, and more recently, for Latinos. The twisted logic of these arguments is that Mexicans did not believe in God—here of course it was the Anglo Protestant God that xenophobes had in mind, as most Mexicans have long been Roman Catholics. Hispanophobes have assumed that the religious life of Mexicans was nothing but a mix of primitive Indian and African cults. Mexicans were mongrels either as mestizos (mix of Spaniard and Indian) or *mulatos* (mix of Spaniard and African). In the racist science of the late nineteenth century half-breeds were believed to inherit all the negative cultural traits of the races they carried in their blood. From such polluted blood, clearly only criminals, imbeciles, heathens, and degenerates could result. Such racial depravity was capable of destroying the purity of Anglo Protestants in the United States, an ugly prospect indeed, as so many of them thought then, and some still do.[24]

Throughout the twentieth century Hispanophobes have viewed ethnic Mexicans as a "problem" that threatens the racial, hygienic, social, and economic basis of life in the United States. Hispanofiles have celebrated the presence of Mexican immigrants as assets that contribute to American prosperity by performing tasks at wages that citizen workers will not accept, by contributing taxes from which they rarely benefit, and by consuming American products. Hispanophobes accordingly have demanded severe immigration restrictions, particularly in moments of economic distress. Hispanofiles have generally favored relatively open borders, more tempered governmental regulation of immigration, believing that Mexican immigrant work and consumption have always led to economic prosperity.

In the 1920s, patriotic societies and eugenicist organizations demanded a stop to Mexican immigration because, as sociologist Robert L. Garis of Vanderbilt University explained:

> Their minds run to nothing higher than animal functions—eat, sleep, and sexual debauchery. In every huddle of Mexican shacks one meets the same idleness, hoards of hungry dogs, and filthy children with faces plastered with flies, disease, lice, human filth, stench, promiscuous fornication, bastardy, lounging, apathetic peons and lazy squaws, beans and dried chili, liquor, general squalor, and envy and hatred of the gringo . . . Yet there are Americans clamoring for more of this human swine to be brought over from Mexico.[25]

Princeton economist Professor Robert F. Foerster opposed Mexican immigration in 1925 on purely racial grounds. Asking rhetorically whether Mexican mestizo and African mulatto racial stocks should be welcomed in the United States, he answered: No! "These groups merely approach but do not attain the race value of the white stocks, and therefore the immigrants from these countries—Latin America—tend to lower the average of the white population of the United States." He warned that it was foolhardy to succumb to the momentary profits derived from cheap Mexican labor while the racial purity of the nation was under attack.[26]

The arguments of labor economist Victor Clark were typical of those in favor of importing more Mexican laborers into the agricultural fields, mines, and railroad yards of the Southwest. Mexicans are "ambitious . . . patient, usually orderly in camp, fairly intelligent under competent supervision, obedient, and cheap," noted Clark.[27] These were the reasons they were so favored as workers.

Over the past thirty years the southwestern United States has experienced a radical racial transformation, perhaps akin to what Spanish America experienced in the eighteenth century. Hardly a day goes by now without news reporters announcing how the ethnic Mexican minority in the United States in many areas is rapidly becoming a majority, and what used to be considered culturally white is quickly becoming brown and particularly spiced. Characteristic of this shift is the fact that ketchup's dominance as a condiment is a thing of the past. Now salsa is king. In April 1990, *Time* magazine purchased an advertisement in *People* magazine announcing a special issue it was about to publish devoted to "America's Changing Color." The picture in the advertisement is as close to the typologies of the Spanish colonial *sistema de castas* as one gets in contemporary times, with thirty-eight smaller pictures of infants of different phenotypes, lying appropriately on pink and blue blankets. The text of the advertisement reads:

HEY WHITEY, YOUR TURN AT THE BACK OF THE BUS. Sometime soon, white Americans will become a distinct minority in a largely brown cultural and racial mix. A hard story for many of our readers. But again, TIME has never tried to be easy. It's what our readers expect. Call it relevance. Call it perspective. If it's important to you, you'll find it on this cover and inside these pages.

Most of these stories reporting America's demographic shift are alarmist and carry all the rhetorical trademarks of Hispanophobia. Their tenor usually vacillates between doom and dread, with reports of the emergence of a paramilitary vigilante group called the Minutemen who patrol the U.S–Mexico border searching for illegal immigrants to take into custody. Hispanofilia, at the beginning of the twentieth century was a glorification of the Mexican worker who endured arduous labor conditions for little pay and even less complaint. Today such workers are despised, but what is praised is their consumption of American-made products. This is the wistful and utopic world of television commercials produced by United Colors of Benetton, which imagine a gloriously democratic multicultural universe of consumption where everyone who has a buck (dollar) is indeed an equal.

One recent *Newsweek* magazine story announced: "By 2005, Latinos will be the largest U.S. minority; they're already shaping pop culture and presidential politics. The Latin wave will change how the country looks—and how it looks at itself."[28] Metaphors in popular literature and the visual media abound describing an approaching Latino "wave," a rising Latino "tide," a Latino population "explosion," "seismic population shifts," and an apocalyptic revolt with

California as "ground zero." While some of these reports target "illegal" immigrants or Latinos more broadly, Mexicans make up about two-thirds of all Latinos. Most of the individuals caught crossing into the United States illegally are from Mexico, so there can be little doubt exactly what population they have in mind.[29] The rhetoric of reaction found in the popular press also suffuses more scholarly representations. Dale Maharidge, a 1990 Pulitzer Prize winner, recently penned a book, *The Coming White Minority: California's Eruption and America's Future,* which is full of descriptions of population seismic shifts and social and cultural explosions. "No white society in the industrial world has ever evolved into a mixed society," he ignorantly declares. "So exercise your right to bear arms. The fight ahead," he predicts, "will not be an easy one."[30]

Harvard Professor Samuel P. Huntington, the highly venerated political theorist who only four years ago was anticipating a clash of civilizations in the Middle East, recently shifted his attention to Latinos in his book, *Who Are We? The Challenges to America's National Identity.* Huntington maintains that the cultural division between Latinos and Anglos will soon replace the racial division between blacks and whites as the most serious cleavage in U.S. society. The vast majority of Latinos, as Huntington so clearly recognizes, are of Mexican immigrant descent. Many entered the country illegally, and are reproducing much more rapidly than whites or blacks, by about a ratio of 5 to 1. They keep speaking Spanish in their home and at work, refuse to learn English, are leading highly segregated lives among their own, and are largely confined in society's lowest economic rungs. These facts portend anarchy, racial war, and separatist sentiments comparable to those of the Quebecois, Huntington warns. Already, nativist whites have responded in California by approving initiatives against benefits for illegal immigrants, affirmative action, and bilingual education, and some like the Minutemen are taking up arms. Mexicans will clearly retaliate; retaking the California they lost in 1848, at the end of the Mexican-American War, plunging the nation into an unprecedented racial war. Patriots will, of course, fight to protect Anglo Protestant culture and the English language from barbaric Mexican assault.[31]

Although this is certainly Hispanophobia at its worst, its hysterical tone is hardly unique. Read the opening words of Peter Brimelow's 1995 book, *Alien Nation: Common Sense About America's Immigration Disaster:*

> There is a sense in which current immigration policy is Adolf Hitler's posthumous revenge on America. The U.S. political elite emerged from the war passionately concerned to cleanse itself from all taints of racism or xenophobia.

Eventually, it enacted the epochal Immigration Act (technically, the Immigration and Nationality Act Amendments) of 1965. And this, quite accidentally, triggered a renewed mass immigration, so huge and so systematically different from anything that had gone before as to transform—and ultimately, perhaps even destroy—the one unquestioned victor of World War II: the American nation, as it had evolved by the middle of the twentieth century.[32]

Brimelow further asserts, "The American nation has always had a specific core. And that core has been white." Americans have a right to demand that their government stop shifting the nation's racial balance. "Indeed, it seems to me that they have a right to insist that it be shifted back."[33]

Although Brimelow's words are incendiary and extreme, they echo many of the anti-Mexican sentiments articulated by Lawrence Auster in *The Path to National Suicide: An Essay on Immigration and Multiculturalism* (1990), and Richard D. Lamm and Gary Imhoff in *The Immigration Time Bomb: The Fragmenting of America* (1985).[34] These pronouncements hail from the political right but increasingly, liberal Democrats such as Arthur Schlesinger Jr. decry how particularistic immigrant loyalties in the United States are leading to "*The Disuniting of America.*" Because Mexicans have been the largest immigrant group that has entered the United States since 1965, it does not take too much arithmetic to conclude who Schlesinger has in mind.[35]

Even scientific racist ideas about the relationship between race and intelligence, dismissed almost a century ago, have reemerged. Latino immigrants, claim Richard J. Hernstein and Charles Murray in their book *The Bell Curve* (1994), on average score 9 percentage points lower on IQ tests than whites. Such disparity, they claim, will lower the overall intelligence of the United States and ultimately lead to more crime, more women on welfare, and more single-parent households.[36]

The Hispanophobia that these authors equate with unfettered racial mixing produced by immigration has tangible effects on individual lives. In 1990, sociologists Edward Telles and Edward Murguía tested the widely reported observation that darker-skinned Chicanos were economically disadvantaged in the United States. Using the 1979 Chicano National Sample drawn from the Southwest, they asked whether those individuals rated as light-skinned by interviewers had higher average earnings than those who were darker. Since the light-skinned group was too small for sound statistical comparisons, it was merged with a group judged to be of medium skin color, and a comparison was then made with the darker-skinned group. The researchers found that there was a strong tendency for the lighter group to earn more than the darker one. As both groups had similar educational levels, this could not explain the differences.[37] Carlos Arce, Edward Murguía, and W. Parker Frisbie, in their 1987 study "Phenotype and Life Chances Among Chicanos," similarly concluded that phenotype—defined in this study as dark skin and Indian facial features—correlated rather closely with socioeconomic status.[38]

William Zweigenhaft and Richard Domhoff tested similar hypotheses about color and class among Latinos with two samples composed mainly of elites. The first sample consisted of photographs of Latino directors of *Fortune* 500 companies. The second sample were photos of the 188 individuals that *Hispanic Business* had identified in its magazine as the "top influential" Latinos in 1993 and 1994. Two independent panels of reviewers concluded that the *Fortune* 500 Latino directors were overwhelmingly "white" or "Anglo." About 50 percent of the influential Latinos were deemed "white," the rest readily identified as "Hispanic."[39] One reader of *Hispanic Business* intuitively drew the same conclusion. Writing to the editor about their November 1996 picture survey of "top influentials," Gustavo E. Gonzales complained that the magazine had "failed to include a single dark face." *Hispanic Business* replied that their list contained Hispanics of "African ancestry" and that one should avoid conclusions based on "visual evidence alone."[40]

This survey of identities in the Southwest would be incomplete without a discussion of the emergence of Chicanos and Chicanas as political identities around 1969. Although previous ethnic Mexican generations had proclaimed their whiteness and European origins as Spaniards, as Spanish Americans, and even as Hispanos fearing their aggregation with African Americans as colored, in 1969 young men and women turned the tables on this logic and began celebrating their denigrated Mexican origin. Defiantly calling themselves Chicanos and Chicanas, these children of assimilated Mexican Americans identified with the oppressed and, in solidarity with Native Americans, laid claim to their own repressed and forgotten racial and indigenous ancestry. They putatively discovered direct genealogical links to the Aztecs, the fiercest warriors that had ever roamed the Americas. They claimed that the Southwest was really Aztlán, the Aztec's ancestral homeland, and demanded its independence from the United States as a sovereign nation. Though these militant Chicanos/as may have been the remote descendants of the Spanish soldiers that had once conquered the Southwest, they wanted no part of this white European Spanish heritage. Chicanos/as instead proclaimed their working-class origins, celebrated Mexican national roots, and were quick to point out that they were racially brown—*la raza de bronce* (the bronze race)—as a result of their mestizo heritage, being as they were products of racial and cultural mixing between Spaniards and Indians. Chicanos were a hybrid people who had long resided in the United States. They had never crossed a border. Rather, at the end of the Texas Revolution in 1836, at the end of the Mexican-American War in 1846–1848, and with the Gadsden Purchase in 1853, the border separating Mexico and the United States had physically crossed them. For Chicano/a activists and scholars in the late 1960s and 1970s, Spain had indeed established the institutions of colonial rule in North America, but that legacy was not a heroic or romantic one. It was a history of plunder, rape, and destruction, or so they opined.

The Mexican American parents and grandparents of Chicanos/as were largely unaccepting of this newly invented political identity. For them "Chicano" had long been a derogatory in-group Spanish-language term for a person of dubious character and for recent immigrants of lower-class standing. The word etymologically derived from *chinaco,* which means "tramp" or "guttersnipe." Much as Negroes began identifying themselves as black during the 1960s, so too militant and politically conscious Chicano/a students embraced this derogatory class identity, inverting its meaning, using it as a badge of racial pride. Examining the social origins of those who called themselves Chicanos reveals that they were young, largely of working-class origin, politically militant, harboring an oppositional stance toward the dominant society and toward assimilation. Within a single extended household in 1970, it was not unusual to find Spanish-speaking monolingual grandparents identifying as *mexicanos,* their bilingual children as Mexican Americans and *mexicanos,* and monolingual English-speaking grandchildren calling themselves Chicanos and Chicanas. Note once again that "Chicano" and "Chicana" were Spanish-language words that were being proclaimed as a defiant identity in English dominant contexts. The rise of Chicana and Chicano identity exemplifies the fact that racial identities can be invented out of thin air and transformed overnight. The transition from a white to brown racial identity occurred in less than a year.[41]

At this moment, dominated as it is by Hispanophobic representations of ethnic Mexicans in the United States, there also exists an emergent Hispanofilia largely focused on the consumption patterns that this emerging majority population will surely produce. "Hispanics are hip, hot and making history," a popular magazine recently announced.[42] Brought to you by Madison

Avenue advertising agencies, consumers are presenting eroticized Hispanic bodies guaranteed to seduce dollars out of pocketbooks. Consume! Consume! Consume! Consume hot Jennifer López records, hip Shakira-styled clothes, Antonio Banderas movies, and *el sabor Latino,* that unique Latin flavor brought to you ice-cold by the Coors Brewing Company of Golden, Colorado. Whatever the popular and indigenous sentiment that gave rise to a Latino identity from below,[43] from above, it has been an invention of Cuban American advertising executives in south Florida and New York who in the 1970s and 1980s were eager to lump and homogenize small Latin American national group identities into a larger unitary market sector. If they could create a clearly identifiable "Latino" market, they stood to profit enormously. They could then persuade large food, beverage, and domestic product manufacturers that Latinos constituted a significant mass market that needed special advertising campaigns only these agents were expertly prepared to address.[44]

This long sweep of the historical genealogy of the social identities we still find in the American Southwest has focused on the process of group formation, on the generation of cultural difference in conditions of conquest and domination. Repeatedly we have seen that while materially and even biologically the individuals who called themselves Spaniards and Indians did not differ much and indeed eked a living in the same ecological zone, the power of brute force that one group uses to dominate another was perpetuated ideologically as innate differences that were rooted in blood, color, and legitimate birth. When Anglo Americans conquered the Southwest in 1848, the process repeated itself. Because the historical sources documenting this period are more extensive, we have been able to illustrate the contestational nature of racial and ethnic identities, their ability to rapidly change and adapt, and the pure genius of invention as a strategy of resistance to domination and control.

7 Race and Erasure

The Hernandez v. Texas *Case*

Ian Haney López

COURTS IN THE UNITED STATES have long wrestled with the racial identity of Mexicans. In 1897, a federal judge in Texas opined that a "pure-blooded Mexican . . . would probably not be classed as white." In contrast, another Texas court, writing in 1951, contended that "Mexican-Americans as a race" are not "a separate race but are white people of Spanish descent."[1] These decisions reflect the liminal position of Mexican Americans, who have historically operated on the cusp between white and non-white identity in U.S. society. But they also tell us about more than just Mexican racial identity, for they provide as well trenchant insight into the nature of race in the United States generally. In that regard, one case stands out. In 1954, just two weeks before issuing the historic decision in *Brown v. Board of Education* that would end de jure school segregation, the U.S. Supreme Court in *Hernandez v. Texas* unanimously declared unconstitutional the practice, widespread in Texas, of excluding Mexican Americans from juries.[2] *Hernandez* deserves our attention partly for reasons of historical accuracy. The Mexican American community has long been an active participant in the struggle for racial justice in the United States, and *Hernandez* brings this fact to the fore. *Hernandez* also has contemporary relevance because it represents the first extension of Constitutional protection to Latinos as a class, no small matter now that Hispanics constitute the largest minority group in the United States. But I concentrate on *Hernandez* here for what it teaches us generally about race and the relationship between categorization and subordination.

Conservative justices on the Supreme Court have been arguing since the mid-1970s for a doctrine of colorblindness, postulating that the achievement

194

of a racially egalitarian society depends on rejecting outright all uses of racial classifications. This commitment to repudiating any use of race has since gained a majority on the Court and, more significantly, has transcended the bounds of law. Today, colorblindness is widely espoused by broad segments of U.S. society as the surest way to combat racism. Yet, the Supreme Court in *Hernandez* understood, in a way we are in danger of letting slip by, that the central dynamic in racial oppression lies not in the explicit use of racial categories. Instead, the essence of race is in the relationships of domination and subordination built upon racial categories. Race as we live it today is only superficially about differentiation. Rather, as *Hernandez* demonstrates, it is centrally about power.

Hernandez, Race, and Racism

In 1954, Earl Warren had just been appointed Chief Justice of the nation's highest court, and on May 14, the Court under his leadership began to issue a series of unanimous opinions repudiating the Jim Crow practices of racial segregation which had so grossly distorted the country's social fabric. That first case was not, as most people believe, *Brown v. Board of Education,* the school desegregation case. Instead, it was *Hernandez v. Texas,* a decision ending the exclusion of Mexican Americans from juries. It is *Hernandez,* and not *Brown,* which counts as the first effort by the newly constituted Warren Court to dismantle racial segregation. And yet, this presents a paradox, for the opinion, written by Chief Justice Warren himself, disclaims race as a basis for its analysis. *Hernandez v. Texas* started the Court on the path to disestablishing Jim Crow, and yet it is not explicitly a race case.

On August 4, 1951, 24-year-old service station attendant Pedro (Pete) Hernández shot and killed tenant farmer Joe Espinosa in Jackson County, Texas.[3] Within twenty-four hours, Hernández was indicted by an all-white grand jury for murder; after a two-day trial and less than three hours of deliberation, an all-white trial jury convicted Hernández and sentenced him to life in prison. The racial compositions of the juries that indicted and convicted Hernández were not an aberration. The county stipulated at trial that no person with a Spanish surname had served on a trial or grand jury in at least a quarter century (and no one could remember any serving before); during that twenty-five-year period, more than six thousand jurors had been seated, but in a county over 15 percent Mexican American, none had been from that group.[4]

The League of United Latin American Citizens, or LULAC, then the most prominent Mexican American civil rights group in the country, agreed to argue Pete Hernández's case as part of a larger legal strategy to attack the systematic exclusion of Mexican Americans from juries throughout Texas.[5] In bringing its challenge, LULAC sought to show that this practice was part of a larger pattern of mistreatment. To that end, they introduced evidence documenting a long list of Jim Crow oppressions: a restaurant in the county seat prominently displayed a sign saying "No Mexicans Served." In addition, Jackson County residents routinely distinguished between "whites" and "Mexicans." Business and civic groups almost entirely excluded Mexican American members. The schools were segregated, at least through the fourth grade, after which almost all Mexican Americans were forced out of school altogether. And finally, on the Jackson County courthouse grounds, there were two men's bathrooms: one was unmarked, while the other said "Colored Men" and "*Hombres Aquí*" (Men Here).[6]

Consider more fully the underlying claim of jury exclusion. LULAC had been founded in Texas in 1929 by Mexican Americans intent on claiming an equal place in U.S. society; then, after the Second World War, returning veterans went back to Texas with a renewed commitment to fight for equal rights.[7] They sought in particular to end three pernicious practices: school segregation, racially restrictive property covenants, and jury exclusion. What ranked jury exclusion with school and residential segregation? To be sure, all-white juries imperiled Mexican American defendants who, like Pete Hernández, risked quick convictions by hostile and biased juries. Moreover, the Mexican American community suffered because white juries rarely and reluctantly convicted whites for depredations against Mexican Americans. But LULAC's determined opposition to jury exclusion arose first and foremost because of its symbolism.[8] Trial by jury rests on the idea of peers judging and being judged by peers. In the context of Texas race politics, however, to put Mexican Americans on juries was tantamount to elevating them to equal status with whites. The idea that "Mexicans" might judge whites deeply violated Texas' racial caste system. LULAC hoped *Hernandez* would help topple a key pillar of Jim Crow: the belief that whites should judge all, but be judged by none but themselves.

There can be no doubt, then, that *Hernandez v. Texas* challenged a Jim Crow practice. This makes it all the more startling that the Supreme Court did not decide *Hernandez* as a race case. At the outset of his opinion, while Chief Justice Warren observed that the Constitution's Fourteenth Amendment primarily protected groups marked by "differences in race or color," he went on to note that "the exclusion of a class of persons from jury service on grounds *other* than race or color may deprive a person of constitutional rights."[9] Why does Warren say that this case is about something *other* than race or color? The answer is simple, though from our perspective today perhaps quite surprising: every party in *Hernandez* argued that Mexican Americans were white.

As the evidence in *Hernandez* suggests, Anglos in Texas in the 1950s generally considered Mexicans an inferior race. This belief originated during the Anglo expansion into what is now the Southwest in the early to mid-1800s, a process that culminated in the expropriation of the northern half of Mexico.[10] At the beginning of the 1800s, Anglos tended to define Mexicans primarily by the cultural and religious aspects of Spanish heritage, and less so by descent-based terms linked to their Spanish and Indian origins.[11] During the 1830s and 1840s, however, as conflict deepened in the Southwest and war between the United States and Mexico loomed, the terms that Anglos used to describe Mexicans shifted sharply from ones noting perceived differences in culture, religion, and language, toward ones stressing skin color and ancestry. In many instances, Anglos simply equated the racial identity of Mexicans with that of Native Americans. Thus, in 1848 Congressman Daniel Dickson justified U.S. expansion into the Southwest by arguing that Mexicans were related to "the fated aboriginal races, who can neither uphold government or be restrained by it; who flourish only amid the haunts of savage indolence, and perish under, if they do not recede before, the influences of civilization."[12] Dickson continued, "Like their doomed brethren, who were once spread over the several States of the Union, they are destined, by the laws above human agency, to give way to a stronger race."[13] Sam Houston expressed the same sentiment, though more bluntly: "The Mexicans are no better than Indians, and I see no reason why we should not go in the same course now, and take their land."[14]

More frequently during this period, Anglos denigrated Mexicans by describing them as a mixed and thereby inferior people. For example, Congressman William Wick opposed the annexation of Mexican territory because, as he said, "I do not want any mixed races in our Union, nor men of any color except white, unless they be slaves. Certainly not as voters or legislators."[15] Or consider Senator John Clayton's opposition to the annexation of Mexican territory: "Yes! Aztecs, Creoles, Half-breeds, Quadroons, Samboes, and I know not what else—'ring streaked and speckled'—all will come in, and instead of us governing them, they, by their votes, will govern *us*."[16] Or note Senator

John Box's opinion that Mexicans were a "mixture of Mediterranean-blooded Spanish peasants with low grade Indians who did not fight to extinction but submitted and multiplied as serfs."[17]

Although racial ideology in this country for the most part has defined races in terms related to the continental division of the world, with Europe, Asia, Africa, and America as the supposed sources of the principal races, the mixed origins of Mexicans did not deter Anglos from regarding them in racial terms. In this, Anglo society clearly drew on its experience with white-black miscegenation. Recall Senator Clayton's invocation of not just "Aztecs" but also "Creoles, Half-breeds, Quadroons, [and] Samboes." Or consider the following editorial from the *Southern Review,* published in 1871:

> An admixture of two unequal races is therefore a cancer, an unpardonable sin against mankind and against nature, which has launched an ever flaming curse on all such connections; inasmuch as she lets the mongrels invariably inherit all the vices and evil traits of both races and rarely, or never, any of the good. Nature absolutely disallows the adulteration of blood; and herein she shows herself to be an aristocrat of the purest water. Every violation of these laws she visits in the most condign and pitiless manner.[18]

But for the fact that this quote comes from an article entitled "The Latin Races in America," one could be forgiven for thinking it yet another screed on the dangers of white and black race-mixing. Predominant cultural conceptions of race emphasized a "great races" logic tied to continental geography, but such logic, particularly in the South, also encompassed specific ideas about racial mixture. As the above excerpt demonstrates, Anglos drew on a developed ideology regarding the evils of racial mixing when they branded Mexicans a mongrel people.[19]

As whites marched westward they believed that the populations they encountered were inferiors destined to fade before them, not through any fault or misdeed on the part of Anglos, but by the laws of nature. Westward expansion was, to use that well-worn phrase, white America's manifest destiny, and the fates of the various peoples on the American continent were determined by their racial characteristics. Thomas Jefferson Farnham, a booster of Anglo expansion into California, made this case in 1840 as follows:

> No one acquainted with the indolent, mixed race of California, will ever believe that they will populate, much less, for any length of time, govern the country. The law of Nature which curses the mulatto here with a constitution

less robust than that of either race from which he sprang, lays a similar penalty upon the mingling of the Indian and white races in California and Mexico. They must fade away.[20]

The U.S. ideology of white racial superiority owes a considerable debt to Anglo-Mexican conflict. This clash came at the critical historical juncture in which Romantic ideals of national particularism and an emerging treatment of race as natural science were becoming widely accepted. In this context, Anglo-Mexican conflict provided a setting for the development and deepening of an ideology of white superiority specifically rooted in nature and revealed through physical differences. "The catalyst in the overt adoption of a *racial* Anglo-Saxonism was the meeting of the Americans and Mexicans in the Southwest, the Texas Revolution, and the war with Mexico," historian Reginald Horsman argues.[21] Consider in this regard that Farnham joined to his indictment of Mexican inferiority, quoted above, a corresponding celebration of Anglo Saxon superiority. With little modesty, Farnham averred that

> [T]he mixing of different branches of the Caucasian family in the States will continue to produce a race of men, who will enlarge from period to period the field of their industry and civil domination, until not only the Northern States of Mexico, but the Californias also, will open their glebe to the pressure of its unconquered arm. The old Saxon blood must stride the continent, must command all its northern shores, must here press the grape and the olive, here eat the orange and the fig, and in their own unaided might, erect the altar of civil and religious freedom on the plains of the Californias.[22]

As Anglos in the mid-1800s pushed into Mexican territory, they brought with them a preoccupation with racial mixing, a conviction that race marked certain peoples as inferior and destined to waste away, and a belief in the specifically racial nature of their own superiority.

For the half-century and more that followed the expansion of the United States into the Southwest, Mexican inhabitants of that region tended to resist their racial subordination by constructing themselves as Mexican nationals and by envisioning an eventual return to Mexico. Rather than directly challenging the racial logic that depicted them as inferiors, they sought to evade it by considering themselves apart from American society.[23] This tendency was exacerbated during the first three decades of the twentieth century, as refugees from Mexico fled north to escape the instability sweeping their homeland, but maintained the hope that they might soon return south.[24] With the onset of the Great Depression, however, immigration from Mexico was cut off, and a removal campaign undertaken that forced half-a-million persons of Mexican descent, Mexican nationals and U.S. citizens alike, back into Mexico.[25] If those who supported the mass expulsions hoped it would remove Mexicans from U.S. society forever, the effect was just the opposite. Those who survived the calamity of forced removals and remained on this side of the border often did so because of deep ties to the United States, measured in terms of generations of residency, familial bonds, and home ownership. Beginning in the 1930s, a new sense of identity emerged among Mexicans in the United States: many came to see themselves as first and foremost Americans. The community shifted from one that dreamed of returning to Mexico to one that identified with remaining in the United States, and U.S. Mexicans increasingly carved out a path of assimilation for themselves and their community.[26] Indeed, the label "Mexican American" emerged during the 1930s, and encapsulated the effort to both retain pride in the community's Mexican cultural origins and to express a fundamentally U.S. national identity.[27]

Inseparable from this new assimilationist identity, however, was an engagement with American racial logic. On this score, the community leaders were certain: Mexican Americans were white. The belief in Mexican whiteness appears rooted in the rise of ethnicity and a broadening conception of who counted as white at the start of the twentieth century. Ethnicity arose as a term of group difference in the early 1900s, when it emerged as a form of identity that would allow expressions of group pride while avoiding the hierarchy central to racial thinking. Ethnicity developed, particularly among Zionists, as a way of capturing what was thought to be "good" about race—a sense of group identity, transmitted by descent, and worthy of loyalty and pride—while eschewing the "bad," the ordering of races and their supposed super- and subordination.[28] Mexican leaders embraced a version of ethnicity in proclaiming at once that they were racially white and so deserved to be free from discrimination, but simultaneously Mexican as a matter of group culture, pride, and political mobilization. To be sure, not all U.S. Mexicans embraced a white racial identity. The elite's ability to claim a white identity partly reflected their elevated class standing and their relatively fair features, attributes that stemmed from race politics not only in the Southwest but also in Mexico, as discussed elsewhere in this volume. Those who were poor or who had dark features were much less likely to insist on a white identity. Similarly, recent immigrants were more likely to identify in cultural or national, rather than racial, terms. No homogenous racial identity existed within the

U.S. Mexican community. Nevertheless, whiteness formed a central component of elite Mexican identity in the Southwest at mid-twentieth century.

These ideas found clear expression in LULAC's arguments in *Hernandez v. Texas.* As in other cases, LULAC followed what it termed its "other white" legal strategy, protesting not segregation itself, but the inappropriate segregation of Mexican Americans as a white racial group.[29] Thus, LULAC objected in its brief to the Supreme Court that, "while legally white," in Jackson County "frequently the term white excludes the Mexicans and is reserved for the rest of the non-Negro population."[30] Hernández's lawyers did not argue principally that segregation was legally wrong, but instead that Mexican Americans should not be segregated because they were legally white. In this, as one of the lead attorneys in the case explained to the Mexican American public, Mexicans were in no different position than other white ethnic groups that had overcome prejudice:

> We are not passing through anything different from that endured at one time or another by other unassimilated population groups: the Irish in Boston (damned micks, they were derisively called); the Polish in the Detroit area (their designation was bohunks and polackers); the Italians in New York (referred to as stinking little wops, dagoes and guineas); the Germans in many sections of the country (called dumb square-heads and krauts); and our much maligned friends of the Jewish faith, who have been persecuted even here, in the land of the free, because to the bigoted they were just "lousy kikes."[31]

The notion of a white ethnic, as opposed to a nonwhite racial, identity was at the root of the legal challenge to jury exclusion against Mexicans in Texas.

Texas, meanwhile, also adopted the claim that Mexican Americans were white—though to preserve segregation. LULAC and others had brought at least seven challenges to jury exclusion in Texas before *Hernandez,* in cases reaching back to 1931. In the initial cases, Texas courts had upheld the all-white juries after accepting evidence that no Mexican Americans were qualified to serve. For example, one court quoted a jury commissioner as saying that "he did not consider the Mexicans . . . as being intelligent enough to make good jurors, so that [he] just disregarded the whole Mexican list and did not consider any of them." The court cited this as showing that "there was no evidence that there was any Mexican in the County who possessed the statutory qualifications of a juror," before concluding that there had been no discrimination "against the Mexican race."[32]

Eventually, this approach proved troublesome for the Texas courts, as their evidence regarding the lack of qualified Mexican Americans seemed to demonstrate rather the prevalence of racial prejudice. In the late 1940s, the Texas courts shifted to a new basis for excluding Mexican Americans. There was no discrimination, the courts held, because like every jury member Mexican Americans were white. As the decision under appeal in *Hernandez* reasoned, "Mexicans are white people . . . The grand jury that indicted [Hernández] and the petit jury that tried him being composed of members of his race, it cannot be said . . . that appellant has been discriminated against in the organization of such juries."[33]

Confronted with contending parties who nevertheless agreed that Mexican Americans were white, how did the Supreme Court react? Immediately, it jettisoned an explicitly racial analysis. The case, Chief Justice Warren said, did not turn on "race or color." But Warren did not then attempt to decide the case in terms of some other form of difference, for instance national origin, ancestry, or ethnicity. Rather, the Court approached this case as concerning group subordination generally. "Community prejudices are not static," Warren wrote, "and from time to time other differences from the community norm may define other groups which need [Constitutional] protection. Whether such a group exists within a community is a question of fact." In this context, Warren reasoned, Hernández's "initial burden in substantiating his charge of group discrimination was to prove that persons of Mexican descent constitute a separate class in Jackson County, distinct from 'whites.' One method by which this might be demonstrated is by showing the attitude of the community."[34]

Hernandez articulated a simple test for when a class deserves Constitutional protection: In the context of the local situation, was this a mistreated group? To answer this question, the Court recapitulated the catalogue of Jim Crow practices adduced by LULAC to demonstrate the social position of Mexicans in Jackson County. *Hernandez* struck down jury discrimination against Mexican Americans not because Mexican Americans were nominally a race, but because in the context of mid-century Texas they were a subordinated group. There's a wonderful irony to this. In *Hernandez v. Texas,* all parties sought to avoid a racial analysis, and the Court claimed to decide the case as if race was not an issue. Nevertheless, the case's holding is perhaps the single most insightful Supreme Court opinion on race ever handed down. *Hernandez* as an opinion captures the fact, not fully understood by Chief Justice Warren as the opinion's author, that race is ultimately a question of community norms and practices—that is, a matter of social domination. No Supreme Court opinion before or since has come so close to this understanding, nor perceived so clearly that subordination should be the touchstone for invoking Constitutional intervention when a state distinguishes between groups.

Classification Versus Subordination

The Supreme Court today emphasizes not a special concern with race as a tool of subordination, however, but with any governmental use of a racial classification whatsoever. The origins of this misplaced emphasis, in turn, can be traced back to 1954, to the *Brown v. Board of Education* case. In *Hernandez,* at issue was whether the Fourteenth Amendment protected Mexican Americans; if it did, their exclusion from juries was clearly prohibited inasmuch as jury exclusion was one of the few forms of segregation struck down by the Reconstruction Court in the wake of the Civil War.[35] Because in *Hernandez* the Court could not rely on race per se, however, it was forced to explain why groups deserve Constitutional protection in general, and thereby pushed to identify social practices rather than the nature of group identity as the core issue. In contrast, *Brown* is in a sense the mirror opposite of *Hernandez.* It was obvious that the Constitution protected African Americans; the troubling question was whether it prohibited the school segregation being challenged by Thurgood Marshall and the National Association for the Advancement of Colored People Legal Defense Fund. Black Americans were indisputably the intended beneficiaries of the Fourteenth Amendment, and their legal protection required no particular justification. In contrast, segregated schools were the norm, and the Court hesitated to condemn such practices in strong terms, for fear of engendering a backlash. Hence, the Court in its decision equivocated.

Any fair reading of the decision would conclude that *Brown* struck down school segregation because it oppressed blacks. But *Brown* did not strongly and unambiguously ground its decision on an anti-subordination rationale. That shortcoming opened the door to the misreading of *Brown* that now dominates Constitutional race law: *Brown,* the contemporary Court insists, stands for the proposition that the Constitution prohibits, not subordination, but virtually any use of racial categories. This distinction is key, for a concern with subordinating practices would lead the Court to strike down government action that harms minorities even if racial classifications are not expressly used, while preserving affirmative action and other race conscious remedies. In contrast, a focus on classifications would do the reverse—immunizing harms to minority communities so long as such harms were produced by institutional rather than purposeful and express racism, and striking down instead affirmative efforts to use race to ameliorate racial inequality. The latter, today, describes current constitutional practice.

Constitutional race law as it operates now is a disaster. On one side, the Court upholds even the most egregious instances of discrimination, so long as no racial categories are invoked. In *McCleskey v. Kemp* (1987), for instance, the Court considered whether the defendant could use the most sophisticated and exhaustive survey of criminal sentencing thus far ever undertaken to prove that racial bias tainted Georgia's death penalty system. In doing so, the Court accepted as uncontroverted fact that Georgia sentences to death blacks who murder whites at *twenty-two times* the rate it orders death for blacks who kill blacks. Nevertheless, the Court ruled that any general statistical showing is irrelevant, holding that there is no Constitutional harm absent the identification of a particular biased actor who made a decision explicitly based on race.[36] On the other, the Court wields the Constitution to strike down virtually every formal use of race, now limited almost exclusively to efforts to ameliorate racism's legacy through affirmative action. *Richmond v. Croson* (1989) tells us that, when a Virginia city once the capital of the Confederacy adopts a set aside program to steer some of its construction dollars to minority owned firms, this is impermissible discrimination—even when, without the program, less than two-thirds of 1 percent of those dollars went to minorities in a city that is 50 percent African American.[37] It is not too strong to say that the current Court uses the Constitution to protect the racial status quo: it principally condones discrimination against minorities, and virtually always condemns efforts to achieve greater racial equality. It does so by focusing not on race as subordination but on race as categorization.

The Supreme Court recently handed down a second *Hernandez* decision, again involving jury discrimination.[38] *Hernandez v. New York* (1991), in comparison to cases like *McCleskey* and *Croson,* is a minor case, but it puts into sharp relief the approach to race that undergirds the Court's contemporary racial jurisprudence. This case involved a Hispanic defendant and the use of a Spanish-language translator, in which the prosecutor peremptorily struck from the jury every Latino. He did so, he said, because where the jurors were supposed to rely on the official translations, the prosecutor did not believe that these potential jurors "could" set aside their familiarity with Spanish. The prosecutor testified: "I felt there was a great deal of uncertainty as to whether they could accept the interpreter as the final arbiter of what was said by each of the witnesses, especially where there were going to be Spanish-speaking witnesses, and I didn't feel, when I asked them whether or not they could accept the interpreter's translation of it, I didn't feel that they could."[39] The word "could," rather than "would," is telling, for while the latter term suggests concern about individual temperament, the former invokes a sense of group disability. Also raising concern, the prosecutor questioned only Hispanic potential jurors but no others about their ability to speak Spanish. Nevertheless, the Court upheld the exclusion, finding no bias on the part of the prosecutor. Justice Sandra Day O'Connor's rationale, offered in a concurring opinion, is especially revealing. She thought it irrelevant that the basis for exclusion correlated closely to Hispanic identity and operated to exclude all and only Latinos. Because the strikes were not explicitly justified in racial terms, O'Connor reasoned, no basis existed for constitutional intervention. The strikes "may have acted like strikes based on race," O'Connor conceded, "but they were not based on race. *No matter how closely tied or significantly correlated to race* the explanation for a peremptory strike may be, the strike does not implicate the Equal Protection Clause unless it is based on race."[40] According to O'Connor, race is not at issue until and unless someone utters that term. Race exists in this conception almost as a magic word: say it, and race suddenly springs into being, but not otherwise. This magic word formalism strips race of all social meaning and of any connection to social practices of group conflict and subordination.

Today's Court gets racism backwards: it denies there is racism no matter how much minorities are harmed so long as a racial term is not specifically invoked by a state actor, even though most racism now occurs through institutionalized practices. And it claims racism amounts to any use of race, when in fact efforts to counteract racial oppression's extensive harms have no choice but to reference race. This misunderstanding of racism is anchored by a narrow, categorical conception of race. It is race-as-a-word-that-must-be-uttered-for-it-to-exist, race-as-skin-disconnected-from-social-practice-or-national-history, race-as-an-empty-category that supports a color-blind jurisprudence best suited to protecting, rather than changing, the racial status quo.

Revealing the made-up nature of racial ideas is fundamental to counteracting regnant racial ideology. Nevertheless, we should be careful not to assume that deconstructing racial categories will necessarily disestablish race. Intellectual efforts to reveal the made-up nature of racial categories, without corresponding political mobilization, lose sight of the fact that race is much more than a set of ideas; it is an ongoing set of social practices and structures. We best oppose racial systems by insisting on the deep connection between ideas of race and social inequality. This, perhaps, is the core insight of *Hernandez v. Texas*. The central issue was not whether race was invoked directly, as the current Court would require, but simply this: did social practices subordinate groups based upon ideas of group difference? For Mexican Americans, as for many other racial minorities, this question has contemporary relevance, and the answer remains a tragic yes.

Conclusion

Today a demographic revolution is underway. Partly as a result of a long history of U.S. expansion, colonial incursions, and gunboat diplomacy throughout the Western Hemisphere, Latin Americans now compose the largest immigrant group in the United States, and this trend will continue, if not accelerate.[41] Not even closing the border would significantly disrupt this development. Domestic births currently outpace immigration as the primary source of Latino population growth, with births to Hispanic mothers outnumbering all other deliveries combined in Bellwether, California. The U.S. Latino population increased 58 percent between 1990 and 2000, and this group, the largest minority in the country, now accounts for more than one of every eight Americans. The Census Bureau conservatively estimates that by 2020 Latinos will number 17 percent of the country.[42]

It is not, perhaps, too strong a statement to say that the future of race in the United States depends on how Hispanics come to be seen, and to see themselves, in racial terms. It is in this context that we should read and reread *Hernandez v. Texas*. In that case the Supreme Court recognized that to dismantle Jim Crow it would not be enough to end the segregation of blacks, but would require too the elimination of discrimination against Latinos, reminding us that Latinos have historically been subject to, and equally long have fought against, racial marginalization in the United States. But perhaps most importantly, *Hernandez* insists that we should be concerned first and foremost not with the categorical basis on which people are mistreated, but with the fact of mistreatment itself. *Hernandez*, it is true, is the leading Latino civil rights case in our nation's history. But it may be much more than that. Read as a call to end subordination, *Hernandez* may be the leading social justice case for us all.

Reconfiguring Race, Gender, and Chicano/a Identity in Film

Adriana Katzew

VISUAL IMAGES bombard us everywhere. Indeed, ours is a "pre-eminently visual culture."[1] Whether through television or film, we are continuously processing both explicit and subliminal visual messages about who we are and what we should be. As a cultural vehicle, the visual media determines the ideas consumed by the audience, and to a large extent also sustains the status quo.[2] Television, for instance, creates ideologies or, at the very least, reflects and fosters the ones that already exist.[3] Furthermore, as psychiatrist Frantz Fanon argues, messages in films "work their way into one's mind and shape one's view of the world of the group to which one belongs."[4] Historian Carlos Cortés states more explicitly that the mass media educates—for better or worse—by disseminating information, images, and ideas regarding race, ethnicity, culture, and foreignness, and that viewers, in turn, learn from the media and construct meanings from their interactions with it both consciously and unconsciously.[5]

Given the importance of the role of the media, how do Mexican Americans see themselves reflected in it? Most tend to see negative, stereotyped, or limited representations of themselves.[6] This is true despite the fact that Mexican Americans comprise a significant percentage of the U.S. population.[7] Since the late 1960s, however, a number of Chicanos/as have worked in film and TV to subvert one-dimensional and stereotyped representations and instead present more complex depictions of people of Mexican origin in terms of racial, ethnic, and cultural identity.[8] In this essay I focus on two films, *Zoot Suit* (1981) and *Real Women Have Curves* (2002). Both films are based on plays written by Chicanos/as and they are directed by Latino/as, still infrequent in

Hollywood. *Zoot Suit* was first written as a play by Luis Valdez, a Chicano activist and founder of the Teatro Campesino (the Farmworkers Theater, associated with César Chávez's United Farm Workers' Movement in the 1960s). Valdez later wrote the screenplay and directed the film, which was the first full-length Hollywood movie by a Chicano. *Real Women Have Curves* was first written as a play by the Chicana playwright and activist Josefina López; she later co-wrote the screenplay for the film, which was directed by the Colombian Patricia Cardoso.

While *Zoot Suit* has been extensively analyzed, it has often been considered on its own, in comparison to other films by Valdez, or in relation to "gang" films.[9] I pair this film with *Real Women Have Curves* to analyze how they each reconfigure representations of race, ethnicity, cultural identity, and gender—issues at the heart of both works. The films approach these issues in divergent ways, reflecting the different points in time in which they were created. *Zoot Suit* was filmed shortly (approximately six years) after the Movimiento Chicano (Chicano Movement), whose goal was to fight for the civil rights of Mexican Americans and reaffirm Chicano identity in positive terms.[10] The film, which focuses on Chicano characters, was based on two historical events in the early 1940s that laid bare the institutional racism against Mexican Americans in the United States. *Real Women* also centers on Mexican Americans, and was filmed nearly thirty years after the Chicano Movement wound down, at a time when younger generations of Mexican Americans have become more acculturated due to the gains made during the Chicano Movement. In addition, these two films also show dramatically different approaches to female characters, especially Chicanas, which can be attributed in part to the fact that *Zoot Suit* was created and directed by a man, and its main protagonists are male, and *Real Women* was created and directed by women, and its main characters are female.

To understand these films and the context from which they emerge, I first provide a brief overview of the history of representations of people of Mexican origin in U.S.-produced film, and also emphasize the emergence of Chicano activism in this media. The essay will then focus on three main issues: first, how these films represent race, both in terms of the casting of actors, as well as their content; second, how the romantic relationships between the white and the Chicano/a characters fit within Hollywood's history of representation of Anglo-Mexican romantic relationships; and third, how the representation of separatism, assimilation, and the "American Dream" is addressed in both films.

Hollywood's History of Racial Stereotyping

Since the inception of film and television in the United States, the portrayal of people of Mexican origin has been based on a series of stereotypes, positive or negative, but nearly always one-dimensional and simplistic. Which stereotypes have been emphasized has generally depended on the political, social, and/or economic context of the United States (as well as international and transnational contexts), and by extension, the Hollywood industry.[11] Tracing the history of some of the stereotypes, film scholar Gary Keller argues that Hollywood films have tended to disparage minorities in order to fit into the Hollywood formula, which placed Anglos as the heroes, reflecting and reinforcing the racial tensions in the United States whereby whites were considered to be superior.[12]

In the early days of film—the silent movies of the 1910s—people of Mexican origin were depicted as "greasers," as well as treacherous criminals, incompetent *bandidos* or bandits, good-hearted simpletons, easy women, and those having a good position or role, but who were nevertheless of low birth.[13] Some of these stereotypes were based on popular novels of the nineteenth century. The "greaser" was one such stereotype. Already in use by the 1850s, "greaser" was a derogatory term applied to non-Anglo or lower-class individuals. In California and the Southwest, the term was specifically applied to Mexicans. There are several conjectures as to the origin of this term, one of which claims that "greaser" derived from Mexican laborers who would put grease on their backs to help with the unloading of cargo and hides.[14] In dime novels, "greaser" denoted "an oily, dark, swarthy villain or bandit who, more often than not, was Mexican or of mixed blood."[15]

The popular literature of the late nineteenth century also cemented the image of Mexicans as *bandidos*. This image was fed by key historical events that created animosity between Anglos and people of Mexican origin: the battle of the Alamo and the annexation of Texas to the U.S. (1836), as well as the Mexican-American War (1846–1848) and the ensuing Treaty of Guadalupe Hidalgo (1848), in which Mexico lost more than fifty percent of its territory to the United States.[16] Anglo mistreatment of Mexicans in the newly acquired territories of the United States, the illegal encroachment upon their land, and the discriminatory legislation against them engendered resentment against the Anglos. In part as a reaction to this discrimination, groups of bandits roamed the countryside in the 1850s raiding and pillaging.[17]

The negative images of people of Mexican origin found in the literature were reflected in one of the earliest films, *Pedro Esquirel and Dionecio Gonzales: Mexican Duel* (1894, directed by W. K. L. Dickson). This was the first film to introduce Mexican characters, and they were portrayed as "violent, treacherous, drunkard, crime oriented, and with the singular inability to control one's primitive passions."[18] These negative images of Mexicans and Chicanos as "greasers" and bandits reverberated in the Westerns, a genre that became popular during the silent film era of the 1910s–1920s, as reflected in film titles such as *Tony the Greaser* (1911) and *Broncho Billy and the Greaser* (1914). The image of the bandit was further bolstered by the Mexican Revolution (1910–1917) and its leader Pancho Villa.[19] Film scholar Charles Ramírez Berg offers a description of the bandit stereotype as developed in films in terms of physical, behavioral, and psychological traits. Physically he is unkempt, dirty, disheveled, and with oily hair. Behaviorally, he is cruel, treacherous, and shifty. Psychologically, he is overly emotional, irrational, and quick to resort to violence. Additionally, he either does not speak English or does so with a heavy accent, which, in Ramírez Berg's analysis, was Hollywood's way of signaling his stupidity and inferior status.[20]

The romantic plots in Westerns from the silent era (and thereon) reflected the racial tension between Anglos and Mexicans/Chicanos and promoted the notion that whites were superior. This happened through what historian Carlos Cortés describes as an "interethnic double standard."[21] While "greasers" could not have successful love affairs with Anglo women, Anglo men could do so with female characters of Mexican origin.[22] Furthermore, Anglo ethnic superiority was asserted in the films by having the Anglo hero steal the heart of the Mexican woman away from the dark-skinned Mexican man with whom she was involved.[23] But, as Cortés points out, "not just any Mexican women would do for an Anglo hero, only classy light-skinned Mexicanas" who were somewhat cultured (for a Latina) and of good Spanish or Latino stock.[24] Dark-skinned Mexican and Chicana female characters were relegated to the role of prostitutes and *cantineras* (bar girls).[25]

"Greasers" and bandits ceased to appear in Hollywood films during World War I (1914–1918), as Hollywood focused instead on a new villain, the Germans—the enemy during the war. Moreover, the export of films to Europe was restricted during the war, which reoriented Hollywood's attention to Latin America as a new market. To appeal to its new audience, Hollywood put aside the "greaser" stereotype. However, when World War I ended with the United States emerging as a world power, Hollywood Westerns reverted to the villains being bandits and greasers of Mexican origin (though the word "greaser" ceased to be used). The negative and disdainful stereotypes of people of Mexican origin after World War I became so strong that, on the domestic front, mutual aid societies asked President Woodrow Wilson (1913–21) to do something about it.[26] In the international arena, several Latin American countries, including Mexico, threatened to boycott the import of films. This threat carried profound implications because Latin America was a significant consumer of U.S. films, and an embargo would have an adverse economic impact on the United States. As a result, President Wilson was compelled to ask the Hollywood movie industry to "please be a little kinder to the Mexicans."[27]

Hollywood did not eliminate negative depictions of Mexican-origin people in the 1920s altogether. The image of the villainous bandit continued, this time reflecting strong nativist sentiment. Nativists wanted to restrict immigrants and keep the United States Nordic, as they believed that immigrants wielded too much power and were responsible for crime, violence, and industrial trouble. And while the Immigration Acts in the first half of the 1920s placed heavy restrictions on Eastern and Southern Europeans, not so on Mexicans. The United States needed Mexicans for cheap labor in agribusiness, and Mexicans immigrated in great numbers. This large influx further fueled racism against Mexicans, who were already getting blamed for the 1921 economic depression and unemployment. Although the discrimination against them was captured by their negative depictions in films, a somewhat more positive stereotype of Mexicans also emerged at this time, that of the *caballero* (gentleman), a good kind of bandit.[28] This stereotype was deployed through two characters: Zorro and the Cisco Kid. Zorro was a light-skinned hero of Spanish or Mexican origin. A Robin Hood-type character, he would fight vicious "mongrels" to help the poor and oppressed Indians and mestizos (people of Indian and Spanish mixed background). Part of the plot (the action typically located in the Southwest) relied on the *caballero* seducing beautiful *señoritas*. *The Mark of Zorro* (1920, directed by Fred Niblo) was the first of a number of films using this character, with most of the roles played by white actors. The *Cisco Kid* was a bandit of Mexican origin, who was both charming and daring, a murderer and a lover. The role of the Cisco Kid was first introduced in *The Caballero's Way* (1914, directed by Webster Cullison), and this character was also played by white actors in this film and several sequels.[29]

The Latin Lover was another stereotype that emerged in the 1920s, a decade marked—prior to the 1929 stock market crash—by economic prosperity, the flappers, jazz, and optimism. It was also the beginning of Hollywood's

Golden Era, when actors became idols.[30] The films in this period tended to be escapist and romantic, giving rise to the stereotype of the Latin Lover—a combination of "eroticism, exoticism, tenderness tinged with violence and danger."[31] This type was first embodied by Rudolph Valentino, an Italian-born actor, who played the role of an Argentinean in the 1921 film *The Four Horsemen of the Apocalypse* (directed by Rex Ingram). It was his black hair, dark complexion and seductive eyes that made him an idol and sent Hollywood studios running in search of other tall, dark, and handsome actors who could play the role of the Latin Lover. It is important to note, however, that the characters were typically European, with the occasional Latin American thrown into the mix. As to the actual actors, studios promoted them as either European-born or of European descent, even in the case of Mexican actors Roland Gilbert and Ramón Novarro, who appealed to audiences partly because they were light-skinned. Some studios went so far as to force actors to change their names to "Latin" sounding ones so as to appeal to audiences.[32]

The stereotype of the "Dark Lady"—Hollywood's female equivalent to the Latin Lover—also emerged in the 1920s. She was "virginal, inscrutable, aristocratic . . . circumspect and aloof."[33] A number of Latin American actresses were associated with this role: Mexican actresses Dolores del Río and Lupe Vélez, as well as actresses Myrtle González and Beatriz Michelena. Because they had light skin and did not fit Hollywood's notion of a Mexican "look," they portrayed exotic, non-Mexican women of various countries and ethnicities.[34]

The Latin Lover films came to an end with the onset of the Great Depression in 1929 and with the transition to movies with sound.[35] In the 1930s, Chicano/Mexican and other Latino/a characters nearly disappeared as a result of several economic circumstances. At a time when jobs were scarce and people were afraid that Mexicans were stealing the jobs of "Americans," nativism reared its ugly head once more, leading to the massive deportation and repatriation of Mexicans and Mexican Americans to Mexico (one-third of the Mexican population was sent back).[36] The eugenics movement further encouraged restrictions on Mexican immigration. In a report prepared by so-called eugenics expert Roy L. Garis, he stated that Mexicans' minds "run to nothing higher than animal functions—eat, sleep, and sexual debauchery." He also referred to Mexicans as "swine," "apathetic peons and lazy squaws."[37] Reports such as this further fueled racist notions about people of Mexican origin, and likely contributed to the disappearance of most Latino/a characters in films of the Latin Lover type.[38] In contrast, the stereotype of the bandit continued (both as a villain and a *caballero*) in a series of sequels featuring the Cisco Kid.[39]

The emergence of "talkies" in 1927 also had a negative impact on many actors due to the quality of their voice. Some Mexican actors were also affected because they did not speak English or spoke with heavy accents. As a result they were demoted from leading to supporting roles. Mexican actresses, however, fared better. Carlos Cortés argues that the representation of Mexican and Chicana women in the 1930s through the mid 1940s can be categorized as sensual and frivolous (when they were not typecast as women of questionable virtue).[40] Sometimes they had a cool sensuality and were restrained and ladylike, as were the characters played by the Mexican actress Dolores del Río. Other characters personified frivolity, as was the case of the roles played by the legendary Brazilian actress Carmen Miranda, dressed in fruit headdresses and singing and dancing to Latin rhythms. And then there was the stereotype of the sensual and frivolous buffoon, as played by Mexican actress Lupe Vélez, whose English pronunciation and manner of speaking amused audiences.[41] Vélez's combination of accent and playful behavior gave rise to the stereotype of the "spitfire," which she embodied in the *Mexican Spitfire* series of eight films made between 1939 and 1943. In them she played a volatile, lively, entertaining woman from Mexico who oftentimes used vulgarity and insults in Spanish. The character was married to an Anglo man, and they lived in the United States. This is especially interesting since the Hays Code, which set the guidelines that governed the production of motion pictures, was in place at that time. The Hays Code specifically prohibited interracial romantic or sexual relationships; yet, it defined race in terms of blacks and whites: "Miscegenation (sex relationships between the white and black races) is forbidden."[42] The fact that the *Spitfire* films feature an Anglo-Mexican couple reflected the nebulous racial classification of people of Mexican origin. For example, the U.S. Census identified Mexicans as white in 1920, as "Mexican" in 1930, and then reclassified them again as white in 1940.[43] While it was clear they were not black, in the world of Hollywood they were not white either. Furthermore, the *Spitfire* films affirmed the romantic paradigm established in the "greaser" films of the silent era: in Anglo Mexican romantic couples, the man was Anglo and the woman was Mexican.

The 1940s brought slight improvements to the representation of Mexicans/ Chicanos, although some stereotypes remained. During the war years, films became more patriotic in tone, and minorities, including Mexican Americans and other Latinos, were depicted as loyal citizens. For instance, *Guadalcanal Diary* (1943, directed by Lewis Seiler) tells the story of a multi-ethnic group of U.S. marines in a battle during World War II. One of the main characters is a Mexican American private, played by Chicano actor Anthony Quinn. Another film that dealt seriously with the subject was *A Medal for Benny* (1945, directed by Irving Pichel)—a story about the heroism of a Mexican American during the war. War films, however, failed to address or mirror the severe segregation that existed within the armed forces.[44]

The representation of Mexicans/Chicanos also improved in the 1940s due to a new U.S. foreign policy. President Franklin D. Roosevelt (1933–45) developed the Good Neighbor Policy in 1933, hoping to create alliances with Latin American countries. This policy, combined with the closing of the European market for films due to World War II, forced Hollywood to turn once more to its Latin American neighbors as potential markets. With the encouragement of the Department of State's newly created Office of the Coordinator of Inter-American affairs in 1940, Hollywood abandoned its negative portrayals of Latinos and Latin Americans as villains, which had thus far alienated Latin American countries, and instead produced films with Latin American themes and locales, where people of Mexican and Latin American origin tended to be shown in a positive light.[45] Romantic musical comedies emerged at this time, and with them the Latin Lover stereotype was resurrected, masking race and ethnic conflicts in the United States.[46] These films were set in Latin American countries, and promoted the idea of the "tropics" as a haven for romance and fun.[47] *Weekend in Havana* (1941, directed by Walter Lang), *Fiesta* (1947, directed by Richard Thorpe), *Holiday in Mexico* (1946, directed by George Sidney), and *Carnival in Costa Rica* (1947, directed by Gregory Ratoff) are a few examples of this genre of musical comedy/Latin Lover films from this period. Postwar films from 1946 to 1949, however, reverted to the old stereotypes of bandits and Latin Lovers. Mexican bandit and hero, the Cisco Kid, returned to the screen from 1939 until 1950, with fourteen films made between 1945 and 1950. But the Anglo actor who had previously starred in them was replaced first by the light-skinned Cuban American actor Cesar Romero, then by Mexican American actor Gilbert Roland, and finally by the Spanish-born Duncan Renaldo.

The disclosure of the atrocities of World War II, the physical and psychological damage that it caused, as well as the problems in the domestic front (i.e., racism) stirred a new level of consciousness in the country in the late 1940s and 1950s. In the film industry, it led a few filmmakers to create movies referred to as "social problem films." These cinematographic works (many of them with a pseudo-documentary style) exposed topical societal problems in the United States and offered a social commentary.[48] A few of these films specifically addressed the conditions of people of Mexican origin, portraying them in a more sympathetic light. The 1949 film *Border Incident* (directed by Anthony Mann), starring Mexican actor Ricardo Montalbán, depicted the condition of *bracero* workers (brought from Mexico and hired by the U.S. government on a temporary basis to supply labor primarily for U.S. agribusiness) and their exploitation at the hands of Anglos. The 1956 film *Giant,* directed by George Stevens, was Hollywood's first major motion picture to expose the racism that Mexican Americans suffered in Texas; it reveals the range of acts waged against them—from doctors denying them services to restaurants and other business establishments refusing to serve them. The film also highlights the transformation of a wealthy Anglo cattle rancher when his son marries a Mexican woman. The father is first outraged, but then embraces her and his new grandchild, a mestizo, whom he now sees as a positive symbol of the integration between Anglo and Mexican cultures through intermarriage.[49] The 1954 film *Salt of the Earth,* directed by Herbert Biberman, was based on a real-life event at the time: the strike by Mexican American miners against a mining company in New Mexico and their exploitation. When the men were forbidden to protest, their wives took over and continued the strike. This is one of the first films to seriously explore issues of race and class between whites and Mexican Americans, and between Mexican American men and women, and which places Chicana women at the forefront of the action and underscores their courage.[50] Initially, however, few people in the United States saw the film because it was suppressed due to the alleged Communist affiliations of the film creators, this at a time when the Cold War, the red (Communist) scare, and McCarthyism defined the political climate of the late 1940s and 1950s. With the fear instilled by the McCarthysm of the 1950s, the development of "social problem" films dealing with Chicanos/as and with other issues of importance was hampered, as actors and filmmakers were blacklisted for any work considered "un-American."

The 1960s did not do much to improve the image of Chicanos, despite being a decade of civil rights and national liberation movements. On the contrary, the Hollywood industry replicated the political status of Chicanos as the invisible minority. With the U.S. policy of containment (of Soviet Union-based communism), a flurry of films depicted Mexicans (and other Latin Americans) as stupid, subservient, ideological disciples of Anglo men from the United States who provide technical and political expertise in Mexico (and other Latin American countries). The 1969 film *The Wild Bunch* (directed by Sam Peckinpah) exemplifies this trend. Not coincidentally, at this time, the greaser and bandit stereotypes also resurfaced with a reappearance of the Western genre. While Anglos were invariably portrayed as superior, Mexican/Chicano men were depicted as amoral villains and cruel, violent, drunken bandits, and women of Mexican origin were portrayed as *cantineras* and prostitutes. The 1960 film *The Magnificent Seven* (directed by John Sturges) typifies these depictions.[51] According to film scholar Rosa Linda Fregoso, this resurgence of the greaser was due to a lack of interest in the Mexican market, as well as Hollywood's realization that, with the emergence and growing strength of the Black Power Movement, African Americans could no longer be as easily depicted in disparaging ways.[52] Hollywood, however, seemed untouched by the civil rights movements of Latinos, especially the Chicano Movement taking place in its own backyard in East Los Angeles. One possible explanation could be the fact that, in terms of sheer numbers, the African American population outnumbered the Mexican population by five to one.[53] In addition, by the mid 1960s the black community had exploded, with riots in Watts, Detroit, and Newark. By contrast, Chicano and other Latino *barrios* remained more quiet and may not have appeared as imminent a threat as did the black rioters.[54]

With the pressure from the civil rights movements of the 1960s, Chicano (and other Latino) characters in film and television increased in the 1970s, yet, as Keller suggests, only as tokens, "coming off as nothing more than stick furniture—functioning as maids, bank tellers, secretaries, cops, a dealer or two—and . . . they seldom do more than take up space, look Latin, and spout either Spanish or stereotypically accented English."[55] In films, the dominant images of Chicanos mirrored those in the news media: illegal aliens, bandits, gang members, and *cantineras*. These images were, in part, the result of the economic recession, with Mexicans accused once more in the history of the United States of stealing jobs.

The 1980s recognized the rapidly growing Chicano and broader Latino market with an increase in the Latino population (by more than fifty percent).[56] Chicanos (and other Latinos) were portrayed in four types of film: mainstream films; films about drug dealing; xenophobia and revenge films;

and films classified as Chicano films.[57] Mainstream films often cast members who played a person of Mexican origin (or other Latinos), but in minor roles. Some of them relied on stereotypes, such as Mexican/Chicanas as sex starved or promiscuous women. Films about drug trafficking proliferated, and in them the Chicanos (as well as other Latinos and Latin Americans) were portrayed as amoral crooks. Gang films, such as *Colors* (1988, directed by Dennis Hopper) and *Bound by Honor* (1993, directed by Taylor Hackford), made their appearance in the 1980s and continued into the 1990s. The 1980s was also the decade in which a large number of Chicano films (films with significant creative input from Chicanos behind the camera) were produced, although this genre has radically decreased.[58]

The Emergence of Chicano Activism in the Film Industry

With the political and social struggles of the 1960s, especially the Civil Rights Movement and the Chicano Movement, Chicano art came into full force.[59] Chicano artist John Valadez describes the 1960s as a time when "we were so starved for any kind of positive identity that any recognition of who we were, that we were even there, caused a deep response."[60] Chicanos took action by creating art because they had "a need to say something about themselves and their community."[61] In response to the marginalization that Mexican Americans experienced, a number of Chicanos got involved in the television and film industries as a means both to make themselves visible and bring about social change.[62]

Between 1968 and 1973 a small number of programs were established for minority students, designed to train them for employment in the film industry. The New Communicators program in Los Angeles, funded by the U.S. Office of Economic Opportunity, was created in 1968, though it lasted only eight months. Longer lived was the University of California, Los Angeles (UCLA) Ethno-Communications Program, which lasted from 1969 to 1973. The University of Southern California also started a special admissions program for minorities during this time; and Stanford University had several Chicano students in its film program in the early 1970s.[63] From these programs emerged a cadre of Chicano/a filmmakers, who, together with other artists in the community, worked to become "producers of visual education."[64] Unlike their Anglo peers, they were not working on personal or private films. As documentary filmmaker Sylvia Morales explained about her work and that of fellow students of color at the Ethno-Communications program: "[F]or us there was a sense of urgency, so we set aside our desire to make personal films in order to make ones which reflected our communities."[65] Their mission was to use their artistic skills to create and produce documentary films and television programs that chronicled the struggles in the Mexican communities around issues that affected them, including educational inequities, racism, and police brutality. One of their fundamental goals was to educate the Mexican American community on these kinds of issues in order to encourage its members to unite and bring about social and political change.[66]

The first documentary film made by a Chicano about Chicanos dates back to 1969 with *I am Joaquin* (*Yo soy Joaquín*) by Luis Valdez, founder of El Teatro Campesino (the Farmworkers Theater) in the mid-1960s, and later director of *Zoot Suit* in 1981.[67] *I am Joaquin* is based on the 1967 poem by Rodolfo "Corky" Gonzales, one of the most important leaders of the Chicano Movement.[68] The technical aspects of the film are simple: still photography while Valdez narrates Gonzales' poem. Yet, the film is powerful in depicting Chicano children, families, and farmworkers with dignity; it also shows close-ups of Mexican murals and pre-Hispanic objects and places, and reveals the faces of great Mexican leaders, including Miguel Hidalgo y Costilla, Benito Juárez, Pancho Villa, and Emiliano Zapata. The film effectively ends with contemporary images of the Chicano Movement, as people of Mexican origin march with posters protesting the Vietnam War and carrying placards that read "Chicano Power" and "Accept me for what I am: Chicano." Indeed, the term "Chicano" was appropriated by Mexican American youth in the 1960s, stripping it from its previous pejorative connotation, when it was used by established Mexican Americans to refer to newly arrived Mexican immigrants who could not transcend their working-class status.[69] The youth, however, vested the term with a positive meaning: the affirmation of their mestizo identity, the claiming of their pre-Hispanic roots, and pride in Mexican culture.

Another important filmmaker from the 1960s was Jesús Salvador Treviño. A Chicano film student in the 1960s, he documented the fight for Chicanos' educational rights. He filmed the events that followed the 1968 walkout of more than ten thousand Chicano high school students in East Los Angeles to protest inferior schooling conditions.[70] In 1972 Treviño wrote and produced another documentary, *Yo Soy Chicano,* which traces Chicano history from its precolonial roots to the civil rights struggles of Mexican Americans in the early 1970s. In this documentary, he interviewed Chicano/a leaders from the late 1960s and 1970s, including Dolores Huerta, Reies López Tijerina, José Angel Gutiérrez, and Rodolfo "Corky" Gonzales, and he recorded their community activism.[71] The documentary was produced by the local PBS station

KCET in Los Angeles, and aired nationally in 1972, receiving accolades from, among others, the *Los Angeles Times* and the *Washington Post*.[72] Treviño went on to write and direct the film *Raíces de Sangre* (1977), a story about the struggles of Mexicans and Chicanos working in *maquiladoras* (labor-intensive factories located in Mexico-U.S. border towns) to create a labor union. Sylvia Morales also contributed to this nascent body of Chicano film with *Chicana* (1979), a documentary that traces the vital contributions of Mexican and Chicana women from Pre-Columbian times to the present.

The late 1960s and 1970s opened the door for these and other Chicano/as to work behind the camera in the film and television industries, and to address their own experiential specificity. Films created by Chicanos, however, flourished in the 1980s. Luis Valdez's 1981 film *Zoot Suit*, to which we will return shortly, broke ground as the first major studio-backed film written and directed by a Chicano. Treviño's film for PBS, *Seguin* (1981), also focused on a true historical story: that of Seguin, a Mexican *tejano* who fought in the Alamo for the American side, became mayor of San Antonio, and was later run out of town by Anglo dissidents. The 1982 film *The Ballad of Gregorio Cortez* (directed by Robert M. Young) is based on a novel written by Chicano writer Américo Paredes and tells the true story of a Chicano cowboy.[73] The 1983 film *El Norte*, directed by Chicano Gregory Nava, tells the story of two Guatemalan Indian siblings as they make their way to Los Angeles illegally in search of a better life. Chicano actor and director Cheech Marin also contributed to this growing body of films with *Born in East L.A.* (1987), a comedy about a Chicano who is mistakenly arrested in an immigration raid and deported to Mexico. The film focuses on his failed attempts to prove his identity and citizenship and return to the United States. That same year, Valdez's *La Bamba* (1987) was released, and it became a top-grossing film; it tells the story of real-life Chicano rock-and-roll star Ritchie Valens. *Break of Dawn* (1989, directed by Isaac Artenstein) chronicles another true story, this time of Pedro González, the first Spanish-language radio and recording star in the 1930s, sent to San Quentin prison on false charges. In *Stand and Deliver* (directed by Ramón Menéndez, 1988), based on a real-life story, Chicano actor Edward James Olmos portrayed the Latino math teacher who successfully worked with underachieving Chicano students in an East Los Angeles high school, despite institutional racism against them.

In the 1990s, there were fewer films by Chicanos about Chicanos. Edward James Olmos starred and directed in *American Me* (1992), a work that portrays with brutal honesty the consequences of gang involvement and violence from the point of view of one gang member. A few years later, Gregory Nava directed *My Family* (1995), a multi-generational saga of the Sanchez family, starring an all-Latino cast. He later directed *Selena* (1997), the story of real-life *tejana* singer, Selena Quintanilla, from her ascent to stardom to her murder. Robert Rodriguez wrote and directed modern day Westerns featuring Chicanos/Mexicans, including *El Mariachi* (1992) and *Desperado* (1995).

The first few years in 2000 have witnessed an even more dramatic decrease of films by Chicanos about Chicanos. Rodriguez did one more film based on his mariachi character in *Once Upon a Time in Mexico* (2003) and a series of films—*Spy Kids* (2001), *Spy Kids 2: Island of Lost Dreams* (2002), and *Spy Kids 3-D: Game Over* (2003) depicting a Latino family of spies. *A Day Without A Mexican* (2004, directed by Sergio Arau) presents a scenario of what would happen in California if Mexicans disappeared. *Walkout* (2006, directed by Edward James Olmos) is one of the most recent made-for-television films based on the 1968 Chicano student protests in East Los Angeles.[74]

Although this overview does not purport to be comprehensive, it provides an idea of the stereotypes of people of Mexican origin that have evolved and resurfaced over time in U.S. film, as well as the unique contributions of Chicano/a and Latino/a filmmakers in bringing Chicano/a characters to the screen. This, in turn, provides a contextual basis to analyze the unique contributions of two critical films: *Zoot Suit* and *Real Women Have Curves*. Central to this discussion is how these films re-present race and situate the Chicano/a characters within the discourse of separatism, acculturation, and the American Dream.

Re-Presenting Race

The films *Zoot Suit* and *Real Women Have Curves* contest Hollywood's traditional representations of race and typecasting. How this contestation manifests itself in the films is related to the points in time in which they were created—closely after the Chicano Movement for *Zoot Suit* (1981) and more than thirty years later for *Real Women* (2002).

Zoot Suit is based largely on two historical events, the Sleepy Lagoon incident and the Zoot Suit Riots. The Sleepy Lagoon incident took place in Los Angeles in 1942, when a gang of Mexican American youth (called *pachucos* or zoot suiters) were wrongly accused and convicted of murdering a Mexican American man. After a couple of years in jail, a court of appeals reversed the lower court's decision and set the young men free. The Zoot Suit Riots took place in June 1943. For several days, sailors on leave or on short-duration passes in Los Angeles would go on searches for men wearing zoot suits—the stylized clothing worn by a number of Mexican American youth—and would beat them up.[75] The event culminated when thousands of soldiers, sailors, and civilians went into Mexican American communities—including bars and movie theaters—to assault *pachucos* and strip them of their zoot suits. The police did not intervene, but instead arrested many of the Mexican Americans who had just been abused. Throughout the incident, the press labeled the sailors "heroes" and encouraged their behavior. The riots ended only with the intervention of the military authorities under pressure from Washington D.C.[76] The film *Zoot Suit* merges both historical events, though it does so in a stylized musical. It tells the story of the Sleepy Lagoon incident from the point of view of the gang leader, Hank Reyna, and his mythic alter ego (and occasionally his super ego) El Pachuco, played by renowned Chicano actor Edward James Olmos. By fusing this incident with the Zoot Suit Riots, the film conveys the institutional racism against Mexican Americans in Los Angeles in the 1940s, especially at the hands of the police, the judicial system, and the press.[77]

The film reconfigures racial representation at many levels; one way is through the story it tells and the casting of actors. Unlike most other Hollywood films, where whites are the protagonists of the story—with characters of Mexican origin in the background or as foils—*Zoot Suit* broke ground by placing Mexican Americans at the center of the story, despite their marginal position in society. Valdez presents a visual landscape of Mexican Americans as mestizos with brown skin and dark-colored eyes and hair. This is striking considering the trend in Hollywood films to depict people of Mexican origin who looked mestizo either as greasers or *bandidos*, or to place them as bodies in the background. Valdez's choice is connected to his deep involvement with the Chicano Movement and its pride in the mestizo identity of Mexican Americans, demonstrated by the slogan "Brown is beautiful." Some Chicanos at the time advocated that this pride be reflected in the film industry. For instance, Francisco Camplis, a film student in the early 1970s, exhorted that Chicano films "must emphasize and reestablish the intelligence, beauty, naturalness, of the *Indígeno, la morena, los prietos.*"[78]

Zoot Suit delves deeper into racial representations by exposing two opposing views of race. While scholars have analyzed the film in terms of its construction of cultural identity, especially through the characters of Hank Reyna and El Pachuco, this essay looks at the contrast of race as biologically determined and race as a cultural and social construction.[79] In the film, it is society's institutions that espouse the view of race as innate or biologically ascribed. The crucial scene that reveals this perspective is when Hank and three other members of his gang are being tried for murder and a white man reads a report in court about the "essence" of Mexicans. The statement asserts that while "Caucasians" use fisticuffs and kicking when fighting each other (acts considered "unsporting"), "the Mexican element considers all this to be a sign of weakness. All he knows and feels is the desire to use a knife to kill or to at least let blood. This inborn characteristic comes down from the blood-thirsty Aztecs."[80] The word "inborn" is a clear indicator of this view of biological determinacy, tacitly categorizing Mexicans as a biological racial group. The white judge's allowance of this report as evidence over the objections of the defense attorney illustrates society's widespread acceptance of such view, represented by its institutions, in this case the so-called justice system.

This scene in the film, closely based on the actual trial during the Sleepy Lagoon incident, needs to be understood in the context of the classification of Mexicans as white in the 1940s, who had been defined as such by a U.S. court since 1897 and in the 1940 U.S. census.[81] Yet, as legal scholar Ian Haney López lucidly demonstrates, legal courts relied on public opinion in determining whether someone was white or not.[82] The court scene in the film highlights the fact that no matter what the census or previous courts had stated, at that point in time mainstream society still believed that Mexicans were a separate racial group based on biological differences.

The biological or Mendelian view of race espoused by most Anglos in the film is set in contrast to the definition of "Chicano" proffered by the character of Tommy, the white, blond-haired *pachuco* member in Hank's gang.[83] In his exchange with Alice Bloomfield, the white woman helping them with their appeal, Tommy senses that, because he is white, Alice expects that he will share information with her that his Mexican American friends will not. He quickly clarifies, however, that he will not reveal any information and explains why he sticks to the same code as his fellows: "I'm in here because I hung around with Mexicans. But I grew up with these *batos,* and I'm a *pachuco* too, see? Simón, esa. You'd better learn what it means to be a Chicano." His words reflect an understanding of Mexicans, specifically Chicanos, as a group bound by social ties. In other words, one does not have to be born a Chicano to be one. This statement provides insight into Valdez's conceptualization of identity formation as one that is socially constructed, and how despite his active participation in the Chicano Movement he does not espouse in this film a narrow, biologi-cally determined, or essentialist definition of Chicano. This position diverges from that of some Chicano "nationalists" from the Movimiento who believed that to be Chicano one had to be of Mexican descent and display physiog-nomic or phenotypic evidence of *mestizaje* or racial mixing.[84] As the Chicana scholar Gloria Anzaldúa so aptly puts it, there is no one type of "real" Chi-cano or a singular Chicano experience.[85] In other words, Chicano is a culture to which anyone can belong given a common experience, shared codes, and understandings, of which language is an important factor. Tommy may be white, but he dresses in zoot suits and speaks Caló, the language of *pachucos,* adhering to Anzaldúa's notion that "ethnic identity is twin skin to linguistic identity—I am my language."[86] Interestingly, the fact that it is a white charac-ter who provides this perspective in the film reinforces the power of whites to decide whether Mexican or Chicano constituted a biological group or was a social construct. The Mexican American characters in the film seem power-less to fight designations imposed upon them, mirroring the reality of many Mexican Americans in the 1940s.

In re-presenting race, *Zoot Suit* inverts Hollywood's long history of de-picting Anglos/whites as heroes and men of Mexican origin as the villains, *bandidos* or criminals. In the film, it is the Mexican American youth who are wrongly accused and mistreated, while many whites—those upholding the racist system—are the bad guys. The white judge personifies the racism against Mexican Americans within the judicial system, as does police brutal-ity, while the press, embodied in a white male reporter, serves to feed racism by fomenting societal fears and anxieties about zoot suiters. In the film (as in the real-life event) it is the press that convicts Hank Reyna and the other *pachucos* before the decision is reached at the end of their trial; and it is the press that incites sailors and other "white" folk to "kill the Pachuco bastard," leading up to the scene that references the actual Zoot Suit Riots, in which zoot suiters were stripped of their clothes and beaten. The film, however, does not simply reverse Hollywood's trend of representing whites as good and Mexicans as their foils. *Zoot Suit* depicts some whites as allies, personified by Mr. Shearer, the gang's male attorney, by Tommy, the white *pachuco,* and by Alice, the Jewish woman who mobilizes the community to help with the gang's appeal and who serves as their link to the world outside of jail. The film, therefore is successful in departing from total "race" separation, allowing for positive interactions between whites and Mexican Americans and for some whites to permeate the Mexican community and adopt a Chicano identity. In doing so, the film allows for different audiences to connect to it. One white viewer, for instance, expressed that "those of us who are Anglos also come to identify with the Anglos in the story who genuinely care for [Mexican Americans] and for justice."[87]

Zoot Suit's reconfiguration of race representations is more complex when it comes to its depictions of romantic interactions. On the one hand, the relationships between Mexican Americans reinforce gender stereotypes. On the other hand, the film's inter-ethnic romantic ties complicate Hollywood's previous history of Anglo Mexican romances, whereby Anglo or white men are allowed to end up with Mexican/Chicana women, but Mexican/Chicano men are not allowed to do so with white women. The emphasis of the Chicano masculinity at the expense of Chicana women, and the stereotyped gender roles of Mexican American women in *Zoot Suit* have been strongly criticized by a number of scholars.[88] Chicana scholars in particular have found the Chicano/a portrayals and the objectification of the female characters problematic.[89] Angie Chabram-Dernersesian, for instance, argues that *Zoot Suit* reflects the Chicano cultural nationalism, which "subsumed the Chicana into a universal ethnic subject that speaks with the masculine instead of the feminine."[90] Similarly, Rosa Linda Fregoso argues that the film offers a masculine discourse because it is "about men, for men."[91] Filmmaker Sylvia Morales further criticizes Valdez for abusing dramatic license by providing stereotypes of Mexican and Chicana women and for his outright exclusion of Mexican American women's political activism in the Sleepy Lagoon case.[92] And scholar Yolanda Broyles-González finds the role of Chicana characters as either inconsequential or shallow, secondary to males, or falling into types: as the virgin or the whore, as the long-suffering mother, or the "cheap broad."[93]

Indeed, both of the Mexican American women romantically linked to Hank Reyna are portrayed through common stereotypes of Mexican women as prostitutes, virgins, or mothers. This is especially the case for his *pachuca* ex-girlfriend Bertha. The film implies that she is a woman of ill repute or a "*puta*," as Hank's mother describes *pachucas*. She is also depicted as a rabble-rouser and bad influence as she tries to incite Hank to kill a member of a rival gang. On the other hand, Hank's new girlfriend, Della, symbolizes the virgin in the trilogy in which Mexican women are often stereotyped. She says as much when she tells Hank that her father makes her feel like a nun. Hank, too, however, protects her status: "I promised to keep you out of trouble, remember?" This is a promise he has made to men—his father and hers—which reveals that rules are made by those in power: men. While initially Della is depicted in simplistic and stereotyped terms, her character, however, does expand beyond the typecast, at least to some degree. After she is released from a juvenile center (to which the judge in Hank's trial forcibly sends her for no apparent reason), she visits Hank in jail. She tells him that she still loves him and is willing to wait for him, but only if there is hope for the relationship: "If you still want me, *órale, suave* [good]. But if you don't that's okay too. But I'm not gonna hang around like a *pendeja* [idiot] all my life." Della's shift from passive to assertive in speaking up to Hank is reminiscent of the strength with which Alice (the gang's advocate) talks to Hank, a feature he finds compelling. The similar courage in Della allows him to fall in love with her a second time. When he kisses her, however, he does so on her hand (a traditional symbol of respect and honoring), without the passion with which he kisses Alice in a previous scene. Again, Hank's treatment of Della reverts back to the stereotyped role of the virgin.

Hank's romantic interest in Alice is more complex. No in-depth analysis of the relationship between Hank as a Chicano man and Alice as a Jewish woman has thus far been undertaken. Some scholars do not even identify her as Jewish but refer to her simply as "white" or erroneously as "Anglo."[94] Other scholars have identified her as Jewish, but their analysis of her place in the film is limited to a critique of Valdez, accusing him of portraying whites as "saviors" at the expense of giving Chicana characters more depth and portraying their involvement in the case with more historical accuracy. Some of Valdez's critics go so far as to question his motivations, suspecting him of trying to "ingratiate himself with the powers that be" or as a means to make the film more palatable to mainstream audiences, appealing especially to Jewish audiences.[95] The scene that marks the beginning of a serious romantic interest on Hank's part towards Alice is when he accuses her of being "just a white broad using Mexicans to play politics." Alice responds angrily, conveying the inequity she has endured in helping his gang's cause, including criticism, distrust, and discrimination from the Mexican community because she is a Jew. Alice's emotional and honest response wins Hank over. He tells her that she has "guts" because no one has ever dared talk to him like that. Implicit in the film is that, while he may be considered inferior in society as a Mexican American, he has courage, a raceless trait. When Alice matches his courage, they become equals in this respect. Hank's romantic interest in Alice reverses the general Hollywood romantic formula of successfully pairing white males with Mexican-origin women. It falls, instead, in the company of very few

Hollywood films prior to *Zoot Suit* where the male romantic protagonist is Mexican American and the woman is white. Yet, similarly to these films, the romance between Hank and Alice is not allowed to flourish. Alice's rejection of Hank, however, is not due to her whiteness nor because she perceives herself as superior. There are multiple interpretations that can be made of the line she utters to signal her rejection: "I can't be your mother, or your sister, or your *huisa* (girlfriend) or your white broad." One reading is that she cannot fulfill the needs she perceives him to have. Another, perhaps more convincing interpretation is that he cannot fulfill her needs because he fixes both Mexican American and white women within prescribed categories. Therefore, Hank's concept of what a woman should be (and, tacitly, the limitations he places on her) does not satisfy Alice's own expectations. But this does not impede Hank from transgressing what was considered a racial boundary, as evident in his response: "nobody's asking you to be a white broad." This line reflects the fact that he no longer thinks of Alice merely as white and as a (sexual) goal to attain, but that his understanding of her identity has become more complex. The fact that she is Jewish—a member of a group that also experienced racism (indeed at points in U.S. history Jews were not considered white)—allows her to cross borders with more ease, or potentially for Hank to see her differently than he does other white people.[96] Furthermore, it is important to understand that the historical period in which the film takes place, 1942 to 1944, falls at the time that Nazism and Hitler's extermination of Jews was taking place, partly under the propaganda that they were racially inferior. While Mexicans were called mongrels or dogs in the United States, Jews were depicted as rats in Nazi Germany. The parallels between Mexican Americans in the United States and Jews under Nazi-sieged nations cannot be ignored in analyzing the film.[97] Ultimately, however, Alice does not reciprocate Hank's feelings, claiming that she falls in love with the causes she fights for, not the people. Although, as mentioned before, the lack of romantic development in the film falls within a long history of thwarted romances between Mexican men and non-Mexican women, Valdez may have chosen it to expose the story between the real-life gang leader in the Sleepy Lagoon case and his Jewish advocate. However, the film also reveals the prevailing social condemnation of some inter-ethnic relationships in the United States during the 1940s.

Like *Zoot Suit*, *Real Women Have Curves* (2002) contributes to reconfiguring the representation of race and gender although it does so in a radically different way, partly because it was created twenty years later. *Real Women* is a "coming-of-age" film from the point of view of a Mexican American girl. It is based on the life of Josefina López, who first wrote the play in 1988 and later co-wrote the screenplay for the film, which was released in 2002.[98] Unlike *Zoot Suit,* which received mixed reviews from scholars and audiences (considered too difficult to grasp by general audiences, especially monocultural or monolingual ones), *Real Women* took the film industry by storm, becoming a box office success and winning the "Audience Award" and a "Special Jury Award for Acting" at the 2002 Sundance Film Festival.[99] It has also received mostly accolades from different audiences, including mainstream white viewers.[100] The film tells the story of Ana, an eighteen year-old Mexican American woman about to graduate from high school, as she negotiates between her Mexican and American worlds in terms of class, education, and prescribed gender roles. Her Mexican world is represented by her family and the Mexican community of East Los Angeles, while her American world is represented by the high school she attends in Beverly Hills and its upper-class white students. Unlike *Zoot Suit,* this film does not focus on direct acts of racism; yet, the issue of race, ethnicity, and cultural identity are at the core of the film.

An essential means by which *Real Women* contests the representation of race is through the casting of actors. In a recent study commissioned by the Screen Actors Guild (2000), Latino actors reported comments from casting directors as to what Mexican actors should look like: "We wanted somebody who was Mexican. We wanted somebody dirty. He (the actor) was white as far as we were concerned" or "You're not Mexican. You have green eyes."[101] *Real Women* challenges this notion by casting Latino/a actors who reflect the physiognomic diversity that exists within the Mexican American community, a result of more than four centuries of *mestizaje* or racial mixing among Indians, blacks, Asians, and Europeans—who in turn have their own history of mixing as well.[102] In *Real Women,* Ana's family and the women working in her sister's clothing factory stand for this heterogeneity. The characters range from having light skin and light-colored eyes to darker skin, hair, and eyes. By showing the phenotypic diversity of people of Mexican origin, the film successfully expands racial casting in ways that other films have not.

Zoot Suit reconfigured racial casting by placing brown bodies at the center, echoing the "Brown is beautiful" motto of the Chicano Movement, and in this sense broke with the Hollywood tradition of privileging light skin to depict non-villainous Mexican/Chicano protagonists. *Real Women* is groundbreaking as it challenges the idea of one look for people of Mexican origin, and does not correlate skin color with class, behavior, or character traits (villain versus hero; honorable versus infamous). Equally significant, the film opposes the race casting encouraged by some Chicano nationalists who have essentialized the mestizo image and fail to realize that they are reproducing the color caste system that harks back to the racial classification system of colonial Spanish America.[103] In this sense, *Real Women*'s wide array of representations more closely aligns with Arturo Aldama's and Gloria Anzaldúa's sophisticated notions of *mestizaje*. For Aldama *mestizaje* goes beyond a mixture of Spanish and Indian. It is an "ethnic, sexual, and political challenge to re-vision systems of being that celebrate the multiplicity of consciousness."[104] Anzaldúa describes a *mestiza* as someone who straddles several cultures.[105]

The reconfiguration of race representations in *Real Women,* however, is more complex when it comes to romantic relationships. The romance between Ana and her classmate Jimmy, a white, affluent young man, complicates the long-standing Hollywood formula, whereby the Mexican woman ends up with her Anglo "savior." The choice of making Ana's boyfriend a white man has not escaped some audience members. One female viewer, for instance, commented: "I was intimidated by the white boyfriend because of what it might say to young Latinos in America."[106] Implicit in this quote is the possibility that Latinos may see themselves as inferior to white men. Screenwriter Josefina López justifies this decision because her own first boyfriend was white, but she is quick to explain that "he doesn't save her" and they do not ride into the sunset, as has been the case in many Westerns.[107] Nevertheless, this explanation does not fully address the multiple and contradictory messages of this romantic representation. Despite López's argument that Ana develops her self-worth on her own, Jimmy is instrumental, perhaps even a catalyst, in helping her gain a sense of self-acceptance and self-worth at a turning point in her life. When Ana shares with him that her mother has called her fat, he tells her, "You're not fat; you're beautiful," contradicting her mother, who embodies her Mexican world. It is through Jimmy's perception of Ana as beautiful that she gains confidence in herself.

However, the representation of the white man/Mexican woman romance breaks away from Hollywood's formulaic portrayal of Mexican women as dependent on white men for their survival.[108] This is established after Ana and Jimmy's love scene, when Jimmy tells her that he will write or e-mail her from college. To this, Ana responds: "No Jimmy, really, don't worry about me anymore." It is clear that she will not sit around pining for him or even contact him. It is implicit that he was her first love, not her only one. Eventually she too leaves California for New York. The film's closing scene reveals a sophisticated-looking Ana strutting confidently in the streets of Manhattan.

Representing Separatism, Assimilation, and the American Dream

Hollywood has tended to depict people of Mexican origin according to three specific and stereotyped narratives. In the first one, individuals of Mexican origin are classified as outsiders who cannot or should not try to cross the symbolic racial border into U.S. white mainstream culture. A second narrative is that of assimilation or the melting pot, where people of Mexican origin can attain the "American Dream" if they follow the individualist ethos established by Anglo society. Third, there is the narrative presented in Hollywood gang movies that classify Mexican Americans as living in communities of color, isolated from white neighborhoods, and inhabiting a world of self-destruction. *Zoot Suit* expands and problematizes these narratives, especially the assimilationist one, while *Real Women* reinforces the narrative of acculturation and assimilation.

In *Zoot Suit* Mexican Americans are represented as an outsider community that is not accepted by the broader U.S. society. The film also reveals how the Mexican American youth subculture of *pachucos* or zoot suiters experiences a double rejection: the first comes from white society at large, and the second from the older generation of Mexican Americans and those working within institutions (e.g., Mexican American police officers). For this subculture of *pachucos,* there is also a dilemma they struggle with: on the one hand a desire to state their difference, and on the other their wish to fit into mainstream society.

This film masterfully presents many of the oppositional practices of this *pachuco* subculture, most evident in the zoot suit clothes or "drapes"—a style of urban survival. As the character of El Pachuco (Hank Reyna's alter-ego) puts it, "Our *pachuco* realities will only make sense if you grasp their stylization." The *pachuco* subculture is also highlighted in the use of its unique language. Anzaldúa explains that the language of the zoot suiters was a language of rebellion against standard Spanish and standard English. It created slang words from both languages, not intended to be understood by those outside the group nor by Mexican American adults.[109] Furthermore, according to Marcos Sánchez-Tranquilino, the *pachuco* culture exemplified a greater *mestizaje* because it was "an assemblage" of multiple dualities—"rural and urban, Eastside and Westside, Mexican and American."[110]

Zoot Suit, however, does more than simply present an anti-assimilation narrative. It presents a complex story that reflects the struggles of the *pachucos* in defining their identity. But while many—such as Hank and his brother— are separatists (and use their clothing and language to mark their distinct identity), they also aspire to the "American Dream," specifically to join the military as a ticket to becoming fully integrated into what is perceived as the broader society. The film highlights the beliefs espoused by some *pachucos* that by joining this institution and risking their lives to serve the country, they would prove their worthiness as "American" and would no longer be classified as "Other." Hank's enlistment in the navy makes this point evident. His father tells him, "I'm glad you're leaving all the pachuco *mierda* [shit] behind you. And I'm proud you're in the navy." The father's words underscore the rigid categories to which young Mexican American men could belong: they could either be *pachuco*s or lowlifes, or be in the navy and prove their patriotism by joining the armed forces.[111]

The illusion of the American Dream further complicates the identity struggles among *pachucos*. This is illustrated in a scene where a Mexican American zoot suiter from another gang wants to beat up a navy man. When Hank does not allow it, the zooter challenges him. "You think you're some kind of hot shit just 'cause the navy accepted you, ah, *ese*?" Hank responds, "As if you didn't try." This exchange tacitly demonstrates that the military represents the "American Dream" where bravery lies in one's character and not in one's race. The navy man that Hank saves becomes the symbol of this dream, for which Hank is ready to kill a Mexican American, a symbol of his own Mexican identity. Through the figure of El Pachuco, the film comments on this ambivalence or liminality: "That's exactly what the show needs right now, *ese,* two more Mexicans killing each other . . . Control yourself, Hank. Don't hate your *raza* [race/people] more than you love the gringo." It is also El Pachuco that gives Hank a reality check: "Forget the war overseas, *carnal* [brother], your war is on the home front." Ironically, while Hank saves the navy man, it is a group of sailors, who epitomize Anglo society in general, that later attack the *pachucos*. This attack reveals that, while Hank wants to become part of American society, society is unwilling to fully embrace him and those like him. The paradox highlighted by the film is that Mexican Americans—both in the film and in real life—did not really have agency to change their classification. The power to allow them to change categories rested in the hands of the Anglo world (e.g., institutions such as the navy, which decided who could join).

Zoot Suit ends with a series of alternative scenarios for Hank after he is released from jail, narrated by different characters. According to the press, he will end up in jail again for robbery and assault with a deadly weapon. In jail he will kill an inmate and when finally released, he will get into hard drugs. The judge, too, will always see Hank as nothing more than a "lowly" zoot suiter. The press and the judge embody the larger U.S. society (and those in power) who perceive Hank as having only one identity—a criminal—and echo an essentialist and racist position. Hank's brother, on the other hand, provides a different ending in which Hank joins the military, is killed in battle, and is awarded a Medal of Honor posthumously. This ending represents society's acceptance of Hank, but only once he has died for the United States, giving up both culture and life (self), as proof that he is indeed an "American." It is Alice Bloomfield, Hank's advocate and romantic interest, who provides an ending that embraces the co-existence of multiple identities for Chicanos, moving beyond essentialist forms of classification. She imagines Hank and Della married with five children, "three of whom are now attending university, speaking *pachuco* slang and calling themselves Chicanos." Her view also redefines education, not the military, as the new banner of the "American Dream."

In contrast to the multiple forms of identity for Mexican Americans posited in *Zoot Suit*, *Real Women* reinforces a discourse of acculturation and assimilation.[112] Ana can reach the "American Dream" by obtaining a good education and going to college.[113] Her teacher, Mr. Guzman—also a Latino—serves as the bridge between Ana's family—the first generation to come to the United States—and Ana's aspirations for a better education and, implicit in that, upward mobility.[114] It is he who insists that she complete her application to Columbia University and uses his contacts with the university to push her application along. And finally, as an acculturated Latino working in a white upper-class environment, Ana's teacher serves to remind her family of the "American Dream." As he tells Ana's father: "Sir, you left your country for a better opportunity. And now it's Ana's turn."

In fostering a narrative of acculturation and assimilation, *Real Women* provides conflicting perspectives on the Mexican American family. On the one hand, the film offers a typical representation of the Mexican American household, whereby some members do not support education and have very prescribed roles for women, exemplified by Ana's mother Carmen.[115] Here, however, the family is not united in this front. When her husband suggests that Ana go to college, Carmen responds: "Yo la puedo educar; yo le enseño a coser, y le enseño a criar a sus hijos, atender a su marido. Esas cosas no le van a enseñar en el colegio" ["I can teach her. I can teach her to sew; I can teach her to raise her kids and take care of her husband. Those are things they won't teach her in school"]. This representation, some would argue, may offer an accurate portrayal of the role of women, for dominant paradigms are transmitted through culture; and though the rules and law are made by those in power, the men, it is the women who transmit them.[116] Indeed, playwright Josefina López speaks of, and writes about, the oppression by men perpetuated and reinforced by mothers.[117] In *Real Women,* it is Ana's mother who transmits the cultural notions of womanhood associated with the Mexican culture (and Catholicism), especially the importance of chastity and of marriage.[118] The film, however, destabilizes the mother's traditionalist notions when Ana goes away to college and espouses the American ethos of individualism to attain the "American Dream." Because U.S. society promotes children going away to college, Ana does exactly that, leaving her family behind. In the closing of the film, as she struts in the streets of New York, she has flourished, now that she is away from her mother's oppression. With her newfound freedom she separates herself from Mexican traditions, those considered limiting and obsolete—such as traditional notions of womanhood—but also the more positive ones, such as collectivity and familial unity.

The film also succeeds in subverting the stereotype of the macho Mexican man (and of Latino men in general) as violent or as non-supportive of women. Through positive representations of Mexican and Latino men, the film presents an alternative to the hierarchical structure of *machismo,* at least in this family—a purposeful decision by those involved in the making of the film, because they wanted to show positive male role models.[119] It is Ana's father who tries to convince his wife that Ana should go to college, and ultimately supports Ana's decision. And it is her grandfather who facilitates her encounters with Jimmy (by lying to the family as to her whereabouts), which allows her to break gender rules and explore her sexuality—part of her process of acculturation.

In tackling the subject of separatism, assimilation, and acculturation, *Zoot Suit* and *Real Women Have Curves* offer glimpses into the liminal or interstitial state in which people of Mexican origin live in the United States—whether they have been in the country for generations or are recent immigrants. *Zoot*

Suit presents Mexican Americans as having a more complex relationship with both U.S. mainstream and with the Mexican American community, simultaneously desiring to assimilate, separate, and obtain the "American Dream." *Real Women* offers a more basic perspective: the main protagonist does not wish to separate but to adapt; to do so it becomes necessary to displace some of the Mexican values she grew up with in order to attain what she views as the "American Dream."

Conclusion

The ways in which *Zoot Suit* and *Real Women Have Curves* configure and reconfigure race, gender, and Chicano/a identity are related to the period in which the films were produced and to the experiences and agendas of their creators. *Zoot Suit* provides a more complex portrayal of race and identity because it was written and filmed close in time to the Chicano Civil Rights Movement by Luis Valdez, who was closely involved with the Movement. Born in 1940, Valdez understood the world in which Mexican Americans lived before the Movimiento, where the youth felt neither Mexican nor American, and where institutional and individual racism were endemic. With the Chicano Movement came a redefinition of identity, in which young Mexican Americans could take pride in their pre-Hispanic roots, reclaim their mestizo identity, own the motto "Brown is beautiful," and leave behind the desire to assimilate.

Real Women was created thirty years after the Chicano Movement, and it was first written as a play by Josefina López in the late 1980s, when she was barely out of high school. As a member of the generation that came after that of the Chicano Movement (she was born in 1969), the issues that concerned her were different than Valdez's. Growing up, López did not know the meaning of the word *Chicano* until she learned about Chicano history in college.[120] Furthermore, issues of racism and civil rights were not in the forefront of American consciousness (or not to the same magnitude as in the 1960s) when the screenplay was written. This is probably why *Real Women* does not portray a struggle over identity with the same intensity as *Zoot Suit*. Here, the main protagonist is both Mexican and American, and there is no institutional racism—at least not in the educational arena—hindering her ability to achieve the "American Dream." The struggle is more on a personal and familial level, instead of a social one. Additionally, the fact that the film director of *Real Women* (Patricia Cardoso) came from Colombia to the United States at the age of twenty-five to study filmmaking at UCLA may limit her understanding of the struggle for many Mexican immigrants and Mexican Americans of low socio-economic status.[121] In other words, she came in a position of privilege. In contrast, Luis Valdez was the son of farmworkers. These experiences certainly color their filmic lens.

The different genres of the films also impact their representation of race. *Zoot Suit* is based on historical events that exposed the blatant institutional racism that existed in the 1940s and shook the Mexican American community to its core. *Real Women* is based on Josefina López's life and belongs to the coming-of-age film genre; as a result, it tackles conflicts that arise at the personal and family level, as opposed to issues that emerge from broader institutional realities. Finally, the gender of both the creators and protagonists of these films sets them apart. *Zoot Suit* presents mostly a male viewpoint at the expense of females, reflecting the male-dominated perspective that plagued the Chicano Movement and alienated many Chicanas, who had a double struggle to contend with: as Mexican Americans fighting racism, and as women battling the sexism within the Chicano community. In *Real Women* the sexism comes from the women, while Mexican men are seen as allies. Also, the film presents contemporary times in which women are considered equal to men (even if often only nominally), and where they no longer have to fit under prescribed roles for them as "virgins, mothers, and whores."[122]

The different perspectives of *Zoot Suit* and *Real Women Have Curves,* as related to their place in history, leave us, then, with an important set of questions. As time continues to pass, and the perception of Mexicans and Chicanos continues to change depending on the political and economic climate of the United States, how will mainstream films (mis)educate viewers as to people of Mexican origin? How will the Hollywood film industry revive old stereotypes or create new ones? And how will Chicano/a filmmakers push back? More pointedly, how will generational differences impact the work of the younger Chicano/a filmmakers, and their desire (or lack thereof) to create identity-based work? We are presently witnessing another wave of nativism, which in the past has brought back to the screen negative and racist stereotypes of Mexicans and Chicanos. The push to seal off the U.S. border as a way to restrict Mexican and other Latin American immigrants has led to draconian laws being debated in Congress, which would punish undocumented immigrants heavily with truly damaging consequences. Already, Mexican filmmaker Sergio Arau has created the 2004 film *A Day Without A Mexican,* which portrays the demise of the California economy should Mexicans leave the state. But we now wait to see how Hollywood mainstream films will portray this issue and how Chicano/a and other filmmakers will contest such representations. As this essay illustrates, it is crucial that we understand such films not in a vacuum, but in the context of the political, economic, social, and cultural climate of the United States and its shifts over time. Only then can we fully grasp Hollywood's response to such changes and, if necessary, counter them. Otherwise, we are left with reels that will appear as real and will further contribute to the miseducation of audiences; reels that perpetrate arbitrary systems of classification with truly damaging effects.

9 Pose and Poseur
The Racial Politics of Guillermo Gómez-Peña's Photo-Performances

Jennifer González and Guillermo Gómez-Peña

(In this conversation, an art theorist and a performance artist discuss race, hybridity, border culture, globalization-gone-wrong, and the politics of representation. This conversation took place during November 2005, via e-mail and phone.)

JG: I'm interested in the way race, as a visual discourse appears in the works you call "photo-performances." These images create the conditions of a non-narrative yet highly iconographic interface between performer and camera. The photo-performance can be seen as an extension of your earlier works, including what you call your first self-conscious performative gesture in the photograph *El vaquero poblano* (fig. 9.1) in which you pose as a young adult astride a children's artificial horse wearing a toy gun and cowboy hat in Puebla, Mexico. Your body is clearly out of scale with the toy horse, and the hat you wear is perched ironically, but the image also exudes a melancholic or a nostalgic yearning for childhood innocence. How does this image encapsulate your interest in the role of the photographic pose? Is it possible to argue that the photo-performance is a new genre? Are there artistic precedents that shape this contemporary practice?

GP: Mexican culture has always been extremely performative. From the dioramas of *santos* found in colonial churches and the *casta* paintings to the pop photographs of the early twentieth century depicting burlesque divas, not to mention the *calendarios* (calendars) of Helguera in the 1940s, Mexico has always been fascinated with the staging of extreme performance personas.

Figure 9.1. *El vaquero poblano.* Shot in
Puebla by a street photographer, 1975.
Photo: Courtesy of La Pocha Nostra.

Sometimes these personas embody idealized or demonized identities; other
times, they depict imaginary identities codified in colonial fantasy. This performativity is in my DNA. My own family has developed a rich iconographic
history of staged photography, which definitely influenced my sensibility.
In fact, I've been working on a long-term project selecting and digitizing
my family photos that go back to the late 1800s. With the help of some relatives I've archived more than three hundred photos, spanning a century of
family history. Many of these images are so self-consciously dramatic and
stylized that they could easily compete in outrageousness with my photo-
performance work. One day, I'd love to publish a book juxtaposing my family
photos with my photo-performances.

Other influences in my performance work include Chicano/border pop
and street culture, specially low-rider and "pinto" iconography, underground

commix, velvet painting, and rare border b-movies. I love this combination of high style and boldness. I'm also interested in the work of Mexican
political activists like Superbarrio, Marcos, and Fray Tormenta, who utilize
performance strategies and symbolic gestures to distribute ideas and generate
public dialogue.

In terms of contemporary art, I feel a certain kinship with other performance artists who have ventured into photography as an extension of their
performance work. Ana Mendieta and Marina Abramovich come to mind;
Ron Athey, and Franco Bas as well . . . And of course, our conceptual grandfather el señor Marcel Duchamp's "Rrose Sélavy" was perhaps the first avant
garde "photo-performance" ever.

JG: There is no spoken or written narrative in the photo-performance, yet
each tableaux produced by the participants suggests scenes or a sequence of
"acts." The camera apparatus participates as the framing device for a series
of elaborate poses on the part of the various players. Each series is comprised
of a set of related images, with costume elements and props being recycled
and shared by different actors so that there's a kind of identity slippage—
across gender and ethnic lines—between the various imaginary characters
portrayed. This sharing and recycling offers viewers a set of clues about the
performance event itself; it's clear that the actors and the photographer play
out their collaboration in real time. We're seeing images that are striking on
their own, but that share with conceptual art an emphasis on the process of
production as much as on the final result; the focus lies on the interface between the performers and the camera, on the act of posing per se, on the simultaneously intimate and public dialog that takes place in this relation of
lens and body. How do you conceive of the relation between the kinds of pose
your performances enact, and the idea of posing in general? How are these
images both like and unlike portraiture?

GP: In my "photo-performance" projects (as in my video projects), my goal
has been to attempt to find a more enlightened and complex "interface" between my live performance work and the camera, one beyond merely witnessing, illustrating, documenting, or even "interpreting" performance. The
main epistemological question infusing these projects has been: how to create a more surprising and "dialogical" relationship between the performance
artist who creates both the concept and the implied narratives and offers his
body/identity/map/arte-facto in sacrifice to the camera, and the photographer

who filters it, frames it and, in doing so, inevitably re-creates it. In this sense, I see the photographer not just as a technician but as an accomplice, and the camera as my implied audience. I constantly challenge them, and invite them to challenge me. I question their power to frame me, to "capture" me, to explicate me. I like to question the power relations inherent in the relationship that exists between the performance artist and the photographer.

More than looking for a pose that works for the camera, I write in advance some conceptual parameters and then, once in the studio, I invite my performance colleagues working with me to play within these parameters. I ask them to develop a sense of being in the space, a certain presence and an attitude, a way of relating to objects and costumes, of connecting symbolically to other bodies. It's like a jamming session indirectly coordinated by me. This is precisely where I feel that the originality of my photographic images lies. They come from a different place than traditional portraiture. They're generated by a different methodology. That's why for me it's extremely important to only work with people I know and like; with artists and photographers who are very familiar with my performance work and whom I trust.

Photo shoots have always helped me clarify my performance personas and have forced me to pay attention to every symbolic detail in my costume and to the political and cultural implications of the human body as a site for creation. In this sense, performance photos are like heightened excerpts of a live performance that never took place. That's precisely why I call them "photo-performances."

We can divide my photographic work into two main periods: prior to 2000, I engaged in all kinds of experiments with the intersection of photography and performance; among others, I photographed my performance personas within the context of an installation. I took these same performance personas and inserted them in public spaces, in politically and historically charged sites and buildings. I juxtaposed them with "normal" people and with local eccentrics I came across during the performance "intervention." I also staged photo shoots in the middle of a live performance and allowed a photographer to shoot a portion of the piece as a performative action to be witnessed by a live audience. I invited fashion and socialite photographers to accompany me and my performance colleagues on public adventures, hitting all types of clubs in costume and staging impromptu tableaux vivants. We asked the photographers to go along with the fiction and behave as if they were part of a "celebrity" event. Once in New York we worked with real paparazzi and crashed all the celebrity parties in our Mexterminator regalia. It was a very sad night because most people in those circles related to us in a very frivolous and at times humiliating manner—to them we were like experimental mariachis—but the photos were fantastic.

Then in 2002 my friend, the Spanish curator Orlando Britto, challenged me to begin to think of my photo-performances as art "objects" in themselves. He invited me to create portfolios strictly for the art world; to think of large formats and complete series; to professionalize my photographic praxis so to speak. He actually commissioned the first five portfolios.

JG: Although the images are clearly well planned and staged, "jamming" implies improvisation. How important is improvisation to this process? Can you say more about this in relation to your performances in general?

GP: The same methodology I utilize to create images in a live performance I tend to use in my photo shoots. Although our performance work is scripted and planned, there's always space for improvisation. In the past few years, we've invited our audiences to co-create the performance with us, right there, as it's taking place. We invite them to try out props and costumes and to develop a fictional identity. Once they've altered their identities in situ, we invite them to insert themselves inside our tableaux vivants and to alter the dynamics of the image and the fate of the performance. It's exciting and dangerous. It can easily turn into bad art, but we take the risk, and most of the time, it works.

Now in the photo sessions it's the same energy and *locura*. If we invite local eccentrics and non-artists to partake in our madness, and we often do, we treat them respectfully as collaborators and not just as models. We invite them to co-create images and play with costumes, props, symbols, nudity, body markings. Besides the core members of La Pocha Nostra (Michele Ceballos, Violeta Luna, Roberto Sifuentes, Emiko R. Lewis, Silvia Antolín Guerra, Orlando Britto, and Gabriela Salgado) and our artist associates in various cities and countries where the photo-shoots have taken place, you can find in my photos all kinds of interesting people with performative personalities, including curators, intellectuals, farm workers, sex radicals, activists, eccentric socialites . . . even lawyers (fig. 9.2). One of the main models in "Post-México en X-paña," Luisa, is a very prominent criminal lawyer in Madrid. In "Ethno-techno," the "neo-Victorian tourist" is Rebecca Solnit, the Pulitzer Prize–winning author.

Figure 9.2. *Telenovela española.* From the portfolio "Post-México en X-paña," created in Madrid with Javier Caballero, 2005. Photo: Courtesy of Orlando Britto-Jinorio and Galería Artificios, Las Palmas de Gran Canaria.

JG: The settings for many of the images are very intimate spaces, small rooms, houses, or even just a simple backdrop. How does the scene in which the actors appear come into play when you're thinking about the constructed universe of the personas? How important is the stage set?

GP: When I began to work more purposely with photographers to develop series for galleries and museums, my aesthetics shifted a bit. I began to place my performance personas in the limbo of a black box theater or against the white walls of a gallery, because I wanted the viewer to concentrate on the complexity of the performance personas. The adorned body, the intervened body, riddled with cultural and political implications was the subject matter. The "space" surrounding them was meant to be a "neutral zone" as opposed to culturally specific locations as in my prior work. In a few instances I've chosen to place these personas inside a house or a highly designed environment, but these surroundings become mere prosthetic extensions of the hyper-identity of the performance persona; the backdrop of the living diorama so to speak.

JG: To date you've conducted three photo-performances specifically for gallery exhibitions: one in Mexico called "Post-Mexicans" with photojournalist Miguel Velasco, one in San Francisco called "Ethno-Techno" with fashion photographer James McCaffrey, and the series "Post-México en X-paña" at the international art fair ARCO Madrid with photographer Javier Caballero.[1] I understand that two more projects are in the works and will appear in 2006. For each photo-performance you select a different kind of photographer and a different set of cultural issues that ground the work in its specific locale. Is the photo-performance always thematically linked to its geographical region? Is the photo-performance ultimately a kind of site-specific practice?

GP: As part of this new process, I've become much more specific in terms of my choice of the photographer, and the guest performers. All these decisions are carefully made, taking into consideration the geographic location and the subject matter I wish to explore. My most recent photographic project took place last month in the Gran Canaria (Canary Islands), one of the main entryways for African and Arab immigrants into Spain. Since I wanted to explore Spain's fear of immigration, I chose to work with a Canarian photographer who was familiar with the issue and with my work, and I invited immigrant artists to work with La Pocha. So you may say that there is a certain site-specificity in the new work, but at the same time I see all my photo-performances as part of a larger project which I'm in the process of articulating. The working title of the overall project is "The New Barbarians." Next year City Lights will publish a catalogue comprising the first five photo-performances.

JG: If theatricality presents the critical point of departure for you, it's not because it's something prized in either documentary or fine art photography—or in its critical reception. Michael Fried's recent essay "Barthes' Punctum" revisits that author's negative discussion of theatricality in photographic production noting that "A further dimension of Barthes' antitheatricalism emerges when we consider his engagement with the pose, the theatrical element in photography par excellence."[2] Fried points out that the theatricality Barthes rejects in photographic practice co-exists with his recognition that photography is, by nature, an inherently theatrical medium. This apparent contradiction is to be found in his discussion of the pose. Fried cites Barthes at length, who writes: "Now, once I feel myself observed by the lens, everything changes; I instantly constitute myself in the process of 'posing,' I instantaneously make another body for myself, I transform myself in advance into an image. This transformation is an active one; I feel that the Photograph creates my body or mortifies it, according to caprice."[3] He also writes, "In front of the lens, I am at the same time; the one I think I am, the one I want others to think I am, the one the photographer thinks I am, and the one he makes use of to exhibit his art. In other words, a strange action: I do not stop imitating myself, and because of this, each time I am (or let myself be) photographed, I invariably suffer from a sensation of inauthenticity, sometimes of imposture (comparable to certain nightmares)."[4] In addition to revealing a productive intellectual paradox concerning photography's theatrical qualities, Barthes' articulation of the experience of the pose could also serve as a remarkably accurate description of the experience of being racially stereotyped: the body is made to perform, to become mortified as a racial type, to be self-imitative as a form of imposture, to live the nightmare of being little more than the projected image of others. How can we think of race as inextricably linked to costumes and the pose? Can you say more about race as a performance?

GP: As a performance artist I'm fully aware of the mechanisms of identity construction. Whether conscious or unconscious, for me, the constructions of race are always connected to the performativity of the racialized body, and in this sense costumes, props, make-up, body paint, cultural artifacts, and the symbolic positions we choose for the body are all part of it. Many "artists of color" are interested in the staging of authenticity; others in the debunking of authenticity. I'm more interested in the conscious staging of artificial authenticity, and in the questioning of this staging process, as it happens in front of an audience or in front of the camera.

JG: What do you see as the links, if any, between the theatricality of the photo-performance and the history of photography as it intersects with racial discourse?

GP: In the late 1980s and early 1990s I was part of that whole generation of artists (James Luna, Coco Fusco, Fred Wilson, etc.) who decided to engage in a dialogue with radical anthropologists such as Barbara Kirschenblatt-Gimblett, James Clifford, Michael Taussig, and Roger Bartra. We were part of the larger project of challenging and deconstructing the colonial gaze of anthropology, which we felt was analogous to the gaze of the "multi-cultural" art world of the time. I called our artistic project "reverse anthropology." The basic premise was for the performance artist to assume a fictional "center" and to push so-called mainstream culture to the margins, and treat it as exotic and unfamiliar. The idea was for us to question the exoticizing gaze of the viewer by placing a distorting mirror between "us" (the insurrected "object" of contemplation or study) and "them." Instead of explaining our artificially constructed "Otherness" to the audience, we were making art in hopes of explaining America to itself through our own displaced sensibilities. To attain this, we placed the audience member/viewer in the position of a "foreigner" or a "minority" in our performance country. This major epistemological insurrection took place from 1988 to 1992. "Border Brujo" and "The Couple in the Cage" were classic pieces of this period.

In 1992, during the heated Columbus debates, Coco Fusco and I decided to remind the United States and Europe of "the other history of intercultural performance": the sinister human exhibits, pseudo-ethnographic tableaux vivants, and living dioramas that were so popular in Europe from the seventeenth century up to the early twentieth century; and that in the United States evolved into more vulgar versions at the turn of the century . . . the dime attractions, roadside museums, and freak shows. However, the premise was similar: "Authentic primitives" were exhibited as human artifacts and mythical specimens in cages, taverns, salons, and fairs, as well as in museums of "Ethnography" and Natural History, next to samples of their homeland's flora and fauna. Their costumes and ritual artifacts were designed by the impresario curator and had nothing to do with reality (fig. 9.3). This sinister practice contributed greatly to the mythologies that Europeans and Americans constructed to rationalize their impression of inhabitants of the New World as cannibals or noble savages. Sadly many of these misperceptions are still present in contemporary mass media and pop cultural depictions of the Latino "Other."

My main concerns have shifted since, but every now and then, my interest in the dark and racist corners of ethnography and anthropology reappears in some of my new images. I recently did a photo shoot in Oaxaca with Mexican photojournalist Antonio Turok, subcomandante Marcos's first photographer. We invited several local and international performance artists to be part of it. Most of the images we created ended up being a commentary on the Orientalist gaze of the North imposed on Oaxaca. I remember asking the indigenous Oaxacan artists working with us in the photo session about their deepest

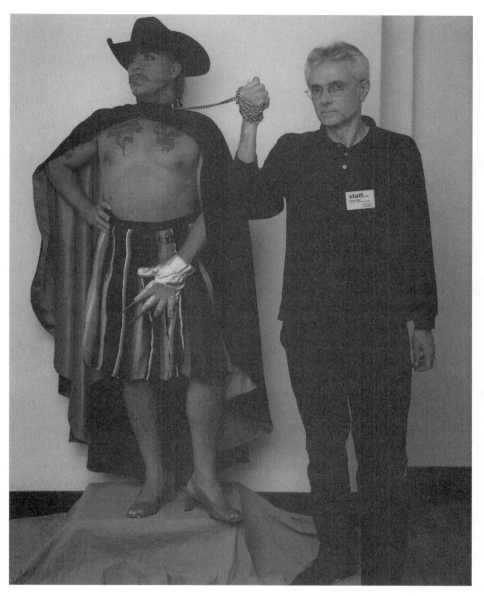

Figure 9.3. *British Curator and Specimen.* Shot in Liverpool by Arturo Vason, 2003. Photo: Courtesy La Pocha Nostra.

concerns. Inevitably all of them wanted to deal with the troubling fascination that foreigners have for the indigenous body, the highly decorated and *folk-loric* body of indigenous Oaxacans. This colonial history never ceases to end.

JG: As you say, the depiction of non-whites as culturally or racially inferior has a long history in which photography plays a central role. Given this history, can you say more about why you chose photography as a medium? Can you articulate how your "living dioramas" are similar to and different from the dioramas and racial typologies of the eugenicists?

GP: They're structurally similar in the sense that they're meant to be seen from all sides and the audience can get really close to the performers/specimens, but their content and conceptual strategies are the opposite. They're meant to question the assumptions of the audience about cultural otherness, to problematize what I call "the intercultural moment."

Race and gender have always been an intrinsic element in everything I do. My aesthetic praxis involves ethnic and gender bending, cultural transvestitism, and power inversions of sorts. In my troupe's universe, so called "people of color," immigrants, women, and gays are in control of the image or the living diorama. It's a performance universe controlled by us. The control is not overt or declared. It's an implied narrative. We try not to be pedagogic or self-righteous in our politics. But it's always there.

This praxis permeates everything I do, my live performances, my videos, my performance texts and my photo-performances. In a sense my photo-performances are an extension of my living dioramas and tableaux vivants. These dioramas were originally inspired by the sinister history of eugenics and human exhibits, but we now use them to deal with more contemporary issues such as racism and sexism as it is expressed in global media, corporate multiculturalism, and tourist culture.

The idea is to heighten features of fear and desire in the dominant imagination and "spectacularize" our "extreme identities," with the clear understanding that these identities have already been distorted by the invisible surgery of global media. We pose in dioramas as "artificial savages" making ourselves available for the audience to "explore" us, change our costumes and props, and even replace us for a short period of time.

As I wrote in *Culturas in Extremis,* "As performance artists, we wish to understand our new role and place in this culture of extreme spectacle that has been forced upon us . . . In the process of detecting the exact placement of the new borders of tolerance (especially since September 11), it becomes necessary to open up a sui generis ceremonial space—a space where the audience may engage in anthro-poetical inquiry and reflect on their new relationship with cultural, racial and political Otherness."[5]

Our aesthetic universe is a kind of Blade Runner in a Tijuana-type world, inhabited by cultural projections and artificial savages, a border zone where old broken myths overlap with brand new mythologies. This Pocha Nostra aesthetic is a pastiche of many things, Norteño and Tex Mex chic intertwined with "Chicano Sci-fi," S&M, Catholic pop, Japanese animé, you name it. It's excessive. A Catalonian art critic labeled it "robo-barroque."

JG: Explain what it means to be "pocha" or "pocho." How does the history of "pocho" culture and (in parallel) Chicano culture in the U.S. influence your work? Do you consider your work "Chicano"? How does the category or identity of the "Chicano" raise specific issues or dilemmas for race politics?

GP: "Pocho" was originally a derogative term coined by Mexicans to describe those who abandon national territory. We were seen as traitors; "bastardized" Mexicans; the forgotten orphans of the omnipotent Mexican nation-state. And so, when I crossed the border, I unwittingly became a Pocho . . . In the 1990s, many of us reclaimed the word and began to use it as a term of empowerment. Remember the legendary Pocho zine created by the Chicano Secret Service performance comedy troupe during those years? This is precisely what my troupe did thirteen years ago. We expropriated the term to baptize ourselves. The Spanglish neologism *"Pocha Nostra"* translates as either "our impurities" or "the cartel of cultural bastards." We love this poetic ambiguity. It reveals an attitude towards art and society: *"Cross-racial, poly-gendered, experi-mental, y qué?"*

Regarding the highly contested term *Chicano,* my position is more complex. Depending on which definition we use, I can be a Chicano . . . or not. Rubén Salazar, the legendary journalist from the *Los Angeles Times* who was killed by the police in 1970, created one of my favorite definitions. He used to say that a Chicano was any politicized Mexican American who didn't have an Anglo image of him/herself. Rubén Guevara, the Chicano ethnomusicologist, took this definition even further. He believes that Chicanismo is a cultural and *espiritual* state of mind, a way of being in the world. I'd add that this way of being in the world, this attitude implies a certain border crossing fluidity, a capability to embrace syncretism and hybridity. It entails a certain border knowledge of how to operate between two or more cultures and languages. In this sense, Chicanismo can be a very useful conceptual model to deal with the complexities of the post 9/11 era . . . I also feel that Chicanismo has become a worldwide phenomenon. The South is moving into the space of the North and redefining it. In a sense all the Arabs, Africans, and South Asians living in Europe are also Chicanos in the widest sense of the term.

JG: This process of redefinition is of course where the struggle for power, for rights, and for recognition takes place, as we can see in the recent youth uprisings in France. Immigrant populations can never simply become "assimilated" as their "host" countries imagine or desire. Instead, the history of colonialism and of economic rapaciousness can be read across the bodies of those it has disenfranchised. Only the ignorant are blind to this scene of cultural engagement and disjunction. Think of all the ideological work that goes into maintaining this ignorance on the part of the general population.

GP: The racist and sexist iconography of corporate multiculturalism and tourist culture and their hidden texts blows my mind. When confronted with these types of images, I'm always thinking to myself, why is it that first we oppress and exterminate other cultures, and then we romanticize them and turn them into exotic icons of consumer desire? How are these images made? The North stereotypes the South. The South internalizes these stereotypes and either reflects them back, mimics them unconsciously to appeal to the consumer appetite of the North, or turns them into "official culture." Meanwhile, identity gets lost or rather "reinvented" in this ricocheting display of reflections and refractions of fear and desire. I'm interested in exploring the intercultural border zone of fear and desire; the realm of the unconscious and the mythical; what lies beneath the geology of First/Third World relations.

JG: Is it not also the case that the South stereotypes the North, both as a form of critical response and conscious emulation?

GP: The South stereotypes the North as a mechanism of self-defense. It does it unconsciously. It's easier to deal with the anguish generated by economic oppression and cultural colonialism this way. It's easier to deal with "dumb gringos" than with ubiquitous corporations. But unlike the North, the South doesn't have the power to broadcast or enforce these stereotypes in the North.

Another interesting phenomenon takes place at the same time: Mexican artists engage in a conscious process of expropriation of dominant cultural forms imposed by the North. We take all the pop cultural garbage sent by the United States, reorganize it, resignify it and turn it into art. As part of this expropriation process, we take the stereotypes generated in the North and turn them inside out and upside down. In my work Superman becomes Supermojado, defendant of migrant worker's rights, and Conan the Barbarian becomes "Chi-conan El Bárbaro."

JG: Your work takes the stereotype as a prototype, and then elaborates it to the point of parody. How is the stereotype crucial to your work?

GP: The engineering process of constructing a performance persona is quite complex, in terms of cutting and pasting and sampling stereotypes, prototypes, archetypes, pop mythology, and social reality.

First comes the process of gathering the information. My collaborators and I are acute observers of both pop culture and social reality. We're like artistic cannibals devouring everything we encounter on the way: Television, film, rock & roll, hip-hop, journalism, anthropology, pornography, religious imagery . . . and of course, the history of the visual and performing arts. We keep diaries. We write down all the ideas and images we come across in the research process, and then we test them in the rehearsal space. What we do as performance artists is to "embody" all this information, and re-interpret it for a live audience, refracting fetishized constructs of otherness through the spectacle of our "heightened" bodies on display. People have described our personas as "intercultural poltergeists."

Now, unlike the hybrids and cyborgs engendered by pop culture, we create our composite creatures with the following formula in mind: one-quarter stereotype, one-quarter audience projection, one-quarter social reality, and one-quarter aesthetic artifact—in the words of cyber-theorist Sandy Stone, we create "poly-cultural cyborgs." Mexican anthropologist Roger Bartra refers to them as "artificial savages."

Why do we do all this? In the American imagination, Mexicans (and by extension other Latinos) are allowed to occupy two different but strangely complementary niches: We're irrationally violent, hypersexual, and highly infectious, or innocent, "natural," and shamanic (fig. 9.4). Often, the political artist simply replaces a negative stereotype with a positive one, without realizing that both are equally colonizing. I hate this oversimplification in so-called "political art" created by non-Anglos. Instead, our work deals with composite images and hybrid personas that embody a multiplicity of symbols, and elicit

Figure 9.4. *Shaman Travesti*. From the portfolio "Ethno-Techno: Evil Others and Identity Thieves," shot in San Francisco with James McCaffrey, 2004. Photo: Courtesy of Orlando Britto-Jinorio and Galería Artificios, Las Palmas de Gran Canaria.

multiple readings. Performance art is a terrain of ambiguity. My audiences and viewers are always asking themselves: What's wrong with this picture or with this tableaux vivant? Why is this supermodel wearing a Zapatista mask? Why are all these designer barbarians rebelling against the gaze of the audience or the photographer?

JG: In addition to asking, "What's wrong with this picture?" your audience may also be thinking "Where do these people exist? What world do they inhabit?"

GP: I want to believe that they inhabit a parallel universe that's both imaginary and "real," a universe that exists somewhere between the phenomenological and the poetic. I see them as complex portraits of an emerging international sub-trans-culture. They're the "new barbarians" invading the North, contaminating their racial purity and destroying their alleged cultural and social order. But they're also part of my psyche. These personas are heightened versions of the multiple selves contained inside my psyche and my body; the other "Others" within me. As a border artist I have multiple selves and voices, some of which are extremely dark and performative and express themselves in my dreams and in my art. Now, going back to your question, do they *really* exist? In a sense they do. Are they mere emblematic or metaphorical representations of my internal life as it intersects with social reality? I'm not sure.

In contemporary art there are well-defined borders between the sociological and the metaphorical realms . . . or between the documentary and the fictional in film, and literature. These borders are meaningless to me. I just don't see them. I'm a bastard child of magical realism and sci-fi, of poetry and activism. For me, realism is just an ideological construction and a mere artistic strategy. I feel a certain discomfort with the kind of social or psychological realism that pretends to capture "reality," in capitals, and assumes that other forms of art are imaginary or fantastic.

JG: Let's talk about how these questions get played out in some specific images. In your "Post Mexicans" series, the image titled "Trio Macabro" raises some of the questions of a cultural or political conflict between Mexico and the U.S. (fig. 9.5). You're in the foreground with your hands in boxing gloves, you gaze at the camera, poised as if ready to fight. One glove is adorned with the U.S. flag, the other the Mexican flag, suggesting that the right hand might be battling the left, or that you are yourself a hybrid of U.S. and Mexican culture ready to defend your complex, mixed identity. You're flanked by a figure

Figure 9.5. *Trio Macabro.* From the portfolio "Post-Mexicans," shot in Mexico City with Miguel Velasco, 2003. Photo: Courtesy of Orlando Britto-Jinorio and Galería Artificios, Las Palmas de Gran Canaria.

wearing feathers, as if from an indigenous tribe, and a woman carrying lilies reminiscent of Diego Rivera's paintings (a recurring motif in your images). They're also both wearing signs of Asian culture: the red sun of Japan tattooed on the arm of the man, and a theatrical Japanese mask on the woman. Finally, a kind of Punk aesthetic of spiked arm bands and metallic accessories gives them a tough exterior. Vaguely menacing, your trio also performs humorously: the man carries a fly swatter as if it were a weapon. Can you say more about how this image and the other images in the "Post Mexicans" series address the question of bicultural life? Why is there an emphasis on "post" in *"Post Mexicans"*?

GP: The "Post Mexicans" are essentially the post-national Mexicans: the millions of uprooted *paisanos* who are constantly crossing the border back and forth, and who are not part of either nation-state. We're an emerging nation, a floating nation, a conceptual country that demands a new cartography to contain us, and a brand-new aesthetic to portray us. As an artist I'm clumsily trying to do both, draft a more enlightened and inclusive poetic cartography and contribute to developing a new aesthetic.

Mestizaje is a thing of the past. Binary models are no longer operative (i.e., Spanish/Indian; North/South; Mexican/Chicano, etc.). The *mestizaje* model was originally created to try to grapple with the fusion between the Spanish and the indigenous. But what do you do with the Post-Mexicanos? We're the product of several racial mixtures and many overlapping subcultures. What are we then? Post-mestizos? Meta-mestizos? We're an expression of a double process; the Chicanoization and Americanization of Mexico and the Mexicanization of the United States. Our identities are in permanent flux. The next generation is a living example of what I'm talking about. More than mestizos, our multiracial and multicultural kids are poly-cultural (and poly-gendered) cyborgs. Neta, they're way beyond conventional notions of *mestizaje*. Take my son Guillermito and his wild multiracial *clica* of friends. They're all fluent in Spanish, English, Spanglish, ebonics, Chiconics, and cybertalk—and they don't even reflect on this. It's a given to them. One day he told me: "Dad, what you theorize in your books, is everyday reality for me."

Is this good or bad, I don't know. All I can say is that as I tour from city to city and from country to country, I witness this phenomenon taking place everywhere I go: a grassroots transnational, transborder culture, which must not be confused with globalization. It's not an imposed phenomenon. It's not created by corporations. It comes from below. It has a different logic of resistance and contamination.

The entire world is experiencing both a profound crisis of national identity and the emergence of multiple repertoires of hybrid identities. We're all clumsily trying to understand what our new place and our new voice is in this hallucinatory cartography. The identities we've inherited all seem dysfunctional and somewhat useless. One of the lessons that performance art has taught me is that we can reinvent our identities; that we're not straight-jacketed by identity. As artists, we have the capability to pick and choose, to move vertically and horizontally, to pastiche and sample from our multiple cultural selves and fragmented identities, in order to hopefully construct a better human being. That's what I'm trying to do in my art. That's what my photo-performances are trying to portray.

JG: In your "Ethno-Techno" series I'm intrigued by the "Geisha Apocalíptica" (Apocalyptic geisha) who stands in a sculptural pose that could have been rendered in marble in the nineteenth century, and whose white face, suggestive of the geisha's makeup, is also a kind of death mask or expression of

Figure 9.6. *Geisha Apocalíptica.* From the portfolio
"Ethno-Techno: Evil Others and Identity Thieves,"
shot in San Francisco with James McCaffrey, 2004.
Photo: Courtesy of Orlando Britto-Jinorio and Galería
Artificios, Las Palmas de Gran Canaria.

desire and identification with "white culture" (fig. 9.6). She stands to the side
of a white cube on the floor, the canonical object of modernist expression and
also a gallery pedestal. What does this signify for you? Why are the words
"nunca regresaremos" scrawled on her back? How does this image relate to
the "Rito Neo-Azteca" (Neo-Aztec Ritual) image of the woman who has the
words "United We Stood" written on her back? (fig. 9.7). In short, how does
the woman's body come to be the mystic writing pad of resistance?

GP: In performance art, the human body, not the stage, is our true site for creation. It's our raw material, our empty canvas, and open book; our navigation
chart and biographical map. It's the vessel for our ever-changing identities.
In performance, our body must be marked, decorated, intervened with culturally, mapped out, chronicled, re-politicized, and re-captured or liberated

Figure 9.7. *Rito Neo-Azteca.* From the portfolio
"Ethno-Techno: Evil Others and Identity Thieves,"
shot in San Francisco with James McCaffrey, 2004.
Photo: Courtesy of Orlando Britto-Jinorio and Galería
Artificios, Las Palmas de Gran Canaria.

by the camera. Our bodies are also occupied territories. The ultimate goal of
performance, especially if one is a woman, gay, or a "person of color," is to de-
colonize one's body and make these decolonizing mechanisms apparent to the
audience in the hope that they'll get inspired to do the same with their own.

When a text is written on the body of a performance artist documented by
the camera, who is really talking? It's a very complex question: In the live performances, my collaborators have more leeway to decide which text to write
on their bodies and how to write it. In the photo-performances the decision is
clearly mine. It's my disembodied voice, but I don't expect the viewer to take it
as such. My hope is that the total image/text functions as a sort of poetic logo,
a conceptual statement that may even spill into the other photos of the series.
You can read on the apocalyptic geisha's back "Nunca regresaremos," which

translates to "We will never return." Where to? Essentialism? To the way our cultures used to be before we became immigrants and nomads? To the way things were before 9/11?

The phrase "United we stood" written on the back of Emiko is also a disembodied poetic statement, and as such it elicits a multiplicity of readings. Is it that she used to be "united," connected to the transvestite Aztec priest holding her scalped hair, and not anymore? Is it about the country, the United States, which is totally disunited under the Bush regime? Is it about the endemic lack of social fabric in multiracial America? Is the statement about "us," the darkies versus "them," those white Christian guys in power? Other readings are also welcome.

JG: I want to pursue the question of the powerful female personas that you have constructed in your photographs. Your image "Against Gauguin" depicts a beautiful woman in something resembling tropical attire who poses with a gun in one hand and one arm across her bare breasts (fig. 9.8). As a critical reprise of Gauguin's exotic and romantic depiction of women from Tahiti, it stands as a challenge to historical (and contemporary) images that sexualize cultural difference. At the same time, the image is strikingly similar to works by Hannah Wilke and Vallie Export, whose self-portraits in the 1970s included half-clothed poses that were simultaneously alluring and threatening. Despite their feminist stance, many thought Wilke and Export's work might simply attract the sexist gaze it claimed to critique. How do you see "Against Gauguin," and other images such as "Guerilla Supermodel," as part of your project to explore power relations as written across the woman's body?

GP: To answer this question I must discuss the specificities of that photoshoot. Those images were generated during the "Tucuman-Chicano" project that took place in Argentina early this year, and *stricto sensu*, they're not part of my photo-performances. I'll explain why. Violeta Luna and I conducted a performance workshop involving fifteen Argentine artists. Most participants (I'd say 70 percent) were women—very powerful rebel actresses, dancers, and intellectuals. What they shared in common was a dissatisfaction with their mono-disciplinary artistic practice and a desire to experiment beyond their *métiers* and to collaborate with us. La Pocha Nostra provided the methodology and the conceptual framework, and each artist developed a couple of performance personas drawn from their own concerns. We invited this amazing young photographer, Ramón Treves, who had been recommended by my

Figure 9.8. *Against Gauguin.* From the portfolio "Tucuman-Chicano," shot in Argentina with Ramón Treves, 2005. Photo: Courtesy of La Pocha Nostra.

friend photographer Julio Pantoja, to document the process, and he showed up with all these amazing backdrops to play with us. We set up an ephemeral photo studio in a room adjacent to the rehearsal space and every time someone would come up with a strong persona, he/she would go and play next door with Ramón for half an hour as the workshop continued. Since we all wanted to support Ramón's career, we decided to not claim authorship of the final portfolio.

Regarding the highly sexualized content of the images, it was a combination of factors: the personas developed by the participating artists themselves, La Pocha's contagious aesthetics, and Ramón's gaze. Perhaps in the current ambiance of *destape* (liberation) in Argentina, these flamboyant and sexualized images of empowered warrioresses and cultural transvestites have different connotations from those being created by artists in the United States.

JG: How do your images unravel the coherence of racial performance? Can you give me your answer with reference to a specific image?

GP: In the late 1990s, my colleagues and I began to surrender our will to the audience in the process of determining the content of our work. For this purpose, we developed "confessional" websites in which we asked Internet users to suggest to us how we should dress as Mexicans and Chicanos, and what kind of performance actions and social rituals we should engage in. We would then carry out their suggestions in a live performance or in a photo shoot. The idea was to use performance as a Rorschach test for people to project their cultural fears and colonial desires, as a mirror for the audience to see the reflection of their own psychological chimeras. The results of our experiment in "reverse anthropology" turned out to be much stranger than anything we could've imagined on our own. In the mid to late 1990s, the "sleepy Mexican" had been banished from the colonial unconscious of contemporary America, deported back to Hollywood, along with Frito Bandito, Speedy González, the "greaser" bandit, and the suffering Frida Kahlo. They had been replaced by a new pantheon of mighty *locos* reflective of the political and media trends of the time, and the anti-immigration rhetoric of politicians. We were perceived to be unnecessarily violent, yet fashionably seductive; techno-literate, yet primeval; politically strident yet gifted with inexplicable spiritual powers. We were contradictory, unpredictable, and at the same time, strangely familiar: a distorted image of the United States: its evil twin. These confessions led to the creation of the "El Mexterminator" project. My techno-shaman personas and Roberto Sifuentes' cyber-vatos come out of that research. These images appear in my book *Dangerous Border Crossers*.[6]

JG: To what extent is your work in a conscious conversation with the history of art?

GP: As a young Mexican artist in a racist U.S. art world I soon realized that the official history of contemporary art was not going to welcome me right away. And I became interested in the other histories of art, the parallel and untold ones . . . My conversation with the history of art has always had a sarcastic and irreverent tone. It's a conversation between an outsider and a functionary. I remember when my work began to be recognized in the late 1980s; art critics were constantly comparing me with famous non-Mexican artists or with the few Mexican artists they were familiar with. They lacked the necessary cultural references and knowledge of Mexican and Chicano art to understand me on my own terms. In their eyes I was always "the Mexican Spalding Gray" . . . or the postmodern grandchild of Diego Rivera. So I began to make fun of their shortsightedness. "Ni Diego Ni Frida" responds to that impulse. So does "El Moctezuma Junior" posing as a rock celebrity and "The Ranchero Stelark."

I have also engaged in an unconscious conversation with historically based Catholic iconography. My Mexican sensibility is permeated with Catholic iconography gone wrong, with female Zapatista Christs, mariachi and low-rider Christs, with immigrant *pietas* and border *madonnas*. My job in this respect has been to problematize my placement in all that history. I see all these historically based images as interventions in the official history of contemporary art.

JG: I'd like to return to the question of race in relationship to the images we've been discussing. How much does the history of Mexico and Mexican conceptions of race figure in your work, and how much is framed by the U.S. context? Here I'm thinking of the recent controversy about the newly minted Mexican postage stamp that depicts Memin Pinguin, a racist cartoon caricature of a black boy. How does the performativity of race differ in the two countries, and how does this influence your work?

GP: I can't escape the fact that I was born and raised in Mexico City. But at the same time, my formative intellectual years took place in the U.S.-Mexico border area and Los Angeles. In this sense I'm a border artist, a *chica-lango* (half *chilango* and half Chicano) with a bicultural sensibility, and a bifocal understanding of culture. Besides, I'm constantly returning to Mexico City, where I have a house and work on several ongoing art projects. It's weird. In a sense I've never left, and in another sense, I'm constantly returning to a place which no longer exists. This dilemma has positioned me in a somewhat strategic place in both countries. In my artwork and in my writings, I often interpret (and purposely misinterpret) Latin American culture for the United States, and U.S. culture for Mexico, and this includes notions of race and identity. Border artists often perform this dual role of vernacular diplomats and intellectual coyotes.

In the 1980s and 1990s, during the culture wars, while the United States was trying to sincerely deal with its multiracial complexities, Mexico was in complete denial. Identity in Mexico was a static construct, intricately connected to national territory and language. A Mexican was someone who lived in Mexico and who spoke Spanish . . . like a Mexican. Despite the fact that we came in all shapes, colors, accents, and even races, *mestizaje* was the master narrative. Whether we liked it or not, we were the bastard children of Hernán Cortés and La Malinche—product of a colonial rape and a cultural cesarean— eternally condemned to come to terms with this historical trauma. The millions of *indios* or Indians, were portrayed as living in a parallel, and mythical time and space outside *our* history and society. As a result of these prevailing static constructs, Mexico saw with perplexity and mistrust all the debates on race and identity taking place in the United States. Now it's quite different.

I believe the change began in 1995 with the Zapatista insurrection. Zapatismo forced Mexico to reflect on its unspoken plural identities and multiple crises. The country's endemic economic distress and racial divides were framed by Marcos in the context of a call for democratic process: for "a place at the table for all Mexicans," not just those affiliated with the oligarchic structure that had ruled the country for so long. The Zapatista lesson was clear: democracy in Mexico could only exist if we recognized and incorporated its diversity. In the words of Subcomandante Marcos, this diversity included not just indigenous peoples, but also women, gays, youth, urban subcultures of sorts, and even those on the other side of the border: the Chicanos and "undocumented" Mexicans. With the rise of the Zapatistas, many forgotten and forbidden Mexicos, including those beyond the border were resurrected. In this sense Zapatistas introduced a national conversation about Mexican racism.

Then Mexico's main political party, the PRI (Partido Revolucionario Institucional), fell in 2000, and with it, all the political, social, and cultural structures sustaining national identity. The great paradox is that as Mexico becomes more open and learns to live with its new democratic complexities and demons, the United States becomes more of a closed society, an authoritarian society ruled by paranoid nationalism, political isolationism, Christian Puritanism and xenophobia, a place where ethnic profiling and censorship have become official policy. In Bush's America most debates on race were eclipsed by the mega-reality of "the war on terror"—that is until [Hurricane] Katrina in 2005 exposed the endemic and unacknowledged racism. Paradoxically, at the same time Mexico is very perplexed and even scared by all these changes. Mexicans know that the ever-expanding connotations of the term "terrorist" now include all brown people. The new enemy is the brown body, America's most wanted inner demon.

All these changes and paradoxes regarding race on both sides of the border express themselves in my work. It's inevitable. I'd say that the current membership of La Pocha Nostra, my performance troupe, is the most obvious example of my conscious decision to deal with the new racial complexities; its members and associates are Mexicans, Chicanos, U.S. Latinos, Asians, Arabs, blacks, "subaltern" Europeans, and hybrids in between.

JG: It seems that the function of "race" is different in both countries, yet your work seems to operate critically within both paradigms. Can you explain how your work is (differently) critical of Mexican race politics and U.S. race politics?

GP: My positionality vis-à-vis identity politics and race politics is contextual and strategic. It shifts from one side of the border to the other, and from context to context. Often my job in Mexico is to question Mexican nationalism and centralism; to question Mexico's racism towards indigenous peoples, Chicanos, and everyone who is not part of the puzzle of national identity. When I go back to Mexico, I do it as a Chicano, and I always try to go back with other Chicano and U.S. Latino artists. It gives me extra moral grounds to overstate my Chicano voice, my hybridity, my otherness. Since Mexico is experiencing an acute process of Chicanoization, my voice now has a context. This process of Chicanoization is produced by the powerful influence of U.S. Latino/Chicano media and by the inevitable cultural influence of the millions of post-Mexicans who constantly return by will or by the force of the *migra*. Mexico is finally trying to deal with this phenomenon. Immigration, border culture, Chicanismo, Spanglish, are now part of the national conversation and the pop imaginary. However, the intellectual and artistic *clicas* are still unwilling to open up.

In the United States my position regarding identity shifts all the time. In Chicano contexts my job is to question Chicanismo in capitals. I try to bring up issues that make Chicano nationalists uncomfortable such as multiple sexualities, experimental aesthetics, and cross-racial collaboration. In Anglo contexts it's different. If the place where I'm speaking or performing is conservative, then I tend to position myself as a hard core Chicano/Latino in order to question the intolerance of Latino otherness. In so-called progressive milieus, especially after 9/11, I either become a Latin American once again, and from the South I question American isolationism, or I assume a pan-ethnic/pan-gendered performance identity to shatter their simplistic views. You know, I'm a coyote, a performance trickster, a border-crosser.

When La Pocha goes to Europe to present work, things get logarithmically more complicated. In order not to be exoticized as the new "urban primitives" from the distant West or from "Mexique," we have to establish strategic alliances with immigrant and deterritorialized groups in Europe; with communities who are experiencing similar processes of transculturation as those experienced by U.S. Latinos in the past. I'm talking about the British Pakistanis, the French Algerians, the Spanish Moroccans, the German Turks, etc. I'm also talking about the Eastern Europeans relocated in Western Europe. These groups are the new European "Chicanos" I was talking about earlier. Collaborating with artists from these communities helps us anchor the piece in a European reality.

JG: Earlier in our conversation you suggested "we can reinvent our identities" and "pick and choose from cultural selves." Yet, as Stuart Hall points out, we live in a world where this reinvention is not a simple matter. Our otherwise fluid identities are often constrained by the material conditions in which we live, both the physical form of our bodies and the economic support they receive. Most people would not choose to find themselves in a racist culture where their skin color or poverty places them in a subaltern position; yet this is a concrete condition for many. As a brown-skinned coyote, as a trickster, as a border-crosser, and as an artist you move between cultural marginalization and economic privilege. For my last question I want to ask: How does class figure explicitly in your images and implicitly in their production? Is the reinvention of identity only an option for the bourgeoisie?

GP: True, there is a global elite that can easily cross borders of race, gender, and class without having to experience the physical, social, or political effects of those border crossings. Their "transcultural fluidity" tends to be superficial and temporary. They're *flaneurs* and cultural tourists in search of extreme otherness and unusual experiences. Subcultures, however, driven by survival and by impulses of resistance, engage in much more daring forms of border crossings. Low riders in Japan are in dialogue with Chicano low riders from the Southwest; DJ's from Latin America and the Arab countries are currently making the music that the white youth dances to; urban tribes from Buenos Aires, São Paolo, or Mexico City are developing similar cultural hybrids as their peers in New York or London. Many of the underground railroads and routes that migrant workers utilize to crisscross the United States go through Indian reservations, Chicano barrios, and progressive white milieux. I'm interested in engaging in a dialogue with all these transnational communities, and I often find them much more open to the reinvention of identity than say, some of my intellectual peers.

My project of reinvention of identity is clearly an art project. And most artistic projects are that, mere prototypes, models which attempt to articulate and chronicle the new complexities of the times. Sadly, we're not activists or politicians and our conceptual models unfortunately don't translate to the social realm, especially in a society, like the United States, which doesn't listen to the voice of its artists. But my audiences do pay attention to what I have to say, and I believe that my ideas have an impact in their lives. In this sense, the pedagogic dimension of performance is where the true political project lies. We always try to conduct workshops for the outsider communities living in the city where we're performing.

As touring artists who experience continuous upward and downward mobility . . . continuous geographical and cultural mobility, we have certain border-crossing privileges that other nomads and migrants lack, and I'm fully aware of it. I only hope to utilize these privileges responsibly, ethically, and to help others to access them as well. La Pocha Nostra is like a Trojan horse: I get invited, and I show up with twenty others. My political project is also to open doors for young rebel artists.

Reference Matter

Notes

Introduction

1. Pedro Alonso O'Crouley, *A Description of The Kingdom of New* Spain (1774), ed. and trans. Seán Galvin (San Francisco: John Howell, 1972), pp. 20–21. It is important to note, however, that there was no consensus as to whether the offspring of Spanish/Portuguese and black mixtures could return to a pure racial pole. See, for example, Lilia Moritz Schwarcz, *The Spectacle of the Races. Scientists, Institutions, and the Race Question in Brazil, 1870–1930,* translated by Leland Guyer (New York: Hill and Wang, 1993); and María Elena Martínez's essay in this volume, note 63.

2. Alfred P. Schultz, *Race or Mongrel: A Brief History of the Rise and Fall of the Ancient Races of Earth: A Theory That the Fall of Nations Is Due to Intermarriage with Alien Stocks: A Demonstration That a Nation's Strength Is Due to Racial Purity: A Prophecy That America Will Sink to Early Decay unless Immigration Is Rigorously Restricted* (Boston: L. C. Page & Company, 1908), pp. 148–51. Schultz's comments exemplify the continuing incorporation of cultural criteria in "scientific" constructions of race. In his analysis of Spain and the Spanish population, he remarks that: "Race impresses its characteristics on the religion that a people profess. The Catholicity of Gothic Spain was not the Catholicity of modern Spain. With the post-Gothic Spaniard, the Iberian-Gothic-Moorish-African mongrel, Catholicity degenerated into the crass fetishism which is the religion of modern Spain" (p. 147).

3. Vasconcelos served twice as Minister of Education, held the position of Rector of the Universidad Nacional Autónoma de México in Mexico City, and exerted a profound influence on Mexican culture by promoting education for the lower classes. He experienced his most productive years as an author during the 1930s, following an unsuccessful campaign for the presidency of Mexico in 1929. His book elaborated on the motto he created in 1921 for the Universidad Nacional Autónoma de México, which is featured in the university's coat of arms—*"Por mi raza hablará el espíritu"* (The

spirit will speak through my race). For an introduction to Vasconcelos's thought, see Marilyn Grace Miller, *Rise and Fall of the Cosmic Race: The Cult of Mestizaje in Latin America* (Austin: University of Texas Press, 2004), pp. 27–44; Nancy Leys Stepan, "*The Hour of Eugenics*": *Race, Gender, and Nation in Latin America* (Ithaca and London: Cornell University Press, 1999), pp. 145–53; and Gabriella de Beer, *Vasconcelos and His World* (New York: Las Americas, 1966).

4. José Vasconcelos, *The Cosmic Race: A Bilingual Edition,* translated and annotated by Didier T. Jaén (Baltimore and London: Johns Hopkins University Press, 1997), pp. 30, 72.

5. Our use of the terms "making" and "marking" of race follows the influential essay by Thomas C. Holt, "Marking: Race, Race-making, and the Writing of History," in *American Historical Review* 100, no. 1 (1995): 1–20.

6. David G. Gutiérrez, "Migration, Emergent Ethnicity, and the 'Third Space': The Shifting Politics of Nationalism in Greater Mexico," *Journal of American History* 86, no. 2 (1999): 481–517. See also Gutiérrez's *Walls and Mirrors: Mexican Americans, Mexican Immigrants, and the Politics of Ethnicity* (Berkeley: University of California Press, 1995).

7. Américo Paredes, "The Folklore of Groups of Mexican Origin in the United States," in Richard Bauman, ed., *Folklore and Culture on the Texas-Mexican Border* (Austin: Center for Mexican-American Studies, 1979), pp. 3–18. According to Ramón Saldívar, Paredes' concept of Greater Mexico should be seen not simply in a cultural-nationalist context but rather as framing a "transnational imaginary." Ramón Saldívar, *The Borderlands of Culture. Américo Paredes and the Transnational Imaginary* (Durham and London: Duke University Press, 2006), pp. 320–21. On the subject of trans- and post-national racial identities, see also the conversation between Jennifer González and Guillermo Gómez-Peña in this volume.

8. The exhibition and symposium were organized by Ilona Katzew. For a discussion of the exhibition within the larger context of representing difference in contemporary museum practice, see Ilona Katzew and Daniel J. Sherman, "Dossier: 'Inventing Race' in Los Angeles," in Daniel J. Sherman, ed., *Museums and Difference* (Bloomington: Indiana University Press, 2008), pp. 289–329.

9. For recent scholarship on *casta* painting, see Ilona Katzew, *Casta Painting: Images of Race in Eighteenth-Century Mexico* (New Haven and London: Yale University Press, 2004); Katzew, ed., *New World Orders: Casta Painting and Colonial Latin America* (New York: Americas Society Art Gallery, 1996); María Concepción García Sáiz, *Las castas mexicanas. Un género pictórico americano* (Milan: Olivetti, 1989); and Susan Deans-Smith, "Creating the Colonial Subject: Casta Painting, Collectors, and Critics in Eighteenth-Century Mexico and Spain," *Colonial Latin American Review* 14, no. 2 (2005): 169–204.

10. For further discussion of this synoptic approach, see Frederick Cooper and Ann Laura Stoler, "Between Metropole and Colony. Rethinking a Research Agenda,"

in Cooper and Stoler, eds., *Tensions of Empire. Colonial Cultures in a Bourgeois World* (Berkeley and Los Angeles: University of California Press, 1997), pp. 1–56.

11. "Scientific racism"—most notably Social Darwinism—included disciplines such as phrenology, physical anthropology, physiognomy, and craniometry. Social Darwinism attempted to demonstrate the laws of human society and to develop understanding of human biological nature including how to improve humanity and thus secure, in theory, the well-being of the collective body. Its origins can be found in the work of Sir Francis Galton (1822–1911), the half-cousin of Charles Darwin (1809–1882), who, in his study *Hereditary Genius* (1869) asserted that intellectual and physical abilities were inborn; he subsequently introduced the term "eugenics" to denote the possibilities for improving the human race.

12. Ania Loomba and Jonathan Burton, eds., *Race in Early Modern England. A Documentary Companion* (New York: Palgrave Macmillan, 2007), p. 8. See also the penetrating reflections on this issue by David Theo Goldberg, *Racist Culture: Philosophy and the Politics of Meaning* (Oxford: Blackwell, 1993); for a lucid discussion of the "distinctiveness" of modern racism, see Nicholas Thomas, *Colonialism's Culture. Anthropology, Travel and Government* (Princeton, N.J.: Princeton University Press, 1994), pp. 66–104. On the continuities and changes in racial discourses in Mexico and Latin America more generally in the late eighteenth and nineteenth centuries, and new scientific taxonomies, see Peter Wade, "Race and Nation in Latin America. An Anthropological View," in Nancy P. Appelbaum, Anne S. Macpherson, and Karin Alejandra Rosemblatt, eds., *Race and Nation in Modern Latin America* (Chapel Hill and London: University of North Carolina Press, 2003), pp. 264–81; and Marisol de la Cadena, "Are Mestizos Hybrid? The Conceptual Politics of Andean Identities," *Journal of Latin American Studies* 37 (2005): 259–84.

13. Peter Wade, "Rethinking Mestizaje: Ideology and Lived Experience," *Journal of Latin American Studies* 37 (2005): pp. 239–57.

14. Appelbaum et al., *Race and Nation;* and Loomba and Burton, *Race in Early Modern England.* For recent examples on colonial Mexico, see R. Douglas Cope, *The Limits of Racial Domination: Plebeian Society in Colonial Mexico City, 1660–1720* (Madison: University of Wisconsin Press, 1994); Ben Vinson III, *Bearing Arms for his Majesty: The Free-Colored Militia in Colonial Mexico* (Stanford, California: Stanford University Press, 2001); and Laura Lewis, *Hall of Mirrors: Power, Witchcraft, and Caste in Colonial Mexico* (Durham and London: Duke University Press, 2003). For colonial Spanish America, see Ann Twinam, *Public Lives, Private Secrets: Gender, Honor, Sexuality, and Illegitimacy in Colonial Spanish America* (Stanford, California: Stanford University Press, 1999).

15. Appelbaum et al., *Race and Nation;* Paul Gilroy, *The Black Atlantic: Modernity and Double Consciousness* (Cambridge: Harvard University Press, 1993); Saldívar, *The Borderlands of Culture;* and Cooper and Stoler, *Tensions of Empire.*

16. For recent discussions of this, see Nancy P. Appelbaum, Anne S. Macpherson, and Karin Alejandra Rosemblatt, "Introduction: Racial Nations," in Appelbaum et al., *Race and Nation*, pp. 2–31; Wade, "Race and Nation"; Wade, "Rethinking Mestizaje"; Florencia Mallon, "Constructing Mestizaje in Latin America: Authenticity, Marginality and Gender in the Claiming of Ethnic Identities," *Journal of Latin American Anthropology* 2, no. 1 (1996): 170–81; Grace Miller, *Rise and Fall of the Cosmic Race*, pp. 22–24; Anani Dzidzienyo and Suzanne Oboler, eds., *Neither Enemies Nor Friends. Latinos, Blacks, Afro-Latinos* (New York: Palgrave Macmillan, 2005); Juliet Hooker, "Indigenous Inclusion/Black Exclusion: Race, Ethnicity and Multicultural Citizenship in Latin America," *Journal of Latin American Studies* 37 (2005): 285–310; and Guillermo de la Peña, "A New Mexican Nationalism? Indigenous Rights, Constitutional Reform and the Conflicting Meanings of Multiculturalism," *Nations and Nationalism* 12, no. 2 (2006): 279–302.

17. Wade, "Race and Nation," pp. 271–75.

18. Cooper and Stoler, *Tensions of Empire*, p. 10.

19. Holt, "Marking: Race, Race-making, and the Writing of History," p. 12.

20. During three centuries of colonial rule, approximately 250,000 Africans were imported as slaves into Mexico. For a discussion of the relative lack of acknowledgment of the importance of black slavery in colonial Mexico, see Bobby Vaughn, "Afro-Mexico: Blacks, Indígenas, Politics, and the Greater Diaspora," in Dzidzienyo and Oboler, eds., *Neither Enemies Nor Friends*, p. 118. For recent works on the lives of African slaves and free blacks in colonial Mexico, see Ben Vinson III and Bobby Vaughn, *Afroméxico. El pulso de la población negra en México. Una historia recordada, olvidada y vuelta a recordar* (Mexico City: CIDE-Fondo de Cultura Económica, 2004); Adriana Naveda Chávez-Hita, ed., *Pardos, mulatos y libertos: sexto encuentro de afromexicanistas* (Xalapa: Universidad Veracruzana, 2001); Hermann Bennett, *Africans in Colonial Mexico: Absolutism, Christianity, and Afro-Creole Consciousness, 1570–1640* (Bloomington: Indiana University Press, 2003); María Elena Martínez, "The Black Blood of New Spain: Limpieza de Sangre, Racial Violence, and Gendered Power in Early Colonial Mexico," *William and Mary Quarterly*, 3rd Series, vol. LCI, no. 3 (July 2004): 479–520; Joan Bristol, *Christians, Blasphemers and Witches: Afro-Mexican Ritual Practice in the Seventeenth Century* (Albuquerque: University of New Mexico Press, 2007); Ben Vinson III and Matthew Restall, eds., *Black Mexico* (Albuquerque: University of New Mexico Press, forthcoming); and Matthew Restall, *The Black Middle: Africans, Mayas, and Spaniards in Colonial Yucatan* (Stanford, California: Stanford University Press, 2009).

21. The Manila Galleons made regular annual crossings between 1573 and 1815, which also facilitated the settlement of free and slave Filipino, Chinese, and Indian immigrants in New Spain. In addition, we know of at least two Japanese embassies to Mexico in 1610 and 1614, respectively. See Jonathan Israel, *Race, Class, and Politics in*

Colonial Mexico, 1610–1670 (London: Oxford University Press, 1975), pp. 75–76; and Virginia González Claverán, "Un documento colonial sobre esclavos asiáticos," *Historia Mexicana* 38, no. 3 (1989): 523–32. The subject of the Asian presence in Mexico during the colonial era, and how Asians were classified and designated in colonial legislation still awaits careful study.

22. Although such protections of indigenous communities were frequently ignored, they nevertheless resulted in the retention of community lands, access to judicial representation through the General Indian Court, and exemption from the Spanish Inquisition after 1570. For an introduction to indigenous responses to Spanish colonial rule, see James Lockhart, *The Nahuas After the Conquest: A Social and Cultural History of the Indians of Central Mexico* (Stanford, California: Stanford University Press, 1992).

23. See Patricia Seed, *To Love, Honor and Obey in Colonial Mexico: Conflicts Over Marriage Choice, 1574–1821* (Stanford, California: Stanford University Press, 1988), and Twinam, *Public Lives, Private Secrets.*

24. For discussion of *gracias al sacar,* particularly as it pertains to the purchase of whiteness in colonial Spanish America, see Ann Twinam, "Racial Passing: Informal and Official 'Whiteness' in Colonial Spanish America," in John Smolenski and Thomas J. Humphrey, eds., *New World Orders. Violence, Sanction, and Authority in the Colonial Americas* (Philadelphia: University of Pennsylvania Press, 2005), pp. 249–72, and Twinam, *Public Lives,* chap. 11.

25. Cooper and Stoler, *Tensions of Empire,* p. 3.

26. One of the most important debates in Latin American historiography is the "caste or estate versus class debate." Proponents of the caste position argue that racially defined estate status was the prime force shaping social relations in colonial Mexico; proponents of the class model suggest that wealth and occupational considerations assumed greater significance than race at the end of the colonial period. Among the defenders of the caste position are Sherburne F. Cook and Woodraw Borah, *The Indian Population of Central Mexico, 1530–1610* (Berkeley: University of California Press, 1960); Lyle N. McAlister, "Social Structure and Social Change in New Spain," *Hispanic American Historical Review* 43, no. 3 (1963): 349–70; Magnus Mörner, *Race Mixture in the History of Latin America* (Boston: Little, Brown & Co., 1967). Favoring the class model are John K. Chance and William B. Taylor, "Estate and Class in a Colonial City: Oaxaca in 1792," *Comparative Studies in Society and History* 19, no. 3 (1977): 454–87; Dennis Nodin Valdés, "The Decline of the Sociedad de Castas" (Ph.D. diss., University of Michigan, 1978). A critique of Chance and Taylor is offered by Robert McCaa, Stuart Schwartz, and Arturo Grubessich, "Race and Class in Colonial Latin America: A Critique," *Comparative Studies in Society and History* 21, no. 3 (1979): 421–33. Patricia Seed has referred to this debate as the "non-debate," and points out that considerations of race, estate, and class in studying the formation of society in

Latin America are not mutually exclusive. She also offers new insights into the discussion: "Social Dimensions of Race: Mexico City: 1753," *Hispanic American Historical Review* 62, no. 4 (1982): 596–606.

27. Matthew Restall, "Black Slaves, Red Paint," in Restall ed., *Beyond Black and Red: African-Native Relations in Colonial Latin America* (Albuquerque: University of New Mexico Press, 2005), p. 5. For examples of arguments that stress the continued and intensified significance of race, see Nicole von Germeten, *Black Blood Brothers. Confraternities and Social Mobility for Afro-Mexicans* (Gainesville: University Press of Florida, 2006); Lewis, *Hall of Mirrors;* and Deans-Smith's essay in this volume.

28. Matthew O'Hara and Andrew Fisher, "Racial Identities and Their Interpreters in Colonial Latin America," in Matthew O'Hara and Andrew Fisher, eds., *Imperial Subjects: Race and Identity in Colonial Latin America* (Durham: Duke University Press, 2009), p. 13.

29. In addition to the Mexican-American War (1846–848), Mexico experienced three other foreign invasions (Spain, 1829; France, 1838 and 1861), and brief subjection to imperial rule once again under the French (1864–1867). Internally, the period was wracked by civil war (the War of the Reform, 1858–1861, and the Mexican Revolution, 1910–1917).

30. Colonial legislation that protected the juridical foundation of the Indian pueblos and village land entailment remained intact, though it quickly became the target—along with the Church—of liberal reformers. For further discussion of the transition of indigenous *repúblicas* to municipalities in the first half of the nineteenth century, see Peter Guardino, *Peasants, Politics, and the Formation of Mexico's National State. Guerrero, 1800–1857* (Stanford, California: Stanford University Press, 1996). For discussion of the expropriation of indigenous lands, see Emilio H. Kourí, "Interpreting the Expropriation of Indian Pueblo Lands in Porfirian Mexico: The Unexamined Legacies of Andrés Molina Enríquez," *Hispanic American Historical Review* 82, no. 1 (2002): 69–117. The classic study of Mexican liberalism is Charles A. Hale, *Mexican Liberalism in the Age of Mora, 1821–1853* (New Haven: Yale University Press, 1968); see also Hale's *The Transformation of Liberalism in Late Nineteenth-Century Mexico* (Princeton, N.J.: Princeton University Press, 1989); and Jaime E. Rodríguez O., ed., *The Divine Charter. Constitutionalism and Liberalism in Nineteenth-Century Mexico* (Oxford: Rowman & Littlefield, 2005).

31. Manuel Dublán and José María Lozano eds., *La legislación mexicana; o colección completa de las disposiciones legislativas expedidas desde la independencia de la República* [1876–1904] (Mexico City: Suprema Corte de Justicia de la Nación, Tribunal Superior de Justicia del Estado de México, El Colegio de México, Escuela Libre de Derecho, 2004), vol. 1, p. 628. For further discussion on the history of anti-slavery legislation in Mexico in the first half of the nineteenth century, see Sean Kelley, " 'Mexico in His Head': Slavery and the Texas-Mexico Border, 1810–1860," *Journal of Social History* 37, no. 3 (2004): 709–723.

32. Claudio Lomnitz, *Exits from the Labyrinth: Culture and Ideology in the Mexican National Space* (Berkeley: University of California Press, 1992), pp. 276–77. Much more research is needed on the transition from a discourse of the *sistema de castas* to one of republican citizenship and the ways in which traditional casta/racial categories continued to be used in different regions in Mexico in the nineteenth century. On this subject, see Claudio Lomnitz, *Deep Mexico, Silent Mexico: An Anthropology of Nationalism* (Minneapolis: University of Minnesota Press. 2001), p. 64.

33. José María Luis Mora, "Catecismo político de la federación mexicana"; quoted in Alicia Hernández Chávez, "From res publicae to Republic," in Rodríguez O., ed., *The Divine Charter*, p. 52.

34. For exceptions to the disappearance of categories of black-Spanish-Indian racial mixtures in the Costa Chica region of southern Mexico, see Vaughn, "Afro-Mexico: Blacks, Indígenas, Politics, and the Greater Diaspora," pp. 122–24. See also Juliet Hooker, "Indigenous Inclusion/Black Exclusion," p. 301.

35. De la Peña, "A New Mexican Nationalism?" p. 281.

36. For discussions of alternative positions to revolutionary *indigenismo,* see Alan Knight, "Racism, Revolution, and Indigenismo: Mexico, 1910–1940," in Richard Graham, ed., *The Idea of Race in Latin America, 1870–1940* (Austin: University of Texas Press, 1990), pp. 80–81.

37. Cultural relativism is usually defined to mean that different beliefs and practices should be interpreted "relative" to one's own culture. For further discussion, see George Marcus and Michael Fischer, *Anthropology as Cultural Critique: an Experimental Moment in the Human Sciences* (Chicago: University of Chicago Press, 1986); and Alexander S. Dawson, *Indian and Nation in Revolutionary Mexico* (Tucson: University of Arizona Press, 2004).

38. For Gamio's seminal work, see his *Forjando patria. Pro-nacionalismo* (1916) (Mexico City: Editorial Porrúa, 1982). Although integration of the indigenous population into the Mexican body politic was not new, the important difference between pre- and post-revolutionary policies of integration resided in the latter's purported "respect" (shaped by Gamio's cultural relativism) of indigenous culture compared with the Porfirian thinkers' emphasis on de-Indianization as a condition of integration into the emerging nation-state and, as a consequence, homogenization of the Mexican population.

39. Institutions established to "Mexicanize" and "acculturate" the Indians include the *Dirección de Antropología* (1918–34), the *Departamento Autónomo de Asuntos Indígenas* (1935–47), and the *Instituto Nacional Indigenista* (1948–2002). See De la Peña, "A New Mexican Nationalism?" p. 282. On rural education, see Stephen E. Lewis, "The Nation, Education, and the "Indian Problem" in Mexico, 1920–1940," in Mary Kay Vaughan and Stephen E. Lewis, eds., *The Eagle and the Virgin. Nation and Cultural Revolution in Mexico, 1920–1940* (Durham and London: Duke University Press, 2006), pp. 176–95; and Mary Kay Vaughan, *Cultural Politics in Revolution:*

Teachers, Peasants and Schools in Mexico, 1930–1940 (Tucson: University of Arizona Press, 1997).

40. Knight, "Racism," p. 82. For a discussion of how *indigenismo* served to reproduce, rather than demolish "many of the racist assumptions of Western European thought, and thus allowed for the continuation of racist paradigms and practices in post-revolutionary Mexico," see Knight, "Racism," pp. 86–88. Also see De la Peña's observations on cultural homogeneity as representing the "official" vision of Mexican citizenship in "A New Mexican Nationalism?" p. 281. For an overview of the modernization strategies in the visual arts and the appropriation of the Indian body for the construction of a national mythology, see Fausto Ramírez, *Saturnino Herrán* (Mexico City: Universidad Nacional Autónoma de México, 1976); and the essays in *Modernidad and modernización en el arte mexicano, 1920–1950*, exh. cat. (Mexico City: Museo Nacional de Arte, 1991).

41. For the visual contestation and hybrid models, see Serge Gruzinski, *Images at War: Mexico From Columbus to Blade Runner (1492–2019)* (Durham: Duke University Press, 2001); and Carolyn Dean and Dana Leibsohn, "Hybridity and Its Discontents: Considering Visual Culture in Spanish America," *Colonial Latin American Review* 12, no, 1 (June 2003): 5–35.

42. De la Peña, "A New Mexican Nationalism?" p. 280. For further discussions of *mestizaje,* see Miller, *Rise and Fall of The Cosmic Race,* pp. 1–26; Lomnitz-Adler, *Exits from the Labyrinth,* pp. 261–81; and Jorge Klor de Alva, "The Postocolonization of the (Latin) American Experience: A Reconsideration of "Colonialism," "Postcolonialism," and "Mestizaje," in Gyan Prakash, ed., *After Colonialism: Imperial Histories and Post-colonial Displacements* (Princeton, N.J.: Princeton University Press, 1995), pp. 241–75.

43. De la Peña, "A New Mexican Nationalism?" p. 293.

44. See David A. Brading's discussion of this issue and particularly his analysis of Molina Enríquez who "fixed upon the mestizo as the basis of nationality." David A. Brading, *Prophecy and Myth in Mexican History* (Cambridge: Centre of Latin American Studies, 1984), p. 66.

45. Justo Sierra, *Evolución política del pueblo mexicano* (1900–1902); quoted in Knight, "Racism," p. 78.

46. Brading, *Prophecy and Myth in Mexican History,* p. 67.

47. Klor de Alva, "The Postocolonization of the (Latin) American Experience," p. 250.

48. Stepan, *"The Hour of Eugenics,"* p. 11.

49. On "behavioral modernization" and the Cultural Revolution in Mexico, see Vaughan and Lewis, eds., *The Eagle and the Virgin,* pp. 9–12.

50. Eugenicists in Mexico drew selectively from Mendelian and Lamarckian systems of racial classification. Mendelian systems derived from the Austrian Gregor Mendel's (1822–1884) laws of the independent assortment and recombination of he-

reditary characters in plants, and postulated that racial differences were biologically determined and passed down from generation to generation. Lamarckian systems were based on the French biologist Jean Baptiste Lamarck's (1744–1829) theory that external influences (e.g., the environment) could permanently alter the germ plasm of an individual; that is, that acquired traits could eventually become inherited. See Alexandra Minna Stern, *Eugenic Nation: Faults and Frontiers of Better Breeding in Modern America* (Los Angeles and Berkeley: University of California Press, 2005), pp. 14–16.

51. For representative works, see Herbert Spencer, *Principles of Biology* (London: W. Norgate, 1866); Gustave Le Bon, *Lois psychologiques de l'évolution des peuples* (Paris, 1902); and Louis Agassiz, *A Journey in Brazil* (Boston: Ticknor and Fields, 1868).

52. Significantly, between the ages of eight and thirteen Vasconcelos crossed the frontier bridge which separated Piedras Negras from Eagle Pass to attend school in the United States. As Brading observes: "As a result, he not only became virtually bi-lingual but also for the remainder of his life entertained a dual, not to say bi-cultural, frame of reference. He exhibited all the attitudes of a frontier nationalist." Brading, *Prophecy and Myth in Mexican History*, p. 75. For Vasconcelos' increasing affinities for eugenics and *blanquemiento* or whitening, see also Miller, *Rise and Fall of the Cosmic Race*, pp. 40–44.

53. Stepan, *"The Hour of Eugenics,"* pp. 145–53.

54. For a discussion of racial categories currently included in the U.S. census, see Steven Harmon Wilson, "Some Are Born White, Some Achieve Whiteness, and Some Have Whiteness Thrust Upon Them: Mexican Americans and the Politics of Racial Classification in the Federal Judicial Bureaucracy, Twenty-five Years After *Hernandez v. Texas*," in Michael A. Olivas, ed., *"Colored Men" and "Hombres Aquí" Hernandez v. Texas and the Emergence of Mexican-American Lawyering* (Houston: Arte Público Press, 2006), pp. 137–38, 141–42. As of 2007 the Office of Management and Budget's categories for race are (1) American Indian or Alaska Native; (2) Asian; (3) Black or African American; (4) Native Hawaiian or Other Pacific Islander; and (5) White. There are also two categories for ethnicity: "Hispanic or Latino" and "not Hispanic or Latino." The Census Bureau's 2000 questionnaires included a sixth racial category: "some other race." As Wilson argues: "This is intended to allow responses from people identifying as Mulatto, Creole, and Mestizo. Reportedly, there are sixty-three possible combinations of the six basic racial categories, including six categories for those who report exactly one race, and fifty-seven categories for those who report two or more races . . . Still unresolved is the basic question, what race should Hispanics check on this form?" (p. 142).

55. Knight, "Racism," p. 97; on anti-Chinese racism in Mexico, see Gerardo Rénique, "Race, Region and Nation: Sonora's anti-Chinese Racism in Mexico's Post-revolutionary Nationalism, 1920s–1930s," in Applebaum et al., *Race and Nation*, pp. 211–36.

56. Andrés Reséndez, *Changing National Identities at the Frontier: Texas and New Mexico, 1800–1850* (Cambridge: Cambridge University Press, 2005), p. 2. Also see Martha Menchaca, *Recovering History, Constructing Race: The Indian, Black, and White Roots of Mexican Americans* (Austin: University of Texas Press, 2001).

57. Gutiérrez, "Migration, Emergent Ethnicity, and the 'Third Space.'" For a discussion of this liminal space as a "relatively coherent in-between region," see Saldívar, *The Borderlands of Culture*, p. 27. Also useful is Samuel Truett and Elliott Young, eds., *Continental Crossroads: Remapping U.S.–Mexico Borderlands History* (Durham and London: Duke University Press, 2004).

58. On this issue see Appelbaum et al., "Racial Nations," p. 17.

59. On the question of race and construction of whiteness in relation to class, see Julie Anne Dowling, "The Lure of Whiteness and the Politics of 'Otherness': Mexican American Racial Identity." (Ph.D. diss., University of Texas, Austin, 2004), chap. 2; and Neil Foley, *The White Scourge: Mexicans, Blacks, and Poor Whites in Texas Cotton Culture* (Berkeley: University of California Press, 1997).

60. For a discussion of the reasons why jury selection remains predominantly white with continued underrepresentation of Latino jurors, see Olivas, "Introduction," in Olivas, ed., *"Colored Men" and "Hombres Aquí,"* p. xx; and Kevin Johnson, *"Hernandez v. Texas:* Legacies of Justice and Injustice" in Olivas ed., *"Colored Men" and "Hombres Aquí,"* pp. 53–90.

61. Klor de Alva, "The Postocolonization of the (Latin) American Experience," pp. 251–52. For an overview of Chicano history, see Rodolfo Acuña, *Occupied America: A History of Chicanos* (New York: Longman, 2006).

62. On this issue see the insightful essay by Josh Kun, "This is Chicano Art?," *LA Times Magazine,* January 9, 2005, pp. 13–15, and 29–32; and the exhibition and accompanying publication *Phantom Sightings: Art after the Chicano Movement,* ed. Rita Gonzalez, Howard N. Fox, and Chon A. Noriega (Los Angeles and Berkeley: Los Angeles County Museum of Art and the University of California Press, 2008).

63. On the obsolescence of the national narrative of *mestizaje* for Mexico, see De la Peña, "A New Mexican Nationalism?" pp. 293–94.

64. Chon A. Noriega, *Shot in America: Television, the State and the Rise of Chicano Cinema* (Minneapolis and London: University of Minnesota Press, 2000), p. xxvi.

65. *Las nuevas memorias del Capitán Jean de Monségur* (1707–08), introd. Jean-Pierre Berthe, translated by Florence Olivier, Blanca Pulido, and Isabelle Véricat (Mexico City: Universidad Nacional Autónoma de México, 1994), pp. 41–42.

Chapter 1

This essay is partly based on an analysis of *probanzas de limpieza de sangre* (proofs of purity of blood) and other research on early modern Spain and New Spain that I conducted for my book, *Genealogical Fictions: Limpieza de Sangre, Religion, and Gender in Colonial Mexico* (Stanford, California: Stanford University Press, 2008).

1. Stuart Hall, "Race, Articulation and Societies Structured in Dominance," *Unesco Reader, Sociological Theories: Race and Colonialism* (Paris: Unesco, 1980), p. 338; Etienne Balibar, "Racism and Nationalism," in *Race, Nation, Class: Ambiguous Identities,* ed. Etienne Balibar and Immanuel Wallerstein (London and New York: Verso, 1991), p. 40; and Cornel West, "Race and Social Theory: Toward a Genealogical Materialist Analysis," in *The Year Left 2: An American Socialist Yearbook,* ed. Mike Davis et al. (London: Verso, 1987), pp. 74–90.

2. Thomas C. Holt, *The Problem of Race in the 21st Century* (Cambridge and London: Harvard University Press, 2000), p. 8.

3. Ibid., 23–24. Also see Peter Wade, *Race, Nature and Culture: An Anthropological Perspective* (London and Sterling, Virginia: Pluto Press, 2002), p. 12; and George M. Fredrickson, *Racism: A Short History* (Princeton and Oxford: Princeton University Press, 2002), pp. 17–47. Whereas Wade links the origin of Western racism to European colonialism and expansion (which began in the fourteenth century), Fredrickson associates it with late medieval religious cosmologies, and in particular with fifteenth-century deployment of notions of "blood" against converted Jews and their descendants in Spain.

4. Paul Gilroy, *The Black Atlantic: Modernity and Double Consciousness* (Cambridge, Massachusetts: Harvard University Press, 1993), p. 14. For a discussion of how Spanish colonialism and its image production forged, and continues to shape Mexico's "hybrid" culture, see Serge Gruzinski, *Images at War: Mexico from Columbus to Blade Runner (1492–2019)* (Durham, N.C.: Duke University Press, 2001).

5. Recent works on the *casta* paintings include Ilona Katzew, *Casta Painting: Images of Race in Eighteenth-Century Mexico* (New Haven and London: Yale University Press, 2004); Magali M. Carrera, *Imagining Identity in New Spain: Race, Lineage, and the Colonial Body in Portraiture and Casta Paintings* (Austin: University of Texas Press, 2003); María Elena Martínez, "The Spanish Concept of *Limpieza de Sangre* and the Emergence of the 'Race/Caste' System in the Viceroyalty of New Spain" (Ph.D. diss., University of Chicago, 2002), pp. 1–42; Ilona Katzew, ed., *New World Orders: Casta Painting and Colonial Latin America* (New York: Americas Society Art Gallery, 1996); and María Concepción García Sáiz, *Las castas mexicanas: un género pictórico americano* (Milan: Olivetti, 1989).

6. Michael Banton, *Racial Theories* (Cambridge and New York: Cambridge University Press, 1998), pp. 4–5, 17–43. Also see Nicholas Hudson, "From 'Nation' to 'Race': The Origin of Racial Classification in Eighteenth-Century Thought," *Eighteenth-Century Studies* 29, no. 3 (1996): 247–48.

7. Paul Freedman, *Images of the Medieval Peasant* (Stanford, California: Stanford University Press, 1999), pp. 59–130. Also refer to Freedman's illuminating discussion

of medieval representations of the peasantry as a lower order of humanity, associated with animals, dirt, and excrement, pp. 133–56. David B. Davis has suggested that this beastilization of the peasantry provided an important antecedent to the early modern racialization of Jews and blacks. David Brion Davis, "Constructing Race: A Reflection" *The William and Mary Quarterly* 54, no. 1 (January 1997): 12–13.

8. See Roberto López Vela, "Estructuras administrativas del Santo Oficio," *Historia de la Inquisición en España y América: las estructuras del Santo Oficio,* vol. II, ed. Joaquín Pérez Villanueva and Bartolomé Escandell Bonet (Madrid: Biblioteca de Autores Cristianos, Centro de Estudios Inquisitoriales, 1993), p. 228; and Elena Postigo Castellanos, *Honor y privilegio en la corona de Castilla: el Consejo de las Órdenes y los Caballeros de Hábito en el s. XVII* (Almazán, Soria: Junta de Castilla y León, 1988), p. 139.

9. The literature on the *limpieza* statutes is too vast to cite here, but for a good introduction to the topic, see Albert A. Sicroff, *Los estatutos de limpieza de sangre: controversias entre los siglos XV y XVII,* trans. Mauro Armiño (Madrid: Tauros Ediciones, S.A., 1985); Jaime Contreras, "Limpieza de sangre, cambio social y manipulación de la memoria," in *Inquisición y conversos* (Toledo: Caja de Castilla–La Mancha, 1994), pp. 81–101; Juan Hernández Franco, *Cultura y limpieza de sangre en la España moderna: puritate sanguinis* (Murcia: Universidad de Murcia, 1996); Antonio Domínguez Ortiz, *Los judeoconversos en la España moderna* (Madrid: Editorial MAPFRE, S.A., 1992); Henry Kamen, *The Spanish Inquisition: A Historical Revision* (New Haven: Yale University Press, 1998); David L. Graizbord, *Souls in Dispute: Converso Identities in Iberia and the Jewish Diaspora, 1580–1700* (Philadelphia: University of Pennsylvania Press, 2004); and Benzion Netanyahu, *The Origins of the Inquisition in Fifteenth Century Spain* (New York: Random House, 1995).

10. According to Joan Corominas, when the word *raza* was being linked to Jewish and Muslim descent, it incorporated the meanings of an older Castilian term (*raça*) that connoted defectiveness (as in "defect in the fabric") and guilt. Joan Corominas, *Diccionario crítico etimológico de la lengua castellana,* vol. III (Berna, Switzerland: Editorial Francke, 1954), pp. 1019–21. Also see Verena Stolcke, "Conquered Women," *Report on the Americas* (NACLA) 24, no. 5 (1991): 23–28.

11. Sebastián de Covarrubias Orozco, *Tesoro de la lengua castellana o española* (1611), ed. Felipe C. R. Maldonado (Madrid: Editorial Castalia, S.A., 1995), p. 851.

12. Huntington Library (hereafter HL), MS. 35150.

13. Biblioteca Nacional (Madrid) (hereafter BNM), MS. 10431, fols. 131–50v.

14. Early modern Spain was not technically a feudal society. Serfdom, which in medieval Castile had been limited, partly due to the nature of colonization and land distribution that accompanied the *Reconquista,* had dwindled by the late fifteenth century. William D. Phillips Jr. and Carla Rahn Phillips, "Spain in the Fifteenth Century," in *Transatlantic Encounters: Europeans and Andeans in the Sixteenth Century,*

ed. Kenneth J. Andrien and Rolena Adorno (Berkeley: University of California Press, 1991), p. 17. Also see Helen Nader, *Liberty in Absolutist Spain: the Habsburg Sale of Towns, 1516–1700* (Baltimore: Johns Hopkins University Press, 1990), pp. 9–15.

15. See, for example, Juan Antonio Maravall, *Poder, honor y élites en el siglo XVII* (Madrid: Siglo Veintiuno, 1984), pp. 173–250; Hernández Franco, *Cultura y limpieza de sangre*, pp. 12–17, 25–26, and 62–65; Henry Kamen, *The Spanish Inquisition: a Historical Revision*, pp. 28–36; and Jaime Contreras, *Sotos contra Riquelmes: regidores, inquisidores y criptojudíos* (Madrid: Anaya & M. Muchnik, 1992), pp. 23–24.

16. Recent studies of the Castilian economy have argued that the traditional social structure was in fact reinforced, especially after 1600. The extension of seigniorialization (which occurred in varying degrees throughout Western Europe) strengthened the bond between the Castilian state and landed aristocracy as well as the idea that nobility was a condition inherited through the blood. The refeudalization of Castilian society did not prevent, however, a certain "bastardization" of the noble estate through the crown's sale of offices (avenues to noble status) and titles to meritorious or wealthy individuals. The phenomenon led Spanish genealogists to make a strong distinction between "nobility of blood" and "nobility of privilege." See Ignacio Atienza Hernández, " 'Refeudalisation' in Castile during the Seventeenth Century: A Cliché?" in *The Castilian Crisis of the Seventeenth Century: New Perspectives on the Economic and Social History of Seventeenth-Century Spain*, ed. I. A. A. Thompson and Bartolomé Yun Casalilla (Cambridge, U.K. and New York: Cambridge University Press, 1994), pp. 249–76, esp. 254–56; in the same volume, Bartolomé Yun Casalilla, "The Castilian Aristocracy in the Seventeenth Century: Crisis, Refeudalisation, or Political Offensive?" pp. 277–300; and I. A. A. Thompson, "The Purchase of Nobility in Castile, 1552–1700," *Journal of European Economic History* 11 (1982): 313–60.

17. Ruth Pike, *Linajudos and Conversos in Seville: Greed and Prejudice in Sixteenth- and Seventeenth-Century Spain* (New York and Washington, D.C.: Peter Lang Publishing, 2000).

18. I. A. A. Thompson, "*Hidalgo* and *pechero*: the language of 'estates' and 'classes' in early-modern Castile," in *Language, History and Class*, ed. Penelope J. Corfield (Cambridge, U.K.: Basil Blackwell, 1991), pp. 70–74. During the Middle Ages and early modern period, images of the trees were often used to represent social estates, genealogies, and even degrees of consanguinity prohibiting marriage. See Freedman, *Images of the Medieval Peasant*, pp. 69–70.

19. BNM, MS. 11576: copy of the patent of nobility and purity of blood of the Calleja family, 1625.

20. On the transatlantic nature of *limpieza de sangre* investigations initiated in New Spain and their implications for both Mexican and Spanish notions of blood, see Martínez, "The Spanish Concept of *Limpieza de Sangre*," chap 5. Ann Laura Stoler has correctly stressed that notions of blood-purity and race operated in imperial contexts,

flowing from the metropolis to the colony and back. Ann Laura Stoler, *Race and the Education of Desire: Foucault's 'History of Sexuality' and the Colonial Order of Things* (Durham and London: Duke University Press, 1995), p. 30.

21. See David Nirenberg, "El concepto de la raza en la España medieval," *Edad Media: Revista de Historia* 3 (Spring 2000): 50–54.

22. Corominas, *Diccionario crítico etimológico de la lengua castellana,* vol. 1, 722–24. Corominas disagreed with Covarrubias's claim that the word *casta* derived from the Latin *castus,* which alluded to chastity.

23. Though the word could refer to the sexual virtue of both women and men, marital fidelity was more central to the definition of the former. "Women who remain loyal to their husbands are called *castas,*" wrote Covarrubias, whereas purity, honesty, and sexual restraint (*"vale puro, continente, opuesto al deshonesto y dado al vicio de la luxuria"*) were the qualities that characterized men who were *castos.* Covarrubias, *Tesoro de la lengu castellana,* p. 283.

24. Ibid., p. 282.

25. See Verena Stolcke, "Invaded Women: Gender, Race, and Class in the Formation of Colonial Society," in *Women, 'Race' & Writing in the Early Modern Period,* ed. Margo Hendricks and Patricia Parker (London and New York: Routledge, 1994), pp. 277–78; Mary Elizabeth Perry, *Gender and Disorder in Early Modern Seville* (Princeton, N.J.: Princeton University Press, 1990), esp. pp. 5–6; and Susan Socolow, *The Women of Colonial Latin America* (Cambridge, U.K.: Cambridge University Press, 2000), pp. 8–9.

26. Julian Pitt-Rivers, "On the Word 'Caste,'" in *The Translation of Culture: Essays to E. E. Evans-Pritchard,* ed. T. O. Beidelman (London: Tavistock Publications, 1971), pp. 234–35. Perhaps because it was used to refer to the place of origin of slaves who had been born in Africa (as in *"casta angola"*), the term *casta* was also applied to "pure" blacks.

27. Archivo General de la Nación (Mexico City) (hereafter AGN), Inquisición, caja 163, fols. 1–37v.

28. Laura A. Lewis, *Hall of Mirrors: Power, Witchcraft, and Caste in Colonial Mexico* (Durham and London: Duke University Press, 2003), pp. 22–25. Lewis's distinction between Spain's metropolitan and colonial discourses of differentiation brings to mind Étienne Balibar's discussion of an "exclusive racism" (of extermination or elimination, as in Nazism) versus an "inclusive" one (of oppression or exploitation resting on the construction and maintenance of hierarchies, as in colonial and slave societies). But as Balibar stresses, the conceptual distinction has limited use, for not only have these two forms of racism (colonial discourses and anti-Semitism) historically exhibited characteristics of the other, but roughly coinciding with the emergence of European protonational identities, they have a "joint descent." Étienne Balibar, "Racism and Nationalism," pp. 39–45.

29. John Carter Brown Library, Libros de Informaciones (hereafter JCB/LI), vol. 1, fols. 487–91. Also see JCB/LI, vol. 2, fols. 207–14: Information (*información*) regarding Alonso Gómez, made in the Villa de Niebla, Spain, fol. 1617.

30. Robin Blackburn, *The Making of New World Slavery: From the Baroque to the Modern, 1492–1800* (London and New York: Verso, 1997), p. 12. For the history and many uses of the Curse of Ham (including justification of serfdom), see Freedman, *Images of the Medieval Peasant*, pp. 86–104; Benjamin Braude, "The Sons of Noah and the Construction of Ethnic and Geographical Identities in the Medieval and Early Modern Periods," *The William and Mary Quarterly* 54, no. 1 (1997): 103–42; and David Goldenberg, *The Curse of Ham: Race and Slavery in early Judaism, Christianity, and Islam* (Princeton, N. J.: Princeton University Press, 2003).

31. See, for example, the early seventeenth-century memorial of the inquisitor don Diego Serrano de Silva. BNM, MS. 10431, fols. 131–50v.

32. A number of laws restricting the rights and privileges of persons of mixed ancestry were passed in the second half of the sixteenth century, especially in the 1570s. See Magnus Mörner, *Race Mixture in the History of Latin America* (Boston: Little, Brown and Company, 1967), pp. 27–29, and 43; C. E. Marshall, "The Birth of the Mestizo in New Spain," *Hispanic American Historical Review* 19 (1939): 160–84; and Richard Konetzke, "El mestizaje y su importancia en el desarrollo de la población hispano–americana durante la época colonial," *Revista de Indias* 7, no. 24 (April–June, 1946): 230.

33. See Gonzalo Aguirre Beltrán, *La población negra de México: estudio etnohistórico* (1st ed. 1946; Mexico City: Fondo de Cultura Económica, 1989), pp. 153–54; R. Douglas Cope, *The Limits of Racial Domination: Plebeian Society in Colonial Mexico City, 1660–1720* (Madison: The University of Wisconsin Press, 1994), pp. 18–24; and J. Jorge Klor de Alva, "*Mestizaje* from New Spain to Aztlán: on the Control and Classification of Collective Identities," in Katzew, ed., *New World Orders*, pp. 60–61. On the rise of the *castas* as a free wage-labor force, see John E. Kicza, "Native American, African, and Hispanic Communities during the Middle Period in the Colonial Americas," *Historical Archaeology* 31, no. 1 (1997): 11–13.

34. Covarrubias, *Tesoro de la lengua castellana*, p. 751. For Corominas, the origin of the word was uncertain, but he speculated that it might have come from the Latin "mixtus." Corominas, *Diccionario crítico etimológico de la lengua castellana*, vol. 3, p. 359.

35. Forbes writes that in Mexico, the term *mulato* continued to be used for the descendants of blacks and Indians into the 1650s and that within the Spanish empire the term generally meant a person who was half African and half something else. As such it could be applied to various combinations. Jack D. Forbes, *Black Africans and Native Americans: Color, Race and Caste in the Evolution of Red-Black Peoples* (New York: Basil Blackwell Ltd., 1988), pp. 162–65.

36. Juan de Solórzano y Pereira, *Política Indiana* (1648) (Madrid: Compañía Ibero–Americana de Publicaciones, 1930), vol. 1, p. 445. Covarrubias also linked the word mulatto to "mule" and wrote that mules were bastard animals, a "third species" produced by the cross of a horse with a donkey that could only reproduce under extraordinary circumstances. Covarrubias, *Tesoro de la lengua castellana*, p. 768.

37. For a good discussion of this topic in the French colonial context, see Doris Garraway, "Race, Reproduction and Family Romance in Moreau de Saint-Méry's *Description . . . de la partie française de l'isle Saint-Domingue*," *Eighteenth-Century Studies* 38, no. 2 (2005): 227–46.

38. Archivo Histórico Nacional (hereafter AHN), Inquisición de México, Libro 1047, fols. 430–434; AHN, Inquisición, Libro 1064; and AHN, Inquisición, Libro 1065.

39. For a few examples refer to Biblioteca Nacional de Antropología e Historia (Mexico City), Microfilm Collection, Serie Puebla, Roll 81, fol. 12v; Condumex (Mexico City), Fondo CMLXI-36, manuscript belonging to the Archivo del Ayuntamiento de Puebla, fol. 46; and Archivo del Ayuntamiento de Puebla, Actas de Cabildo, vol. 1, doc. 234.

40. See AHN, Inquisición, Libro 1064; AHN, Inquisición, Libro 1065; AGN, Inquisición, vol. 372, exp. 14; and AGN, Inquisición, vol. 684, exp. 4.

41. AHN, Inquisición de México, Libro 1047, fols. 430–34: Correspondence from the Mexican Inquisition to the Supreme Council of the Inquisition, November 5, 1576.

42. See AGN, Inquisición, vol. 82, exp. 4, fol. 118; and AHN, Inquisición de México, Libro 1057.

43. For more on this topic, see María Elena Martínez, "The Black Blood of New Spain: *Limpieza de Sangre*, Racial Violence, and Gendered Power in Early Colonial Mexico," *William and Mary Quarterly* 3rd Series, vol. LCI, no. 3 (July 2004): 479–520.

44. The European use of archives and censuses to transform colonial knowledge into colonial power has received considerable attention from scholars of nineteenth-century India. The literature includes Bernard Cohen, *Colonialism and its Forms of Knowledge: The British in India* (Princeton, N.J.: Princeton University Press, 1996); Partha Chatterjee, *The Nation and its Fragments: Colonial and Postcolonial Histories* (Princeton, N.J.: Princeton University Press, 1993); Nicholas B. Dirks, *Castes of Mind: Colonialism and the Making of Modern India* (Princeton, N.J.: Princeton University Press, 2001); and Nicholas B. Dirks, "Annals of the Archive: Ethnographic Notes on the Sources of History," in *From the Margins: Historical Anthropology and its Futures,* ed. Brian Keith Axel (Durham, N.C.: Duke University Press, 2002), pp. 47–65.

45. See, for example, Patricia Seed, *To Love, Honor, and Obey in Colonial Mexico: Conflicts Over Marriage Choice, 1574–1821* (Stanford, California: Stanford University Press, 1988), p. 251, n. 25; and Cope, *The Limits of Racial Domination*, p. 24.

46. AGN, Bienes Nacionales, vol. 578, exp. 21; and AHN, Inquisición, Libro 1067, fols. 316–18, and 500–500v.

47. Ramón A. Gutiérrez, *When Jesus Came, the Corn Mothers Went Away: Marriage, Sexuality and Power in New Mexico, 1500–1846* (Stanford, California: Stanford University Press, 1991), pp. 196–200; Robert H. Jackson, "Race/caste and the Creation and Meaning of Identity," *Revista de Indias* 55, no. 203 (1995): 155; and Steven W. Hackel, *Children of Coyote, Missionaries of Saint Francis: Indian-Spanish relations in Colonial California, 1769–1850* (Chapel Hill: Omohundro Institute of Early American History and Culture and University of North Carolina Press, 2005), pp. 59–60.

48. See, among others, Patricia Seed, "Social Dimensions of Race: Mexico City, 1753," *Hispanic American Historical Review* 62, no. 4 (1982): 568–606; Cope, *The Limits of Racial Domination*, pp. 49–67; Stuart B. Schwartz, "Colonial Identities and the *Sociedad de Castas*," *Colonial Latin America Review* 4, no. 1 (1995): 185–201; and Richard Boyer, *Cast and Identity in Colonial Mexico: A Proposal and an Example* (Storrs, Providence, and Amherst: Latin American Studies Consortium of New England, 1997).

49. Refer to Richard L. Garner and Spiro E. Stefanou, *Economic Growth and Change in Bourbon Mexico* (Gainesville: University Press of Florida, 1993); Richard Salvucci, "Economic Growth and Change in Bourbon Mexico: A Review Essay," *The Americas* 51, no. 4 (1994): 219–31; Paul Gootenberg, "On Salamanders, Pyramids, and Mexico's 'Growth-without-Change': Anachronistic Reflections on a Case of Bourbon New Spain," *Colonial Latin America Review* 4, no. 1 (1995): 117–27; and Josefina Zoraida Vázquez, ed., *Interpretaciones del siglo XVIII mexicano: el impacto de las reformas borbónicas* (Mexico City: Nueva Imagen, 1992), esp. the articles by Brian R. Hamnett and Carlos Marichal.

50. Seed, *To Love, Honor, and Obey,* pp. 25, 96–8, and 146–47. Also see Dennis Nodin Valdés, "The Decline of the *Sociedad de Castas* in Mexico City" (Ph.D. diss., University of Michigan, 1978), pp. 40–42. For examples of late seventeenth-century petitions by mulatto slaves and mestizos to marry Spanish and *castiza* women in Mexico City, see AGN, Inquisición, Caja 163, Folder 16, exps. 4–6.

51. The issue of whether the expansion of mercantile capitalism in New Spain made "class" more important than "caste" at the end of the colonial period was extensively debated in the 1970s and 1980s. Despite disagreement about which one became more salient, most scholars agreed that the former had become more significant than it had been in previous centuries. See, for example, John K. Chance and William B. Taylor "Estate and Class in a Colonial City: Oaxaca in 1792," *Comparative Studies in Society and History* 19 (1977): 454–87; Robert McCaa, Stuart B. Schwartz, and Arturo Grubessich, "Race and Class in Colonial Latin America: A Critique," *Comparative Studies of Society and History* 21, no. 3 (July 1979): 421–42, esp. 433; with reply from John K. Chance and William B. Taylor, "Estate *and* Class: A Reply," *Comparative Studies of Society and History* 21, no. 3 (July 1979): 434–41; Patricia Seed and Philip F. Rust, "Estate and Class in Colonial Oaxaca Revisited," *Comparative Studies of Society and History* 25, no. 4 (October 1983): 703–10; and Robert McCaa and Stuart B. Schwartz,

"Measuring Marriage Patterns: Percentages, Cohen's Kappa, and Log-Linear Models," *Comparative Studies of Society and History* 25, no. 4 (October 1983): 711–20.

52. See JCB/LI, Vol. IV, fols. 395–401 and subsequent volumes.

53. *Oficios viles* essentially referred to trade and money lending. In Spanish sources, the phrase was usually accompanied by allusions to *oficios mecánicos* ("mechanical trades"), which included silversmiths, painters, embroiderers, stonemasons, innkeepers, tavern owners, and scribes (except royal ones).

54. Attesting to the growing application of *limpieza* policies are Inquisition records, which contain purity of blood documents for aldermen, *alcaldes* (judges), and university professors that were not produced by the Holy Office itself but by town councils, royal officials, colleges, seminaries, and so forth. See AHN, Inquisición, Leg. 2284. For examples of town councils with purity requirements, see AGN, Ayuntamientos, vol. 197, fols. 1–22v, 49 and 65. And for examples of educational stipends for which the applicant submitted proof of purity, see AGN, Archivo Histórico de Hacienda, vol. 2019, exp. 5; and AGN, Archivo Histórico de Hacienda, vol. 2019, exp. 9.

55. This information became part of a report of his professional and academic merits he compiled in 1752, when he was serving as a judge (*oidor*) in Guadalajara's *audiencia* or high court. AHN, Inquisición, Leg. 2282.

56. AHN, Inquisición, Leg. 2284.

57. Although the concept of *calidad* was already used in the sixteenth century, it became much more common in the eighteenth century. As Robert McCaa has observed, in the late colonial period it referred to a number of factors, including economic status, occupation, purity of blood, and birthplace, to "reputation as a whole." Robert McCaa, "Calidad, Clase, and Marriage in Colonial Mexico: The Case of Parral, 1788–90," *Hispanic American Historical Review* 64, no. 3 (1984): 477–501. In *probanzas de limpieza de sangre* the term *calidad* began to compete with that of *casta*. Phrases such as *calidad de mulato* and *calidad de español* started to appear almost as often *as casta de mulato* and *casta de español,* and Inquisition officials and witnesses tended to use "calidad" and "casta" interchangeably. For a few examples, see AHN, Inquisición, Leg. 2282; AHN, Inquisición, Leg. 2286 (1); and AGN, Bienes Nacionales, vol. 578, exp. 21.

58. See BNM, MS. 18701.

59. A key moment in the history of the Spanish crown's curtailment of the church's independence on matters of marriage, the passage of the Real Pragmática of 1776 (extended to the colonies in 1778) made parental consent necessary for marriage for people under twenty-five, stressed the importance of marriages between "equals," and shifted the power to mediate disputes between parents and children from ecclesiastical to royal courts. On its implications in Mexico, see Seed, *To Love, Honor, and Obey,* esp. pp. 200–04.

60. Michel Foucault first discussed the shift (which he also referred to as the transition from a "deployment of alliance" to a "deployment of sexuality") in *The His-*

tory of Sexuality, trans. Robert Hurley (New York: Vintage Books, 1990), esp. vol. 1, pp. 106–10, and 147–49.

61. AGN, Bienes Nacionales, vol. 578, exp. 21.

62. Carrera, *Imagining Identity in New Spain,* p. 9. For a more thorough discussion on the concept of physiognomy, refer to Rebecca Haidt, *Embodying the Enlightenment: Knowing the Body in Eighteenth-Century Spanish Literature and Culture* (New York: St. Martin's Press, 1998).

63. See, for example, AGI, México 684; AGN, Ayuntamientos, vol. 197; and AGN, Indiferente de Guerra, vol. 30. David Cahill has reproduced a list of Andean *casta* categories that was included in an eighteenth-century colonial description of the Peruvian population. Titled "genealogía de la Plebeya gente" ("Genealogy of the Plebeian People"), it begins with a Spanish male and black female and also allows for the descendants of the Spanish-African union to return to the Spanish pole. Why the possibility that black blood could be completely whitened was contemplated in the Andean colonial context and not in Mexico's visual or written records is difficult to answer, but perhaps the large number of the African-descended population in the viceroyalty of Peru (especially in Lima) prior to independence offers a clue. See David Cahill, "Colour by Numbers: Racial and Ethnic Categories in the Viceroyalty of Peru, 1532–1824," *Journal of Latin American Studies* 26 (1994): 339.

64. AHN, Inquisición, Leg. 2288.

Chapter 2

An earlier version of this essay appeared in Susan Deans-Smith and Eric Van Young, eds., *Mexican Soundings: Essays in Honour of David A. Brading* (London: Institute for the Study of the Americas, 2007), and is reprinted by kind permission of the Institute for the Study of the Americas, University of London. My thanks to Ilona Katzew for her patient and insightful critique of this essay.

1. Archivo Antiguo de la Academia de San Carlos (hereafter AAASC) 10038, Instancia de los Profesores de Pintura y Escultura de esta N.C. sobre que se les releve de la contribucion que se les exive para la Jura de Nuestro Augusto Soberano, 1789, fol. 6. The Royal Academy of San Carlos was the first and only royal academy of fine arts (painting, sculpture, architecture, and engraving) established in Spain's American colonies. For a brief introduction to the Academy's history, see Jean Charlot, *Mexican Art and the Academy of San Carlos, 1785–1915* (Austin: University of Texas Press, 1962). Four of the painters had worked as "correctors" or tutors in drawing in the provisional school of engraving that eventually became the Royal Academy of San Carlos: Andrés López, Mariano Vázquez, Rafael Gutiérrez, and Juan Sáenz.

2. AAASC 10038, Instancia de los Profesores de Pintura y Escultura de esta N.C., 1789, fol. 6.

3. AAASC Gav 9/doc. 1030, Memorial de los profesores de la Noble Arte de Pintura to Ex Sr, 1799. One of the petitioners, Francisco Clapera, had been employed as

an Assistant Director of Painting; the four "correctors" who signed the petition of 1789 also signed this petition. The places where illicit painting and selling of artworks was conducted included carriage builders' workshops, carpenters' workshops, public auctions, and "other public and secret places."

4. Ibid.

5. Ibid.

6. Instructive on this point is Matthew O'Hara and Andrew Fisher's discussion of how identity "also embraces self-understanding, that is, the affective meaning of social categories, the sense of groupness as experienced by an individual, the lived reality of sameness or difference." See their "Racial Identities and Their Interpreters in Colonial Latin America," in Matthew O'Hara and Andrew Fisher eds., *Imperial Subjects: Race and Identity in Colonial Latin America* (Durham: Duke University Press, 2009), p. 21. I use the terms *race* and *racial* with the same qualification as expressed by Stuart Schwartz to signify "general markers of distinction and hierarchy without necessarily implying their modern definitions." Stuart Schwartz, "Colonial Identities and the *Sociedad de Castas,*" *Colonial Latin American Review* 4, no. 1 (1995): 196, note 1. Also see Antonio Feros, "Reflexiones atlánticas: identidades étnicas y nacionales en el mundo hispano moderno," *Cultura Escrita & Sociedad* 2 (2006): 77–107.

7. Research on guilds and artisans in colonial Latin America in general remains underdeveloped. The classic study on colonial Mexico is Manuel Carrera Stampa, *Los gremios mexicanos: la organización gremial en Nueva España, 1521–1861* (Mexico City: Edición y Distribución Ibero-Americana de Publicaciones, S.A., 1954). See also R. Douglas Cope, *The Limits of Racial Domination: Plebeian Society in Colonial Mexico City, 1660–1720* (Madison: University of Wisconsin Press, 1994); Sonia Pérez Toledo, *Los hijos del trabajo. Los artesanos de la ciudad de México, 1780–1853* (Mexico City: El Colegio de México, 1996). Social historians have virtually ignored artists in their studies of artisans and colonial societies. One exception is Lyman Johnson, "The Silversmiths of Buenos Aires: A Case Study in the Failure of Corporate Social Organization," *Journal of Latin American Studies* 8, no. 2 (1976): 181–213. Despite substantial art historical literature on painting and painters in colonial Mexico, the social history of painters remains embryonic. The most important essays to date are Rogelio Ruiz Gomar, "El gremio y la cofradía de pintores en la Nueva España," in Elisa Vargas Lugo and Gustavo Curiel, eds., *Juan Correa: su vida y su obra,* vol. 3 (Mexico City: Universidad Nacional Autónoma de México, 1991) (hereafter *Correa,* vol. 3), pp. 203–22, and Ruiz Gomar's "Unique Expressions: Painting in New Spain," in *Painting a New World: Mexican Art and Life 1521–1821,* exh. cat. (Denver and Austin: Denver Art Museum, and University of Texas Press, 2004), pp. 47–78; Jaime Cuadriello, "El obrador Trinitario: María de Guadalupe creada en idea, imagen y materia," in *El Divino Pintor: la creación de María de Guadalupe en el taller Celestial,* exh. cat. (Mexico City: Museo de la Basílica de Guadalupe, 2001), pp. 61–205; Paula Mues Orts, "Merezca ser hidalgo

y libre el que pintó lo santo y respetado: la defensa novohispana del arte de la pintura," in *El Divino Pintor,* pp. 29–59; Clara Bargellini, "Originality and Invention in the Painting of New Spain," in *Painting a New World,* pp. 79–91; Ilona Katzew, *Casta Painting: Images of Race in Eighteenth-Century Mexico* (London and New Haven: Yale University Press, 2004), chap.1. The classic survey of colonial painters is Manuel Toussaint, *Pintura Colonial en México* (Mexico City: Universidad Nacional Autónoma de México, 1982). Useful reference works include Guillermo Tovar de Teresa, *Repertorio de artistas en México,* 3 vols. (Mexico City: Grupo Financiero Bancomer, 1995–1997) (hereafter *Repertorio*); Glorinela González Franco et al., *Artistas y artesanos a través de fuentes documentales. Ciudad de México,* vol. 1 (Mexico City: Instituto Nacional de Antropología e Historia, 1994) (hereafter *Artistas*); Virginia Armella de Aspe and Mercedes Meade de Angulo, *Tesoros de la Pinacoteca Virreinal* (Mexico City: Fomento Cultural Banamex, 1993) (hereafter *Tesoros*); Paula Mues Orts, *La libertad del pincel. Los discursos sobre la nobleza de la pintura en Nueva España* (Mexico City: Universidad Iberoamericana, 2008).

8. Ruth MacKay, *"Lazy, Improvident People." Myth and Reality in the Writing of Spanish History* (Ithaca and London: Cornell University Press, 2006), p. 195. See also Charles Gibson, *The Aztecs under Spanish Rule* (Stanford, California: Stanford University Press, 1964), and Cope, *The Limits of Racial Domination,* p. 21. Examples of guilds which requested enforcement of existing ordinances prohibiting both ownership of workshops and apprenticeships to people of "*color quebrado*" ("broken color"), or which sought to include new ordinances to introduce such restrictions include silver and gold beaters (1669), carvers (1704), silk spinners (1729), architects (1746), and silversmiths (1746). On the importance of *limpieza de sangre* (pure and untainted blood) and its revival in the late seventeenth and eighteenth centuries in Spain among certain guilds and artisans, and the "slippage between racial and occupational categories of exclusion," see MacKay, *"Lazy, Improvident People,"* p. 159.

9. Ruiz Gomar, "El gremio," pp. 203–22.

10. Ibid., pp. 209–10. For regulations in Spain concerning the prohibition of teaching painting to Jews and Moors in the 1607 statutes of the Colegio de Valencia, see Miguel Falomir Faus, "Artists' Responses to the Emergence of Markets for Paintings in Spain, c. 1600," in Neil De Marchi, and Hans J. Van Miegroet, eds., *Mapping Markets for Paintings in Europe, 1450–1750* (Turnhout: Brepols Publishers, 2006), pp. 135–65.

11. Katzew, *Casta Painting,* chap. 3.

12. See, for example, Mues Orts, "Merezca ser hidalgo," and Bargellini, "Originality and Invention."

13. On the shifting attitudes toward artists and artisans in Spain and Spanish America, see Mackay *"Lazy, Improvident People,"* pp. 182–97.

14. Javier Portús Pérez, *Pintura y pensamiento en la España de Lope de Vega* (Guipúzcoa: Nerea, 1999), pp. 79–80.

15. On the possible apprenticeship of Luis Juárez with Echave Orio, see Rogelio Ruiz Gomar, *El pintor Luis Juárez. Su vida y su obra* (Mexico City: Universidad Nacional Autónoma de México, 1987), pp. 92–96.

16. Marcus B. Burke, *Treasures of Mexican Colonial Painting: the Davenport Museum of Art Collection* (Santa Fe, New Mexico: Museum of New Mexico Press, 1998), p. 30.

17. Juana Gutiérrez Haces et al., *Cristóbal de Villalpando, ca. 1649–1714* (Mexico City: Fomento Cultural Banamex, 1997), pp. 39, 51; Tovar de Teresa, *Repertorio*, vol. 3, p. 286. Echave y Rioja was the great-grandson of Baltasar de Echave Orio (c. 1558–c. 1623) and son of Baltasar de Echave Ibía (1583–c. 1644).

18. Ibarra refers to Juan Correa as "my master." Quoted by Miguel Cabrera in his *Maravilla americana y conjunto de raras maravillas observadas con la dirección de las reglas del arte de la pintura en la prodigiosa imagen de Ntra. Sra. de Guadalupe de México* (1756) (Mexico City: Editorial Jus, 1977), p. 10. Ibarra may also have trained with Juan Rodríguez Juárez. See Ruiz Gomar, "Unique Expressions," p. 71.

19. *Artistas*, p. 233.

20. For Villalpando, see *Repertorio*, vol. 3, p. 386; for Correa, *Repertorio*, vol. 1, p. 286; for Rodríguez Carnero, Francisco Pérez de Salazar y Haro, *Historia de la pintura en Puebla y otras investigaciones sobre historia y arte* (Mexico City: PERPAL, 1990), pp. 165–66; and Rogelio Ruiz Gomar, "El pintor José Rodríguez Carnero (1649–1725). Nuevas noticias y bosquejo biográfico," *Anales del Instituto de Investigaciones Estéticas* 70 (Mexico City, 1997): 45–76.

21. For further discussion of such networks, see Susan Deans-Smith, " 'This Noble and Illustrious Art:' Painters and the Politics of Guild Reform in Early Modern Mexico City, 1674–1768," in Deans-Smith and Van Young, eds., *Mexican Soundings*, pp. 72–73. On the transmission of the "secrets of the trade," see Bargellini, "Originality and Invention," p. 88; and Cabrera's comment on Ibarra in *Maravilla americana*, p. 9.

22. See Toussaint, *Pintura Colonial;* the biographical entries for painters in *Repertorio;* and *Tesoros*.

23. In 1739, Cabrera described himself as an *"español"* in the *libro de amonestaciones* prior to his marriage to Ana Solano; *Tesoros*, p. 181. Note that José de Alcíbar seems to be responsible for a long-standing assumption that his colleague Cabrera was an Indian; see D. A. Brading's discussion of this point in *Mexican Phoenix. Our Lady of Guadalupe: Image and Tradition Across Five Centuries* (Cambridge: Cambridge University Press, 2001), p. 196.

24. Ibarra's father was a *morisco* (offspring of Spanish and mulatto) and his mother was a free mulatta (offspring of Spanish and black). On the "euphemistic" nature of terms such as *moreno* and *pardo*, see Ben Vinson III, *Bearing Arms for His Majesty: The Free-Colored Militia in Colonial Mexico* (Stanford, California: Stanford University Press, 2001), p. 200. For Ibarra, see *Tesoros*, p. 137; *Repertorio*, vol. 2, p. 180; and Xavier Moyssén, "El testamento de José de Ibarra," *Boletín de Monumentos Históricos*

6 (1981): 42–52. Morlete Ruíz' godparents were free mulattos; *Tesoros,* p. 191; and *Repertorio,* vol. 2, p. 388.

25. Ruiz Gomar, "El gremio," p. 216.

26. For discussion of the election of guild inspectors in the late sixteenth century, see Nelly Sigaut, "Pintores indígenas en la ciudad de México," *Historias* 37 (1997): 137–51; Toussaint, *Arte Colonial,* pp. 66–67, and Toussaint, *Pintura Colonial,* pp. 33–38.

27. See Ruiz Gomar, "El pintor José Rodríguez Carnero," pp. 45–76; and Toussaint, *Pintura Colonial,* p. 113.

28. For extensive documentation on Correa's commercial activities, see *Correa,* vol. 3. One of Villalpando's *fiadores* (bondsman), for example, was a merchant, don Manuel Ruiz de Prado y Cabrero. Haces, *Cristóbal de Villalpando,* p. 81. For a deeper discussion of the economic profiles of painters, see Deans-Smith, "'This Noble and Illustrious Art,'" pp. 74–76.

29. For a discussion of painting as a high-risk occupation, see John Michael Montias, *Artists and Artisans in Delft: A Socio-Economic Study of the Seventeenth Century* (Princeton, N.J.: Princeton University Press, 1982).

30. For short biographies on these painters, see Tovar de Teresa, *Repertorio.* On Miguel Cabrera's possible membership in the prestigious Jesuit religious brotherhood of the Congregación de la Purísima in Mexico City (Cabrera in general appears to be an exceptional case), see Luisa Elena Alcalá, "Miguel Cabrera y la Congregación de la Purísima," forthcoming in *Anales del Instituto de Investigaciones Estéticas.* I wish to thank the author for sharing with me a copy of her essay.

31. James S. Amelang, *The Flight of Icarus: Artisan Autobiography in Early Modern Europe* (Stanford, California: Stanford University Press, 1998), pp. 233–37.

32. For good overviews of the painters' situation in Spain, see Jonathan Brown, "Academies of Painting in Seventeenth-Century Spain," in Anton W. A. Boschloo et al., eds., *Academies of Art Between Renaissance and Romanticism,* Leids Kunsthistorisch Jaarboek V–VI (1986–87) (The Hague: SDU Uitgeverij): 177–85; and Brown, *Images and Ideas in Seventeenth-Century Spanish Painting* (Princeton, N.J.: Princeton University Press, 1978). See also Portús Pérez, *Pintura y pensamiento,* and Falomir Faus, "Artists' Responses."

33. Portús Pérez, *Pintura y pensamiento.*

34. Andrés Úbeda de los Cobos argues that the intention of Spanish painters was not to suppress the guild but to provide an additional source of academic training. Úbeda de los Cobos, "Pintura, mentalidad e ideología en la Real Academia de Bellas Artes de San Fernando, 1741–1800" (Ph.D. diss., Universidad Complutense de Madrid, 1988), p. 168; see also his *Pensamiento artístico español del siglo XVIII. De Antonio Palomino a Francisco de Goya* (Madrid: Museo Nacional del Prado, 2001).

35. For the painters' attempts to secure exemption from the sales tax in Spain, see Falomir Faus, "Artists' Responses," pp. 156–59. The evidence related to the question

of *alcabalas* and painters in Mexico is equivocal. There is the important case of the painter Pedro de Benavides, who in 1655 petitioned (unsuccessfully) the Puebla City council to exempt painters from payment of this tax; see Juan Miguel Serrera, "La defensa novohispana de la ingenuidad de la pintura," *Boletín de la Real Academia de Bellas Artes de San Fernando* 81 (1995): 275–88. Worth noting is that Benavides submitted his petition in 1655, some twenty years after painters in Spain received exemption from the *alcabala* (albeit of a qualified nature) in 1633; this suggests that such exemption was not granted automatically to all painters in Spain and its colonies. The only other explicit reference to *alcabalas* that I have found appears in the petition submitted by José de Ibarra and several other painters and engravers in 1753 to the viceroy, in which they refer to painters in Spain and their exemption from payment of the sales tax. The petition is reprinted in Mina Ramírez Montes, "En defensa de la pintura. Ciudad de México, 1753," *Anales del Instituto de Investigaciones Estéticas* 78 (2001): 119. For further discussion of this petition, see endnote 104. For an alternative interpretation of the significance of the *alcabalas,* see Paula Mues Orts, *La libertad del pincel,* pp. 209–217. What is certain is that by 1794, painters' exemption from the *alcabala* was codified in the instructions distributed to customs officials in New Spain. See Article 70, *Instruccion de 31 de marzo de 1794* ... HM 508, vol. I, Huntington Library, San Marino, CA.

36.   For good overviews in general of the question of painters' self-representations, see James Clifton, "A Portrait of the Artist," in *A Portrait of the Artist, 1525–1825: Prints from the Collection of the Sarah Campbell Blaffer Foundation,* exh. cat. (Houston: The Museum of Fine Arts, 2005); and Zirka Zaremba Filipczak, *Picturing Art in Antwerp 1550–1700* (Princeton, N.J.: Princeton University Press, 1987).

37.   In a contract for two paintings signed in 1719, for example, Juan Rodríguez Juárez is referred to or refers to himself as "professor in the art of painting"; see Toussaint, *Pintura Colonial,* p. 264, note. 29. Cabrera describes himself in his will as "don Miguel Cabrera, Professor of the Noble Art of Painting"; see Tovar de Teresa, *Miguel Cabrera. Pintor de Cámara de la reina celestial* (Mexico City: Grupo Financiero Inver-México, 1995), p. 269.

38.   Luis Bertucat's identity remains unclear. He appears to have been a painter, but no examples of his work are known. Although the issue is beyond the scope of this essay, the criteria by which the painters chose their representatives are not always clear.

39.   Archivo de Notarias de la Ciudad de México (hereafter ANCM), Antonio José Olaondo, #472, 1768, fol. 41v. For additional examples of such terms, see the documents reprinted by Xavier Moyssén in "La primera academia de pintura en México," *Anales del Instituto de Investigaciones Estéticas* 9, no. 34 (1965): 15–29.

40.   Rensselaer W. Lee, "*Ut Pictura Poesis:* The Humanistic Theory of Painting," *The Art Bulletin* XXII, no. 4 (1940): 197–269; and Portús Pérez, *Pintura y pensamiento.* Also see the useful discussion by Mindy N. Taggard, "Ut Pictura Poesis": Artists' Status in Early Modern Córdoba," *Artibus et Historiae* 17, no. 34 (1996): 69–82.

41. These verses were included in a pamphlet authored in 1742 by the canon of the cathedral of Guadalajara Dr. Lucas de la Casas Mota y Flores to acknowledge the Franciscan Pedro Antonio Buzeta's efforts in the construction of an aqueduct. For further discussion of this subject and the reprinting of one of Ibarra's poems, see Paula Mues Orts, *El Arte Maestra: traducción novohispana de un tratado pictórico italiano* (Mexico City: Museo de la Basílica de Guadalupe, 2006), pp. 78–79.

42. Cabrera, *Maravilla americana;* numerous allusions to the association between poetry and painting are peppered throughout the text.

43. Haces, *Cristóbal de Villalpando,* p. 81. See also the suggestive analysis by Clara Bargellini of the possible relationship between Villalpando's decoration of the dome of the Capilla de los Reyes, cathedral of Puebla, and the eight *villancicos* composed by Sor Juana Inés de la Cruz for the celebration of the Feast of the Immaculate Conception in 1689 in the same cathedral; Haces, *Cristóbal de Villalpando,* pp. 218–21.

44. Francisco de la Maza, *La mitología clásica en el arte colonial de México* (Mexico City: Universidad Nacional Autónoma de México, 1968), p. 13; and Joaquín Velázquez de León, *Arcos de triunfo* (Mexico City: Universidad Nacional Autónoma de México, 1978).

45. Guillermo Tovar de Teresa, *Bibliografía Novohispana de Arte. Segunda Parte. Impresos mexicanos relativos al arte del siglo XVIII* (Mexico City: Fondo de Cultura Económica, 1988) (hereafter *BNA,* II), pp. 221, 260.

46. The Creole Jesuit Pedro José Mariano de Abarca describes the painters' triumphal arch in his *El Sol en León . . .* (Mexico, 1748), *BNA,* II, pp. 264–65; Joan Stack, "Artists into heroes: The Commemoration of Artists in the Art of Giorgio Vasari," in Mary Rogers, ed., *Fashioning Identities in Renaissance Art* (Aldershot: Ashgate, 2000), pp. 163–75.

47. For greater elaboration on this argument, see Portús Pérez, *Pintura y pensamiento,* p. 88.

48. See Bargellini, "Originality and Invention," pp. 87–90; and Cuadriello, "El obrador Trinitario," pp. 189–98. Other examples of examinations include the Virgen de Santa María la Redonda described by Cabrera y Quintero in 1746 (*BNA,* II, p. 242); and Ibarra and Francisco Martínez participated in the inspection of the Cristo de los Desagravios (*Artistas,* pp. 232–33).

49. Cayetano de Cabrera y Quintero, *Breve Razón de la Idea, Estatuas, e Inscripciones, que el Nobilíssimo Arte de la Pintura . . .* (Mexico, 1733), Biblioteca Nacional, Manuscritos de Fondo Reservado, Borradores de Cayetano de Cabrera y Quintero, MS. 26, fols. 1r–6v.

50. *Gazetas de México,* 61, Dec. 1732, *BNA,* II, pp. 385–86.

51. Abarca, *El Sol en León . . . , BNA,* II, p. 265.

52. Toussaint, *Pintura Colonial,* p. 112; *El Segundo Quince de Enero de la Corte Mexicana* (1730), *BNA,* II, p. 143.

53. *Explicacion de el arco erigido en la puerta de el Palacio Arzobispal de Mexico, a la gloria de el Rey N. Señor D. Carlos III . . . 25 June, 1760, BNA,* II, 353–55.

54. Useful here is James Clifton's discussion about the ways in which "corporate intrusion into the ego-documents . . . of artists might occur . . . for example, through reference either to groups to which the artist belongs or to other artists to be imitated. Artists occasionally signed paintings with reference to their membership in a group, especially as an academician, or their nationality." Clifton, "A Portrait of the Artist," p. 5.

55. It is important to note that both paintings are attributions. See Ruiz Gomar's discussion of Rodríguez Juárez' portrait in "Unique Expressions," pp. 238–39. Mues Orts suggests that Ibarra's portrait may, in fact, have been painted by his student Miguel Rudecindo Contreras: "Merezca ser hidalgo," p. 52. Also important but beyond the scope of this essay are the "self-portraits-as-witness" or bystander portraits by painters. One example is that of Villalpando who placed himself among the bishop and clerics of the cathedral chapter in the *Apparition of Saint Michael on Mount Gargano* which represents an allegory of the church in New Spain (this is one of six large canvases created for the sacristy of the cathedral of Mexico City dated around 1685). See Bargellini, "Painting in Colonial Latin America," in *The Arts in Latin America, 1492–1820,* exh. cat. (Philadelphia and New Haven: The Philadelphia Museum of Art, and Yale University Press, 2006), p. 330.

56. Clifton, "A Portrait of the Artist," pp. 18, 22. Note also Clifton's important reminder that "Representations of artists—whether specific or generic—should never be taken as unmediated 'snapshots' of actual appearance or practice. They aim at various kinds of effect which may require a lack of, or selective, realism in portrayal. For example, they might be intended to demonstrate an artist's exalted status (or obscure a less exalted status)." See also Filipczak's observation that it is only after painters' gain a secure sense of their elevated status that they could "embrace their manual work in portraiture and depictions of their studios." Filipczak, *Picturing Art in Antwerp,* p. 9.

57. Abelardo Carrillo y Gariel, *Autógrafos de pintores coloniales* (Mexico City: Universidad Nacional Autónoma de México, 1953), pp. 13–14.

58. Carrillo y Gariel, *Autógrafos,* p. 61, and Mues Orts, "Merezca ser hidalgo," p. 51.

59. Tovar de Teresa, *Miguel Cabrera,* p. 326.

60. Bargellini, "Consideraciones sobre algunas firmas de pintores novohispanos. El proceso creativo," in Alberto Dallal, ed., *El proceso creativo: XXVI Coloquio internacional de historia del arte* (Mexico City: Universidad Nacional Autónoma de México, Instituto de Investigaciones Estéticas, 2006), pp. 203–22.

61. Additional depictions of divinely created images by Juan Correa (Saint Luke Painting the Virgina of Nieves), Juan Sánchez Salmerón (The Holy Spirit Painting the Virgin of Guadalupe), and Miguel Cabrera (God Painting the Virgin of Guadalupe) are reproduced in *El Divino Pintor,* pp. 121, 151, 163. For a discussion of the concept of the "Divine Painter" (*"Divino Pintor"*), see Cuadriello, "El obrador Trinitario," p. 66; and Portús Pérez, *Pintura y pensamiento,* p. 89.

62. Examples of art treatises produced in Spain include Gaspar Gutiérrez de los Ríos, *Noticia general para la estimación de las artes* . . . (1600); Juan de Butrón, *Discursos apologéticos* . . . (1626); Vicente Carducho, *Diálogos de la Pintura* (1633); Francisco Pacheco, *Arte de la Pintura* (1649), and Acislo Antonio Palomino y Velasco, *El Museo Pictórico* . . . (1715-1724).

63. Miguel Cabrera, *Maravilla americana*.

64. *El Arte Maestra. Discurso sobre la Pintura. Muestra el modo de perficionarla con varias invenciones y reglas practicas pertenecientes a esta materia.* For a discussion of this treatise and Ibarra's association with the translation, see Mues Orts, *El Arte Maestra*, pp. 70-83. For an alternative interpretation that Ibarra authored the treatise, see Myrna Soto, *El Arte Maestra: Un tratado de pintura novohispano* (Mexico City: Universidad Nacional Autónoma de México, Instituto de Investigaciones Bibliográficas, 2005).

65. Presumably *Arte de la Pintura* refers to Francisco Pacheco's treatise of 1649. For a reproduction of this portrait, see Noemí Atamoros Zeller, *Nueva iconografía: Sor Juana Inés de la Cruz* (Mexico City: Hoechst Marion Roussel, 1995), p. 15.

66. Bargellini, "Originality and Invention," p. 83; see also her discussion of the concept of invention and the intellectual foundations of painting in "Painting in Colonial Latin America," p. 331; and Mues Orts, "Merezca ser hidalgo," p. 52.

67. My discussion here is influenced by Leonard Bell, "Colonial Eyes Transformed: Looking at/in Paintings: An Exploratory Essay," *Australian and New Zealand Journal of Art* 1 (2000): 40-62.

68. For a discussion of "seeing" and "knowing a place," see Bell, "Colonial Eyes Transformed," p. 50. María Concepción García Sáiz argues that this particular composition demonstrates Cabrera's "awareness of sources which other [painters] lacked or chose not to use." García Sáiz, *Las castas mexicanas: un género pictórico americano* (Milan: Olivetti, 1989), p. 80.

69. García Sáiz identified the engraving as Adriaen Brouwer's "The Fat Man." See García Sáiz, "Pinturas 'costumbristas' del mexicano Miguel Cabrera," *Goya. Revista de Arte* 142 (1978): 186-93. For a reproduction of the "Fat Man" print, see Wilhem von Bode, *Adriaen Brouwer. Sein Lebure und seine werke* (Berlin: Euphorion Verlag, 1924), p. 32.

70. Toussaint, *Pintura Colonial*, p. 136.

71. Archivo Histórico del Distrito Federal (hereafter AHDF), Francisco Barrio Lorenzot, *Colección de Ordenanzas de la muy noble e insigne y muy leal e imperial Ciudad de México* (hereafter *Ordenanzas*), 431-A, fols. 50v-64. On the relationship between the production of pictures and the concern with orthodoxy, see Bargellini, "Painting in Colonial Latin America," p. 331.

72. The issue here is not whether the painters' assessments of the generally poor quality of paintings was accurate, but to understand their reasons to justify reform of their guild regulations.

73. Gibson, *The Aztecs under Spanish Rule,* p. 400; Tovar de Teresa, "Consideraciones sobre retablos, gremios y artífices de la Nueva España en los siglos XVII y XVIII," *Historia Mexicana* 34, no. 1 (1984): 16–18.

74. See Toussaint, *Arte Colonial,* p. 80. Unlike the painters' original ordinances of 1557, which contained no explicit prohibitions against non-Spanish craftsmen, the ordinances of the carpenters, carvers, joiners, and viol makers of 1568 prohibited blacks and slaves from owning a workshop and from taking the guild examination; AHDF, *Ordenanzas,* 431–A, fol. 193, and fols. 208–208v.

75. Lyle N. McAlister, *Spain & Portugal in the New World, 1492–1700* (Minneapolis: University of Minnesota Press, 1984), p. 395; Woodrow Borah, *Justice By Insurance: The General Indian Court of Colonial Mexico and the Legal Aides of the Half-Real* (Berkeley: University of California Press, 1983), pp. 80–83. For the increasing use of the term *miserables* in the eighteenth century, see William B. Taylor, "'. . . de corazón pequeño y ánimo apocado': Conceptos de los curas párrocos sobre los indios en la Nueva España del siglo XVIII," *Relaciones* 39 (El Colegio de Michoacán, 1989): 5–67.

76. Tovar de Teresa, "Consideraciones," pp. 5–40. Marcus Burke also argues that such large-scale decorative commissions as *retablos* increasingly placed stress on guild structures and the position of painters; Burke, *Treasures,* pp. 59–60. See also Bargellini, "Painting in Colonial Latin America," pp. 332–33.

77. For a thorough discussion of the complexity of *retablo* fabrications and the craftsmen involved, see Heinrich Berlin, "Salvador de Ocampo: A Mexican Sculptor," *The Americas* IV, no. 4 (1948): 415–28.

78. Painters refer to several different types of individuals whom they perceived to be illicit producers, contractors, or sellers of artworks such as *trapaleros* and *tratantes* who were neither trained nor licensed by the guild, or subsequently, by the Royal Academy of San Carlos. Much more research is required on these individuals, not only to have a better understanding of who they were and what they did, but because they point to two important issues: (1) the development of the market for artworks in colonial Mexico City which may be more significant than has been traditionally acknowledged; (2) the mechanisms employed for the regulation of sales of artworks. For excellent discussions of both of these issues in relation to Spain and Europe in the early modern period, see the essays in De Marchi and Van Miegroet, eds., *Mapping Markets for Paintings in Europe, 1450–1750.*

79. AAASC Gav. 5/Exp. 632, fol. 24, "Testimonio de las Ordenanzas del Arte de la Pintura y Dorado," Cristóbal de Villalpando, José Sánchez, José de Rojas–V. Ex., 3 October 1686 (hereafter Testimonio). On the *tratantes de pintura* in seventeenth-century Spain and the commerce in artworks, see Falomir Faus, "Artists' Responses," pp. 135–65.

80. Edelmira Ramírez Layva, "La censura inquisitorial novohispana sobre imágenes y objetos," in *Arte y coerción. Primer coloquio del comité mexicano de historia*

de arte (Mexico City: Universidad Nacional Autónoma de México, Instituto de Investigaciones Estéticas, 1992), p. 158.

81. Duncan Kinkead argues that the greatest increase in exports of paintings to Spanish America from Seville occurred in the 1670s; see his "Juan de Luzón and the Sevillian Painting Trade with the New World in the Second Half of the Seventeenth Century," *The Art Bulletin* LXVI, no. 2 (1984): 307. See also De Marchi and Van Miegroet, "Exploring Markets for Netherlandish Paintings in Spain and Nueva España," *Nederlands Kunsthistorisch Jaarboek* 50 (1999): 81–111. On the significance of the Jesuits in introducing artworks into colonial Mexico, see Luisa Elena Alcalá, "'De compras por Europa': Procuradores jesuitas y cultura material en Nueva España," *Goya. Revista de Arte* 318 (2007): 141–58.

82. ANCM, 1–VIII–1674, Nicolás Bernal, "Poder para pleitos y defensas que otorga el gremio de pintores representado en los maestros de dho arte . . ." fol. 117. Note that López Dávalos was one of the painters who inspected the Virgin de Guadalupe in 1666. See Gustavo Curiel, "Fiestas para un virrey. La entrada triunfal a la ciudad de México del Conde de Baños. El caso de un patrocinio oficial, 1660," in Gustavo Curiel, ed., *Patrocinio, colección y circulación de las artes* (Mexico City: Universidad Nacional Autónoma de México, Instituto de Investigaciones Estéticas, 1997), p. 187.

83. AHDF, *Ordenanzas,* 431–A, fols. 50v–64.

84. It is worth noting that the painters' petition for approval of the original set of ordinances of 1557 was submitted in the name of "*some oficiales* of the craft and art of the painter" [my emphasis].

85. AHDF, *Ordenanzas,* 431–A, fols. 50v–51. After Rodríguez Carnero moved from Mexico City to Puebla sometime between 1684 and 1687, eight painters in Puebla also petitioned the *alcalde mayor* (royal district governor) of Puebla, probably in the 1690s or early 1700s, for the approval and implementation of ordinances for the painters' guild; one of the petitioners was Rodríguez Carnero. See Ruiz Gomar, "El pintor," p. 66.

86. The exam covered two areas: theory (definition of lines, circles, points, and angles), and an exercise to be performed in front of the inspectors and two masters; see Ruiz Gomar, "El gremio," p. 211. For an example of an examination and procedures, see ANCM, Joseph de Anaya y Bonillo, 22 April 1698, fols. 231–32; *Correa,* vol. 3, doc. LXVII, p. 102.

87. Clause four stipulated the components of the theoretical and practical examination that must be mastered by anyone who wished to practice "such an illustrious art as that of a painter." See Mues Orts' discussion of this point, "Merezca ser hidalgo y libre," pp. 34–35.

88. Although the painters and gilders involved in the reform efforts attempted to demarcate the differences and boundaries among crafts, in practice painters frequently worked in different media.

89. Only gilders, in theory, could work with sculpted images "which is a distinct craft to that of joiners and wood carvers which belong to the occupation of carpenter." AHDF, *Ordenanzas,* 431–A, fols. 50v–64.

90. AHDF, *Ordenanzas,* 431–A, fols. 50v–64.

91. The term *españoles* in all likelihood referred to both Creoles and Spaniards born in the Iberian Peninsula.

92. On the development of the secondhand market, the importance of auctions to this market, and the level of fraud involved in such auctions in Spain, see Falomir Faus, "Artists' Responses," pp. 143–44.

93. AHDF, *Ordenanzas,* 431–A, fols. 57–64.

94. See the entries in *Artistas,* pp. 375, 376, 406, 416; Haces, *Cristóbal de Villalpando,* pp. 82, 94, 118, 120; *Correa,* vol. 3, doc. LXXXIII, pp. 136–137; *Repertorio,* vol. 3, p. 196.

95. AAASC Gav. 5/Exp. 632, Testimonio, fols. 1–104v. Inspections of twenty-five workshops in Mexico City, Tlatelolco, and Xochimilco can be grouped into clusters for the years 1689, 1695, and 1717. Only five workshop owners, two of whom were Indian, were found not to be in violation of the new ordinances. The main violations prosecuted included the illegal practice of painting and gilding (mainly gilding) by craftsmen (primarily *ensambladores*) and their untrained workers, and the operation of painting and gilding workshops by unlicensed owners. For further discussion, see Deans-Smith, "'This Noble and Illustrious Art,'" pp. 87–90.

96. Complaints about the ineffectiveness of the guild ordinances began as early as 1698. See AAASC, Gav. 5/Exp. 632, fols. 27v–30, for the concerns of Antonio de Salcedo, a master gilder, about unexamined indigenous painters and gilders who "make the most imperfect Holy Images that I have ever seen."

97. AAASC, Gav. 5/Exp. 652, fols. 102–103.

98. As Portús Pérez observed in the case of the Spanish painters, "The academy is the most palpable manifestation that the painter has ceased to be a simple artisan and that his position on the social and professional plane has improved;" Portús Pérez, *Pintura y pensamiento,* p. 68. See also Mues Orts' discussion of the relationship between the impulse to "modernize" pictorial style in colonial Mexico and the need to adopt new forms of associations and apprenticeship among the painters such as academies in order to facilitate such innovation: *El Arte Maestra,* p. 68.

99. Jonathan Brown observes that after 1650 a few academies appeared in other parts of Spain but they were local affairs with limited aims and duration. The academy founded in Seville in 1660, with Murillo as one of its founding members, was the most important. Brown, "Academies of Painting," pp. 175–85.

100. ANCM, Libro 2577, 4 Sept. 1722, Felipe Muñoz de Castro, fol. 222. A recently discovered document suggests that Ibarra took a leading role in attempts to establish an academy in 1722; see Bargellini, "Originality and Invention," p. 281, note 50.

101. ANCM, Libro 2583, 7 Sept. 1728, Felipe Muñoz de Castro, fols. 347–50. Of the nine signatories on the petition eight were Spanish and one, Carlos Clemente López, was an Indian *cacique*. I have been unable to locate biographical data on Clemente del Campo that would allow a clearer assessment of the nature of his relationship to the painters.

102. Ibid. Note that in 1697 a Spanish decree stipulated that descendants of the pre-Hispanic indigenous nobility should be recognized as *hidalgos* or nobles and that the indigenous population in general was deemed to be "pure." Reprinted in Richard Konetzke, *Colección de documentos para la historia de la formación social de Hispano-américa, 1493–1810* (Madrid: Consejo Superior de Investigaciones Científicas, 1962), vol. 3, pp. 66–69.

103. Ibid.

104. Twelve painters signed the petition including, in addition to Ibarra, some of the most recognized painters of the time such as Francisco Martínez, Francisco Vallejo, Miguel Cabrera, and Juan Patricio Morlete Ruiz. The engravers Baltasar Troncoso y Sotomayor and Baltasar Rodríguez Medrano and the architect Miguel Espinosa de los Monteros also signed the document. See Ramírez Montes, "En defensa de la pintura," pp. 103–128.

105. AHDF, Actas de Cabildo, 30 July 1753, fols. 27v–28. Fragmentary data from the 1753 census indicates that at the level of master painter, nineteen of twenty-one masters were classified as Spanish, one was a mestizo, and no race was stated for the other one. Seven out of eight apprentices listed were classified as Spanish. The breakdown by racial classification for the total number of painters, including apprentices, is as follows: españoles 60 percent, indios 3 percent, castizos 5 percent, mestizos 8 percent, mulattos 5 percent, and 19 percent stated no race (Archivo General de la Nación, Padrones, vol. 52, and Civil, vol. 1496). Note that the only parts of the 1753 census that survive cover approximately three-quarters of the central area of Mexico City, which was predominantly Spanish. Specific groups were excluded from the census, such as male and female religious, and Indians without fixed employment. For a discussion of the census, see Irene Vázquez Valle, "Los habitantes de la ciudad de México en 1753" (Master's thesis, El Colegio de México, 1975).

106. For a useful comparative study that examines efforts to define and tighten regulations that excluded mulattos and blacks from universities in Spanish America, see John Tate Lanning, *The Royal Protomedicato: The Regulation of the Medical Profession in the Spanish Empire*, ed. John Jay (Durham: Duke University Press, 1985).

107. Moyssén, "La primera academia." Moyssén reprints four notarial documents related to efforts to establish an academy. What is interesting about three of these, is the changing composition of the petitioners in terms of numbers and of individual painters. What the turnover of petitioners means is not clear. Some painters may have been working outside of Mexico City; others may have died or decided against

participation for personal reasons. One possibility is that the financial obligation of the transactions may have dissuaded some from continued participation. For further discussion, see Deans-Smith, "'This Noble and Illustrious Art,'" p. 93.

108. José Ventura Arnáez (active 1756–1771) was the exception.

109. See Jaime Cuadriello's assessment of Cabrera's growing success following the inspection of the Virgin of Guadalupe in "El obrador Trinitario," pp. 61–205. Also interesting is his discussion of the links between the emergence of the cult of the Virgin of Guadalupe, Creole patriotism, and the elevation of the painters' status.

110. Moyssén, "La primera academia," doc. 1, p. 23. The location where the painters met is not specified.

111. Ibid., p. 24.

112. Ibid., p. 23.

113. Ibid., p. 24. Note the similarities of the painters' rhetoric to that of painters in Spain. In justifying the need for an academy, painters in Madrid emphasized the importance of correct representations and that "If holy scenes are poorly painted, the faithful will be led into error, and good painting can only be guaranteed through instruction in the proper precepts of the art. The dangers posed by bad painting, which abounds in Spain, should be remedied by the foundation of a royal academy so that the art can be scientifically learned." See Brown, "Academies of Painting," pp. 177–85.

114. Moyssén, doc. 1, p. 24.

115. Where Couto derives this information from is unclear, but presumably it was included in the statutes of the academy he mentions. See José Bernardo Couto, *Diálogo sobre la historia de la pintura en México* (1872) (Mexico City: Fondo de Cultura Económica, 1995).

116. Couto, *Diálogo*, p. 141.

117. Moyssén, "La primera academia," doc. IV, pp. 28–29.

118. Ramírez Montes correctly notes that Couto was mistaken in dating the *Estatutos* to 1753 as evidenced by the difference in positions described in the petitions of 1754–1755 and those cited by Couto. See her "En defensa de la pintura," p. 104. The five directors were José Manuel Domínguez, first director; Morlete Ruiz, second director; Pedro Quintana, director; Vallejo, third director; and Alcíbar, director. Couto, *Diálogo*, p. 141.

119. AAASC doc. 502, Alcíbar to Ex. Sr., 1789. Mues Orts has observed that despite the scarce evidence about these "academies," rather than being ephemeral and with little influence, they may in fact, have exercised a significant role in the development and articulation of opinions about style and composition. See Mues Orts, *El Arte Maestra*, p. 68.

120. Whether they ever received a response to their petitions is unknown.

121. For a discussion of the importance in consolidating the painters' corporate status in tandem with individual artists' success in early modern Europe, see James Clifton, "A Portrait of the Artist," p. 7.

122. ANCM, Antonio José Olaondo, 1768, fol. 22. An important question for future consideration is whether Cabrera and his associates continued to press for royal approval of a Mexican academy of painting and/or continued with their own "academy" between 1754 and up until Cabrera's death in 1768.

123. The term *pardo* could refer to the offspring of Africans and Indians but came to be used synonymously with mulatto; it is also used to describe free-colored militiamen. See Vinson, *Bearing Arms for His Majesty,* p. 200. For an example of a legal document in which Correa is categorized as a *"mulato libre"* ("free mulatto") see a rental contract of 1676 reprinted in *Correa,* vol. III, doc. XXVI, p. 46.

124. Cope, *Limits of Racial Domination,* p. 53.

125. For a persuasive argument on this point for the seventeenth century, see Laura Lewis, *Hall of Mirrors: Power, Witchcraft, and Caste in Colonial Mexico* (Durham: Duke University Press, 2003).

126. AAASC/Gav 9/Doc. 1030, Memorial de los profesores de la Noble Arte de Pintura to Ex Sr, 1799.

127. AAASC/Gav 9/Doc 1031, Rafael Ximeno y Planes, Ginés de Andrés y de Aguirre, Manuel Tolsá, Joaquín Fabregat to Ex Sr, 3 August, 1799.

128. AAASC/Gav 9/Doc. 1034, El Fiscal Protector de Indios to Ex Sr, 31 December, 1799.

129. The dress of the assistant may be that of a *tlacuilo* or indigenous artist. I wish to thank Ilona Katzew for pointing this out to me.

130. MacKay, *"Lazy, Improvident People,"* p. 183.

131. AGN Casa de Moneda vol. 271, fols. 121–346, for numerous examples of guild examinations and declarations that make specific use of the term *limpieza de sangre.* See also Carlos Rubén Ruiz Medrano, *El gremio de plateros en Nueva España* (San Luis Potosí: El Colegio de San Luis, 2001).

132. For the case of Puebla, Mexico, for example, see José María Lorenzo Macías, "De mecánico a liberal. La creación del gremio de "las nobles y muy liberales artes de ensamblar, esculpir, tallar y dorar" en la ciudad de Puebla, *Boletín de Monumentos Históricos* 6 (2006): 42–59. In Cuzco, Peru, in 1688, the indigenous painters successfully sought complete separation from the Spanish painters' guild, a consequence of which was the foundation of the Cuzco school of painting. For further discussion of this, see Marcus Burke, "The Parallel Course of Latin American and European Art in the Viceregal Era," in *The Arts of Latin America,* p. 78. According to Burke the separation was based on cultural and stylistic differences and not the result of a "racial process." It may be premature, however, to disregard the economic and racial underpinnings of this important separation.

Chapter 3

I am grateful to the Getty Foundation and the John Carter Brown library (Brown University) for their generous funding which allowed me to conduct research for this essay. I also wish to thank Susan Deans-Smith and María Elena Martínez for their careful reading of the manuscript. I am particularly grateful to William B. Taylor for his insightful comments, and for the generous spirit with which they were proffered. All translations are my own.

1. The discussions between Friar Bartolomé de las Casas and the humanist Juan Ginés de Sepúlveda about the humanity of the Indians, set in Valladolid in 1550–55, is legendary. While Las Casas set out to prove that the Indians were fully rational, Sepúlveda argued that they were no more than slaves by nature. See Lewis Hanke, *La humanidad es una. Estudio acerca de la querella sobre la capacidad intelectual y religiosa de los indígenas americanos que sostuvieron en 1550 Bartolomé de las Casas y Juan Ginés de Sepúlveda* (Mexico City: Fondo de Cultura Económica, 1985; 1st ed. in English 1974); Anthony Pagden, *The Fall of Natural Man: The American Indian and the Origins of Comparative Ethnography* (Cambridge: Cambridge University Press, 1986); and Patricia Seed, "'Are These Not Also Men' The Indians' Humanity and Capacity for Spanish Civilisation," *Journal of Latin American Studies* 24, part. 3 (1993): 629–52.

2. William Robertson, *The History of America,* 2 vols. (Dublin: Printed for Messrs, 1777), vol. 1, preface, p. ix.

3. José de Acosta, *Historia natural y moral de las* indias . . . (1590) (Madrid: Pantaleón Aznar, 1792; facs. Seville: Hispano-Americana de Publicaciones, S.A., 1987), pp. 154, 268.

4. On Acosta's evolutionism and his two most influential works, *De procuranda indorum salute* (1587) and *Historia natural y moral de las Indias* (1590), see Pagden, *The Fall of Natural Man,* chap. 7.

5. For an overview of Spanish scholarship after García, see Lee Eldridge Huddleston, *Origins of the American Indians. European Concepts, 1492–1729* (Austin and London: University of Texas Press, Institute of Latin American Studies, 1967), pp. 77–109. García's book is featured in many libraries of the time; see, for example, the 1779 inventory of Viceroy Antonio María Bucareli y Ursúa (1771–1779), Archivo General de la Nación, Mexico (hereafter AGN), Intestados, vol. 80, 2a parte, exps. 1–7, fol. 63v.

6. For the theory of monogenesis and polygenesis, see Margaret T. Hodgen, *Early Anthropology in the Sixteenth and Seventeenth Centuries* (Philadelphia: University of Pennsylvania Press, 1971; 1st ed., 1964), chap. 6. In his *De Civitas Dei* (413–412 CE) Saint Augustine had vehemently countered the Greco-Roman notion of a multiplicity of origins and lineages for humankind. See Nicolás Wey Gómez, *The Tropics of Empire: Why Columbus Sailed South to the Indies* (Cambridge, Masssachusstes, and London: The MIT Press, 2008), pp. 119, and 123. I wish to thank the author for sharing an advance copy of his book.

7. Gregorio García, *Origen de los indios de el Nuevo Mundo, e Indias Occidentales* (Madrid: Imprenta de Francisco Martínez Abad, 1729; facs., Mexico City: Fondo de Cultura Económica, 1981).

8. For the somewhat popular theory that the Indians came from the Ten Lost Tribes of Israel, see Richard H. Popkin, "The Rise and Fall of the Jewish Indian Theory," in Yosef Kaplan, Henry Méchoulan and Richard H. Popkin, eds., *Mennaseh Ben Israel and His World* (Leiden: E. J. Brill, 1989), pp. 63–82. This theory was sometimes used to link the Indians with the "impure" Jews and thus curtail their rights, such as being ordained priests. See Stafford Poole, "Church Law and the Ordination of the Indians and *Castas* in New Spain," *Hispanic American Historical Review* 61, no. 4 (1981): 637–50.

9. García, *Origen de los Indios*, bk. 3, p. 81.

10. Ibid., bk. 3, p. 100.

11. See, for example, Londa Schiebinger, *Nature's Body: Gender in the Making of Modern Science* (Boston: Beacon Press, 1993), pp. 134–35; and Schiebinger, *The Mind Has No Sex? Women in the Origin of Modern Science* (Cambridge, Massachusetts: Harvard University Press, 1989), pp. 160–61.

12. García, *Origen de los Indios*, bk. 2, pp. 72–73. The idea that nations were sovereign or subject based on where they were located on the globe goes back to the ancient world with authors such as Pliny and Aristotle. On this subject, see Wey Gómez, *The Tropics of Empire*. On the alleged humidity of the Americas and its negative effect on Amerindians and Creoles, see also Jorge Cañizares-Esguerra, "New World, New Stars: Patriotic Astrology and the Invention of Amerindian and Creoles Bodies in Colonial Spanish America, 1600–1650," in Cañizares-Esguerra, *Nature, Empire, and Nation: Explorations of the History of Science in the Iberian World* (Stanford, California: Stanford University Press, 2006), pp. 64–95.

13. García, *Origen de los indios*, bk. 3, pp. 100–02. On the Aristotelian distinction between male and female, see Wey Gómez, *The Tropics of Empire*, pp. 244–251.

14. García, *Origen de los indios*, bk. 4, pp. 313–16.

15. On this subject, see also Cañizares-Esguerra, "New World, New Stars," pp. 75–77.

16. The 1729 edition contains several additions and modifications to the original version of 1607 published in Valencia. It has been suggested that the changes were made to emphasize the Spanish patriotic tone of the book at a time when the Spanish monarchy was losing its power. See Teresa Martínez Terán, *Los antípodas. El Origen de los Indios en la razón política del siglo XVI* (Puebla, Mexico: Instituto de Ciencias Sociales y Humanidades, Benemérita Universidad Autónoma de Puebla, 2001).

17. "Discurso sobre los indios de la Nueva España," in *Recolección de varios curiosos papeles no menos gustosos que útiles a ilustrar en asuntos morales, políticos, históricos y otros* (Cádiz, Spain, 1762), Biblioteca Nacional de México, MS. 21, fol. 1. I published the manuscript in Ilona Katzew, *Una visión del México del Siglo de las Luces. La codificación de Joaquín Antonio de Basarás* (Mexico City: Landucci, 2006), pp. 341–68.

18. Lorenzo Boturini Benaducci, *Idea de una nueva historia general de la America septentrional. Fundada sobre material copioso de Figuras, Símbolos, Caracteres, y Jeroglíficos, Cantares y Manuscritos de Autores Indios, últimamente descubiertos* (Madrid: Imprenta de Juan de Zúñiga, 1746), p. 110.

19. Ibid., pp. 99–100.

20. Ibid., pp. 99–106

21. Ibid., pp. 110–34.

22. Ibid., p. 104. Gregorio García, *Predicación del Evangelio en el Nuevo Mundo viviendo los Apóstoles* (Baeza, Spain: Impreso por P. de la Cuesta, 1625).

23. Huddleston, *Origins of the American Indians,* pp. 138–41. See also Richard H. Popkin, *Isaac La Peyrère (1596–1676): His Life, Work and Influence* (Leiden: E. J. Brill, 1987).

24. Benito Jerónimo Feijoo, "Solución del gran problema histórico sobre la población de América, y revoluciones del Orbe Terráqueo," (1733) in *Dos discursos de Feijoo sobre América,* introd. Agustín Millares Carlo (Mexico City: Biblioteca Enciclopédica Popular, Secretaría de Educación Pública, 1945), p. 40. Here I disagree with Cañizares-Esguerra who notes that New World intellectuals "avoided the contemporaneous rancorous debates on the subject in Europe." Cañizares-Esguerra, "New World, New Stars," p. 66.

25. Joseph Torrubia, *Aparato para la historia natural española. Tomo Primero. Contiene muchas disertaciones physicas, especialmente sobre el Diluvio* ... (Madrid: En la Imprenta de los Herederos de Don Agustín de Gordejuela y Sierra, 1754), esp. the unpaginated *aprobación* of friar Jerónimo de Salamanca, and pp. 151–65.

26. Francisco Xavier Alejo, *Solucion del gran problema acerca de las Americas, en que sobre el fundamento de los Libros se descubre facil camino á la transmigracion de los Hombres del uno al otro Continente; y como pudieron pasar al Nuevo Mundo, no solamente las Bestias de servicio sino tambien las Fieras, y nocivas. Y con esta ocasión se satisface plenamente el delirio de los Pre-Adamitas, apoyado con esta dificil objeción hasta ahora no bien desatada* (Mexico City: Imprenta Real del Superior Gobierno, y del Nuevo Rezado, de los Herederos de Doña María de Ribera, 1763), unpaginated preface by Francisco Carmona Godoy y Bucareli.

27. Ibid., unpaginated *aprobación* by Hipólito Díaz.

28. Ibid., pp. 66–67. The view that the darker, or "tawny" color of the Indians originated from Noha's curse of Ham's descendants was fairly common at the turn of the seventeenth century. See Benjamin Braude, "The Sons of Noah and the Construction of Ethnic and Geographical Identities In Medieval and Early Modern Periods," *William and Mary Quarterly,* 3rd, ser., 54 (1997): 103–42; and William McKee Evans, "From the Land of Canaan to the Land of Guinea: The Strange Odyssey of the 'Sons of Ham,'" *American Historical Review* 85 (1980): 15–43.

29. Wey Gómez, *The Tropics of Empire,* pp. 67–70; 220–23; and 278–83.

30. Agustín de Vetancurt, *Teatro Mexicano* . . . (Mexico City: Doña María Benavides Viuda de Juan de Ribera, 1698; facs. Mexico City: Editorial Porrúa, 1982), treatise 1, chap. VI, p. 12.

31. See, for example, Antonio de León Pinelo, *El Paraíso en el Nuevo Mundo. Comentario apologético, Historia natural y Peregrina de las Indias Occidentales Islas de Tierra Firme del Mar Océano* . . . (ca. 1650–56), 2 vols., ed. Raúl Porras Barrenechea (Lima: Comité del IV Centenario del Descubrimiento del Amazonas, 1943).

32. On this subject, see the lucid discussion of Cañizares-Esguerra, "New World, New Stars."

33. The literature on the European historiography of the New World is vast. The classic and pioneering study on the subject is Antonello Gerbi, *La disputa del Nuevo Mundo. Historia de una polémica, 1750–1900* (Mexico City: Fondo de Cultura Económica, 1993; 1st ed. in Italian, 1955); see also Benjamin Keen, *The Aztec Image in Western Thought* (New Brunswick, N.J.: Rutgers University Press, 1990; 1st ed., 1971), chaps. 8–9; David Brading, *The First America. The Spanish Monarchy, Creole Patriots, and the Liberal State, 1492–1867* (Cambridge: Cambridge University Press, 1993), pp. 422–64; and Jorge Cañizares-Esguerra, *How to Write the History of the New World. Histories, Epistemologies, and Identities in the Eighteenth-Century Atlantic World* (Stanford, California: Stanford University Press, 2001).

34. Anthony Pagden, *Lords of the World: Ideologies of Empire in Spain, Britain and France, c. 1500–c. 1800* (New Haven: Yale University Press, 1995), pp. 163–77; see also Cañizares-Esguerra, *How to Write the History of the New World*, pp. 35–38.

35. Raynal reprinted his work several times, each time introducing substantial modifications. The edition of 1780 is the most important and complete. The citations are from the 1788 English translation. Guillaume Thomas François Raynal, *A Philosophical and Political History of the Settlements and Trade of the Europeans in the East and West Indies* . . . 8 vols. (London: Printed for A. Strahn and T. Cadell, in the Strand, 1788), vol. 3, bk. 4, p. 253.

36. Ibid., vol. 3, bk. 6, pp. 304, and 309–10; vol. 4, bk. 7, pp. 34–39; vol. 8, bk. 19, p. 314.

37. Ibid., vol. 3, bk. 6, p. 275.

38. Ibid., vol. 8, bk. 19, pp. 366–67.

39. In the Spanish version of Raynal's work of 1784, the translator Eduardo Malo de Luque praised Raynal's work for its useful information, prodigious style, and clear method, but also emphasized the lengths he went to purge it from the profusion of ill-intended remarks: "My sole intention is to bring good to my nation and to the public . . . I am not so proud as to conceal that this most useful work is the result of the painstaking labor of an author whose pen, often tainted by harmful blood, is deadly poison. I have labored not little to purify it of its poisonous outpours, and to correct it from the pride and haughtiness that befits the thoughts of a man who calls himself

the *defender of humanity, of truth, and of liberty.*" The role of translators frequently entailed a degree of purging and semantic alteration to remove antipatriotic commentaries and ensure publication. *Historia política de los establecimientos ultramarinos de las naciones europeas.* Por Eduardo Malo de Luque, 5 vols. (Madrid: Por D. Antonio de Sancha, 1784), preface, p. 5.

40. Robertson mentions obtaining a good share of printed and unpublished materials from Lord Grantham who was appointed ambassador to the court of Madrid. Robertson, *The History of America,* vol. 1, preface, pp. vii–viii.

41. Ibid., vol. 2, bk. 4, pp. 18–25.

42. Ibid., vol. 2, bk. 4, p. 16.

43. Ibid., vol. 3, bk. 7, pp. 220–21.

44. Although plans were underway much earlier and in 1755 the Council of Indies entrusted the project to the Royal Academy of History in Madrid, ensuing debates about methodology delayed its fulfillment several years. For a detailed discussion of the Real Academia de la Historia's protracted methodological debates, see Cañizares-Esguerra, *How to Write the History of the New World,* pp. 160–69.

45. Juan Bautista Muñoz, *Historia del Nuevo Mundo* (Madrid: Por la Viuda de Ibarra, 1793), pp. 1–26.

46. Brading, *The First America;* Cañizares-Esguerra, *How to Write the History of the New World.*

47. Cañizares-Esguerra, *How to Write the History of the New World,* p. 217.

48. Juan José de Eguiara y Eguren, *Biblioteca mexicana* (1755), ed. Ernesto de la Torre Villar (Mexico City: Universidad Nacional Autónoma de México, 1986), vol. 1, p. 55.

49. Juan de Espinosa y Medrano, *La nobena maravilla nuebamaente hallada en los Panergiricos Sagrados . . .* (Valladolid: Joseph de Rueda, 1695), parecer of M.R.O. Fray Ignacio de Quesada, n.p.

50. Jorge Juan y Antonio de Ulloa, *Noticias secretas de América* (1772), Ed. Luis J. Ramos, 2 vols. (Madrid: Consejo Superior de Investigaciones Científicas, Instituto Fernández de Oviedo, 1985), vol. 2, pp. 333–37.

51. José Joaquín Granados y Gálvez, *Tardes americanas: Gobierno gentil y católico: Breve y particular noticia de toda la historia Indiana . . .* (Mexico City: En la Nueva Imprenta Matritense de D. Felipe de Zúñiga y Ontiveros, 1778), pp. 128–29.

52. Ibid., p. 399.

53. Doris M. Ladd, *The Mexican Nobility at Independence, 1780–1826* (Austin: Institute of Latin American Studies, University of Texas, 1976), pp. 21, 235, n. 28. See also Cañizares-Esguerra, *How to Write the History of the New World,* p. 233.

54. Moxó's work was written between 1804 and 1805 but first published in 1839 in Geneva. See Benito María de Moxó, *Cartas mejicanas. Facsímil de la edición de Génova, 1839.* Introd. by Elías Trabulse (Mexico City: Fundación Miguel Alemán, Fondo

de Cultura Económica, 1999). The work was not published in Spain because imperial authorities deemed it antipatriotic.

55. Ibid., pp. 91–92.

56. Ibid., pp. 40–41.

57. Ibid., p. 146. See note 1 for additional references.

58. The image appeared in *Entretenimientos de un prisionero en las provinicias del Río de la Plata* (Barcelona: Imprenta de José Torner, 1828), a pastiche of Moxó's *Cartas* published by his nephew Luis María de Moxó y López under the name Barón de Juras Reales.

59. William B. Taylor, *Magistrates of the Sacred, Priests, and Parishioners in Eighteenth-Century Mexico* (Stanford, California: Stanford University Press, 1996), pp. 173–75.

60. Alzate's awareness of foreign scientific novelties and his affiliation with European scientific societies led to accusations of being antipatriotic (*extrangerismo*), a charge that he dismissed in several of his publications: "I will always take pride in having been born a Spanish vassal. This nation boasts of sufficient merits, which only profound ignorance or a ridiculous type of preoccupation would try to slander." José Antonio de Alzate y Ramírez, *Asuntos varios sobre ciencias, y artes* (Mexico City: Imprenta de la Biblioteca Mexicana del Lic. D. Josef de Jáuregui, 1772), December 28, 1772, no. 11, p. 74.

61. Alzate y Ramírez, *Gazetas de literatura de México,* 3 vols. (Mexico City: Felipe de Zúñiga y Ontiveros, 1790), January 15, 1788, vol. 1, no. 1.

62. Ibid., December 9, 1789, vol. 1, no. 7.

63. Alzate y Ramírez, *Descripción de las antigüedades de Xochicalco . . .* (Mexico City: Felipe Zúñiga y Ontiveros, 1791), dedication, n.p.

64. Alzate y Ramírez, *Descripción de las antigüedades de Xochicalco,* p. 2.

65. Cañizares-Esguerra, *How to Write the History of the New World,* pp. 281–87.

66. Alzate y Ramírez, *Gazetas de Literatura de México,* January 15, 1788, vol. 1, no. 1, pp. 3–4. He also cites Boturini and Clavijero.

67. Alzate, *Gazetas de literatura,* December 9, 1787, vol. 1, no. 7, p. 55.

68. Ibid., Alzate, "Descripción de los indios de la Nueva España," in *La expedición de Malaspina, 1789–1794,* 9 vols. (Madrid: Ministerio de Defensa, Museo Naval, 1999), pp. 77–83. Alzate does not explictly mention Juan de Cárdenas's *Problemas y secretos maravillosos de las Indias* (Mexico, 1591) nor Enrico Martínez's *Repertorio de los tiempos y historia natural desta Nueva España* (Mexico, 1606), but his theory of separate bodies for Amerindians, Spaniards, and blacks appears to be modeled after their work. For the work of Cárdenas and Martínez, see Cañizares-Esguerra, "New World, New Stars," pp. 87–91.

69. See, for instance, García, *Origen de los Indios,* bk. 2, p. 69.

70. The notion of "staining by desire" was often invoked in the early modern world to explain the different coloration of people and how blackness extended through the

generations. See Barbara Maria Stafford, *Body Criticism: Imagining the Unseen in Enlightenment Art and Medicine* (Cambridge, Massachusetts: MIT Press, 1997), p. 306.

71. The four qualities of the human body corresponded to the four elements of the cosmos: fire (hot), air (dry), earth (cold), and water (wet); their combination was supposed to form the body's humors: yellow bile (hot and dry), blood (hot and wet), phlegm (wet and cold), black bile (cold and dry).

72. Alzate, *Observaciones sobre la física, historia natural, y artes útiles* (Mexico City: En la Oficina de Don José Francisco Rangel, 1787), vol. 1. no. 5, pp. 42–46.

73. Antonio León y Gama, *Descripción histórica cronológica de las dos piedras que en ocasión del nuevo empedrado que se está formando en la plaza principal de México, se hallaron en el año de 1790* ... (Mexico City: Imprenta de Don Felipe de Zúñiga y Ontiveros, 1792), p. 4.

74. Francisco Javier Clavijero, *Storia antica del Messico*, 4 vols. (Cesena, Italy, 1780–1781); the quotes are taken from the Spanish version *Historia Antigua de México* (1780–1781) (Mexico City: Porrúa, 1991), pp. XXI–XXII, XXXIII, and XXXV.

75. Ibid.

76. Ibid.

77. Ibid., p. 45.

78. Ibid, p. 47.

79. Ibid., p. 213. On this subject, see also John Leddy Phelan, "Neo-Aztecism in the Eighteenth Century and the Genesis of Mexican Nationalism," in Stanley Diamond, ed., *Culture in History: Essays in Honor of Paul Radin* (New York: Columbia University Press, 1960), pp. 760–70.

80. At some point there were plans to publish Clavijero's work in Spain. Alzate mentions being charged with the task of annotating the Spanish translation. See *Gazetas de Literatura de México*, October 2, 1792, p. 377.

81. Clavijero's work attracted numerous readers and was quickly translated into several languages. In the preface of the 1787 English version, the translator took the Spaniards to task by emphasizing the many pitfalls of their own chronicles of the New World. "The discovery of America constitutes one of the most remarkable areas of the world; and the history of it a subject not only curious but universally interesting, from its various connections with almost every other part of the globe. The Spanish historians of the two preceding centuries have done little towards elucidating this point. Partiality, prejudice, ignorance, and credulity, have occasioned them all to blend the many absurdities and improbabilities with their accounts, that it has not been merely difficult, but altogether impossible to ascertain the truth." He also contended that while authors like Robertson had exerted a great deal of attention in writing their books, the distance that separated them from the subject of study and the lack of first-hand knowledge of the people and culture of the region was the reason for leaving "the American side of the picture still greatly in the dark." *The History of Mexico Collected from Spanish and Mexican Historians from Manuscripts, and Ancient Paintings of the*

Indians. Illustrated by Charts, and Other Copper Plates. To which are added Critical Dissertations on the Land, the Animals, and Inhabitants for Mexico. By Abbé D. Francesco Saverio Clavigero. Translated from the Original Italian by Charles Cullen, Esq. In Two Volumes (London: Printed for G. G. and J. Robinson, No. 25, Pater-noster Row, 1787.), preface, pp. III–IV.

82. José Mariano Díaz de la Vega, "Memorias piadosas de la nación yndiana recogidas de varios Autores por el P. F. Joseph Díaz de la Vega Predicador grāl è Hijo de la Prov.ª del Santo Evangelio de Mexico" (1782), Real Academia de la Historia, Madrid, Col. Boturini, MS 9/4886. Another copy of the manuscript is at the AGN, Historia, vol. 32, and an 1849 copy of the latter is at the Bancroft Library, University of California at Berkeley, MSS M–M240. The citations are from the Madrid copy.

83. The biographical information on Díaz de la Vega derives from the Madrid manuscript, fol. 44v, and from father Francisco Antonio de la Rosa Figueroa, "Bezerro general menológico y chronológico de todos los religiosos que ha havido en la Provincia," University of Texas, Benson Library, MS. No. 1641 (G–25), fols. 85, 147, 351, and a loose piece of paper between fols. 248–249. De la Rosa gives two dates for Díaz de la Vega's taking of vows: March and April 23, 1736, and also states that he was from Huichapan. Father de la Rosa's project included an ambitious catalogue of all the Franciscans of his province up to 1763. On de la Rosa's work, see William B. Taylor, "Between Nativitas and Mexico City: An Eighteenth-Century Pastor's Local Religion," in Martin Austin Nesvig, ed., *Local Religion in Colonial Mexico* (Albuquerque: University of New Mexico Press, 2006), pp. 90–117.

84. Díaz de la Vega, "Memorias piadosas de la nación yndiana," fols. 1r–4v, 8r–9r, 62v–63r.

85. This is a recourse found frequently in the literature of the period to attest to the miraculous origin of images. Díaz de la Vega mentions several crucifixions and images of Christ in Mexico City at the Church of Santo Domingo, Balvanera (Cristo Crucificado), San Agustín (Santo Cristo de Totolapa), Regina Coeli (Santo Ecce Homo); the convents of San Juan de la Penitencia (Santo Niño de San Juan), and of Jesús María (Santo Cristo de Jesús María); the Hospital de la Purísima Concepción (Jesús Nazareno); and the sanctuary of Chalma outside of Mexico City (Santo Cristo de Chalma).

86. Juan Antonio de Paredes, *Carta edificante . . . la vida exemplar de la Hermana Salvadora de los Santos, India Otomí . . .* (Mexico City: Imprenta Nueva Madrileña de los Herederos del Lic. D. Joseph de Jáuregui, 1784).

87. Ibid., pp. 111–12.

88. Díaz de la Vega, "Memorias piadosas de la nación yndiana," chaps. 15–18. In Juan de Urtassumm, *La gracia triunfante en la vida de Catharina Tegakovita. India iroquesa, y en las de otras, assi de su nacion, como de esta Nueva España . . .* (Mexico City: Imprenta de Joseph Bernardo de Hogal, 1724). For the polemical history of this text and its unusual circulation from the northern empire of France to New Spain, see the

excellent study by Allan Greer, "Iroquois Virgin: The Story of Catherine Tekakwitha in New France and New Spain," in Allan Greer and Jodi Blinkoff, eds., *Colonial Saints: Discovering the Holy in the Americas, 1500–1800* (New York and London: Routledge, 2003), pp. 235–50. See also Allan Greer, *Mohawk Saint: Catherina Tekakwitha and the Jesuits* (New York: Oxford University Press, 2005).

89. Urtassumm, *La gracia* triunfante, pp. 209–33.

90. Ibid., n.p.

91. Allan Greer, "Iroquois Virgin," pp. 235–50.

92. Paredes, *Carta edificante*, pp. 110–11.

93. Ibid., n.p.

94. Díaz de la Vega, "Memorias piadosas de la nación yndiana," chap. 13.

95. Poole, "Church Law on the Ordination of the Indians." There were, however, various decrees permitting the ordination of Indians issued in 1697, 1725, and 1766. I wish to thank Dorothy Tanck Estrada for this observation.

96. Díaz de la Vega, "Memorias piadosas de la nación yndiana," fol. 128r.

97. The history of the Colegio de Indias is documented in José María Marroqui, *La ciudad de México* (1900), 3 vols. (Mexico City: Jesús Medina Editor, 1963), vol. 3, pp. 11–19.

98. Apparently a fifth canvas was commissioned, but upon the death of the painter the work was effaced "without any consideration" and the canvas was placed in public auction; no information was therefore known of the sitter. Juan de Merlo is described as born in Tlaxcala; he received his doctorate in canon law from the University of Mexico, and was canon of the cathedral of Puebla and bishop of Honduras. Nicolás del Puerto is described as a Zapotec Indian born in Chichicapa (Oaxaca), who studied at the Colegio Mayor de Todos Santos in Mexico City, and occupied important posts at the university, the cathedral, and the Holy Tribunal of the Inquisition. For the paintings' inscriptions, see Díaz de la Vega, "Memorias piadosas de la nación yndiana," fols. 128v–133v.

99. Stafford Poole, *Our Lady of Guadalupe: The Origins and Sources of a Mexican National Symbol, 1531–1797* (Tucson: The University of Arizona Press, 1997), pp. 83–84. Although the first four canvases were commissioned in the second half of the eighteenth century, there is no telling whether Valeriano's could have been earlier.

100. Ibid., pp. 104, 128–29, 142.

101. The racial identity of El Lunarejo remains unknown. See Luis Jaime Cisneros and Pedro Guibovich Pérez, "Juan de Espinoza Medrano, un intelectual cuzqueño del seiscientos: nuevos datos biográficos," *Revista de Indias* 48, nos. 182–183 (1998): 327–47. For a description of a portrait of El Lunarejo at the Dominican convent of Lima, see Juan de Velasco, *Historia del Reino de Quito en la América Meridional* (Quito: Imprenta del Gobierno de 1844), vol. 1, p. 198. A seventeenth-century portrait of a dark-complexioned Lunarejo can be found today at the Hotel Monasterio, Cuzco, Peru.

102. The Colegio de Indias was eventually turned into a convent. According to Marroqui the portraits were still in the possession of the nuns following the secularization of the church in the nineteenth century. See Marroqui, *La ciudad de México,* p. 13. A seventeenth-century portrait of Juan de Merlo is in the collection of the Museo Nacional de Historia, Mexico City. See María E. Ciancas and Bárbara Meyer, *La pintura de retrato colonial (siglos XVI–XVIII): catálogo del Museo Nacional de Historia* (Mexico City: Museo Nacional de Historia, 1994), p. 107.

103. The stories of these images were closely modeled on European hagiographies, where the patron saint usually appears to a shepherd. For the context of the apparition of miraculous images in Spain, see William Christian, Jr., *Apparitions in Late Medieval and Renaissance Spain* (Princeton, N.J.: Princeton University Press, 1981).

104. Moved by a strong patriotic sentiment, Florencia penned a sequence of books about miraculous images in Mexico. The enormous popularity of his works stemmed from the way he synthesized the stories found in several earlier sources and from his clear and accessible prose. Serge Gruzinski, *La guerra de las imágenes. De Cristóbal Colón a "Blade Runner"* (1492–2019) (Mexico City: Fondo de Cultura Económica, 1995), pp. 139–41. For Florencia's role in spreading the history of these images, see Antonio Rubial's introduction to Francisco de Florencia and Juan Antonio de Oviedo's *Zodíaco Mariano* (1755) (Mexico City: Consejo Nacional para la Cultura y las Artes, 1995), p. 18; and Luisa Elena Alcalá, "The Jesuits and the Visual Arts in New Spain, 1670–1767" (Ph.D. diss., New York University, New York, 1998), chaps. 1–2. The literature on the Virgin of Guadalupe is extensive. A few useful sources include Poole, *Our Lady of Guadalupe;* Taylor, "The Virgin of Guadalupe in New Spain: An Inquiry into the Social History of Marian Devotion," *American Ethnologist* 14, no. 2 (1987): 9–33; Francisco de la Maza, *El guadalupanismo mexicano* (Mexico City: Fondo de Cultura Económica, 1981); and Brading, *Mexican Phoenix. Our Lady of Guadalupe: Image and Tradition Across Five* Centuries (Cambridge: Cambridge University Press, 2001). For the development of Guadalupe's iconography, see *Imágenes guadalupanas,* exh. cat. (Mexico City: Centro Cultural de Arte Contemporáneo, 1987); Jaime Cuadriello, ed., *El Divino Pintor: la creación de María Guadalupe en el taller Celestial,* exh. cat. (Mexico City: Museo de la Basílica de Guadalupe, 2002); and Jaime Cuadriello, ed., *Zodíaco Mariano, 250 años de la declaración pontificia de María de Guadalupe como patrona de México,* exh. cat. (Mexico City: Museo de la Basílica de Guadalupe, Museo Soumaya, 2004).

105. Although the visual tradition of the Virgin of Guadalupe was fixed in the mid-seventeenth century, her images proliferated in an unprecedented way in the eighteenth. This came about in part through her proclamation as Mexico City's patroness in 1737; a second inspection of the original image in 1751 by a group of prominent painters led by Miguel Cabrera (1713/1718–1768), who declared that it was not painted by a human hand; and Pope Benedict XIV's 1754 confirmation of the Virgin of Guadalupe's patronage (*patronato*) and his concession of a proper mass and office

in her name. Miguel Cabrera became the most acclaimed painter of the Guadalupe after 1750.

106. Luis de Cisneros, *Historia de el principio y origen, progresos, venidas a México, y milagros de la Santa Imagen de Nuestra Señora de los Remedios* (1621), ed. Francisco Miranda (Mexico City: El Colegio de Michoacán, 1999); Francisco de Florencia, *La milagrosa invencion de un Thesoro Escondido . . .* (1685) (Seville: Imprenta de las Siete Revueltas, 1754). Some of New Spain's most prominent Marian images were also catalogued by Florencia and Oviedo in their *Zodíaco Mariano* (1755); this work was begun by Florencia and completed by Oviedo in the eighteenth century.

107. On the Virgin of Remedios, see Linda A. Curcio-Nagy, "Native Icon to City Protectress to Royal Patroness: Ritual, Political Symbolism, and the Virgin of Remedies," *The Americas* 52, no. 3 (1996):367–91. On the relationship of the Virgins of Remedios and Guadalupe, see Solange Alberro, "Remedios y Guadalupe. De la unión a la discordia," in Clara García Ayluardo and Manuel Ramos Mediana, eds., *Manifestaciones religiosas en el mundo colonial americano* (Mexico City: INAH, CONDUMEX, Universidad Iberoamericana, 1997), pp. 315–29. The Archivo Histórico del Distrito Federal (formerly Archivo Histórico del Ayuntamiento de la Ciudad de México), Mexico City, is a rich repository of documents about the sanctuary and the devotion of Remedios. William Taylor's current research on the devotional landscape of New Spain relies extensively on this archival source. See his "La Virgen de Guadalupe, Nuestra Señora de los Remedios y la cultura política del período de Independencia," in Alicia Mayer, ed., *México en tres momentos: 1810–1820–2010*, 3 vols. (Mexico City: Instituto de Investigaciones Históricas, Universidad Nacional Autónoma de México, 2007), vol. 2, pp. 213–239.

108. On the Virgin as a unifying element of society, see Cisneros, *Historia de el principio . . . de Nuestra Señora de los Remedios*, p. 153.

109. Díaz de la Vega offers useful information for assessing the popular following of the Virgin of Remedios in the eighteenth century and the sense of pride the image continued to instill in Juan Ceteutil's family. He mentions visiting Juan Ceteutil's house where the image was originally housed, which remained in the family for generations. When Díaz de la Vega saw it in 1745 (he was in contact with Juan Ceteutil's grandchildren Guillermo, between 1745 and 1753, and Pascuala de Tovar, between 1745 and 1747), the small room of the Virgin was still preserved. Pascuala de Tovar also began building a beautiful chapel where the image was once kept, but upon her death the project was left unfinished. According to Díaz de la Vega, the house had a sculpted tablet with an eagle with extended wings—the coat of arms of the Ceteutil family; by the 1780s the house was in a state of complete disarray. Díaz de la Vega, "Memorias piadosas de la nación yndiana," fols. 54r, 58r–59v.

110. See the excellent study of Jaime Cuadriello, *Las glorias de la República de Tlaxcala o la conciencia como imagen sublime* (Mexico City: Museo Nacional de Arte,

Instituto de Investigaciones Estéticas, Universidad Nacional Autónoma de México, 2004).

111. Francisco de Florencia, *Narracion de la marabillosa aparicion que hizo San Miguel a Diego Lazaro de San Francisco* . . . (Seville: Imprenta de las Siete Revueltas, 1692). Florencia mentions deriving part of his information from an earlier text by Father Pedro Salmerón.

112. The great flurry of miraculous images in the Catholic world led Pope Urban VIII (1623–44) to impose strict restrictions regarding their acceptance. For the context in New Spain, see Antonio Rubial García, "Los santos milagreros y malogrados de la Nueva España," in Clara García Ayluardo and Manuel Ramos Medina, *Manifestaciones religiosas*, p. 56.

113. The paintings were probably inspired by those commissioned by Diego Lázaro to record the event. See Eduardo Báez-Macías, *El arcángel San Miguel: su patrocinio, la ermita en el santo desierto de Cuajimalpa y el santuario de Tlaxcala* (Mexico City: Universidad Nacional Autónoma de México, 1979); Cuadriello, "Tierra de prodigios: la ventura como destino," in *Los pinceles de la historia: el origen del reino de la Nueva España, 1680–1750*, exh. cat. (Mexico City: Museo Nacional de Arte, 1999), pp. 199–204; Alcalá, "The Jesuits and the Visual Arts," pp. 85–95.

114. Manuel Loayzaga, *Historia de la Milagrosissima Imagen de N.ra S.ra de Occotlan que se venera extramuros de la ciudad de Tlaxcala* (Mexico City: Reimpreso por la viuda de D. Joseph Hogal, 1750). The book was first printed in 1745. Ocotlán's devotion was integrated to Oviedo's *Zodíaco Mariano*, pp. 256–71. Loayzaga was the key figure in the promotion of the cult of Ocotlán; in addition to publishing the account, he devoted his life to caring for the sanctuary, which he embellished with a lavish *camarín* (the image's octagonal chamber behind the altar) and elaborate paintings. On the painted cycles, see Cuadriello, *Las glorias de la República de Tlaxcala*, pp. 269–87.

115. The first two chapters of Loayzaga's account of the Virgin of Ocotlán are devoted to this subject.

116. Cuadriello, *Las glorias de la República de Tlaxcala*, pp. 303–15.

117. Díaz de la Vega, "Memorias piadosas de la nación yndiana," chap. 8. The source cited by Díaz de la Vega is Francisco Xavier de Santa Gertrudis, *La cruz de piedra, imán de la devoción venerada en el Colegio de misioneros apostólicos de la ciudad de Santiago de Querétaro* . . . (Mexico City: Francisco Ortega y Bonilla, 1722). For the history of the cross and its diffusion in the eighteenth century by the Franciscans based on indigenous sources, see Antonio Rubial García, "Santiago y la cruz de piedra: la mítica y milagrosa fundación de Querétaro, ¿una elaboración del Siglo de las Luces?," in Juan Ricardo Jiménez Gómez, ed., *Creencias y prácticas religiosas en Querétaro* (Mexico: Universidad Autónoma de Querétaro, 2005), pp. 25–58.

118. Ibid., p. 56.

119. Díaz de la Vega, "Memorias piadosas de la nación yndiana," fols. 47r–48v.

120. Florencia, *Narracion de la marabillosa aparicion que hizo San Miguel,* p. 80.

121. Guillermo Tovar de Teresa, *Miguel Cabrera: pintor de Cámara de la Reina Celestial* (Mexico City: Espejo de Obsidiana, 1995), pp. 102–06; 122–23.

122. Jaime Cuadriello offers a compelling case of the artistic patronage of a noble indigenous family in Tlaxcala in the late eighteenth century. The elaborate decorative program commissioned by Don Ignacio Faustinos Mazihcatzin Calmecahua Escobar, priest of San Simón Yehualtepec from 1785 to 1803, included paintings of the Virgin of Ocotlán, San Miguel del Milagro, Catherine Tekakwitha, and the martyrdoms of Cristobalito, Juan, and Antonio, among others. As Cuadriello has noted, this was a veritable indigenous ensemble of ethnic, familial, and regional pride. Jaime Cuadriello, *Las glorias de la República de Tlaxcala.*

123. Díaz de la Vega, "Memorias piadosas de la nación yndiana," fol. 9v.

124. For a corpus of many of these images, see *Los pinceles de la historia. El origen del reino de la Nueva España, 1680–1750,* exh. cat. (Mexico City: Museo Nacional de Arte, 1999).

125. Gathering Boturini's documents proved more difficult than expected as the collection underwent many vicissitudes, first moving from the viceregal palace— where it lost many volumes in the process—later being transferred to the university where it was housed with the holdings that belonged to the Jesuits prior to their expulsion in 1767, and finally to the Franciscan convent in Mexico City. In addition, several copies commissioned by reputed Mexican antiquarians circulated in the viceroyalty, making it difficult to distinguish between the originals and the copies.

126. John B. Glass, *The Boturini Collection and the Council of Indies, 1780–1800.* Contributions to the Ethnohistory of Mexico, no. 4, Lincoln Center (Massachusetts: Conmex Associates, 1976); and Cañizares-Esguerra, *How to Write the History of the New World,* pp. 300–05.

127. AGN, Historia, vol. 1, fol. 13v.

128. The viceroy of Mexico Juan Vicente de Güemes Pacheco de Padilla, count of Revillagigedo (1789–94) commissioned father Francisco García de Figueroa the task of collecting the documents, a duplicate of which is housed at the AGN, Historia, vol. 32.

129. Preface by Friar Francisco García Figueroa, AGN, Historia, vol. 32, fol. 4.

130. On subaltern forms of power contestation, see Ann Laura Stoler, *Race and the Education of Desire: Foucault's History of Sexuality and the Colonial Order of Things* (Durham, N.C.: Duke University Press, 1995).

131. AGN, Historia, vol. 1, fol. 13v.

132. Moxó, *Cartas mejicanas,* p. 149.

Chapter 4

An earlier version of this essay was published in Spanish, Jaime Cuadriello, "Moctezuma a través de los siglos," in Víctor Mínguez and Manuel Chust, eds., *El imperio sublevado*. *Monarquía y naciones en España e Hispanoamérica* (Madrid: Consejo Superior de Investigaciones Científicas, 2004), pp. 95–122.

1. Fernando R. de la Flor, *Barroco, representación e ideología en el mundo hispánico* (Madrid: Cátedra, 2002), pp. 13–76, 161–217. On the subject of public festivals, see also Linda Curcio-Nagy A., *The Great Festivals of Colonial Mexico City: Performing Power and Identity* (Albuquerque: University of New Mexico Press, 2004).

2. Keith Moxey, *Teoría, práctica y persuasión. Estudios sobre historia del arte* (Madrid: Ediciones del Serbal, 2004), pp. 137–48.

3. Aldred Gell, *Art and Agency: An Anthropological Theory* (Oxford: Clarendon, 1988), pp. 1–28.

4. Ernst Gombrich, *Imágenes simbólicas, estudios sobre el arte del Renacimiento* (Madrid: Editorial Debate, 2001), p. 4.

5. One only needs to recall the view of Moctezuma's descendants in our times, who continue to lay claim to the ideological genealogy of their illustrious ancestor from the moral perspective of *indigenismo* or Hispanism. See Pablo Moctezuma Barragán, *Moctezuma y el Anáhuac. Una visión mexicana* (Mexico City: Editorial Limusa, 1999); and José Miguel Carrillo de Albornoz y Muñoz de San Pedro, *Memorias de doña Isabel de Moctezuma* (Mexico City: Editorial Nueva Imagen, 1999).

6. Baltasar Dorantes de Carranza's testimony is highly revealing, as he is one of the first directly to characterize Quetzalcóatl as a prophecy, and to allude to the illegitimately occupied throne: "He told [Cortés] through Marina's tongue: tell this god that he is welcome in this city, whose presence and sight I am enjoying, since I have been in his place ruling and governing this kingdom which his father the god Quetzalcóatl had left, in whose seat and hall I have unworthily sat, and whose vassals I have ruled and governed; and that if he comes to enjoy this kingdom which is his, that is here at his service, let me then relinquish it to him, since in our ancestors' prophecies I have found it foretold and written, and may he take it in a fair hour, and let me subject myself to his service and will." Baltasar Dorantes de Carranza, *Sumaria relación de las cosas de la Nueva España* (1602) (Mexico City: Editorial Porrúa, 1987), p. 169.

7. Francisco Cervantes de Salazar, *Crónica de la Nueva España* (1514) (Mexico City: Editorial Porrúa, 1985), pp. 461–84; Bernal Díaz del Castillo, *Historia verdadera de la conquista de la Nueva España* (1630) (Mexico City: Editorial Porrúa, 2004), pp. 286–97.

8. Antonio de Solís, *Historia de la conquista de México* (1684) (Mexico City: Miguel Ángel Porrúa, 1988), pp. 327–34.

9. Ibid., p. 18.

10. Ibid., p. 334.

11. Ibid.

12. Accusations were made against Cortés by his enemies in Mexico and Spain that included misuse of crown monies, illegally hoarding Aztec treasure, the murder of his wife Catalina, debts, doubts about his loyalty to the King, and general abuse

of power. Cortés traveled to Spain in 1528 and again in 1541 in order to lay his case personally before the king. None of the charges were substantiated but neither was Cortés reinstated as governor of Mexico. He was, however, confirmed as captain general and received the noble title of the Marqués del Valle de Oaxaca returning to Mexico in 1530. After his second journey to Spain in 1541 to defend himself against the continued accusations, Cortés remained there until 1547, when having decided to return to Mexico once more, he died while making preparations for his trip.

13. Diego Muñoz Camargo, *Descripción de la ciudad y provincia de Tlaxcala* (c. 1580) (San Luis Potosí: Gobierno del Estado, El Colegio de San Luis, 2000), plate 20.

14. For the paintings of the Inca kings, see Luis Eduardo Wuffarden, "La descendencia real y el renacimiento inca en el virreinato," in *Los incas: reyes del Perú* (Lima: Banco de Crédito, 2005), pp. 162–95.

15. See Helga von Kugelgen, "La estructuración emblemática de unos tableros en el arco de triunfo," in *Juegos de Ingenio y Agudeza: La pintura emblemática de la Nueva España,* exh. cat. (Mexico City: Museo Nacional de Arte, 1997), pp. 94–97.

16. The Turk and the Tatar were the models of vice and cruelty against whom European chroniclers measured the barbarity of other rulers and polities. See Sonia V. Rose, "Moctezuma, varón ilustre: su retrato en López de Gómara, Cervantes de Salazar y Díaz del Castillo," in Karl Kohut and Sonia V. Rose, eds., *Pensamiento europeo y cultura colonial* (Frankfurt: Editorial Vervuert, 1997), pp. 69–97.

17. Jean Hani, *La realeza sagrada, del faraón al cristianísimo rey* (Barcelona: Editorial Sophia Perennis, 1998), p. 82.

18. Salazar, *Crónica de la Nueva España,* pp. 301, 485.

19. This portrait, which was discovered in 1999, was published in Jaime Cuadriello, ed., *Los pinceles de la historia. El origen del reino de la Nueva España,* exh. cat. (Mexico City: Museo Nacional de Arte, 1999). When I first published my research on the portrait's iconography, I had not yet fully grasped its many meanings, especially in relation to its patronage.

20. For the juridical expression of royal symbols in the viceroyalties of America, see the lucid study of Altuve-Febres Lores, *Los reinos del Perú. Apuntes sobre la monarquía peruana* (Lima: Edición del autor, 1996).

21. Hani, *La realeza sagrada,* pp. 91–105.

22. One of the model biblical kings similarly depicted as reverential and in the act of relinquishing his attributes, is illustrated by Juan Bautista Villalpando, *El Templo de Salomón* (c. 1604). In keeping with the vision of Zechariah's prophesy of the advent of Christ and his church, the king is shown before the candelabrum in the tabernacle, offering up his scepter, and placing his hand on his chest to symbolize his state as an "embodied" Christian prince. In Andean art, extant paintings from the first half of the seventeenth century depict the Inca approaching the gate of Bethlehem like a Magi,

thus representing in ecumenical fashion the "fourth part of the world." The overt "acculturated" missionary intent, which was characteristic of Jesuit iconographical programs (e.g., paintings of St. Francis Xavier baptizing Moctezuma or the Inca), also applies to pre-Hispanic symbolism. A case in point is the *copilli* (royal diadem) worn by Moctezuma. This headdress, which the Jesuit Manuel Duarte called "a half-mitre" in reference to its almond-shaped form, was seen as evidence of America's ancient apostolic Christianity. It was believed to be one of the signs that the Apostle St. Thomas Quetzalcóatl had left behind on his journey through the continent, preaching and appointing priests. In Andean dynastic portraits of the Inca kings that were popular among the Cuzco nobility, Atahualpa is often depicted at the end; he is distinguished from his predecessors because he is shown in the act of surrendering his club of command to his successor—Charles V himself. See Carlos V. Guy Rozat, "Lecturas de Moctezuma, revisión del proceso de un cobarde," *Historias* 31 (Mexico City: Dirección de Estudios Históricos del INAH, 1994): 37; Teresa Gisbert, *Iconografía y mitos indígenas en el arte* (La Paz: Ediciones Gisbert, 1994), pp. 77–78; and Manuel Duarte, "Pluma rica, Nuevo fénix de América," in Nicolás León, *Bibliografía mexicana del siglo XVIII* (Mexico City: 1906), vol. 3, p. 437.

23. Juan de Torquemada, *Monarquía Indiana* (1615) (Mexico City: Editorial Porrúa, 1986), vol. 1, p. 193.

24. Ibid.

25. Francisco López de Gómara, *Historia general de las Indias* (1553) (Barcelona: Ediciones Orbis, 1985), vol. 2, p. 136.

26. Isidro Rafael Gondra, *Explicación a las láminas pertenecientes a la Historia Antigua de México y a la de su Conquista, que se la ha agregado a la traducción mexicana de W. H. Prescott* (Mexico City: Ignacio Cumplido, 1846), p. 151. Gondra states the following: "Plate 64. The portrait of Moctezuma II, which has served as a model for this plate, was engraved in North America, although I am unaware of the original from which it was copied. In the Tecpan of Santiago there was a very old portrait, although its date was also unknown. Either that painting or another very similar may be found today in the collection of Licenciado Mariano Riva Palacio; but both suffer excessively from the time at which they were painted, and two minor details are sufficient proof of the overall inaccuracy of the works: the club placed on the right side in the style of a Spanish sword and the scepter the monarch holds in his right hand, fashioned in a completely Spanish style, prove that it is a modern copy."

27. Iván Escamilla, "Razones de la lealtad, cláusulas de la fineza: poderes, consensos y conflictos en la oratoria sagrada novohispana ante la sucesión de Felipe V," in Alicia Mayer, ed., *Poder, religión y autoridad en la Nueva España* (Mexico City: Universidad Nacional Autónoma de México, 2004), pp. 179–204.

28. Charles Gibson, *The Aztecs under Spanish Rule: A History of the Indians of the Valley of Mexico, 1519–1810* (Stanford, California: Stanford University Press, 1964), p. 191.

29. Detlef Heikamp, *Mexico and the Medici* (Florence: Editrice Edam, 1972), pp. 23, 42.

30. Jaime Cuadriello, "El origen del reino y la configuración de su empresa. Episodios y alegorías de triunfo y fundación," in Cuadriello, ed., *Los pinceles de la historia*, p. 60.

31. Elías Trabulse, *Los manuscritos perdidos de Sigüenza y Góngora* (Mexico City: El Colegio de México, 1988), pp. 29–32. The portrait closely resembles the image of Netzahualpilli in the Códice Ixtlixóchitl in the Bibliothèque National de France, Paris.

32. Giovanni Francesco Gemelli Careri, *Viaje a la Nueva España* (1728) (Mexico City: Universidad Nacional Autónoma de México, 1983), pp. 24–64.

33. Archivo General de la Nación (AGN), Mexico City, Tierras, vol. 2692, exp.19, fols. 64v–65.

34. Jaime Cuadriello, *Las glorias de la República de Tlaxcala, o la conciencia como imagen sublime* (Mexico City: Universidad Nacional Autónoma de México, Instituto de Investigaciones Estéticas, Museo Nacional de Arte, 2004), pp. 344–72.

35. Elsewhere I address the figure of Moctezuma in baroque political rituals, especially in the thematic *mitote,* or dance of Moctezuma, where the dramatized surrender of weapons symbolized the renewal of the colonial pact. However, this was a polyvalent ritual that, on the one hand, evoked the renunciation of Mexico's crown and the forging of a universal Catholic empire, and on the other hand, continued to underscore New Spain's foundational role as rooted in antiquity. Through this dance, the kingdom was born and reborn, with all of its juridical and political credentials, into historical and territorial reality. Jaime Cuadriello, "El encuentro de Cortés y Moctezuma como escena de concordia," in *Amor y desamor en las artes, XXIII Coloquio Internacional de Historia del Arte* (Mexico City: Instituto de Investigaciones Estéticas, Universidad Nacional Autónoma de México, 2001), pp. 263–92.

36. In the presence of the viceroy and the Indian authorities, "the festival was enlivened by the dances of Indians covered in feathers and holding in one hand a rattle, referred to as *ayacastle* in the Mexican language, and in the other a type of feather fan." See Manuel Rivera Cambas, *México pintoresco, artístico y monumental* (1880–83) (Mexico City: Editorial del Valle de México, 1974), vol. 2, p. 80. For the context of the image of Moctezuma's dance reproduced here, see Ilona Katzew, *Una visión del México del Siglo de las Luces. La codificación de Joaquín Antonio de Basarás* (Mexico City: Landucci, 2006).

37. The Cádiz Cortes put communal property at risk, especially because of the revenues derived from its management. The government's absorption of indigenous communal property was tantamount to the administrative and governmental collapse of Indian towns. In addition, the eradication of the Indian court made any dispute over land exceedingly difficult. Although the intention was to create a system based on the

equality of its citizens, the Indians were increasingly dislocated from their previous forms of government as a polity. On this subject see Dorothy Tanck Estrada, *Pueblos de indios y educación en el México colonial* (Mexico City: El Colegio de México, 1999), pp. 545–54; and Bartolomé Portillo and José María Clavero, *Pueblos, nación, constitución: en torno a 1812* (Vitoria, Spain: Ikusager Ediciones, 2004), pp. 11–51.

38. See Andrés Lira, *Comunidades indígenas de frente a la ciudad de México: Tenochtitlan y Tlatelolco, sus pueblos y barrios, 1812–1919* (Mexico City: El Colegio de México, 1983).

39. The Carbonari were members of a secret political association in Italy, organized in the early part of the nineteenth century for the purpose of changing the government into a republic. The origin of the Carbonari is uncertain, but the society is said to have first met, in 1808, among the charcoal burners of the mountains, whose phraseology they adopted.

40. Esther Acevedo, Fausto Ramírez, and Jaime Cuadriello, Introduction to *Los pinceles de la historia: De la patria criolla a la nación mexicana,* exh. cat. (Mexico City: Museo Nacional del Arte, 2000), p. 24.

41. See Joel R. Poinsett, *Notas sobre México* (Mexico City: Editorial Jus, 1973); José Fuentes Mares, *Poinsett, historia de una gran intriga* (Mexico City: Editorial Jus, 1958), unpaginated. The major post-independence rival political factions in Mexico identified themselves with freemasonry; they were divided between the York Rite Masons (or *Yorquinos*), who supported federalism, and the Scottish Rite (or *Escoceses*), who favored centralism.

42. "At El Águila, there is talk of the dance held on Saturday night in the home of the North American envoy, and it is added that by happenstance the image of the Emperor Moctezuma Xocoyotzín was hung at the front of the hall; perhaps it is the full-length portrait that was in the house of the Andrade *mazyorazgo,* the descendant of that Emperor, a very old painting that depicts him richly dressed, which was on sale at public auction for 25 pesos on the second Calle del Relox, and there was nobody who wanted to buy it. Now he [Moctezuma] receives the applause that had been denied him and from a foreign nation." Carlos María de Bustamante, *Diario histórico de México* [May 29, 1825] (Mexico City: Instituto Nacional de Antropología e Historia, 1982), vol. 3, pp. 1, 79.

43. See Rafael Isidro Gondra, *Explicación de las láminas pertencientes a la "Historia Antigua de México y la de su Conquista" que se han agregado a la traducción mexicana de la de William H. Prescott* (Mexico City: Imprenta Lito-tipográfica de Ignacio Cumplido, 1846).

44. For the history of these editions, see Elena Estrada de Gerlero, "La litografía y el Museo Nacional como armas del nacionalismo," in *Los pinceles de las historia. De la patria criolla a la nación mexicana,* exh. cat. (Mexico City: Museo Nacional de Arte, 2000), pp. 152–69. In 1849, a French traveler in Mexico named Ronde drew a sketch of this painting (which is now housed in the Bibliothèque Nationale de France, Paris),

and markedly idealized the full-length figure. The sketch was subsequently disseminated in the French press.

45. Manuel González Ramírez, *La revolución social de México* (Mexico City: Fondo de Cultura Económica, 1974), vol. 1, pp. 136–50.

46. Throughout the colonial period, based on ancient medical understanding, the Indians' lack of facial hair (e.g., beards) was seen as a sign of their supposed effete and cowardly nature.

47. Gondra, *Explicación a las láminas pertenecientes a la Historia Antigua*, p. 151.

48. Fritz Saxl, *La vida de las imágenes* (Madrid: Alianza Forma, 1989), p. 11.

49. Michael Baxandall, *Modelos de intención* (Madrid: Hermann Blume, 1989), pp. 127–29.

50. Hugh Thomas, *Yo, Moctezuma, Biografía novelada* (Mexico City: Planeta, 1995).

51. Quoted in Elsa Cecilia Frost, *Este Nuevo orbe* (Mexico City: Universidad Nacional Autónoma de México, Centro Coordinador y Difusor de Estudios Latinoamericanos, 1996), pp. 155–64.

52. I wish to thank Mercedes Iturbe for sharing this information. She bought the painting in Paris from a prominent member of André Breton's circle, Madame Geo Dupin. See Mercedes Iturbe, *Espíritos cómplices* (Mexico City: Grupo Editorial, 1997), pp. 71–277.

53. Such curatorial delirium merited the scathing critique of, among others, Francisco Reyes Palma: "Treinta Siglos + × = México Eterno," in *Curare, espacio crítico para las artes* 14 (Mexico City, 1999), pp. 14–17.

54. See Cuadriello, ed., *Los pinceles de la historia,* pp. 60–61.

Chapter 5

1. U.S. Department of Commerce, Bureau of the Census, *Abstract of the Fifteenth Census of the United States: 1930* (Washington, D.C.: Government Printing Office, 1933), p. 5.

2. Melissa Nobles, *Shades of Citizenship: Race and the Census in Modern Politics* (Stanford, California: Stanford University Press, 2000), p. 44. *Mulatto* was removed in 1900 but reinstated in 1910.

3. Secretaría de la Economía Nacional, Dirección General de Estadística, *Quinto censo de población, 15 de Mayo de 1930, resumen general* (Mexico City, 1930), p. xvi; also see Luis A. Astorga A., "La razón demográfica de estado," in *Revista Mexicana de Sociología* (1989): 193–210.

4. For a more extensive discussion of the development of eugenics in the early twentieth century, see also Alexandra Minna Stern, *Eugenic Nation: Faults and Frontiers of Better Breeding in Modern America* (Berkeley and Los Angeles: University of California Press, 2005).

5. See Suzanne Oboler, *Ethnic Labels, Latino Lives: Identity and the Politics of (Re)presentation in the United States* (Minneapolis: University of Minnesota Press, 1995).

6. See David Theo Goldberg, *The Racial State* (Maiden, Massachusetts: Blackwell, 2002); Tukufu Zuberi, *Thicker than Blood: How Racial Statistics Lie* (Minneapolis: University of Minnesota Press, 2001).

7. See Martha Hodes, "The Mercurial and Abiding Power of Race: A Transnational Family Story," *American Historical Review* 108, no. 1 (2003): 84–118; Ann Laura Stoler, "Racial Histories and their Regimes of Truth," *Political Power and Social Theory* 11 (1997): 183–206.

8. See Ilona Katzew, *Casta Painting: Images of Race in Eighteenth-Century Mexico* (New Haven and London: Yale University Press, 2004); Ann Twinam, *Public Lives, Private Secrets: Gender, Honor, and Illegitimacy in Colonial Spanish America* (Stanford, California: Stanford University Press, 1999); Martha Menchaca, *Recovering History, Constructing Race: The Indian, Black, and White Roots of Mexican Americans* (Austin: University of Texas Press, 2001).

9. See Donna J. Haraway, *Modest_Witness@Second_Millennium.FemaleMan@_Meets_OncoMouse(tm): Feminism and Technoscience* (New York: Routledge, 1997).

10. See Alexandra Minna Stern, "From Mestizophilia to Biotypology: Racialization and Science in Mexico, 1920–1960," in Nancy Appelbaum, Anne S. MacPherson, and Karin Alejandra Rosemblatt, eds., *Race and Nation in Modern Latin America* (Chapel Hill: University of North Carolina Press, 2003), pp. 187–210; Alexander Dawson, *Indian and Nation in Revolutionary Mexico* (Albuquerque: University of New Mexico Press, 2003).

11. See Matthew Frye Jacobson, *Whiteness of a Different Color: European Immigrants and the Alchemy of Race* (Cambridge, Massachusetts: Harvard University Press, 1998); Mae M. Ngai, *Impossible Subjects: Illegal Aliens and the Making of Modern America* (Princeton, N.J.: Princeton University Press, 2004).

12. Geoffrey C. Bowker and Susan Leigh Star, *Sorting Things Out: Classification and its Consequences* (Cambridge, Massachusetts: The MIT Press, 1999).

13. Ibid, p. 10.

14. See Ronald Bayer, *Homosexuality and American Psychiatry: The Politics of Diagnosis* (Princeton, N.J.: Princeton University Press, 1987).

15. See Kenneth Prewitt, "Racial Classification in America: Where Do We Go from Here?" *Daedalus* 134, no. 1 (2005): 5–18; C. Matthew Snipp, "Racial Measurement in the American Census: Past Practices and Implications for the Future," *Annual Review of Sociology* 29 (2003): 563–99.

16. See María Elena Martínez, this volume.

17. See Goldberg, *The Racial State;* Ian Hacking, *The Taming of Chance* (Cambridge: Cambridge University Press, 1990).

18. See Londa Schiebinger, *Nature's Body: Gender in the Making of Modern Science* (Boston: Beacon Press, 1993).

19. See Paul Starr, "The Sociology of Official Statistics," in William Alonso and Paul Starr, eds., *The Politics of Numbers* (New York: Russell Sage Foundation, 1987),

pp. 7–57; Nobles, *Shades of Citizenship;* David Theo Goldberg, *Racial Subjects: Writing on Race in America* (New York: Routledge, 1997).

20. Nobles, *Shades of Citizenship,* chap. 2.

21. Nobles, *Shades of Citizenship,* p. 44; on mulattos and census enumeration, see also Joel Williamson, *New People: Miscegenation and Mulattos in the United States* (Baton Rouge: Louisiana State University Press, 1995).

22. Antonio García Cubas, *The Republic of Mexico in 1876: A Political and Ethnographical Division of the Population, Character, Habits, Customs and Vocations of Its Inhabitants.* Trans. George F. Henderson (Mexico City: "La Enseñanza" Printing Office, 1876). This tract was published only in English. See Casey Walsh, "Statistics and Ecologies of Power in Mexican Anthropology," *Nueva Antropología* 19, no. 64 (2005): 53–73.

23. García Cubas, *The Republic of Mexico in 1876,* p. 20.

24. Ibid, p. 20.

25. See Secretaría de Economía, Dirección General de Estadística, *Estadísticas sociales del porfiriato, 1877–1910* (Mexico City: Dirección General de Estadística, 1956); Departamento de la Estadística Nacional, *Resumen del censo general de habitantes, de 30 de Noviembre de 1921* (Mexico City: Talleres Gráficos de la Nación, 1928).

26. See Stephen Jay Gould, *The Mismeasure of Man* (2d. ed; New York: Penguin 1996); Sander Gilman, *Difference and Pathology: Stereotypes of Sexuality, Race, and Madness* (Ithaca: Cornell University Press, 1988).

27. Martin S. Pernick, *The Black Stock: Eugenics and the Death of "Defective" Babies in American Medicine and Motion Pictures Since 1915* (New York: Oxford University Press, 1996).

28. Ian F. Haney López, *White by Law: The Legal Construction of Race* (New York: New York University Press, 1997); Sarah Gualtieri, "Becoming 'White': Race, Religion and the Foundations of Syrian/Lebanese Ethnicity in the United States," *Journal of American Ethnic History* 20, no. 4 (2001): 29–58. In the case of adjudications on jury makeup, court rulings that Mexicans were white (and whites counted for Mexicans) functioned as a kind of veiled discrimination that complicated arguments against the unconstitutionality of Mexican segregation based on racial status and group identification. See Haney López, this volume. Also see Ariela J. Gross, "Texas Mexicans and the Politics of Whiteness," *Law and History Review* 21, no. 1 accessed at www.history-cooperative.org on May 3, 2005; George A. Martinez, "The Legal Construction of Race: Mexican Americans and Whiteness," *Harvard Latino Law Review* 2 Rev. 321 (Fall 1997), accessed at http://www.lexis-nexis.com on May 5, 2005.

29. See Stoler, "Racial Histories;" Thomas Holt, "Marking: Race, Race Making and the Writing of History," *American Historical Review* 100, no. 1 (1995): 1–20.

30. Sir Francis Galton, *Essays in Eugenics* (London: Eugenics Education Society, 1909), p. 35; Diane Paul, *Controlling Human Heredity: 1865 to the Present* (Atlantic Highlands, N.J.: Humanities Press, 1995), chap. 1.

31. See Daniel J. Kevles, *In the Name of Eugenics: Genetics and the Uses of Human Heredity* (2nd. ed; Cambridge: Harvard University Press, 1995), p. 14.

32. For an excellent summary of Mendel's experiments and theories, see Kevles, *In the Name of Eugenics.* On this subject see also Stern, *Eugenic Nation.*

33. For example, eugenicists played a key role in the infant and child hygiene organizations and agencies developed in Mexico starting in the early twentieth century; their counterparts did the same on the state level in the United States, directing infant and maternal welfare programs on the state and federal levels.

34. J. Joaquín Izquierdo, "Necesidad de que en México emprenda el estado estudios de eugenesia," *Medicina* 3, no. 32 (1923): 189–92, quote from p. 190. Unless otherwise noted, all translations are mine.

35. Rafael Carrillo, "Tres problemas mexicanos de eugenesia: etnografía y etnología, herencia e inmigración," *Revista Mexicana de Puericultura* 3, no. 25 (1932): 1–15, quote from p. 3.

36. See "Bases mínimas de política demográfica, que presentan el Comité Mexicano para el Estudio de los Problemas de Población y la Sociedad Mexicana de Eugenesia, a la nación y al gobierno," *Eugenesia* 2nd series vol. 1, no. 1 (1939): 2–4.

37. *Ley general de población* (Mexico City: Ediciones Botas, 1936), p. 1. Also see Gilberto Loyo, *Las deficiencias cuantitativas de la población de México y una política demográfica nacional* (Mexico City: Partido Nacional Revolucionario, 1934). This law was based largely on the demographic policy recommendations contained in Loyo's *La política demográfica de México,* endorsing a combination of campaigns against infant mortality and general public health measures, prenuptial certificates, the selective immigration of "assimilable" foreigners, the repatriation of Mexican nationals from the United States, and the invigoration of the mestizo through programs aimed at modernizing the Indian.

38. On "Latin" eugenics, see Nancy Leys Stepan, *"The Hour of Eugenics": Race, Gender, and Nation in Latin America* (Ithaca: Cornell University Press, 1991).

39. See Agustín Basave Benítez, *México mestizo: análisis del nacionalismo mexicano en torno a la mestizofilia de Andrés Molina Enríquez* (Mexico City: Fondo de Cultura Económica, 1992); also see David A. Brading, "Social Darwinism and Romantic Idealism: Andrés Molina Enríquez and José Vasconcelos in the Mexican Revolution," *Prophecy and Myth in Mexican History* (Cambridge: Center of Latin American Studies, 1984); Alan Knight, "Racism, Revolution, and *Indigenismo*: Mexico, 1910–1940," in Richard Graham, ed., *The Idea of Race in Latin America, 1870–1940* (Austin: University of Texas Press, 1990), pp. 71–107.

40. On the aesthetic dimensions, see Ana María Alonso, "Conforming Disconformity: 'Mestizaje,' Hybridity, and the Aesthetics of Mexican Nationalism," *Cultural Anthropology* 19, no. 4 (Nov. 2004): 459–90; Tace Hedrick, "Blood-Lines that Waver South: Hybridity, the "South," and American Bodies," *Southern Quarterly* 42, no. 1 (2003):

39–52; Marilyn Grace Miller, *Rise and Fall of the Cosmic Race: The Cult of Mestizaje in Latin America* (Austin: University of Texas Press, 2004).

41. Alonso, "Conforming Disconformity," p. 466.

42. Ibid, p. 463.

43. See Dawson, *Indian and Nation.*

44. Many scholars have insightfully analyzed *Forjando Patria* and Gamio's indigenism. See, for example, Walsh, "Statistics and Ecologies"; Walsh, "Eugenic Acculturation: Manuel Gamio, Migration Studies, and the Anthropology of Development in Mexico, 1910–1940," *Latin American Perspectives* 138, no. 31–5 (2004): 118–45; Dawson, *Indian and Nation;* Alonso, "Conforming Disconformity"; and Robert M. Buffington, *Criminal and Citizen in Modern Mexico* (Lincoln: University of Nebraska Press, 2000), just to mention a few of the most recent.

45. See José Vasconcelos, *La raza cósmica* (1925) (Mexico: Espasa, 1943).

46. Ibid, p. 42.

47. Ibid, p. 47.

48. For excellent discussion of "distant" versus "proximate" race-mixing, see Lourdes Martínez-Echazábal, "*Mestizaje* and the Discourse of National/Cultural Identity in Latin America, 1845–1959," *Latin American Perspectives* 25, no. 3 (1998): 21–42.

49. José Vasconcelos, *The Cosmic Race: A Bilingual Edition,* translated and annotated by Didier T. Jaén (Baltimore and London: Johns Hopkins Press, 1997), pp. 3–5.

50. On similar patterns in Ecuador, see A. Kim Clark, "Race, 'Culture', and Mestizaje: The Statistical Construction of the Ecuadorian Nation, 1930–1950," *Journal of Historical Sociology* 11, no. 2 (1998): 185–211.

51. A review of the rosters of the Mexican Eugenics Society and the Pro-Race Committee of Mexico City from the 1920s to the 1940s—which drafted racist legislation and continuously pathologized Chinese Mexicans and later, Jews fleeing Nazi Germany—reveals just one member of both organizations: Cristóbal Rodríguez, a military general and editor of the anti-clerical and jingoistic journal, *La Patria.* On Sinophobia and nationalism in Mexico, see Gerardo Rénique, "Race, Region, and Mestizaje: Sonora's Anti-Chinese Movement and Mexico's Post-Revolutionary Nationalism, 1920–1930s," in Appelbaum, MacPherson, and Rosemblatt, eds., *Race and Nation in Modern Latin America,* pp. 211–36.

52. Alfredo Correa, "La eugenesia y su importancia," *Pasteur* 9, no. 2–4 (1936): 73–76. See also Correa, "Importancia de la eugenesia ante el criterio del estado," *Pasteur* 6, no. 2–6 (1933): 151–64.

53. Alfredo Saavedra, *Eugenesia y medicina social* (Mexico City, 1934), p. 119.

54. For a longer discussion of biotypology in Mexico in terms of science, race, and gender, see Stern, "From Mestizophilia to Biotypology."

55. Charles B. Davenport, *The Trait Book* (Cold Spring Harbor, N.Y.: Eugenics Record Office Bulletin No. 6, 1912).

56. Garland E. Allen, "The Eugenics Records Office at Cold Spring Harbor, 1910–1940," *Osiris,* 2nd series, vol. 2 (1986): 225–64. The Dewey decimal system is used in libraries to classify materials by dividing them into ten classes (000 for Generalities, 100 for Philosophy and Psychology, and so on), which are then sub-divided further until an item is assigned a precise numerical classification.

57. Davenport, *The Trait Book.*

58. Allen, "The Eugenics Record Office," p. 239.

59. See Stern, *Eugenic Nation,* chap. 1.

60. Harry H. Laughlin, "Population Schedule for the Census of 1920," *Journal of Heredity* 10, no. 5 (1919): 208–10.

61. Ibid, p. 208.

62. See, for example, Paul, *Controlling Human Heredity;* and Steven Selden, *Inheriting Shame: The Story of Eugenics and Racism in America* (New York: Teachers College, Columbia University, 1999).

63. See Nancy Ordover, *American Eugenics: Race, Queer Anatomy, and the Science of Nationalism* (Minneapolis: University of Minnesota Press, 2003); Daylanne K. English, *Unnatural Selections: Eugenics in American Modernism and the Harlem Renaissance* (Chapel Hill: University of North Carolina Press, 2004).

64. See John Higham, *Strangers in the Land: Patterns of American Nativism, 1860–1925* (1955) (New Brunswick, N.J.: Rutgers University Press, 1988).

65. See Michael Omi and Howard Winant, *Racial Formation in the United States: From the 1960s to the 1980s* (New York: Routledge, 1986).

66. Paul, *Controlling Human Heredity,* p. 105.

67. See Mae M. Ngai, "The Architecture of Race in American Immigration Law: A Reexamination of the Immigration Act of 1924," *Journal of American History* 86, no. 1 (1999): 67–92.

68. See Gabriela F. Arredondo, *Mexican Chicago: Race, Identity and Nation, 1916–1939* (Urbana-Champaign: University of Illinois Press, 2006).

69. One of the best discussions of these hearings can be found in Mark Reisler, *By the Sweat of Their Brow: Mexican Immigrant Labor in the United States, 1900–1940* (Westport, Connecticut: Greenwood Press, 1976).

70. *Congressional Record* 69:3, 70th Congress, 1st Session (1928), pp. 817–18.

71. *Hearings Before the Committee of the Census, House of Representatives,* 70th Congress, *Fifteenth and Subsequent Censuses* (Washington, D.C.: Government Printing Office, 1928).

72. "American History in Terms of Human Migration," Statement of Harry H. Laughlin, Extracts from Hearings Before the Committee on Immigration and Naturalization, House of Representatives, 70th Congress, March 7, 1928 (Washington, D.C.: GPO, 1928), contained in D-4-5, Papers of Harry H. Laughlin (HHL), Special Collections (SC), Truman State University (TSU), Kirksville, Missouri.

73. Ibid, p. 18.

74. Ibid.

75. See Neil Foley, *The White Scourge: Mexicans, Blacks, and Poor Whites in Texas Cotton Culture* (Berkeley: University of California Press, 1997); for an excellent discussion of how these racial politics played out in Chicago, see Gabriela F. Arredondo, *Mexican Chicago*.

76. "Population Schedule for the Census of 1930," C-4-6, HHL, SC, TSU.

77. See David G. Gutiérrez, *Walls and Mirrors: Mexican Americans, Mexican Immigrants, and the Politics of Ethnicity* (Berkeley: University of California Press, 1995); Julie Anne Dowling, "The Lure of Whiteness and the Politics of 'Otherness': Mexican American Racial Identity." (Ph.D. diss., University of Texas, Austin, 2004), chap. 2. The history of Mexicans and the 1930 and 1940 censuses deserve much more scholarly attention.

78. See Harvey M. Choldin, "Statistics and Politics: The 'Hispanic Issue' in the 1980 Census," *Demography* 23, no. 3 (1986): 403–18; Laura E. Gómez, "The Birth of the 'Hispanic' Generation: Attitudes of Mexican-American Political Elites toward the Hispanic Label," *Latin American Perspectives* 19, no. 4 (1992): 45–58.

79. See Stepan, "*The Hour of Eugenics,*" chap. 6.

80. Charles Davenport, "Race Crossing," First Pan American Conference on Eugenics and Homiculture, Folder: Pan American Conference (1st), Charles B. Davenport Papers (CBD), B/D27, American Philosophical Society (APS), Philadelphia.

81. Charles Davenport, "The Eugenical Principles of Immigration," Folder: Panamerican Conference (1st), CBD, B/D27, APS.

82. "Primera sesión de la Primera Conferencia Panamericana de Eugenesia y Homicultura," Folder: Panamerican Conference (1st), CBD, B/D27, APS, "una exposición histérica de la evolución de las leyes de inmigración en los Estados Unidos." Santamarina's participation in the conference is detailed in III-36-10, Archivo Histórico de la Secretaría de Relaciones Exteriores (AHSRE), Mexico City.

83. Ibid.

84. Transcription of evening address by Santamarina, Folder: Pan American Congress (1st), CBD, B/D27, APS.

85. Ibid.

86. Veronica Guerrero Mothelet and Stephan Herrera, "Mexico launches bold genome project," *Nature Biotechnology* 23, no. 9 (2005): 1030.

Chapter 6

1. Américo Castro, *The Spaniards: An Introduction to their History* (Berkeley: University of California Press, 1971), pp. 1–94. See also María Elena Martínez, "The Black Blood of New Spain: *Limpieza de Sangre*, Racial Violence, and Gendered Power in Early Colonial Mexico," *William and Mary Quarterly*, 3rd Series, vol. LCI, no. 3 (July 2004): 479–520.

2. Gaspar Pérez de Villagrá, *History of New Mexico*, translated by Gilberto Espinosa (Alcalá, 1610; reprinted, Los Angeles: The Quivira Society, 1933), p. 173. See also Aurelio M. Espinosa, "El desarrollo de la palabra Castilla en la lengua de los indios Hopis de Arizona," *Revista de Filología Española* 22 (1935): 298–300.

3. The details of contact between Spaniards and Indians can be found in Ramón A. Gutiérrez, *When Jesus Came, the Corn Mothers Went Away: Marriage, Sexuality and Power in New Mexico, 1500–1846* (Stanford, California: Stanford University Press, 1992).

4. Fredrich Katz, *The Ancient American Civilizations* (New York: Praeger, 1972); Eric R. Wolf, *Sons of the Shaking Earth* (Chicago: University of Chicago Press, 1966); Sherburne R. Cook and Woodrow W. Borah, *The Indian Population of Central Mexico, 1531–1610* (Berkeley: University of California Press, 1960).

5. The history of the *sistema de castas* can be studied in Magnus Mörner, *Race Mixture in the History of Latin America* (Boston: Little, Brown and Company, 1967); Claudio Esteva-Fabregat, *Mestizaje in Ibero-America* (Tucson: University of Arizona Press, 1995); Silvio Zavala, *Las instituciones jurídacas en la conquista de América* (Madrid: Imprenta Helénica, 1935); Ilona Katzew, *Casta Painting: Images of Race in Eighteenth-Century Mexico* (London and New Haven: Yale University Press, 2004); María Elena Martínez, *Genealogical Fictions: Limpieza de Sangre, Religion, and Gender in Colonial Mexico* (Stanford, California: Stanford University Press, 2008).

6. Magnus Mörner, *Race Mixture*; Ann Twinam, *Public Lives, Private Secrets: Gender, Honor, Sexuality, and Illegitimacy in Colonial Spanish America* (Stanford, California: Stanford University Press, 1999).

7. Quoted in Verena Martínez-Alier, *Marriage, Class and Colour in Nineteenth-Century Cuba* (London: Cambridge University Press, 1974), pp. 83–84.

8. Spanish Archives of New Mexico, microfilm edition, Reel 9: frames 789–820.

9. Fray Angélico Chávez, "Genízaros," in *Handbook of North American Indians*, vol. 9, ed. William C. Sturtevant (Washington, D.C.: Smithsonian Institution, 1979), pp. 198–201; Steven M. Horvath, "The Social and Political Organization of the Genízaros of Plaza de Nuestra Señora de los Dolores de Belén, New Mexico 1740–1812" (Ph.D. diss., Brown University, 1979); David M. Brugge, *Navajos in the Catholic Church Records of New Mexico 1694–1875*, Research Report no. 1 (Window Rock, Arizona: The Navajo Tribe, 1968), p. 30

10. Archivo General de la Nación (Mexico City): Historia, vol. 25, exp. 25, fol. 229.

11. Frances Leon Swadesh, *Los Primeros Pobladores: Hispanic Americans of the Ute Frontier* (Notre Dame, Indiana: Notre Dame University Press, 1974), p. 45. Florence Hawley Ellis, "Tomé and Father J.B.R.," *New Mexico Historical Review* 30 (1955): 89–114, quotation from p. 94.

12. Elsie C. Parsons, "Tewa Mothers and Children," *Man* 24 (1924): 149; Edward H. Spicer, *The Yaquis: A Cultural History* (Tucson: University of Arizona Press, 1980),

pp. 22–23; N. Ross Crumrine, *The Mayo Indians of Sonora: A People Who Refuse to Die* (Tucson: University of Arizona Press, 1977), p. 69.

13. Gutiérrez, *When Jesus Came, the Corn Mothers Went Away*, pp. 193–94.

14. Américo Paredes, "The Problem of Identity in a Changing Culture: Popular Expressions of Culture Conflict Along the Lower Rio Grande Border," in Stanley R. Ross, ed., *Views Across the Border: The United States and Mexico* (Albuquerque: University of New Mexico Press, 1978), pp. 68–94.

15. Ibid., pp. 72–75.

16. Raymund A. Paredes, "The Mexican Image in American Travel Literature, 1831–1869," *New Mexico Historical Quarterly* 1 (1977): 5–29; Deena Gonzáles, "The Spanish-Mexican Women of Santa Fe: Patterns of Their Resistance and Accommodation, 1820–1880" (Ph.D. diss., University of California, Berkeley, 1986); John R. Chávez, *The Lost Land: The Chicano Image of the Southwest* (Albuquerque: University of New Mexico Press, 1984); Phillip A. Hernández, "The Other Americans: The American Image of Mexico and Mexicans, 1550–1850" (Ph.D. diss., University of California, Berkeley, 1974); Susan R. Kenneson, "Through the Looking Glass: A History of Anglo-American Attitudes Toward the Spanish-Americans and Indians of New Mexico" (Ph.D. diss., Yale University, 1978); Jack D. Forbes, "Race and Color in Mexican-American Problems," *Journal of Human Relations* 16 (1968): 55–68; Manuel Gamio, *Mexican Immigration to the United States* (Chicago: University of Chicago Press, 1930), pp. 129, 209.

17. Leonard Pitt, *The Decline of the Californios: A Social History of the Spanish-Speaking Californians, 1846–1890* (Berkeley: University of California Press, 1966), pp. 53, 157, 174, 188, 204, 259, 267, 309; Arthur L. Campa, *Hispanic Culture in the Southwest* (Norman: University of Oklahoma Press, 1979), p. 5.

18. Joseph V. Metzgar, "The Ethnic Sensitivity of Spanish New Mexicans: A Survey and Analysis," *New Mexico Historical Review* 49 (1974): 52.

19. Ibid., p. 60.

20. Erna Fergusson, *New Mexico: A Pageant of Three Peoples* (New York: Knopf, 1964), p. 218; Nancie González, *The Spanish-Americans of New Mexico: A Heritage of Pride* (Albuquerque: University of New Mexico Press, 1969), pp. 80–81.

21. Gamio, *Mexican Immigration to the United States*, p. 133.

22. Richard Norstrand, "Mexican American and Chicano: Emerging Terms for a People Coming of Age," *Pacific Historical Review* 42, no. 3 (1973): 396.

23. The various forms Hispanofilia and Hispanophobia have taken in the United States can be studied in Richard L. Kagan, ed., *Spain in America: The Origins of Hispanism in the United States* (Urbana and Chicago: University of Illinois Press, 2002).

24. These ideas can be studied in Robert E. Bieder, *Science Encounters the Indian, 1820–1880: The Early Years of American Ethnology* (Norman: University of Oklahoma Press, 1986); and George W. Stocking, Jr., *Race, Culture and Evolution: Essays in the History of Anthropology* (New York: The Free Press, 1968).

25. Roy L. Garis, *Mexican Immigration: A Report by Roy L. Garis for the Information of Members of Congress,* United States House of Representatives, 1930, p. 436.

26. Robert F. Foerster, *The Racial Problems Involved in the Immigration from Latin America and the West Indies to the United States: A Report to the Secretary of Labor* (Washington: Government Printing Office, 1925), pp. 55, 57.

27. Victor S. Clark, "Mexican Labor in the United States," *United States Bureau of Labor Bulletin* 78 (1908): 496.

28. "Latin U.S.A.," *Newsweek,* July 12, 1999.

29. Otto Santa Ana, *Brown Tide Rising: Metaphors of Latinos in American Public Discourse* (Austin: University of Texas Press, 2002).

30. Dale Maharidge, *The Coming White Minority: California's Eruptions and America's Future* (New York: Times Books, 1996).

31. Samuel P. Huntington, *Who Are We? The Challenges to America's National Identity* (New York: Simon & Schuster, 2004).

32. Peter Brimelow, *Alien Nation: Common Sense About America's Immigration Disaster* (New York: HarperPerennial, 1996), p. xv.

33. Ibid., pp. 10, 265.

34. Lawrence Auster, *The Path to National Suicide: An Essay on Immigration and Multiculturalism* (Monterey: American Immigration Control Foundation, 1990); Richard D. Lamm and Gary Imhoff, *The Immigration Time Bomb: The Fragmenting of America* (New York: Truman Talley Books, 1985).

35. Arthur Schlesinger, Jr., *The Disuniting of America: Reflections on a Multicultural Society* (New York: W.W. Norton, 1992).

36. Richard J. Hernstein and Charles Murray, *The Bell Curve: Intelligence, and Class Structure in American Life* (New York: Free Press, 1994), pp. 362–65.

37. Edward A. Telles and Edward Murguía, "Phenotypic Discrimination and Income Differences Among Mexican Americans," *Social Science Quarterly* 71 (1990): 682–96.

38. Carlos H. Arce, Edward Murguía, and W. Parker Frisbie, "Phenotype and Life Chances Among Chicanos," *Hispanic Journal of Behavioral Sciences* 9, no. 1 (1987): 19–32.

39. Richard L. Zweigenhaft and G. William Domhoff, *Diversity in the Power Elite: Have Women and Minorities Reached the Top?* (New Haven: Yale University Press, 1998), pp. 130–31.

40. Gustavo E. Gonzales, "Are Black Hispanics Being Ignored?" *Hispanic Business* (November 1996): 6.

41. Michael V. Miller, "Mexican Americans, Chicanos, and Others: Ethnic Self-Identification and Selected Social Attributes of Rural Texas Youth," *Rural Sociology* 41 (1976): 234–47; Tino Villanueva, "Sobre el término 'chicano,'" *Cuadernos Hispano-Americanos* 336 (1978): 387–410; Joseph V. Metzgar, "The Ethnic Sensitivity of Spanish New Mexicans: A Survey and Analysis," *New Mexico Historical Review* 49 (1974): 51–72;

Armando Gutiérrez and Herbert Hirsch, "The Militant Challenge to the American Ethnos: 'Chicanos' and 'Mexican Americans,'" *Social Science Quarterly* 53 (1973): 830–45.

42. "Latin U.S.A.," *Newsweek*, July 12, 1999.

43. Felix Padilla, *Latino Ethnic Consciousness: The Case of Mexican Americans and Puerto Ricans in Chicago* (Notre Dame, Indiana: University of Notre Dame Press, 1985).

44. Arlene Dávila, *Latinos Inc.: The Marketing and Making of a People* (Berkeley: University of California Press, 2002).

Chapter 7

1. *Sanchez v. Texas*, 243 S.W.2d 700, 701 (Tex. Crim. App. 1951).

2. *Hernandez v. Texas*, 347 U.S. 475 (1954).

3. For background facts on the *Hernandez* case, see generally Ian Haney López and Michael A. Olivas, "*Hernandez v. Texas:* Jim Crow, Mexican Americans, and the Anti-subordination Constitution," in Devon W. Carbado and Rachel F. Moran, eds., *Race and Law Stories* (New York: Foundation Press, 2008).

4. *Hernandez v. Texas*, 251 S.W.2d 531, 533 (Tex. Crim. App. 1952).

5. Gustavo C. García, "An Informal Report to the People," in Ruben Munguía, ed., *A Cotton Picker Finds Justice: The Saga of the Hernandez Case* (1954) (no page numbers in original). See also Mario T. García, *Mexican Americans: Leadership, Ideology, and Identity, 1930–1960* (New Haven: Yale University Press, 1989), p. 49.

6. 347 U.S. at 479–480.

7. Ian Haney López, *Racism on Trial: The Chicano Fight for Justice* (Cambridge: Belknap and Harvard University Press, 2003), pp. 71, 75–76.

8. Clare Sheridan, "'Another White Race': Mexican Americans and the Paradox of Whiteness in Jury Selection," *Law & History Review* 21 (2003): 109, 138–39.

9. 347 U.S. at 478 (emphasis added).

10. I discuss the early racialization of Mexicans at length in Haney López, *Racism on Trial*, especially chapter three, from which the following discussion is taken.

11. Arnoldo De León, *They Called Them Greasers: Anglo Attitudes Toward Mexicans In Texas, 1821–1900* (Austin: University of Texas Press, 1983), p. 4.

12. Reginald Horsman, *Race and Manifest Destiny: The Origins of Racial Anglo-Saxonism* (Cambridge: Harvard University Press, 1981), pp. 243–44.

13. Ibid.

14. Ibid., p. 243.

15. Ibid., p. 238.

16. Ibid., p. 246.

17. Joan Moore, *Mexican Americans* (New York: Prentice-Hall, 1970), p. 47.

18. De León, *Greasers*, p. 22.

19. Note that a census taken in 1834 reported that four out of five of the Anglo settlers in Texas came from slave states. Cecil Robinson, *With the Ears of Strangers: The Mexican in American Literature* (Tucson: University of Arizona Press, 1963), p. 67.

20. Robert Heizer and Alan Almquist, *The Other Californians: Prejudice and Discrimination Under Spain, Mexico, and the United States to 1920* (Berkeley: University of California Press, 1971), p. 140.

21. Horsman, *Race and Manifest Destiny* (emphasis added), p. 208.

22. Heizer and Almquist, *The Other Californians*, p. 140.

23. García, *Mexican Americans*, p. 14.

24. Ibid., pp. 210–12.

25. George J. Sánchez, *Becoming Mexican American: Ethnicity, Culture, and Identity in Chicano Los Angeles, 1900–1945* (New York: Oxford University Press, 1993), p. 12.

26. Haney López, *Racism on Trial*, pp. 70–72.

27. García, *Mexican Americans*, p. 16.

28. Victoria Hattam, "Ethnicity: An American Genealogy," in Nancy Foner and George M. Fredrickson, eds., *Not Just Black and White* (New York: Russell Sage Foundation Publications, 2004). See also Mathew Frye Jacobson, *Whiteness of a Different Color: European Immigrants and the Alchemy of Race* (Cambridge: Harvard University Press, 1998).

29. On the "other white" legal strategy, see Steven H. Wilson, "Brown over 'Other White': Mexican Americans' Legal Arguments and Litigation Strategy in School Desegregation Lawsuits," *Law & History Review* 21 (2003): 145.

30. Brief of Petitioner at 38, *Hernandez v. Texas*, 347 U.S. 475 (No. 406). See also Neil Foley, "Becoming Hispanic: Mexican Americans and the Faustian Pact with Whiteness," in Neil Foley, ed., *Reflexiones 1997: New Directions in Mexican American Studies* (Austin: University of Texas Press, 1997), p. 53.

31. García, "An Informal Report to the People."

32. *Ramirez v. State*, 40 S.W.2d 138, 139, 140 (Tex. Crim. App. 1931).

33. *Hernandez v. State*, 251 S.W.2d 531, 536 (Tex. Crim. App. 1951).

34. 347 U.S. at 478, 479.

35. *Strauder v. West Virginia*, 100 U.S. 303 (1880).

36. *McCleskey v. Kemp*, 481 U.S. 279 (1987).

37. *City of Richmond v. Croson*, 488 U.S. 469 (1989).

38. *Hernandez v. New York*, 500 U.S. 352 (1991).

39. Ibid., at 404.

40. Ibid., at 404 (O'Connor, J., concurring) (emphasis added).

41. For further discussion of the future of race, with special reference to changes in the Latino population, see Ian Haney López, "Race on the 2010 Census: Hispanics and the Shrinking White Majority," *Daedalus* (Winter 2005): 42; and Ian Haney

López, *White by Law: The Legal Construction of Race* (New York: New York University Press, revised edition 2006), esp. chap. 8.

42. U.S. Bureau of the Census, *The Hispanic Population, Census 2000 Brief* (May 2001), p. 2.

Chapter 8

1. Paul du Gay et al., *Doing Cultural Studies: The Story of the Sony Walkman* (London: Sage Publications, 1997), p. 19.

2. David Held, *Introduction to Critical Theory* (Berkeley: University of California Press, 1980).

3. Todd Gitlin, "Prime Time TV: The Hegemonic Process in TV," *Television and Its Influence among African-Americans and Hispanics* (1979): 251–66.

4. Frantz Fanon, *Black Skin, White Masks* (New York: Grove Press, 1967), p. 152.

5. Carlos E. Cortés, "Knowledge Construction and Popular Culture: The Media as Multicultural Education," in James C. Banks and Cherry A. McGee Banks, eds., *Handbook of Research on Multicultural Education* (San Francisco: Jossey-Bass, 2001), p. 169.

6. Several reports have found that prime time television continues "to fall short reflecting the rich diversity of our society." See Children Now, "Fall Colors 2003–2004: Prime Time Diversity Report" (Oakland, California: Children Now, 2004), p. 12. Also, content analyses of television programs tend to group all Latinos together (i.e., Mexican Americans, Puerto Ricans, Cubans, Dominicans, etc.) because television programs do not offer enough information to further distinguish characters as members of a particular group. See Children Now, "Fall Colors 2003–2004: Prime Time Diversity Report" (Oakland, California: Children Now, 2004); Children Now, "Latinos on Prime Time. Report III: 2001–02 Prime Time Television Season" (Oakland, California: Children Now, 2002); Alison R. Hoffman and Chon A. Noriega, "Looking for Latino Regulars on Prime-Time Television: The Fall 2003 Season" (Los Angeles: UCLA Chicano Studies Research Center, 2004); Darnell Hunt, "Prime Time in Black and White: Not Much Is New for 2002" (Los Angeles: UCLA, 2003); Chon A. Noriega, "Ready for Prime Time: Minorities on Network Entertainment Television" (Los Angeles: UCLA Chicano Studies Research Center, 2002); Harry P. Pachon et al., "Missing in Action: Latinos in and out of Hollywood" (Claremont, California: The Tomás Rivera Policy Institute, 1999); and Harry P. Pachon et al., "Still Missing: Latinos in and out of Hollywood" (Claremont, California: The Tomás Rivera Policy Institute, 2000). On the subject of how the media can be seen as both reflecting and educating toward a culture of exclusion of culturally and politically subordinated groups, see Henry A. Giroux, "Doing Cultural Studies: Youth and the Challenge of Pedagogy," in Pepi Leistyna, Arlie Woodrum, and Stephen A. Sherblom, eds., *Breaking Free: The Transformative Power of Critical Pedagogy* (Cambridge, Massachusetts: Harvard Educational Review, 1996).

7. Latinos are the fastest growing group in the United States. According to the U.S. census, they comprise 37.4 million people or 13.3 percent of the total U.S. population. Within this group, people of Mexican origin comprise 66.9% of all Latinos. See Roberto Ramirez and G. Patricia de la Cruz, "The Hispanic Population in the United States: March 2002" (Washington, D.C.: Current Population Reports, P20–545, U.S. Census Bureau, 2002), pp. 1–2.

8. I use the terms "Chicano/a" and "Mexican American" to refer to people of Mexican ancestry living in the United States. When using the term "Mexican," I refer to people in Mexico. The term "of Mexican origin" refers to both Chicanos/as and Mexicans. For stylistic purposes, I use "Chicano(s)" to mean both male and female. "Latino" is a broad umbrella term, which comprises Mexican Americans, as well as people of Latin American descent in general.

9. See Norman K. Denzin, "Zoot Suits and Homeboys (and Girls)," *The Review of Education/Pedagogy/Cultural Studies* 23, no. 2 (2001): 167–99; Rosa Linda Fregoso, "The Representation of Cultural Identity in 'Zoot Suit' (1981)," *Theory and Society* 22, no. 5 (1993): 659–74; Christine List, *Chicano Images: Refiguring Ethnicity in Mainstream Film* (New York: Garland Publishing, 1996); Mark Pizzato, "Brechtian and Aztec Violence in Valdez's Zoot Suit," *Journal of Popular Film & Television* 26, no. 2 (1998): 52–61.

10. The Chicano Movement lasted approximately from 1965 to 1975, although it began to wind down after the National Chicano Moratorium in 1970—a peaceful demonstration with an estimated 20,000 to 30,000 participants that ended violently. For more on this subject, see Rodolfo Acuña, *Occupied America: A History of Chicanos* (New York: Longman, 2004), chap. 13.

11. The U.S. context must be understood within international and transnational contexts. As Seth Fein states, "The history of U.S. international relations is central to the study of U.S. culture and society . . . the history of the rest of the world must be seen as part of the history of the United States." See Seth Fein, "New Empire Into Old: Making Mexican Newsreels the Cold War Way," *Diplomatic History* 28, no. 5 (2004): 703–48.

12. I use the term "Anglo" to mean a white person from the United States.

13. For a detailed explanation of "greaser," see Gary D. Keller, *Hispanics and United States Film: An Overview and Handbook* (Tempe, Arizona: Bilingual Review/Press, 1994), pp. 48–53. Also see Gary D. Keller, "The Image of the Chicano in Mexican, United States, and Chicano Cinema: An Overview," in Gary D. Keller, ed., *Chicano Cinema: Research, Reviews, and Resources* (Tempe, Arizona: Bilingual Review/Press, 1985), p. 45; *Bronze Screen: 100 Years of the Latino Image in Hollywood Cinema* (2002, directed by Susan Racho, Nancy De Los Santos, and Alberto Dominguez).

14. For a discussion on the origins of the term "greaser," see Steven W. Bender, *Greasers and Gringos: Latinos, Law, and the American Imagination* (New York: New York University Press, 2003). See also Leonard Pitt, *The Decline of the Californios: A*

Social History of the Spanish-Speaking Californians, 1846–1890 (Berkeley: University of California Press, 1966).

15. Luis Reyes and Peter Rubie, *Hispanics in Hollywood: A Celebration of 100 Years in Film and Television* (Hollywood, Calif.: Lone Eagle, 2000), p. 5.

16. For the particulars of these historical events, see Acuña, *Occupied America: A History of Chicanos.*

17. Reyes and Rubie, *Hispanics in Hollywood,* p. 5.

18. Frank Javier Garcia Berumen, *The Chicano/Hispanic Image in American Film* (New York: Vantage Press, 1995), p. 2.

19. Reyes and Rubie, *Hispanics in Hollywood,* p. 5.

20. Charles Ramírez Berg, *Latino Images in Film: Stereotypes, Subversion, Resistance* (Austin: University of Texas Press, 2002), p. 68.

21. Carlos E. Cortés, "Chicanas in Film: History of an Image," in Clara E. Rodríguez, ed., *Latin Looks: Images of Latinas and Latinos in the U.S. Media* (Boulder, Colorado: Westview Press, 1997), p. 128.

22. Ibid., p. 127.

23. Ibid. See also George Hadley-Garcia, *Hispanic Hollywood: The Latins in Motion Pictures* (New York: Citadel Press, 1990), p. 35. Some films that depicted this idea that the "greaser" loses his Mexican/Chicana woman to the Anglo include *The Mexican's Revenge* (1909), *Carmenita the Faithful* (1911), and *Chiquita the Dancer* (1912).

24. Carlos E. Cortés, "Chicanas in Film: History of an Image," p. 128.

25. Ibid.

26. Acuña, *Occupied America: A History of Chicanos,* p. 180.

27. Racho, De Los Santos, and Dominguez, "Bronze Screen."

28. See Acuña, *Occupied America: A History of Chicanos,* chap. 9.

29. For a comprehensive history of films featuring the characters of the Zorro and the Cisco Kid, see Reyes and Rubie, *Hispanics in Hollywood,* pp. 387–410.

30. Berumen, *The Chicano/Hispanic Image in American Film,* pp. 5–7.

31. Ramírez Berg, *Latino Images in Film,* p. 76.

32. For instance, a Hollywood studio changed the name of Jacob Krantz, an Austrian Jewish actor to that of Ricardo Cortez, as well as his birthplace as Spain. See Racho, De los Santos, and Domínguez, "Bronze Screen."

33. Ramírez Berg, *Latino Images in Film,* p. 76.

34. Rosa Linda Fregoso, *MeXicana Encounters: The Making of Social Identities on the Borderlands* (Berkeley: University of California Press, 2003), esp. chap. 6.

35. For more on the history of the Latin Lover stereotype, see Berumen, *The Chicano/Hispanic Image in American Film,* chap. 2; Hadley-Garcia, *Hispanic Hollywood: The Latins in Motion Pictures,* chap. 1; Reyes and Rubie, *Hispanics in Hollywood,* p. 12.

36. Acuña, *Occupied America: A History of Chicanos,* p. 208.

37. Quoted by Acuña from the Committee on Immigration and Naturalization. Ibid., p. 209.

38. In the few instances when Latinos/as were portrayed, they were depicted as aristocrats from South America. See Racho, De los Santos, and Dominguez, "Bronze Screen."

39. *In Old Arizona* (1929, directed by Raoul Walsh) was the first sequel. For a listing of the Cisco Kid films, see Reyes and Rubie, *Hispanics in Hollywood*, pp. 401–10.

40. Cortés, "Chicanas in Film: History of an Image," pp. 128–31.

41. Hadley-Garcia, *Hispanic Hollywood: The Latins in Motion Pictures*, p. 40.

42. See Leonard J. Leff and Jerodl L. Simmons, *The Dame in the Kimono: Hollywood, Censorship, and the Production Code* (New York: Grove Press, 1990). The Hays Code was voluntarily adopted in 1930 by the Motion Pictures Producers and Distributors Association (later to become the Motion Picture Association of America or MPAA) to avoid governmental censorship.

43. Acuña, *Occupied America: A History of Chicanos*, pp. 201–02, 242, 262.

44. Berumen, *The Chicano/Hispanic Image in American Film*, p. 47.

45. Examples of these kinds of films are Walt Disney's *Saludos Amigos* (1942), and the 1940 remake of *The Mark of Zorro* (directed by Rouben Mamoulian). The latter was translated into several Spanish dialects to match the Spanish spoken in different South American countries. The reception in Latin America of many other films that utilized Latin America as a backdrop, however, varied. See Reyes and Rubie, *Hispanics in Hollywood*, pp. 18–22.

46. Ibid., p. 21.

47. For an excellent discussion on North Americans' notion of Cuba as the land of the "Latin Lovers," see Louis A. Pérez Jr., *On Becoming Cuban: Identity, Nationality, and Culture* (Chapel Hill: University of North Carolina Press, 1999), chap. 3.

48. Charles Ramírez Berg, "Bordertown, the Assimilation Narrative, and the Chicano Social Problem Film," in Chon A. Noriega, ed., *Chicanos and Film: Representation and Resistance* (Minneapolis: University of Minnesota Press, 1992), pp. 29–46. See also Ramírez Berg, *Latino Images in Film*, pp. 111–27. Ramirez Berg considers *Bordertown*, a 1935 film directed by Archie Mayo, as the beginning of the genre of "social problem" films.

49. Ramírez Berg, *Latino Images in Film*, p. 126. See also Reyes and Rubie, *Hispanics in Hollywood*, pp. 138–39.

50. See James J. Lorence, *The Suppression of Salt of the Earth: How Hollywood, Big Labor, and Politicians Blacklisted a Movie in Cold War America* (Albuquerque: The University of New Mexico Press, 1999).

51. The 1961 film *One-Eyed Jacks* (directed by Marlon Brando) was also a Western, but it portrayed Chicanos in a more favorable light by highlighting the Mexican influence in California and portraying Mexican/Chicana women as strong and independent.

52. Racho, De Los Santos, and Dominguez, "Bronze Screen."

53. Acuña, *Occupied America: A History of Chicanos,* p. 298.

54. Ibid., p. 309.

55. Keller, "The Image of the Chicano in Mexican, United States, and Chicano Cinema: An Overview," p. 43. See also Carlos E. Cortés, "Chicanas in Film," in Gary D. Keller, ed., *Chicano Cinema: Research, Reviews, and Resources* (Tempe, Arizona: Bilingual Review/Press, 1985), pp. 102–06.

56. Berumen, *The Chicano/Hispanic Image in American Film,* p. 190. Also see the U.S. Census for 1970 and 1980.

57. Ibid., pp. 189–231.

58. Film scholar Chon Noriega proffers the definition of Chicano film as "a film (or video) by and about Chicanos" whereby the word "by" means that the writer, producer, or director is Chicano. There are some movies by non-Chicanos that are considered to be Chicano films because their cultural sensibility is considered to be Chicano-like. Chon A. Noriega, ed., *Chicanos and Film: Representation and Resistance* (Minneapolis: University of Minnesota Press, 1992), p. xix.

59. Max Benavidez, "Chicano Art: Culture, Myth, and Sensibility," in Cheech Marin, ed., *Chicano Visions: American Painters on the Verge* (Boston: Bulfinch Press, 2002); Juan D. Bruce-Novoa, *Retrospace* (Houston: Arte Público Press, 1990); Shifra M. Goldman and Tomás Ybarra-Frausto, "The Political and Social Contexts of Chicano Art," in Dennis J. Bixler-Márquez et al., eds., *Chicano Studies: Survey and Analysis* (Dubuque, Iowa: Kendall/Hunt Publishing Company, 2001).

60. Max Benavidez, "Chicano Art: Culture, Myth, and Sensibility," p. 18.

61. Ibid., p. 17.

62. Goldman and Ybarra-Frausto, "The Political and Social Contexts of Chicano Art"; Marin, *Chicano Visions;* George Vargas, "A Historical Overview/Update on the State of Chicano Art," in David R. Maciel, Isidro D. Ortiz, and María Herrera-Sobek, eds., *Chicano Renaissance: Contemporary Cultural Trends* (Tucson: The University of Arizona Press, 2000).

63. For a more detailed account of the two programs, see Chon A. Noriega, *Shot in America: Television, the State, and the Rise of Chicano Cinema* (Minneapolis: University of Minnesota Press, 2000), chap. 6.

64. Ibid. See also, Tomás Ybarra-Frausto, "Arte Chicano: Images of a Community," in Eva Sperling Cockcroft and Holly Barnet-Sánchez, eds., *Signs from the Heart: California Chicano Murals* (Venice, California: Social and Public Art Resource Center, 1990), p. 56.

65. Renee Tajima, "Ethno-Communications: The Film School Program That Changed the Color of Independent Filmmaking," in Renee Tajima, ed., *The Anthology of Asian Pacific American Film and Video* (New York: Third World Newsreel, 1985), p. 38. Quoted in Noriega, *Shot in America,* p. 101.

66. Goldman and Ybarra-Frausto, "The Political and Social Contexts of Chicano Art"; Francisco J. Lewels Jr., *The Uses of the Media by the Chicano Movement: A Study in Minority Access* (New York: Praeger Publishers, 1974); Noriega, *Shot in America;* Jesús Salvador Treviño, *Eyewitness: A Filmmaker's Memoir of the Chicano Movement* (Houston: Arte Público Press, 2001).

67. Valdez has continued to work in the Hollywood industry since he directed *Zoot Suit* in 1981. He also wrote and directed *La Bamba* in 1987. More recently he directed the 1994 version of the *Cisco Kid* starring Latino actor Jimmy Smitts and Chicano actor Cheech Marin.

68. Luis Valdez, "I Am Joaquin" (1969). For a discussion on the relationship between the poem and the film, see Rolando Hinojosa, "*I Am Joaquin:* Relationships between the Text and the Film," in Gary D. Keller, ed., *Chicano Cinema: Research, Reviews, and Resources,* pp. 142–45.

69. Francisco Arturo Rosales, *Chicano! The History of the Mexican American Civil Rights Movement* (Houston: Arte Público Press, 1996).

70. Treviño, *Eyewitness: A Filmmaker's Memoir.* For more on the 1968 Blowouts, see Dolores Delgado Bernal, "Chicana/o Education from the Civil Rights Era to the Present," in José F. Moreno, ed., *The Elusive Quest for Equality: 150 Years of Chicano/Chicana Education* (Cambridge: Harvard Educational Review, 1998), pp. 77–108. While the Blowouts took place in March 1968, in October student demonstrators in Tlatelolco, Mexico City, were massacred by soldiers and police. The news of the massacre was spread worldwide, further angering Chicano youth. See Acuña, *Occupied America: A History of Chicanos,* pp. 321–22. That was a key year globally in terms of student riots.

71. Treviño later became the executive producer for the acclaimed 1996 PBS series *Chicano! The History of the Mexican American Civil Rights Movement.* Although his repertoire has expanded to include mainstream television series, his connection to Chicano filmmaking continues, as evidenced in one of his latest projects, *Resurrection Boulevard* (2000–2002). Other filmmakers of Mexican origin have been working since the 1970s, including Moctesuma Esparza and Gregory Nava, who directed *El Norte, Selena,* and *My Family.*

72. Treviño, *Eyewitness: A Filmmaker's Memoir,* p. 268. For more on Treviño's film work, see also Noriega, *Shot in America,* pp. 103, 115, 135–38, 145–52, 162.

73. Paredes' novel was titled *With His Pistol in His Hand,* written in 1958.

74. Chicanos/as have also been active in the television arena helping to change the prevailing fact that, outside of documentaries, few programs have centered on Chicano themes or characters. *Chico and the Man* (1974–1978), *The George Lopez Show* (2002–2007), *Resurrection Boulevard* (2000–2002), *American Family* (2002–2004), and *Ugly Betty* (2006–present) focus on Chicano/a characters.

75. Holly Alford, "The Zoot Suit: Its History and Influence," *Fashion Theory* 8, no. 2 (2004): 225–36.

76. See Richard Griswold del Castillo, "The Los Angeles 'Zoot Suit Riots' Revisited: Mexican and Latin American Perspectives," *Mexican Studies/Estudios Mexicanos* 16, no. 2 (2000): 367–91; Mauricio Mazón, *The Zoot-Suit Riots: The Psychology of Symbolic Annihilation* (Austin: University of Texas Press, 1984); Eduardo Obregón Pagán, *Murder at the Sleepy Lagoon: Zoot Suits, Race, and Riot in Wartime L.A.* (Chapel Hill: The University of North Carolina Press, 2003).

77. For a detailed story line of the film, see Christine List, *Chicano Images*.

78. Francisco X. Camplis, "Towards the Development of a Raza Cinema (1975)," in Chon A. Noriega, ed., *Chicanos and Film: Representation and Resistance* (Minneapolis: University of Minnesota Press, 1992), p. 299. Camplis was a film student at Stanford's film program in the early 1970s. See Noriega, *Shot in America*, p. 240, n. 108.

79. See Fregoso, "The Representation of Cultural Identity in 'Zoot Suit' (1981)." See also Rosa Linda Fregoso, *The Bronze Screen: Chicana and Chicano Film and Culture* (Minneapolis: University of Minnesota Press, 1993), chap. 2.

80. The report read in the film was almost identical to the report read by the chief of the sheriff's Foreign Relations Bureau during the actual *Sleepy Lagoon* trial. See Ian Haney López, *Racism on Trial: The Chicano Fight for Justice* (Cambridge, Massachusetts: Belknap Press, 2003), p. 74.

81. Ian Haney López, *White by Law: The Legal Construction of Race* (New York: New York University Press, 1996), p. 204.

82. Ibid. See also his essay in this volume.

83. On Mendelian systems of racial classification that posit that racial traits are inherent and passed from generation to generation, see Alexandra Minna Stern, *Eugenic Nation: Faults and Frontiers of Better Breeding in Modern America* (Berkeley and Los Angeles: University of California Press, 2005), pp. 14–16.

84. Fregoso, *The Bronze Screen*, p. xviii.

85. Gloria Anzaldúa, *Borderlands La Frontera: The New Mestiza* (2nd ed; San Francisco: Aunt Lute Books, 1999), p. 80.

86. Ibid., p. 81.

87. See www.imdb.com/title/tt0083365. Comments from viewers throughout this essay were obtained from IMDb, a film database (www.imdb.com/), and from www.amazon.com since there are no audience reception studies on these films. While I do not claim that these comments are representative of all audiences, they are a legitimate source that reflects individuals' opinions.

88. Pizzato, "Brechtian and Aztec Violence in Valdez's Zoot Suit."

89. Fregoso, *The Bronze Screen*, p. 24.

90. Ibid., p. 38.

91. Ibid., p. 33.

92. Sylvia Morales, "Celluloid Mujeres," in Gary D. Keller, ed., *Chicano Cinema: Research, Review & Resources* (Tempe, Arizona: Bilingual Review/Press, 1985), p. 91.

93. Yolanda Broyles-González, *El Teatro Campesino: Theater in the Chicano Movement* (Austin: University of Texas Press, 1994), p. 203.

94. The following authors refer to Alice differently, either as white (List), or Anglo (Denzin). Denzin, "Zoot Suits and Homeboys (and Girls)"; List, *Chicano Images;* Pizzato, "Brechtian and Aztec Violence in Valdez's Zoot Suit."

95. Broyles-González, *El Teatro Campesino,* p. 203; Fregoso, *The Bronze Screen,* p. 23.

96. Haney López, *White by Law,* p. 104.

97. The character of Alice Bloomfield is based on Alice McGrath, the executive secretary of the Sleepy Lagoon Defense Committee, the daughter of Russian Jewish immigrants. Valdez most likely had a good understanding of the role people had played in Chicano politics, certainly as a member of César Chávez's United Farmworkers Movement. For one, Chávez based his grassroots strategies from his involvement with Jewish activist Fred Ross of the Community Service Organization (CSO), headed by Sal Alinsky, also a Jewish activist. See Acuña, *Occupied America: A History of Chicanos,* pp. 276–77, 279, 313, 385.

98. Josefina López's play is more political. She co-wrote the screenplay for the film with George LaVoo.

99. Fregoso discusses the mixed reception and low box office returns for *Zoot Suit.* See Fregoso, *The Bronze Screen,* pp. 23–24. Her argument that the film was difficult to grasp by monocultural/monolingual audiences extends to other scholars. See Denzin, "Zoot Suits and Homeboys (and Girls)."

100. See http://www.imdb.com/title/tt0296166/ for viewers' comments.

101. Pachon et al., "Still Missing: Latinos in and out of Hollywood," pp. 4–5.

102. The Spanish process of *mestizaje,* for one, included Jews and Moors.

103. Fregoso, *The Bronze Screen,* p. xviii.

104. Arturo Aldama, "Visions in the Four Directions: Five Hundred Years of Resistance and Beyond," in W. S. Penn, ed., *As We Are Now: Mixblood Essays on Race and Identity* (Los Angeles: University of California Press, 1997), p. 161. Quoted in Cynthia L. Bejarano, *¿Qué Onda? Urban Youth Cultures and Border Identities* (Tucson: University of Arizona Press, 2005), p. 208.

105. Anzaldúa, *Borderlands La Frontera,* p. 102.

106. See http://www.imdb/com/title/tt0296166/usercomments?start=60.

107. The film's DVD provides commentaries made by Josefina López, as well as those of the others involved in the making of the film.

108. *High Noon* (1952, directed by Fred Zinnemann) and *Lone Star* (1996, directed by John Sayles) are examples of films where Mexican women depend economically on Anglo men.

109. Anzaldúa, *Borderlands La Frontera,* p. 78.

110. Quoted in List, *Chicano Images,* p. 70.

111. Indeed, the number of Chicanos who served in the armed forces has been estimated to be somewhere between 375,000 and 500,000. For a discussion on Mexican Americans and their experiences with the armed forces, see Acuña, *Occupied America: A History of Chicanos,* chap. 11; George Mariscal, ed., *Aztlán and Viet Nam: Chicano and Chicana Experiences of the War* (Berkeley: University of California Press, 1999).

112. Valencia explains acculturation as the process that takes place when individuals are exposed to a new culture and, as a result, cultural learning and adaptation occur. Richard R. Valencia, ed., *Chicano School Failure and Success: Past, Present, and Future* (London: RoutledgeFalmer, 2002), p. 241.

113. This fits within a genre already established in Hollywood whereby youth of color can only escape poverty and the dangers of their *barrios* or ghettos through education. See, for instance, *Blackboard Jungle* (1955, directed by Richard Brooks); *To Sir with Love* (1967, directed by James Clavell); *Stand and Deliver* (1988, directed by Ramón Menéndez); and *Dangerous Minds* (1995, directed by John Smith).

114. In a presentation at Wellesley College in 2004, Josefina López shared how her own high school teachers encouraged her to apply to college.

115. In a personal interview with Josefina López on September 7, 2004, she indicated that in real life, it was her father who did not want her to go to college.

116. Anzaldúa, *Borderlands La Frontera: The New Mestiza,* p. 38.

117. See the chapter on Josefina López in Adriana Katzew, "'No Chicanos on TV': Learning from Chicana/o Artists-Activists Countering Invisibility and Stereotypes in the Media through Art" (Ed.D. diss., Harvard University, 2005), pp. 117–58.

118. See Maria Elena Martínez's discussion in this volume.

119. Josefina López, however, usually writes about the oppression by men of their wives and daughters, while at the same time acknowledges that women are the transmitters of men's values. Personal interview with Josefina López, February 22 and September 7, 2004.

120. Personal interview with Josefina López, February 22, 2004.

121. See http://www.oprah.com/rys/omag/rys_omag_200308_aha.jhtml.

122. López used this phrase in speaking of the depiction of Chicana/Mexicana women by Luis Valdez in his work. See Katzew, "'No Chicanos on TV,'" p. 127.

Chapter 9

1. The models in the photographs reproduced here were members of Gómez-Peña's performance troupe, La Pocha Nostra (Juan Ybarra, Violeta Luna, Emiko R. Lewis, etc.), as well as artists, intellectuals, sex radicals, activists, curators, and local eccentrics from the site where the photo-shoot took place. The first three portfolios were commissioned by Canarian curator Orlando Britto-Jinorio and printed by BRH Editions at Daylight Professional Laboratory, Madrid. "Post-México en X-paña" premiered last February as part of ARCO, Madrid, and is now in the permanent collection of DAROS (Zurich).

2. Michael Fried, "Barthes's Punctum," *Critical Inquiry* 31, no. 3 (Spring 2005): 564.

3. Ibid.

4. Ibid.

5. Guillermo Gómez-Peña, "Culturas-in-extremis: Performing Against the Cultural Backdrop of The Mainstream Bizarre," in *Ethno-Techno: Writings on Performance, Activism, and Pedagogy* (New York: Routledge, 2005), pp. 45–64.

6. Guillermo Gómez-Peña, *Dangerous Border Crossers: The Artist Talks Back* (New York: Routledge, 2000).

Index